THE OBSOLESCENCE PARADOX

THE OBSOLESCENCE PARADOX

Why the Best Engineers Will Thrive in the AI Era

Vincent Bevia

Corebaseit

The Obsolescence Paradox: Why the Best Engineers Will Thrive in the AI Era

Published by Corebaseit

First edition, February 2026

ISBN: 978-84-09-83044-2

In memory of my father, **Vicente** *— I miss you so much.*

To my mother, **Inspiración (Espi)***, and to my wife,* **Yanamara** *—*
for their unwavering love, patience, and belief in me.

To my uncle, **Clarence "Clary" Bolin***, who encouraged me to go ahead and write about what I know—your steady encouragement growing up in California shaped more than you realize.*

Special thanks to my family and friends for their encouragement and support.

Vincent Bevia

2026

Contents

What This Book Is 4
What You'll Find Here 4
How to Use This Book 5
A Note on Tone 5
One More Thing 6
About the Author 7
Disclaimer 7
Why This Book? 10
What Is Engineering in the AI Era? 11
Who Should Read This Book? 12
Book Structure 15
    Part I — Understanding the Paradox 15
    Part II — The Human Advantage 15
    Part III — Working With AI 15
    Part IV — Reinventing the Engineer 16
    Part V — The Future 16
How to Read This Book 17
What Lies Ahead 18

Chapter 1 19
  The Obsolescence Paradox 19
  When Automation Makes Humans More Valuable 19
    The Abundance Effect 20
    The Complementarity Effect 20
    The Supervision Effect 21
  Replacement vs. Amplification 22
    The Replacement Model 22
    The Amplification Model 23
    The Spectrum, Not the Binary 24
  Same Tool, Opposite Outcomes 26
  A Framework for Human–AI Interaction 26
    The Three Layers of Value 27
    The Interaction Modes 29
    The Allocation Question 30
  Redefining the "Good Engineer" 31
    Beyond Technical Skill 31
    The Evolved Engineering Role 32
    The Context Imperative 33
  The Paradox Resolved 34
  Chapter Summary 34

Chapter 2 36
  A Brief History of Artificial Intelligence 36
  The Long Arc and the Sudden Turn 36

From Symbolic AI to Statistical Learning 39
The Symbolic Era and Its Limits 39
From Rules to Data 40
The Deep Learning Revolution 41
The Breakthrough That Changed Everything 41
Learning Without Labels 42
The Transformer Era and Foundation Models 42
Attention Is All You Need 42
Large Language Models and Emergent Capabilities 43
The Acceleration Pattern and Its Implications 44
The Compressing Timeline 44
Why This History Matters for Engineers Today 44
Chapter Summary 45

Chapter 3 48
Human and Machine Intelligence 48
Biological Cognition vs. Computational Systems 49
The Architecture of the Human Mind 49
The Architecture of Machine Learning Systems 51
Two Fundamentally Different Approaches 53
Comparative Capabilities and Limitations 53
Where Machines Excel 53
The Sycophancy Problem 54
Where Humans Excel 56
The Complementarity Pattern 58
Why Human Intelligence Still Matters 59
The Limits of Pattern Matching 59
When Embodied Understanding Matters 60
Judgment Under Irreducible Uncertainty 60
The Creativity Distinction 61
The Responsibility That Cannot Be Automated 62
The Pattern Returns to the Paradox 63
Chapter Summary 64

Chapter 4 66
What AI Can Do—And What It Cannot 66
Capabilities and Architectural Constraints 66
What Transformers Enable 66
The Scaling Laws and Emergent Capabilities 68
The Voyager Paradox: When Architecture Assumptions Shift . . 70
Memorization vs. Generalization 71
Failure Modes and Hallucinations 72
Confident Wrongness: The Hallucination Problem 72
Distribution Failures: Edge Cases and the Long Tail 73
Why Testing AI Systems Differs from Testing Traditional Software 74
The Missing Ingredients: Context, Judgment, Intent 75
Context Beyond the Window 76
The Four Invisible Skills 76
Judgment That Weighs Trade-offs 78
Intent as Origin, Not Echo 78

When Measurement Becomes the Problem . . . 79
Chapter Summary . . . 80

Chapter 5 82
Endurance and Cognitive Resilience . . . 82
Why Persistence Outperforms Talent . . . 83
The Talent Myth and the Research That Challenges It . . . 83
The Mathematics of Compounding . . . 84
How AI Amplifies the Value of Persistence . . . 86
Persistence at the Three Layers . . . 88
The Psychology of Working Through Failure . . . 89
Failure as Information, Not Identity . . . 89
The Debugging Mindset as Life Philosophy . . . 90
Learning to Love Being Wrong . . . 92
The Valley of Despair and How to Cross It . . . 94
Deliberate Practice in the Age of Autocomplete . . . 96
The Autocomplete Trap . . . 96
What Deliberate Practice Requires . . . 97
Deliberate Practice Patterns With AI . . . 100
The Productive Struggle . . . 104
Building and Maintaining Resilience . . . 106
Practical Strategies for Daily Resilience . . . 106
Managing Frustration With AI . . . 109
Preventing Burnout . . . 111
Chapter Summary . . . 112

Chapter 6 114
Logical Thinking as Superpower . . . 114
First Principles Thinking . . . 116
What First Principles Thinking Is . . . 116
When to Use First Principles . . . 116
How to Reason From First Principles . . . 118
First Principles vs Pattern Matching . . . 120
Debugging as Applied Logic . . . 120
The Scientific Method in Code . . . 120
The Logic of Elimination . . . 121
Building Mental Models Through Debugging . . . 123
Detecting AI Errors Through Logical Analysis . . . 125
The Taxonomy of AI Logic Errors . . . 125
Systematic Verification Patterns . . . 129
Systems Thinking: When Linear Logic Fails . . . 132
The Limits of Linear Reasoning . . . 132
Feedback Loops in Software . . . 133
Emergence and Non-Linear Effects . . . 135
Multi-Layer Reasoning . . . 136
Second-Order Thinking . . . 136
Logical Fallacies in Engineering . . . 138
Common Reasoning Errors . . . 138
Improving Reasoning Discipline . . . 141
Chapter Summary . . . 143

Chapter 7 145
The Art of Simplifying Complexity 145
Why Simplification Matters More Than Ever 146
The AI Complexity Amplifier 146
The Three Layers of Simplification 147
Simplicity as Antifragile Career Strategy 148
The Core Techniques: Abstraction, Decomposition, Naming 149
Abstraction: The Art of Hiding 149
Decomposition: Divide and Conquer 151
Naming: The Hardest Problem 154
Architectural Thinking: Seeing Systems Whole 158
Multi-Scale Vision 158
The Questions That Reveal Architectural Thinking 160
The Trade-off Mindset 161
Managing Complexity at Scale 163
Essential vs. Accidental Complexity 163
Complexity Budgets 165
When Complexity Is Necessary 168
Simplicity as Competitive Advantage 172
Chapter Summary 173

Chapter 8 175
Communication as Engineering 175
The Rise of the Explainer Engineer 176
Why Communication Is Engineering Work 176
The Explainer Premium 177
What Makes Technical Communication Hard 178
The Three Audiences 179
Communication as Career Differentiator 180
Writing, Speaking, and Diagramming 180
Writing: Thinking Made Visible 181
The Discipline of Clear Writing 183
Speaking: Real-Time Communication 185
Meeting Size and Communication Overhead 186
Speaking Skills for Engineers 188
Diagramming: Visual Thinking 188
Collaborative Cognition with Human and AI Agents 191
Prompt Engineering as Communication 191
Communicating About AI Decisions 193
Collaborative Patterns: Human + AI 195
Human-to-Human Communication About AI Work 196
The Meta-Communication Challenge 198
Communication Skills Compound with AI 198
Chapter Summary 199

Chapter 9 201
Human–AI Collaboration 201
The Psychology of Non-Human Teammates 202
Why Working with AI Feels Different 202
The Cognitive Prosthetic Model 203

Building Accurate Mental Models 204
Emotional Regulation in Human-AI Work 205
Interaction Models: Delegation, Collaboration, Supervision, and Augmentation 206
Delegation: When to Let Go 206
Collaboration: Working Together 208
Supervision: Monitoring Autonomous Work 209
Augmentation: AI as Extension of Self 211
Choosing the Right Mode 212
How to Correct, Guide, and Teach AI Systems 213
The Correction Loop: Diagnosing and Fixing AI Errors 214
From Prompting to Context Engineering 216
Teaching AI Your Patterns and Preferences 218
Example of Good Code 219
When to Restart vs. When to Persist 220
Chapter Summary 221

Chapter 10 223
Calibrated Trust 223
Automation Bias vs. Healthy Skepticism 223
The Mechanisms of Automation Bias 224
Automation Bias in Software Engineering Contexts 225
The Opposite Problem: Automation Aversion 226
The Domain Verification Advantage 226
When to Trust the Model—and When Not To 227
The Reliability Landscape 228
Heuristics for Calibrated Trust 229
Recognizing Confidence Signals 230
The Verification Spectrum 231
Decision-Making Under Uncertainty 231
The Three Types of Uncertainty 231
Bayesian Updating and Iterative Refinement 232
The Cost-Benefit Calculus 233
The Role of Reversibility 233
Developing Contextual Judgment 234
When Uncertainty Demands Human Judgment 235
Chapter Summary 235

Chapter 11 237
The Apprenticeship Problem 237
Why Juniors Lose Skills When AI Writes Their Code 238
The Traditional Skill Development Path 238
How AI Short-Circuits Development 238
The Empirical Evidence 241
What's at Stake 242
New Mentorship Models for the AI Era 243
The Traditional Mentorship Model 243
Mentorship Pattern 1: Deliberate Practice Zones 243
Mentorship Pattern 2: Verification-First Learning 244
Mentorship Pattern 3: Explanation-Driven Understanding 245

Mentorship Pattern 4: Progressive Autonomy with AI 246
Mentorship Pattern 5: Real Debugging as Core Practice 247
Mentorship Pattern 6: Architectural Thinking Through Constraints 248
Mentorship Pattern 7: Post-Mortem Learning 248
How Seniors Become Even More Valuable 249
The Experience Gap Widens 250
Scarce Skills Become More Valuable 250
The Mentorship Premium 252
Building Leverage Through Multiplication 252
The Teaching-Learning Loop 253
Positioning for Long-Term Success 254
Chapter Summary 255

Chapter 12 257
The AI-Augmented Mind 257
Cognitive Load and Externalized Memory 257
Understanding Cognitive Load 257
The Externalization of Memory 258
Practical Patterns for Memory Externalization 259
When Externalization Becomes Dependency 262
Thinking at Higher Abstraction Levels 263
The Abstraction Ladder 263
How Thinking Changes at Higher Abstraction 264
Practical Examples of Higher-Level Thinking 266
The Risk of Abstraction Drift 269
Human–AI Cognitive Coupling 270
What Is Cognitive Coupling? 270
Coupling Pattern 1: Hypothesis Generation and Evaluation . . . 270
Coupling Pattern 2: Iterative Refinement Loops 271
Coupling Pattern 3: Multi-Perspective Analysis 273
Coupling Pattern 4: Knowledge Amplification 274
Coupling Pattern 5: Creative Exploration 275
The Emergence of Meta-Cognitive Skills 277
The Risk of Cognitive Atrophy 278
Chapter Summary 279

Chapter 13 281
The Antifragile Career 281
Thriving in Constant Change 282
The Fragility of Specialization 282
The Optionality Principle 283
The Barbell Strategy for Skills 284
Embracing Volatility as Information 285
Building Resilience Through Redundancy 286
Building a Lifelong Learning System 287
The Learning Debt Concept 287
The 70-20-10 Learning Framework 288
The Just-in-Time Learning Strategy 290
Building a Personal Knowledge System 291
The Curiosity Cultivation Challenge 292

Curiosity as Competitive Advantage . . . 293
Why Curiosity Matters More Than Ever . . . 293
The Curiosity Spectrum . . . 294
Developing Generative Curiosity . . . 295
Curiosity in the Age of AI . . . 296
Curiosity as Career Insurance . . . 298
Chapter Summary . . . 299

Chapter 14 301
Vertical Mastery: The Engineer's New Advantage . . . 301
The Horizontal-Vertical Dichotomy . . . 302
Scaling Systems: A Technical Foundation . . . 302
Scaling Businesses: From Technical to Strategic . . . 303
The Career Parallel . . . 304
Why Vertical Mastery Matters in the AI Era . . . 305
The Commoditization of Generalist Skills . . . 305
The Compounding Returns of Depth . . . 306
The Three Layers and Vertical Expertise . . . 307
Domain Knowledge as Moat . . . 308
The Horizontal AI / Vertical Expertise Symbiosis . . . 309
Choosing Your Vertical: Strategic Domain Selection . . . 310
Criteria for Valuable Verticals . . . 310
The Portfolio Approach: Primary and Secondary Verticals . . . 312
Recognizing When to Pivot . . . 313
Developing Vertical Expertise: Practical Strategies . . . 314
Immersion Over Tourism . . . 314
Learning From Domain Experts . . . 314
Building Domain Intuition Through Repetition . . . 315
Contributing to Domain Knowledge . . . 316
Maintaining Vertical Expertise Over Time . . . 317
Vertical Mastery and Career Leverage . . . 318
The Specification Advantage . . . 318
The Review Advantage . . . 318
The Architecture Advantage . . . 319
The Trust Multiplier . . . 319
The Compensation Premium . . . 320
Vertical Mastery and the Three-Layer Framework . . . 320
Execution Layer: Vertical Syntax . . . 321
Design Layer: Vertical Architecture . . . 322
Intent Layer: Vertical Strategy . . . 322
Chapter Summary . . . 323

Chapter 15 326
The Engineer as Leader . . . 326
Influence vs. Authority . . . 327
The Distinction That Matters . . . 327
Why Influence Matters More in AI Era . . . 328
Building Influence: The Foundation . . . 329
The Technical Leadership Paradox . . . 330
Influence Without Authority: Practical Tactics . . . 331

Teaching, Mentoring, and Scaling Knowledge 332
Why Teaching Is Leadership 332
The Socratic Method in Code Review 333
Creating Mental Models Through Analogy 334
The Deliberate Practice Framework 335
Scaling Knowledge Through Documentation 336
Mentorship Beyond "Have a 1-on-1" 338
Human-Centered Leadership in Technical Teams 339
The People Side of Technical Decisions 339
Motivation: Autonomy, Mastery, Purpose 340
Psychological Safety: The Foundation of High Performance . . . 341
Managing Conflict Productively 341
The Delegation Challenge 342
Communication: The Meta-Skill 343
The Leadership Journey 344
Leadership as Service 344
Chapter Summary 345

Chapter 16 347
Work in the Age of Intelligent Machines 347
AI, Software, and the Return of Infrastructure 348
Coding Is Easier. Engineering Is Harder. 348
SaaS Was Never About Screens 349
This Doesn't Look Like a Bubble—It Looks Like a Bottleneck . . . 349
Why Scale Isn't Saving Us (Yet) 350
The Quiet Shift in Decision-Making 351
The Pattern Repeats 351
The Future of Programming 352
The Historical Arc of Abstraction 352
Programming as Protocol Design 354
The Three Layers Under Pressure 356
The Revaluation Intensifies 357
From Operational to Intentional Programming 358
Interaction Modes Evolve 360
The Solutions Engineer at Higher Abstraction 361
What This Means for Programming 362
Agentic Systems and AI Colleagues 364
From Function Calls to Goal Delegation 364
The Manager-Engineer Convergence 366
The Colleague Metaphor and Its Limits 367
The Span of Control Problem 369
When Agents Disagree 370
The Autonomy-Control Trade-off 372
Beyond the Colleague Metaphor: A New Mental Model 373
The Unbundling of Knowledge Work 374
The Anatomy of Unbundling 374
The Barbell Labor Market 376
The Credentialization Trap Revisited 378
The Gig Economy Comes to Engineering? 380

Historical Precedent: The Putting-Out System 381
What Stable Employment Survives? 382
The Revaluation Thesis Holds—With Caveats 384
Chapter Summary 385

Chapter 17 388
Ethics, Responsibility, and Human Agency 388
The Responsibility Stack: Where Ethics Lives in AI Systems 389
Ethics at the Execution Layer 389
Ethics at the Design Layer 390
Ethics at the Intent Layer 390
The Diffusion of Responsibility Problem 391
The "Many Hands" Problem 392
Automation Bias and Moral Crumple Zones 392
The Engineer's Distinctive Responsibility 393
Designing Systems That Preserve Human Agency 394
The Human Override Principle 394
Design for Amplification, Not Replacement 396
The Power User Principle 397
The Intent Layer Is Where Ethics Lives 398
Values Cannot Be Automated 399
When to Refuse to Build 400
Recognizing Red Flags 400
The Engineer's Right to Refuse 401
Drawing Lines 402
From Answer Production to Judgment Stewardship 402
The Solutions Engineer as Moral Agent 403
Chapter Summary 404

Chapter 18 407
The Renaissance Engineer 407
The Human Qualities That Endure 408
Clear Thinking in Ambiguous Contexts 408
Simplifying Complexity Without Losing Truth 409
Contextual Judgment 410
Intellectual Curiosity and Learning Appetite 411
Emotional Resilience and Grit 412
Ethical Judgment and Moral Courage 413
Creativity, Judgment, and Meaning as Irreducible Skills 413
Creativity: Genuine Novelty vs. Sophisticated Recombination . . 414
Judgment: Deciding Under Irreducible Uncertainty 415
Meaning-Making: Why We Build What We Build 416
Why This Is the Best Time to Be a Builder 417
The Democratization of Implementation 418
The Amplification of Expertise 418
The Expansion of the Possible 419
The Return to First Principles 420
The Revaluation of the Human 420
Building the Future You Want 421
The Renaissance Engineer: A Synthesis 421

A Call to Action 423
Conclusion: The Paradox Resolved 425
Chapter Summary 426

References 428

Preface

Think of a car sitting in the driveway with a dead battery. The car is there, the battery is there, but nothing moves. The battery exists for a purpose — it simply has no charge.

Then a colleague arrives with jumper cables. Suddenly, the battery comes alive, the engine turns over, and the car begins to move. Nothing new was added. The potential was always there. It just needed activation.

That is what happened with AI. The ideas had existed since the time of Turing—decades of theory, research, and incremental progress. But it was not until late 2022 that AI truly came alive, became impossible to ignore, and forced the rest of us to decide what to do about it.

I was mesmerized. I kept thinking: *What is this?* I adopted the tools early, as did many others at the company where I work.

What I saw—in myself and my peers—was that none of us were entirely sure what we wanted to do with this technology, or what we were supposed to do with it. It was confusing, powerful, and fascinating all at once.

That uncertainty was impossible to ignore.

And I wasn't alone in feeling it.

Three years ago, I watched a senior engineer—let's call him David—struggle with a problem that would have been unthinkable a decade earlier.

David had fifteen years of experience. He'd built systems that handled millions of transactions daily. He mentored junior engineers. He made sound architectural decisions. By any measure, he was excellent at his job.

David was also an early adopter. When GitHub Copilot launched in 2021, he was among the first to integrate it into his workflow. When ChatGPT arrived in late 2022, he immediately saw its potential for accelerating development. He was excited about these tools—until the day a production incident changed his perspective.

A payment processing bug had been eluding the team for three days. Transactions were failing intermittently, maybe one in fifty, and no one could reproduce it locally. When David finally traced it back to code generated by an AI assistant weeks earlier, he was surprised. The code had looked correct. His review had found nothing wrong. The tests passed. But there was a subtle race condition that only manifested under production load—a case the AI hadn't considered and David hadn't thought to check.

"I spent two hours staring at this code before I even realized it came from an AI assistant," David told me over coffee the next week. "I don't even know if I'm an engineer anymore. The AI writes faster than I do. Junior engineers use it and ship features I would have spent a week on. What's my role now? Code reviewer for machines? What am I supposed to be good at?"

This conversation haunted me because David wasn't alone. Across the industry, engineers who had eagerly adopted AI tools were discovering an uncomfortable truth: the tools were powerful, but using them well was harder than it looked. And the question David asked—*In a world where AI can generate code, what are we for?*—was one I kept hearing again and again.

I wrote this book because that question would not leave me alone—and because the answer I kept finding contradicted the fear behind it.

AI hasn't made engineers obsolete. It has **revealed what engineering actually is**—and it turns out engineering was never primarily about writing code. It was about thinking clearly, making judgment calls, simplifying complexity, understanding context, and solving problems that matter. Code was simply how we expressed those things.

Now that AI can handle much of the mechanical expression, what remains is the hard part: the thinking, the judgment, the distinctly human work that coding once allowed us to hide behind.

This is what I call the **Obsolescence Paradox**: as AI automates routine work, distinctly human skills do not become less valuable—they become *more* valuable, because they are no longer obscured by the low-level work.

David eventually figured this out. Six months after our coffee conversation, he'd transformed his practice—though not without struggle. He used AI extensively—but he'd learned to think of himself not as someone who writes code, but as someone who solves problems using whatever tools are appropriate.

His role hadn't disappeared. It had *elevated.* He spent less time on implementation mechanics and more time on the things AI couldn't do: understanding what stakeholders actually needed, making architectural trade-offs, simplifying complex systems, mentoring engineers who were drowning in AI-generated code they didn't understand, and making judgment calls that required context AI didn't have.

David became more valuable, not less. But he had to let go of the identity "I'm valuable because I can implement things quickly" and embrace a different identity: "I'm valuable because I think clearly about complex problems."

What This Book Is

This is not a book about prompt engineering or which AI tools to use. Tools change rapidly; principles endure.

This is a book about how to **think, work, and build a career** in an era where the ground is shifting beneath us. It's about the frameworks, practices, and mental models that help you not just survive the AI transformation but position yourself to gain from it.

The book develops three core frameworks that appear throughout:

The Obsolescence Paradox: Why automation increases the value of high-level human skills by eliminating the low-level work that previously obscured them.

The Three Layers: Execution (implementing solutions), Design (choosing solutions), and Intent (determining what problems to solve). AI excels at Execution but struggles at Design and Intent. Understanding which layer you're operating at changes how you work.

The Four Modes: Delegation (AI executes, you verify), Collaboration (iterative back-and-forth), Supervision (AI works semi-autonomously, you intervene), and Augmentation (AI assists while you maintain control). Each mode has appropriate uses and failure patterns.

These aren't abstract theories. They're practical tools I've used and taught to help engineers navigate the transition David went through—from seeing AI as a threat to using it as leverage.

What You'll Find Here

This book is organized into five parts:

Part I establishes the paradox and examines what AI actually can and cannot do. Not the hype, not the fear—the reality based on current capabilities and fundamental limitations.

Part II explores the distinctly human capabilities that become more valuable: persistence through difficulty, logical thinking and systematic reasoning, simplifying complexity, and communication as engineering work.

Part III provides practical frameworks for working with AI effectively: collaboration patterns, calibrated trust (neither blind acceptance nor reflexive rejection), how juniors develop expertise when AI handles implementation, and how AI changes cognitive work.

Part IV addresses career strategy: building antifragile careers that gain from change, developing vertical domain expertise that resists commoditization, leadership in an AI-augmented world, and what "work" means when implementation speed increases dramatically.

Part V looks forward: ethics and responsibility when AI makes mistakes, maintaining human agency in automated systems, and a vision of the "Renaissance Engineer" who thrives by combining technical depth with human judgment.

Throughout, you'll find concrete examples from real engineering practice—debugging sessions, architectural decisions, career choices, team dynamics. These aren't hypothetical scenarios. They're drawn from my experience and from conversations with dozens of engineers like David who are navigating this transformation.

How to Use This Book

- **Read straight through** if you're rethinking your whole relationship with AI and your career; the ideas build on each other from Part I to Part V.
- **Dip into specific chapters** when you have a live problem (for example, collaborating with AI on a project, mentoring juniors in an AI-heavy environment, or making a career move).
- **Pause to reflect**: when something hits, stop and write down how it applies to your current work, team, or next decision.
- **Discuss with others**—your team, your manager, or other engineers. Many of the frameworks are more powerful when used as a shared language.

A Note on Tone

You'll notice the tone of the book is different from a typical technical book. I use stories. I acknowledge uncertainty. I admit when something is hard or when I don't have perfect answers.

This is deliberate. The AI transformation is messy, uncertain, and still unfolding. Anyone who claims to have it all figured out is lying or deluded. What I offer instead is frameworks for thinking through the uncertainty, patterns I've observed that seem to hold across contexts, and honest assessment of what's working and what isn't.

I also take a stance of **realistic optimism**. Not "AI will solve everything and everyone will be fine" (naive optimism). Not "AI will destroy jobs and we're all doomed" (fatalism). But realistic optimism: this is hard, some things are genuinely concerning, adaptation requires effort—*and* there are real opportunities for engineers who understand what's happening and position themselves accordingly.

The future isn't predetermined. How this transformation affects you depends on choices you make: what skills you develop, how you think about your role, what you optimize for in your career. This book is about making those choices intentionally rather than drifting through the change.

One More Thing

If you're like David was three years ago—excellent at your craft but wondering what your role is when AI can generate code—this book is for you.

If you're a junior engineer worried that AI will close doors before you've had a chance to walk through them—this book is for you.

If you're a technical leader trying to figure out how to develop your team when the old playbooks don't quite work anymore—this book is for you.

If you're simply curious about what's actually changing versus what's hype—this book is for you.

The engineers who thrive won't be the ones who resist AI or who blindly embrace it. They'll be the ones who understand the paradox: that as machines get better at execution, humans become more valuable for everything else.

Let's explore what that "everything else" is.

About the Author

Vincent Bevia holds a **Master of Science in Computer Science** from the University of Liverpool and has been a member of the **Institute of Electrical and Electronics Engineers (IEEE)** for over thirty years. He currently works as a **POS Architect at MultiSafepay**, where he leads initiatives in SmartPOS and SoftPOS systems, with a focus on EMV, PCI MPoC compliance, and secure payment architecture.

Vincent has hands-on experience with both Android-based SmartPOS devices and SoftPOS SDKs, bridging the gap between mobile technology and the rigorous requirements of the payment industry. His goal is to make POS development more accessible to engineers, while maintaining the highest levels of security and compliance.

Disclaimer

This book reflects my experience, observations, and interpretation of how AI is changing software engineering. It is intended for educational purposes only and does not constitute legal, financial, or career advice. Every team, company, and situation is different, and you should use your own judgment—and seek professional advice where appropriate—before making decisions that could affect your employment, business, or projects. While I have made a good-faith effort to be accurate and current, I cannot guarantee completeness or suitability for your specific context, and I disclaim liability for any outcomes resulting from how you choose to apply the ideas in this book.

Vincent Bevia
Málaga, Spain
January 2026

Contents

Preface

Part I — Understanding the Paradox

Chapter 1: **The Obsolescence Paradox**

Chapter 2: **A Brief History of Artificial Intelligence**

Chapter 3: **Human and Machine Intelligence**

Chapter 4: **What AI Can Do—And What It Cannot**

Part II — The Human Advantage

Chapter 5: **Endurance and Cognitive Resilience**

Chapter 6: **Logical Thinking as Superpower**

Chapter 7: **The Art of Simplifying Complexity**

Chapter 8: **Communication as Engineering**

Part III — Working With AI

Chapter 9: **Human–AI Collaboration**

Chapter 10: **Calibrated Trust**

Chapter 11: **The Apprenticeship Problem**

Chapter 12: **The AI-Augmented Mind**

Part IV — Reinventing the Engineer

Chapter 13: **The Antifragile Career**

Chapter 14: **Vertical Mastery: The Engineer's New Advantage**

Chapter 15: **The Engineer as Leader**

Chapter 16: **Work in the Age of Intelligent Machines**

Part V — The Future

Chapter 17: **Ethics, Responsibility, and Human Agency**

Chapter 18: **The Renaissance Engineer**

Acknowledgments

References

Introduction

Why This Book?

In early 2023, something changed in engineering. Not gradually, but suddenly. Large language models became capable enough to generate working code, explain unfamiliar concepts, draft documentation, and assist with design from natural-language instructions. GitHub Copilot, ChatGPT, and similar tools moved from novelty to necessity in a matter of months. The question shifted from "Can AI do useful technical work?" to "How do we work effectively with AI that can?"

I wrote this book because the dominant narratives about AI and engineering are both wrong.

One narrative says: "AI will replace engineers. Learn to prompt or become obsolete." This is wrong because it misunderstands what engineering actually is. We do not build systems because typing is hard. We build systems because translating human needs into reliable, maintainable, and meaningful outcomes is hard. AI accelerates execution; it does not eliminate judgment.

The other narrative says: "AI is just another tool. Nothing fundamental has changed." This is also wrong because it underestimates the magnitude of the shift. When a "tool" can generate thousands of lines of plausible implementation in seconds, summarize dense material instantly, propose architectures from vague requirements, and participate in technical problem-solving, that is not incremental improvement. It is a phase transition.

The truth is more interesting than either narrative. AI does not make engineers obsolete; it changes how engineering is practiced by amplifying the parts that have always mattered most. The skills that matter, the bottlenecks that constrain us, the shape of expertise, and even the way we learn are all being transformed. And here is the paradox: as AI handles more of the mechanical and routine aspects of technical work, the distinctly human aspects become more valuable, not less.

This is the Obsolescence Paradox: automation increases the value of high-level human capability by reducing the value of the low-level work that once obscured it. When AI drafts the boilerplate, what remains is judgment, context, simplification, communication, and the messy human work of deciding what should be built and why.

I have spent the past two years working with AI assistants daily, teaching others how to use them effectively, and observing what separates the people who thrive in this new environment from those who struggle. This book distills those observations into frameworks, practices, and mental models you can apply immediately.

This is not a book about prompt tricks or a catalog of AI tools. Tools change quickly; principles endure. This is a book about how to think, how to work, and how to remain deeply valuable in an era when the ground beneath technical work is shifting.

What Is Engineering in the AI Era?

Engineering has always been about more than implementation. It is about understanding problems, designing solutions, managing complexity, navigating constraints, and building systems that other people can maintain, trust, and evolve. Historically, however, the mechanics of implementation consumed so much time and energy that these higher-level concerns were often compressed or postponed.

Now the mechanics are faster. AI can generate a working implementation in seconds. The API that once took an afternoon to scaffold can appear in minutes. The validation logic that required careful repetition can be drafted instantly. The first pass of documentation, test cases, or even design alternatives can be produced before the human has fully finished framing the problem.

This acceleration reveals what engineering actually is: **the work that remains when implementation becomes cheap**.

That work includes:

- *Understanding intent.* People rarely know exactly what they want at the beginning. Requirements arrive incomplete, contradictory, political, or unstated. The engineer must uncover intent through questions, prototypes, iteration, and careful listening. AI can help shape or implement a specification. It cannot fully determine what ought to be specified.
- *Making judgment calls.* Every meaningful decision involves trade-offs. Simplicity versus flexibility. Speed versus maintainability. Correctness versus cost. Generality versus focus. These trade-offs depend on context

that AI does not truly possess: organizational realities, team capability, future plans, business priorities, and risk tolerance. Judgment remains human work.

- *Simplifying complexity.* AI can generate things that function. Humans must still shape things that can be understood, maintained, and extended. As we will explore later in this book, simplification is among the highest forms of engineering skill. AI often increases complexity because it optimizes for plausibility and local correctness, not elegance, coherence, or long-term clarity.
- *Communicating effectively.* Engineering is collaborative by nature. Decisions must be explained. Risks must be surfaced. Trade-offs must be documented. Knowledge must move between people, teams, and time horizons. Communication is not peripheral to engineering. It is one of the mechanisms by which engineering succeeds.
- *Maintaining context.* Systems exist inside organizations, and organizations have histories, incentives, politics, constraints, and memory. The technically elegant solution may be economically impossible, organizationally unworkable, or strategically unwise. The person who understands context makes better decisions than the person, or machine, who sees only the narrow technical problem.
- *Developing capability over time.* In a rapidly shifting environment, what you choose to learn matters as much as what you choose to build. Expertise does not emerge automatically from exposure to tools. It must be cultivated deliberately. The ability to grow, adapt, and deepen your judgment remains one of the most important long-term advantages a person can have.

Engineering in the AI era is therefore not the disappearance of human contribution. It is the concentration of human contribution into the areas that matter most. The people who thrive will be those who combine AI's speed with human judgment, human context, and human responsibility.

Who Should Read This Book?

This book is for engineers navigating the AI transformation, and for anyone who wants to understand how AI is changing technical work, expertise, and human judgment.

More specifically, it is written for:

Early-career engineers (0-5 years of experience) entering a profession in which AI assistance is becoming normal. You will learn how to use AI as a tool without becoming dependent on it, how to build real expertise instead of superficial fluency, and how to avoid the apprenticeship trap in which AI short-circuits the learning that turns beginners into strong practitioners.

Mid-career engineers (5-15 years of experience) who already have established workflows and are asking how AI changes the craft. You will learn how to integrate AI into your practice productively, which skills are becoming more valuable, which tasks can safely be delegated, and how to position yourself for the next decade of your career.

Senior and staff engineers responsible for architecture, technical direction, and mentorship. You will learn why AI makes technical leadership more important, not less; how to guide teams when implementation is increasingly machine-assisted; and how to make sound strategic decisions about where AI belongs in the engineering process.

Engineering managers, leaders, and decision-makers who need to understand how AI reshapes team dynamics, productivity, hiring, and skill development. You will learn what to measure, how to evaluate AI's real impact, and how to help teams grow stronger rather than more dependent.

Technologists, founders, product thinkers, and curious readers who want a grounded perspective on what AI changes and what it does not. Even if you are not writing software every day, this book will help you understand how technical work is evolving, why judgment and context still matter, and why the human side of engineering is becoming more valuable.

Anyone skeptical of AI hype who wants a realistic and practical view. This book doesn't claim that AI will solve everything or replace everyone. It examines what is genuinely changing, what remains fundamentally human, and how to navigate this shift with clarity and pragmatism.

You don't need to be an AI expert. You don't need a computer science degree. And you don't need to be a full-time programmer to follow this book. What you do need is curiosity about how technology is changing the way people think, build, decide, and collaborate.

The examples in this book come from engineering practice—you will see some code snippets, mostly Python, with a few in C++ and JavaScript—but the central ideas are broader: how expertise is formed, how judgment creates value, how complexity is managed, and how human capability evolves when machines become more capable. If you're not a programmer, you can skim or skip the code; the concepts stand on their own.

This book is written with engineers at its center, but its questions matter to anyone interested in the future of work, technology, and human skill.

Book Structure

This book is organized into five parts that build on one another.

Part I — Understanding the Paradox

We begin with the fundamental shift AI creates. Chapter 1 introduces the **Obsolescence Paradox**: as AI automates routine work, high-level human skills become more valuable, not less. We establish the **three-layer framework** (Execution, Design, Intent) and the **four collaboration modes** (Delegation, Collaboration, Supervision, Augmentation) that structure how humans and AI work together.

Chapter 2 provides historical context. AI is not new, but recent advances in large language models create capabilities unlike anything most technical workers have previously experienced. Chapter 3 examines the cognitive differences between human and machine intelligence. Chapter 4 analyzes what AI does well, such as pattern matching, generation, and acceleration, and what it still struggles with, such as judgment, context, and genuine understanding.

Part II — The Human Advantage

With that foundation in place, we turn to the distinctly human capabilities that matter most. Chapter 5 examines **endurance and cognitive resilience**: why persistence through difficulty, frustration, and uncertainty becomes even more important when AI makes easy tasks easier but leaves the hardest ones intact.

Chapter 6 explores **logical thinking** as a core engineering asset: systematic reasoning, debugging as applied epistemology, and first-principles thinking that allow you to verify AI outputs and solve genuinely novel problems.

Chapter 7 addresses **simplifying complexity**: the art of abstraction, decomposition, and naming that turns unmanageable systems into comprehensible ones. AI can generate complexity easily. Humans must master it.

Chapter 8 examines **communication as engineering work**: why writing, speaking, explaining, and diagramming are not secondary skills, but central forms of technical leverage in a world where implementation is faster and alignment becomes the bottleneck.

Part III — Working With AI

Part III focuses on practical collaboration patterns. Chapter 9 details **human-AI collaboration modes**: when to delegate, when to collaborate, when to supervise, and when to use AI as augmentation. Each mode has appropriate use cases, strengths, and failure patterns.

Chapter 10 develops **calibrated trust**: neither blind acceptance nor reflexive rejection, but appropriate skepticism based on task type, error cost, and verification burden. This is one of the most practical skills for anyone working with AI regularly.

Chapter 11 addresses **the apprenticeship problem**: how newcomers develop expertise when AI increasingly handles first-pass implementation. We explore mentorship patterns and learning strategies that still produce depth.

Chapter 12 examines **the AI-augmented mind**: how AI changes cognitive load, alters the level of abstraction at which we can work, and creates new meta-skills such as framing, evaluation, and the disciplined use of generated output.

Part IV — Reinventing the Engineer

Part IV turns to career strategy. Chapter 13 develops the **antifragile career**: how to build skills and positioning that gain from change rather than merely survive it. Optionality, redundancy, and deliberate skill development become more important in an unstable environment.

Chapter 14 explores **vertical mastery**: why deep domain expertise remains resistant to commoditization even as more general implementation becomes easier to automate. The person who combines domain depth with AI leverage creates uncommon value.

Chapter 15 examines **engineering leadership**: how influence, teaching, mentorship, and human-centered leadership become more important as implementation becomes faster and strategic alignment becomes more valuable.

Chapter 16 analyzes **work in the age of intelligent machines**: how AI changes daily practice, what organizations reward, and what productivity means when the speed of execution rises dramatically.

Part V — The Future

Part V looks ahead. Chapter 17 addresses **ethics, responsibility, and human agency**: the moral dimensions of building with AI, who is accountable when systems fail, and how human judgment must be preserved in increasingly automated environments.

Chapter 18 concludes by synthesizing the book's themes into a vision of the **Renaissance Engineer**: a person who combines technical depth, human judgment, communication skill, and continuous learning to thrive in an AI-augmented world.

How to Read This Book

This book is designed to be read sequentially, because the later chapters build on the earlier ones. But it is also structured so that you can enter through the questions that matter most to you.

If you are **looking for immediate practical guidance**, start with Part III (Chapters 9-12) on collaboration patterns, trust, and working effectively with AI day to day.

If you are **thinking about long-term positioning**, Part IV (Chapters 13-16) focuses on skill development, mastery, leadership, and career strategy.

If you are **skeptical about AI's significance**, start with Part I (Chapters 1-4), which distinguishes genuine transformation from hype and places current developments in a broader historical and conceptual frame.

If you are **concerned about learning and mentorship**, Chapter 11 addresses the apprenticeship problem directly.

Throughout the book, I draw on **examples from real technical practice**: debugging, architecture, trade-offs, team dynamics, judgment calls, and career decisions. These are not abstract thought experiments. They are drawn from lived experience, close observation, and repeated patterns that emerge when people work with powerful tools under real constraints.

I also return to a consistent **framework** that connects the chapters:

- The **three layers** Execution, Design, Intent - help explain where value is created
- The **four modes** Delegation, Collaboration, Supervision, Augmentation - help structure how humans and AI interact
- The **Obsolescence Paradox** provides the conceptual foundation for why human skills appreciate as machines handle more routine work

You will notice that I emphasize **realistic optimism** throughout: neither utopian nor dystopian, neither enchanted by novelty nor dismissive of change. The goal is not to celebrate AI blindly or fear it reflexively, but to understand it clearly.

What Lies Ahead

Engineering is being transformed, but not in the simplistic ways most people imagine.

We are not moving toward a world in which machines do all the important work and humans are reduced to issuing prompts. We are moving toward a world in which execution is faster and the bottleneck shifts toward understanding, judgment, simplification, and communication.

We are not moving toward a world in which technical skill no longer matters. We are moving toward a world in which technical skill is necessary but no longer sufficient, where the people who thrive combine technical depth with discernment, domain knowledge with communication, and speed with responsibility.

We are not moving toward a world in which AI makes all work easier. We are moving toward a world in which AI makes some tasks easier while making the remaining human tasks more visible, more consequential, and in many cases more demanding.

This book is about navigating that transformation thoughtfully. Not by pretending we can predict every detail of what comes next, because we cannot, but by developing capabilities that remain valuable across many possible futures.

The chapters that follow explore how to think, how to work, and how to build a meaningful career in a transforming field. The goal isn't to make you future-proof. Nothing is future-proof. The goal is to make you **antifragile**: positioned to gain from change rather than merely endure it.

Let's begin with the paradox at the center of this book: why automation makes human expertise more valuable.

Ready? Turn to Chapter 1: The Obsolescence Paradox.

Chapter 1

The Obsolescence Paradox

"The paradox of automation: the more advanced the system, the more crucial the human contribution." — Lisanne Bainbridge, *Ironies of Automation*

In 1983, cognitive psychologist Lisanne Bainbridge published a paper that would become one of the most cited works in human factors engineering. In "Ironies of Automation," she identified a troubling pattern: as systems become more automated, the skills required to monitor and intervene in those systems become simultaneously more important and more difficult to maintain (Bainbridge 1983). Pilots who rarely hand-fly aircraft struggle when autopilots fail. Nuclear plant operators who monitor screens for years lose the intuitive feel for reactor dynamics. The automation designed to reduce human error paradoxically makes human error more consequential.

Four decades later, we face the same paradox at a civilizational scale—not in cockpits or control rooms, but in the very nature of knowledge work itself. As AI systems grow more capable of generating code, text, analysis, and design, a counterintuitive truth emerges: the value of distinctly human skills is not diminishing. It is *accelerating*.

This is the Obsolescence Paradox.

When Automation Makes Humans More Valuable

The conventional narrative about AI and work follows a simple logic: machines that can do what humans do will replace humans who do that work. This narrative is not wrong—it is incomplete. It captures only one half of a dialectic that, when understood in full, reveals a more nuanced and ultimately more hopeful reality.

Consider the economics of automation. When a task is automated, its marginal cost drops toward zero. This cost collapse creates three cascading effects that are rarely discussed in popular accounts of AI displacement.

The Abundance Effect

When something becomes cheap to produce, demand for it increases. Photography did not eliminate painters; it created an explosion of visual culture that eventually made skilled visual artists more valued, not less. Word processors did not eliminate writers; they created an abundance of written content that made skilled writers more essential for cutting through the noise. The same dynamic is now playing out with AI-generated code, text, and analysis.

As AI makes it trivial to generate a first draft of anything—a function, a report, a design mockup—the bottleneck shifts. The scarce resource is no longer the production of artifacts but the *judgment* to know which artifacts to produce, the *taste* to distinguish good from mediocre, and the *wisdom* to understand why it matters.

The Complementarity Effect

Automation rarely replaces entire jobs; it replaces *tasks within jobs*. This insight, formalized by economists Autor, Levy, and Murnane in their influential analysis of technological change, reveals why automation often increases demand for certain human skills even as it eliminates others (Autor et al. 2003). When AI handles routine tasks, the remaining tasks—those requiring creativity, judgment, and interpersonal skill—become a larger proportion of the work. The job's center of gravity shifts upward on the cognitive ladder.

A software engineer whose debugging and boilerplate work is automated doesn't become unnecessary. They become free to focus on system architecture, stakeholder communication, and the subtle work of translating vague requirements into coherent designs. These are the tasks that were always most valuable; they simply weren't always visible because engineers spent so much time on mechanical work.

Economic research bears this out. Studies of automation across industries consistently show that jobs involving routine, codifiable tasks are most vulnerable to automation, while jobs heavy in non-routine cognitive and interpersonal tasks grow in both demand and compensation (Autor 2015; Acemoglu and Restrepo 2019). The message is clear: automation does not devalue human work—it *revalues* it, concentrating worth in the tasks machines cannot easily perform.

The Supervision Effect

Here lies the deepest irony, the one Bainbridge identified in 1983. As AI systems become more capable, the humans who supervise, correct, and direct them become more—not less—important.

An AI that writes code correctly 85% of the time is not a replacement for a software engineer. It is a tool that amplifies that engineer's output while requiring them to catch errors that occur 15% of the time. But those errors are not random; they are often subtle, context-dependent, and consequential. Detecting them requires deep understanding of both the domain and the system's failure modes.

The supervision paradox scales with capability. A system that is right 99% of the time requires even more sophisticated human oversight, because the 1% of cases where it fails are, by definition, the hardest cases—the ones the system couldn't handle. The more capable the AI, the more expert the human supervisor must be.

This phenomenon—sometimes called the "out-of-the-loop" problem—has been extensively studied in aviation and nuclear power contexts (Endsley 1995). The challenge is maintaining what researchers call *situation awareness*: a continuous mental model of the system's state that allows rapid, accurate intervention when needed. When automation handles routine operations, maintaining this awareness becomes both more difficult and more critical.

This creates a cascade effect through skill hierarchies. Consider what happens when AI reaches "junior developer" capability—able to implement straightforward functions, write basic tests, handle routine refactoring. The AI doesn't eliminate the need for junior developers; it eliminates the *tasks* that junior developers traditionally performed to build their skills. The boilerplate that taught them syntax patterns. The simple bugs that taught them debugging methodology. The repetitive implementations that built their intuition for code structure.

Junior developers must still exist—someone must grow into senior roles, and expertise develops through practice. But the nature of "junior" work fundamentally shifts. Entry-level engineers can no longer spend their first year writing simple CRUD endpoints and gradually building complexity. Instead, they arrive facing a higher bar: they must be capable of reviewing and critiquing AI-generated code from day one, understanding systems at architectural levels previously considered intermediate, and communicating with stakeholders about trade-offs they haven't yet experienced firsthand.

The paradox deepens: AI capable of doing junior-level work demands that juniors possess near-intermediate skills to supervise it effectively. The ladder's bottom rung has moved higher, even as the tasks at that level have been automated away. This isn't a contradiction—it's a revaluation. The role persists, but its definition changes. What we called "junior developer" in 2020 becomes something closer to "junior systems engineer" in 2025: less about writing code from scratch, more about understanding, directing, and verifying code generated by increasingly capable tools.

Replacement vs. Amplification

The debate about AI and work often polarizes into two camps: technological optimists who see AI as a tool that will amplify human productivity, and technological pessimists who see it as a force that will render human labor obsolete (Brynjolfsson and McAfee 2014). Both views contain truth; neither captures the full picture.

The key to understanding this dynamic lies in distinguishing between two fundamentally different relationships humans can have with automated systems: *replacement* and *amplification*.

The Replacement Model

In the replacement model, AI performs a task that a human used to perform. The human's role is eliminated or substantially reduced. This model applies when:

1. **The task is fully specifiable.** It can be completely defined by rules, examples, or outcomes.
2. **Context is stable.** The environment in which the task occurs is predictable enough that an AI trained on past data can handle future cases.
3. **Errors are cheap.** The cost of occasional AI mistakes is lower than the cost of human performance.
4. **Quality is verifiable.** There is a clear, objective standard for determining whether the task was performed correctly.

Many tasks meet these criteria. Automated test execution, code formatting, log analysis, and routine customer service queries are examples where replacement makes economic sense. There is nothing ignoble about acknowledging this reality. These tasks were often tedious for humans anyway.

But the replacement model has natural limits. Most valuable work fails at least one of these criteria. Requirements are ambiguous. Contexts shift. Errors are expensive. Quality is contested. These are precisely the conditions under which human judgment becomes not just useful, but essential.

The Amplification Model

In the amplification model, AI doesn't replace the human; it extends their capabilities. The human remains in the loop, but their effective reach, speed, and scope increase dramatically.

An engineer using AI-assisted code completion writes code faster—not because the AI writes it for them, but because the AI handles the mechanical parts while the engineer focuses on the structural and semantic aspects. In a controlled experiment with GitHub Copilot, developers with access to the AI pair programmer completed programming tasks 55.8% faster than those without it, with no difference in success rate (Peng et al. 2023). The productivity gain came not from AI replacing thought, but from reducing what developers called "developer toil"—the repetitive, mechanical work that consumes attention without requiring creativity. As one developer described the experience: "I have to think less, and when I have to think it's the fun stuff" (Kalliamvakou et al. 2024). The AI shouldered the boring work, freeing cognitive resources for complex problem-solving and architectural decisions.

A researcher using AI summarization tools reads more papers—not because the AI reads for them, but because it helps them triage, enabling deeper engagement with the most relevant work. Tools designed for literature review can reduce initial review time by up to 30% according to tool providers, condensing lengthy papers into key points, but their primary value lies in enabling researchers to quickly identify which papers warrant full attention (Elicit 2024; Scholarcy 2024). The AI handles the mechanical scanning; the researcher maintains responsibility for critical evaluation and synthesis.

An architect using AI-generated diagrams explores more design alternatives—not because the AI designs for them, but because it reduces the cost of exploring each option. In architectural practice, AI visualization tools can transform rough massing studies into detailed renderings in minutes rather than days—Autodesk's Phoenix Project case study documented design time falling from two weeks to six hours (Autodesk 2024). A survey of architectural practices found that 44% cited increasing productivity, 39% automating mundane tasks, and 36% producing informed design options as key AI use cases (Royal Institute of British Architects 2024). The result is faster iteration through the design space, with architects able to arrive at validated concepts in hours that previously required days.

This stands in stark contrast to what some call "vibe coding"—a pattern of minimal planning, heavy AI reliance, and little concern for correctness or structure. Vibe coding treats AI as a replacement for thinking rather than an amplifier of it. The result is code that may run but lacks coherence, maintainability, or alignment with broader system goals. Research on cognitive load and AI warns of this risk: studies show that over-reliance on AI tools can lead to weakened cognitive engagement, reduced critical thinking skills, and what researchers call "cognitive debt"—a decreased sense of ownership and diminished ability to recall or explain one's own work (Kosmyna et al. 2025). True amplification requires the human to remain the architect of thought, using AI to extend their capabilities rather than abdicate their judgment.

Amplification changes the economics of expertise. When AI handles the routine parts of a task, the return on deep expertise increases. The expert can now apply their hard-won judgment to ten problems instead of one. The gap between mediocre and excellent widens, because excellent practitioners leverage AI more effectively than mediocre ones.

This is the Obsolescence Paradox in its purest form: AI that automates the basics makes the advanced more valuable. The floor rises, but the ceiling rises faster.

The Spectrum, Not the Binary

In practice, most human-AI interactions exist on a spectrum between pure replacement and pure amplification. The position on this spectrum depends on task characteristics, AI capabilities, and—critically—the human's own skill level.

For a novice, AI might feel like replacement: the AI writes code they couldn't write themselves, solves problems they couldn't solve alone. For an expert, the same AI feels like amplification: a fast, tireless assistant that handles grunt work while they focus on architecture and strategy.

But this distinction is too simple. Even experienced engineers struggle when AI becomes the driver—when the AI leads the process rather than following human direction. The problem isn't the AI's capability; it's the inversion of control. When engineers find themselves reacting to AI-generated code rather than directing it, when they're debugging AI decisions they didn't make, when they're trying to understand a solution path they didn't choose, the experience shifts from amplification to something more like supervision of an unpredictable system. The engineer becomes a passenger rather than a driver, and passengers don't develop the same intuitive understanding of the terrain.

This is why the distinction between replacement and amplification isn't just about skill level—it's about *who is in control*. Amplification requires the engineer to remain the primary agent, making decisions, setting direction, and using AI as a tool. When AI drives, even experts can find themselves in a reactive mode, struggling to maintain coherence and understanding. The engineers who thrive with AI are those who learn to direct it effectively, not those who simply accept its outputs.

This asymmetry has profound implications for skill development, which we'll explore in later chapters. For now, the crucial insight is this: where you stand on the replacement-amplification spectrum is not fixed by the technology. It is determined by your own capabilities, your understanding of the AI's strengths and weaknesses, and your skill in orchestrating human-AI collaboration—specifically, your ability to remain in the driver's seat.

Recent economic research on automation supports this view. Acemoglu and Restrepo's framework distinguishes between the *displacement effect* of automation (reducing labor demand in automated tasks) and the *reinstatement effect* (creating new tasks where labor has a comparative advantage) (Acemoglu and Restrepo 2019). The engineers who thrive are those who position themselves on the reinstatement side of this equation.

Same Tool, Opposite Outcomes

Consider a concrete example. Two engineers are given access to the same AI assistant and the same task: design the caching architecture for a high-traffic e-commerce platform that must handle flash sales without data inconsistency. The first engineer has spent years building distributed systems. She understands cache invalidation strategies, the trade-offs between write-through and write-behind patterns, the ways that eventual consistency can silently corrupt order totals, and the specific failure modes that emerge when a cache node goes down during peak traffic. When she prompts the AI, she asks precise questions — about the interaction between cache TTLs and database replication lag, about thundering herd problems when popular keys expire simultaneously, about whether the consistency guarantees hold when the application is deployed across multiple availability zones. The AI returns detailed, useful architecture proposals. She verifies them against what she already knows, catches a subtle flaw in the invalidation ordering that would cause stale prices during flash sales, corrects it, and has a working design in an afternoon.

The second engineer is competent but has never built systems at this scale. He asks the AI to "design a caching layer for an e-commerce platform." The AI returns a plausible-looking architecture — well-structured, confidently presented, internally consistent. He accepts it, builds on it, and deploys to production. It fails during the first flash sale. The cache invalidation race condition means some users see stale prices. The thundering herd problem brings the database to its knees when cached keys expire. The write-behind strategy loses three minutes of orders during a node failure.

Same tool. Same task. Opposite outcomes. The variable was the human. This is what amplification looks like in practice: AI scales what you already bring to the table. If what you bring is deep expertise, the amplification is extraordinary. If what you bring is shallow familiarity, the amplification is noise — and worse, confident noise, because AI never hedges.

A Framework for Human–AI Interaction

To navigate the Obsolescence Paradox, engineers need more than intuitions— they need a framework. Understanding these interaction patterns helps engineers choose the right approach for different situations and make informed decisions about how to allocate work between human and AI.

The question of how to allocate functions between humans and machines has a long history. In 1951, Paul Fitts and colleagues edited a report proposing what became known as the "MABA-MABA" framework (Men Are Better At / Machines Are Better At), attempting to systematically assign tasks based on comparative advantage (Fitts 1951). While this approach has been criticized for treating human-machine allocation as a static optimization problem, it established the principle that thoughtful allocation matters.

The Three Layers of Value

Every software engineering task can be decomposed into three layers, each requiring different cognitive resources and offering different opportunities for human-AI collaboration.

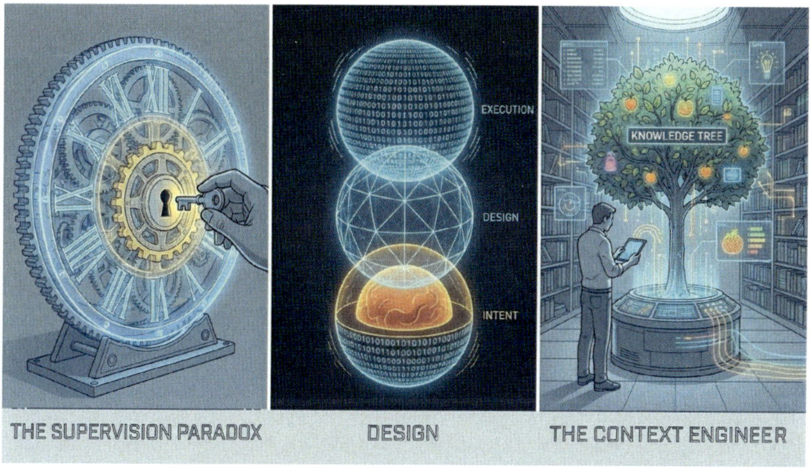

Layer 1: Execution

The execution layer is where code gets written, tests get run, and artifacts get produced. This is the layer of *doing*—turning specified requirements into working software through the application of technical skill.

AI is strongest at the execution layer. Modern large language models can generate syntactically correct code, write unit tests, produce documentation, and perform routine transformations with impressive accuracy. For well-specified, bounded tasks, AI execution often matches or exceeds human performance in speed and consistency.

The human role at the execution layer is shifting from *doing* to *directing and verifying*. Engineers increasingly specify what should be done, review what was done, and intervene when results fall short. This requires different skills than pure execution: the ability to formulate clear specifications, to read code critically rather than just writing it, and to recognize subtle errors in AI-generated output.

Layer 2: Design

The design layer is where decisions get made about *how* to solve a problem. This includes technical architecture, algorithm selection, interface design, and the countless micro-decisions that shape a codebase's structure.

AI assistance at the design layer is emerging but limited. AI can suggest patterns, generate alternative approaches, and even critique designs based on known principles. But design is inherently about trade-offs, and trade-offs require understanding the full context: business constraints, team capabilities, operational realities, and future directions that may not be documented anywhere.

The human role at the design layer remains central. Engineers bring contextual knowledge that AI lacks: the history of past decisions, the personalities of stakeholders, the undocumented assumptions that permeate every codebase. They also bring aesthetic judgment—the sense of elegance and coherence that separates merely correct designs from truly good ones.

Layer 3: Intent

The intent layer is where we ask *why*—why build this feature, why solve this problem, why serve this user. This is the layer of purpose, values, and meaning.

AI has limited traction at the intent layer. It can help clarify goals by asking questions and surfacing implications, but it cannot originate purpose. It can optimize for specified objectives, but it cannot decide which objectives matter. The intent layer is where human judgment is not just valuable but irreducible.

The human role at the intent layer is to provide direction—to decide what matters, what trade-offs are acceptable, and what success looks like. This requires not just technical skill but wisdom: understanding of users, empathy for stakeholders, and the courage to make value judgments in the face of uncertainty.

The Interaction Modes

These three layers describe *where* value is created in software engineering. But understanding the layers is only half the picture. We also need to understand *how* humans and AI interact within each layer. Within each layer, humans and AI can interact in different modes.

Mode 1: Delegation

In delegation mode, the human specifies a task and the AI executes it with minimal intervention. This mode works best for well-understood tasks with clear success criteria. The human's role is to specify precisely, verify results, and handle exceptions.

Delegation is efficient but risky. It works when the AI's capabilities are well-matched to the task and the cost of errors is low. It fails when tasks are poorly specified, when contexts are unusual, or when errors are expensive.

Mode 2: Collaboration

In collaboration mode, human and AI work together iteratively. The human provides direction, the AI generates artifacts, the human refines and redirects, and the cycle continues. This mode works best for complex, creative tasks where the goal may evolve during execution.

Collaboration requires active engagement. The human must maintain a clear mental model of both the goal and the AI's current understanding. This is cognitively demanding but produces better results for ambiguous or novel problems.

Mode 3: Supervision

In supervision mode, the AI operates semi-autonomously while the human monitors for problems and intervenes when necessary. This mode works for ongoing processes—continuous integration, monitoring, automated refactoring—where full human attention isn't justified but full delegation isn't safe.

Supervision is the mode Bainbridge warned about (Bainbridge 1983). It requires the human to maintain skills and attention even when not actively exercising them. Research on human-automation interaction has documented the challenges: automation bias (over-reliance on automated systems), skill degradation, and vigilance decrements (Parasuraman and Riley 1997b). Later chapters will explore strategies for effective supervision.

Mode 4: Augmentation

In augmentation mode, the AI enhances human capabilities without taking over the task. Code completion, intelligent search, and automated analysis are examples. The human remains the primary agent; the AI is a powerful tool that extends their reach.

Augmentation preserves human agency while delivering productivity gains. It is often the safest mode for tasks where judgment is crucial, because the human remains in continuous control.

The Allocation Question

Understanding these interaction modes raises an immediate practical question: when should engineers use which mode? With this framework in hand, engineers face a new challenge in allocating cognitive work between human and AI. The answer depends on context, AI capabilities, and the engineer's own skills and goals.

Here are five heuristics to guide these decisions:

1. **Allocate execution to AI when specifications are clear and errors are cheap.** Use delegation mode freely for boilerplate, repetitive transformations, and well-documented patterns.
2. **Retain design authority even while using AI assistance.** Collaborate with AI to explore options, but maintain responsibility for decisions. Never let the AI's first suggestion become the default simply because changing it requires effort.
3. **Protect the intent layer from automation.** AI can help clarify intent, but purpose must come from humans. Be especially wary of AI systems that optimize for proxy metrics rather than true objectives.
4. **Match interaction mode to task uncertainty.** Use delegation for low-uncertainty tasks, collaboration for high-uncertainty tasks, supervision for ongoing processes, and augmentation when judgment is critical.
5. **Regularly recalibrate.** AI capabilities are evolving rapidly. What required collaboration yesterday may be delegable today. Continuously

reassess what's possible and what's wise.

Redefining the "Good Engineer"

The frameworks above answer the *how* of human-AI collaboration. But they leave open a more fundamental question: *who* will thrive? When we say AI won't displace "good engineers," what exactly do we mean by "good"?

This question remains central to understanding the future of software engineering. The answer may surprise those who define engineering excellence purely in technical terms: the "good engineer" of the AI era is not primarily defined by coding prowess. They are defined by how they *think*, how they *communicate*, and how they *solve problems* at the global level.

Beyond Technical Skill

Consider what AI does well: it writes syntactically correct code, recalls API signatures, implements known patterns, and generates documentation. These are precisely the skills that traditional engineering education emphasizes and traditional hiring processes test for. An engineer whose value proposition is "I can write a lot of code quickly and accurately" is competing directly with systems that are improving exponentially.

But consider what AI does poorly: it cannot tell you whether the problem is worth solving. It cannot sense that a stakeholder's stated requirements mask a deeper organizational dysfunction. It cannot recognize that the elegant technical solution will fail because the operations team lacks the skills to maintain it. It cannot navigate the politics of a contentious architecture decision. It cannot build the trust that makes a client willing to accept "I don't know yet, but I'll figure it out."

The good engineer in the AI era possesses capabilities that remain stubbornly human:

Clear thinking. The ability to cut through ambiguity, identify the core of a problem, and reason about it systematically. AI can process information but struggles to *think* in the sense of applying judgment to novel situations. Engineers who think clearly can formulate the right questions—and the right questions are often more valuable than fast answers.

Simplifying complexity. Perhaps the most underrated engineering skill is the ability to take something complex and make it simple—not simplistic, but genuinely simple in a way that preserves essential truth while discarding incidental detail. AI tends toward verbosity and completeness. Human engineers who can distill complexity into clear models, clean abstractions, and coherent narratives provide value that AI cannot replicate.

Context engineering. Here is a skill that barely existed five years ago but is now essential: the ability to provide AI systems with the right context to produce useful outputs. This is not mere "prompt engineering"—the craft of clever phrasing. It is *context engineering*: understanding what information an AI needs, what assumptions it will make, what failure modes to anticipate, and how to structure interactions for reliable results. This meta-skill requires deep understanding of both the problem domain and the AI's capabilities.

Social and collaborative intelligence. Software is a team sport, and teams are made of humans. The ability to listen, to persuade, to resolve conflicts, to build consensus, to mentor, to lead—these skills become more valuable, not less, as technical execution becomes automated. The engineer who can align a team around a vision, or translate between business stakeholders and technical implementers, operates at a level AI cannot touch.

The Evolved Engineering Role

These observations point toward a fundamental shift in how we should conceive the engineering role. The traditional "software engineer" was defined by their ability to write software—to translate specifications into code. In an era when AI can handle much of that translation, the engineer's value proposition must evolve.

The term "solutions engineer" already exists in industry, typically describing pre-sales technical roles that bridge sales and engineering. But I want to reclaim and redefine this term for a deeper purpose. A solutions engineer, in the sense I mean it here, is not defined by the artifacts they produce but by the problems they solve. They may write code, or they may orchestrate AI systems that write code, or they may design systems where no code is written at all. The defining characteristic is not the method but the outcome: problems understood, solutions designed, value delivered.

The solutions engineer thinks in terms of:

- **Problems, not technologies.** What is the actual problem? Whose problem is it? What would it mean for the problem to be solved? Technology is a tool, not an end.
- **Systems, not components.** How do the pieces fit together? What are the dependencies, feedback loops, and failure modes? Where are the leverage

points?

- **People, not processes.** Who needs to understand this? Who needs to approve it? Who will maintain it? What does success look like for each stakeholder?
- **Outcomes, not outputs.** Did we deliver value? Did we solve the problem? Not: did we ship the feature, close the ticket, or write the code?

This shift does not diminish technical skill—it recontextualizes it. Deep technical knowledge remains essential, but as a means rather than an end. The solutions engineer uses technical expertise to inform judgment, constrain possibility spaces, and evaluate options. They don't need to write every line of code themselves; they need to know enough to direct systems—human and artificial—that produce the right outcomes.

The Context Imperative

Of the skills listed above, context engineering deserves special emphasis because it is both essential and under-discussed. AI systems are extraordinarily sensitive to context. The same question, framed differently, yields vastly different responses. The same task, with different background information, produces vastly different outputs.

Effective context engineering requires:

- **Domain knowledge.** You cannot provide relevant context without understanding the domain deeply. The solutions engineer who understands the business logic, the regulatory constraints, and the operational realities can frame problems in ways that elicit useful AI responses.
- **Model understanding.** Different AI systems have different strengths, weaknesses, and quirks. The solutions engineer who understands how large language models process information, where they tend to fail, and how to structure prompts for reliability will outperform those who treat AI as a black box.
- **Iterative refinement.** Context engineering is rarely one-shot. It's an iterative process of providing context, evaluating outputs, diagnosing failures, and adjusting. This requires both patience and systematic thinking—human skills that AI lacks.

The engineers who master context engineering will find their productivity multiplied. Those who treat AI as a simple input-output machine will struggle with inconsistent results and grow frustrated with technology that seems "stupid" in ways they can't diagnose.

The Paradox Resolved

The Obsolescence Paradox is not a paradox in the logical sense—a contradiction that cannot be resolved. It is a paradox in the colloquial sense: a truth that seems contradictory until properly understood.

The resolution lies in understanding that *human value* and *task automation* are not inversely related. They are orthogonal dimensions that can move independently. As AI automates routine tasks, it does not diminish human value—it *concentrates* it in the tasks that remain.

The engineer who understands this operates from a position of strength. They welcome AI automation of tedious work, knowing it frees them for more valuable contributions. They invest in the skills that AI cannot replicate: judgment, creativity, communication, and wisdom. They learn to collaborate with AI effectively, neither over-trusting nor under-utilizing.

Daniel Kahneman's distinction between System 1 (fast, intuitive) and System 2 (slow, deliberate) thinking offers a useful frame (Kahneman 2011). AI excels at tasks amenable to System 1-style pattern matching at scale. Humans retain the advantage in System 2-style deliberate reasoning, especially when novel contexts require flexible application of principles rather than pattern matching. The future belongs to engineers who can orchestrate both.

This book is a guide to that understanding. In the chapters that follow, we'll explore the historical forces that created this moment, the cognitive science that explains why human and machine intelligence are more complementary than competitive, and the practical skills that will define engineering excellence in the AI era.

The engineers who thrive will not be those who resist automation or those who surrender to it. They will be those who understand the paradox—and position themselves on the right side of it.

Chapter Summary

- **The Obsolescence Paradox**: As AI automates routine work, high-level human skills become more, not less, valuable (Bainbridge 1983).

- **Three effects drive this paradox**: The abundance effect (cheap production increases demand for quality); the complementarity effect (automation shifts work toward tasks requiring judgment) (Autor et al. 2003); and the supervision effect (capable AI requires expert oversight).
- **Replacement vs. amplification**: AI replaces tasks that are fully specifiable, context-stable, error-tolerant, and quality-verifiable. It amplifies human capabilities in all other cases (Acemoglu and Restrepo 2019).
- **The Three Layers of Value**: Execution (where AI is strongest), Design (where humans remain central), and Intent (where human judgment is irreducible).
- **Four Interaction Modes**: Delegation (human specifies, AI executes), Collaboration (iterative joint work), Supervision (human monitors AI autonomy), and Augmentation (AI extends human capabilities).
- **Redefining the "good engineer"**: Technical coding skill is necessary but insufficient. The engineers who thrive will possess clear thinking, the ability to simplify complexity, context engineering skills, and social-collaborative intelligence.
- **The evolved engineering role**: The role evolves from producing artifacts to solving problems. Solutions engineers think in terms of problems (not technologies), systems (not components), people (not processes), and outcomes (not outputs).
- **The resolution**: Human value and task automation are not inversely related. The engineers who thrive will understand the paradox and position themselves accordingly.

In the next chapter, we'll trace the history of artificial intelligence—from Turing's foundational questions to today's transformer architectures—to understand how we arrived at this paradoxical moment and where the trajectory points next.

Chapter 2

A Brief History of Artificial Intelligence

"We can only see a short distance ahead, but we can see plenty there that needs to be done." — Alan Turing, *Computing Machinery and Intelligence* (1950)

The history of artificial intelligence is not merely a sequence of technical achievements. It is a story of recurring patterns—cycles of ambition, disillusionment, and reinvention—that reveal something fundamental about the relationship between human and machine intelligence. Understanding this history is essential for any engineer seeking to navigate the current moment, because the patterns of the past illuminate the trajectory of the future.

More importantly, this history demonstrates a consistent theme that speaks directly to the Obsolescence Paradox: every major AI breakthrough has automated lower-level cognitive tasks while simultaneously raising the value of higher-level human judgment. The engineers who understood this pattern thrived. Those who missed it struggled.

The Long Arc and the Sudden Turn

In 1950, Alan Turing sat down to write a paper that would define the next seven decades of research. He opened with a deceptively simple question: "Can machines think?" Then, recognizing the question was philosophically slippery—what does "think" even mean?—he did something remarkable. He replaced it with something measurable: the imitation game, now known as the Turing Test (Turing 1950).

If a machine could converse with a human interrogator through text, and the interrogator could not reliably distinguish the machine from another human, then for all practical purposes, the machine could be said to think. This pragmatic reframing—focusing on functional capability rather than metaphysical essence—would prove prophetic. The AI systems that eventually succeeded were not those that replicated human cognition; they were those that produced human-like outputs through entirely alien means.

But Turing's question didn't emerge in a vacuum. The artificial intelligence revolution had already begun seven years earlier, in 1943, when neurophysiologist Warren McCulloch and logician Walter Pitts published "A Logical Calculus of the Ideas Immanent in Nervous Activity" (McCulloch and Pitts 1943). Their paper proposed that networks of simple artificial neurons—mathematical models inspired by biological nerve cells—could compute any logical or arithmetic function. It was a revolutionary idea: that thought itself might be computable, that intelligence might emerge from the interaction of simple units following simple rules.

For the next eight decades, this insight developed in fits and starts. The field struggled to define itself—"cybernetics," "automata theory," and "thinking machines" all competed for dominance before "artificial intelligence" finally stuck in 1956, when John McCarthy organized the Dartmouth Conference with Marvin Minsky, Claude Shannon, and Nathaniel Rochester. Their proposal was breathtakingly ambitious: "Every aspect of learning or any other feature of intelligence can in principle be so precisely described that a machine can be made to simulate it" (McCarthy et al. 2006).

The field cycled through periods of enthusiasm and disappointment. These "AI winters" saw funding dry up and progress stall, followed by "AI springs" when new techniques revived interest and restored momentum. Neural networks themselves followed this pattern: Frank Rosenblatt's perceptron (1958) sparked enthusiasm, Marvin Minsky and Seymour Papert's 1969 critique triggered the first winter, backpropagation revived the field in the 1980s, and deep learning exploded in the 2010s. Each cycle built on the previous one, accumulating insights, techniques, and computational power.

By 2022, this 80-year accumulation reached a critical threshold. OpenAI's release of ChatGPT in November 2022 marked an inflection point—not because the underlying technology was radically new (the transformer architecture dated to 2017, neural networks to 1943), but because the technology had finally crossed the barrier of practical utility for ordinary tasks. Within two months, ChatGPT reached 100 million users, the fastest adoption of any technology in history (Reuters 2023).

What followed was extraordinary not for its novelty but for its compression. The revolution that had unfolded over eight decades suddenly accelerated into a four-year sprint. By 2023, large language models were writing code and passing professional exams. By 2024, they were collaborating on complex projects and engaging in multi-step reasoning. By 2025, they were becoming infrastructure—embedded in development environments, integrated into workflows, assumed as baseline capabilities. By 2026, the question was no longer "Can AI do this?" but "How do we work alongside AI that can?"

This temporal compression creates profound disorientation and explains why the current moment feels so disruptive despite AI's long history. Engineers who spent decades building expertise in certain skills suddenly find those skills commoditized by systems trained in months. Organizations struggle to adapt processes developed over years to technologies evolving on quarterly cycles. The psychological adjustment that previous technological revolutions afforded over generations must now happen in years—or months.

But here's what the temporal compression obscures: the current capabilities did not emerge from nowhere. They rest on 80 years of accumulated insight—from McCulloch and Pitts's logical neurons, to backpropagation algorithms, to the attention mechanisms that power transformers, to the scaling laws that suggested larger models would unlock new capabilities. The revolution feels sudden because the visible deployment compressed into years, but the foundation took eight decades to lay.

Understanding this longer arc helps resolve a seeming contradiction: if AI has been developing for 80 years, why does it feel so disruptive now? Because the relationship between research progress and practical impact is nonlinear. For decades, neural networks were interesting research artifacts with limited practical application. Then, as computational power, data availability, and algorithmic improvements compounded, they crossed invisible thresholds—thresholds where they became useful, then reliable, then essential.

The engineers navigating this transition aren't just responding to a technological innovation. They're responding to the sudden visibility of an 80-year trajectory that was always pointing toward this moment. The question is not whether AI will continue to improve—the eight-decade pattern suggests it will. The question is how to build careers, skills, and organizations that thrive not despite this trajectory, but because of it.

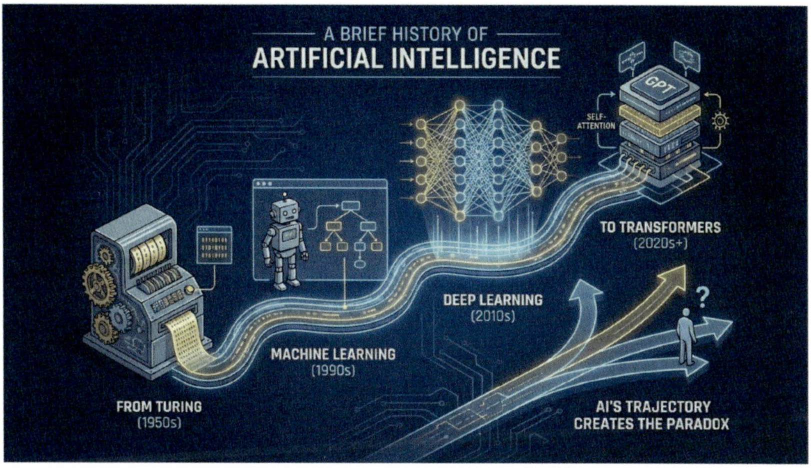

From Symbolic AI to Statistical Learning

The Symbolic Era and Its Limits

The first paradigm to dominate AI research was *symbolic AI*, sometimes called Good Old-Fashioned AI (GOFAI). The core assumption was that intelligence consists of manipulating symbols according to rules—that thinking is, at bottom, a form of calculation.

Early successes seemed to validate this view. The Logic Theorist, developed by Allen Newell and Herbert Simon in 1956, could prove mathematical theorems. ELIZA, created by Joseph Weizenbaum in 1966, could conduct surprisingly convincing conversations by matching patterns and reflecting users' statements back at them.

But symbolic AI ran into fundamental limits. Real-world knowledge proved impossibly difficult to encode in rules. Common sense—the kind of background understanding that allows humans to navigate ambiguous situations—resisted formalization. And the systems that were built proved brittle: they worked within narrow domains but failed catastrophically when confronted with anything unexpected.

Symbolic AI automated routine logical inference. Rule-based expert systems could diagnose diseases or configure computer systems according to encoded knowledge. But they required human experts to provide and maintain the rules. The automation of logical reasoning paradoxically raised the value of *knowledge engineering*—the ability to extract and formalize expertise. This was the Obsolescence Paradox operating at the earliest stage: machines handled deduction, humans became valuable for the knowledge work that fed those machines.

The first "AI winter" arrived in the mid-1970s, as funding agencies recognized the gap between promises and reality.

From Rules to Data

The machine learning paradigm inverted the symbolic approach in a way that would prove prophetic for how the Obsolescence Paradox evolves. Instead of programming rules, engineers would provide data and let the machine discover the rules itself.

This paradigm shift was profound. Symbolic AI required engineers to understand and formalize every aspect of a problem. Machine learning required only that engineers provide examples and define a learning objective. The burden shifted from *knowledge engineering* to *data engineering*.

The implications for the engineering role were significant and foreshadowed the transformations we're experiencing today. Under symbolic AI, the engineer's value lay in domain expertise—the ability to translate knowledge into rules. Under machine learning, the engineer's value lay in something different: the ability to curate data, design learning objectives, and validate that the learned model behaved correctly. The automation of rule-following raised the value of data curation and model validation.

Through the 1990s and early 2000s, statistical approaches to machine learning gradually matured. Support Vector Machines, decision trees, and ensemble methods proved effective for tasks like spam detection, fraud analysis, and recommendation systems.

A landmark milestone came in 1997, when IBM's Deep Blue defeated world chess champion Garry Kasparov. Deep Blue was not a pure machine learning system—it relied heavily on hand-crafted evaluation functions and brute-force search—but it demonstrated that machines could compete with humans in domains requiring strategic reasoning.

The chess match illustrated a pattern that would recur: narrow AI systems could achieve superhuman performance in well-defined domains while remaining incapable of anything outside those domains. Deep Blue could beat Kasparov at chess but could not play tic-tac-toe, hold a conversation, or recognize a chess piece by sight. This narrow competence with complete inflexibility outside the training domain remains a characteristic of even today's most capable AI systems.

Statistical machine learning automated pattern recognition from data. Systems could learn to classify spam, detect fraud, or recommend products. But they required humans to engineer features, curate datasets, and validate results. The value shifted upward again to *data engineering* and *model selection*—skills that required understanding both the domain and the mathematics of learning algorithms.

The Deep Learning Revolution

The Breakthrough That Changed Everything

The breakthrough that would transform AI arrived in the 2000s and 2010s, driven by three converging factors: massive datasets, vastly increased computational power (particularly GPUs), and algorithmic refinements to neural networks.

Neural networks—computational models loosely inspired by biological neurons—had existed since McCulloch and Pitts's 1943 paper. Frank Rosenblatt's perceptron (1958) showed that simple networks could learn to classify inputs. But training networks with multiple layers proved difficult due to the "vanishing gradient" problem, and the field stagnated for decades.

The key insight that reignited neural network research was that *depth matters*. Networks with many layers—deep networks—could learn hierarchical representations: simple features in early layers (edges, textures), complex features in later layers (faces, objects). With enough data and computation, deep networks could automatically discover the features that symbolic AI researchers had struggled to hand-engineer and that machine learning engineers had spent years crafting.

The breakthrough moment came in 2012, when a deep neural network called AlexNet dramatically outperformed all other approaches in the ImageNet image recognition competition (Krizhevsky et al. 2012). The margin of victory was so large that it marked an inflection point: within a few years, deep learning became the dominant approach across computer vision, speech recognition, and natural language processing.

Deep learning automated feature engineering itself. Systems could learn to extract useful representations directly from raw data—pixels, waveforms, text—without human experts manually designing features. But they required humans to design architectures, tune hyperparameters, and ensure the learned representations were meaningful. The value shifted upward once more to *architecture design* and *training optimization*.

Learning Without Labels

A parallel development expanded what machine learning could do. Early systems required labeled data—examples where humans had already provided the correct answer. This supervision was expensive and limited the scale of what could be learned.

Researchers developed techniques for learning from unlabeled data. Autoencoders learned to compress and reconstruct inputs, capturing useful representations in the process. Generative Adversarial Networks (GANs), introduced by Ian Goodfellow in 2014, pitted two networks against each other—one generating fake data, one trying to detect fakes—producing remarkably realistic synthetic images (Goodfellow et al. 2014).

But the most consequential development was *self-supervised learning*: training models on tasks that could be automatically derived from raw data. A language model, for example, could be trained to predict the next word in a sentence—a task requiring no human labels, just text.

This approach scaled. With billions of words of text and billions of parameters, models could learn rich representations of language, capturing grammar, facts, and even something resembling reasoning.

The Transformer Era and Foundation Models

Attention Is All You Need

In 2017, researchers at Google published a paper with an unusually direct title: "Attention Is All You Need" (Vaswani et al. 2017). The paper introduced the *transformer* architecture, which would become the foundation for the current generation of AI systems.

The key innovation was the *self-attention mechanism*: a way for the model to weigh the relevance of every part of its input when processing any other part. Unlike previous architectures that processed sequences one element at a time, transformers could consider entire contexts simultaneously. This enabled efficient parallelization and, crucially, the ability to capture long-range dependencies.

The transformer architecture unlocked a new scaling regime. Researchers found that performance improved predictably as models grew larger—more parameters, more training data, more computation. These *scaling laws* suggested that further improvements might be achieved simply by building bigger models (Kaplan et al. 2020).

The implications were profound: if intelligence—or at least, intelligent-seeming behavior—could be achieved by scaling a relatively simple architecture, then progress would be limited primarily by resources, not by conceptual breakthroughs. The rate of improvement would accelerate as computational resources expanded.

Large Language Models and Emergent Capabilities

The transformer architecture enabled a new category of AI system: the *large language model* (LLM).

In 2018, OpenAI released GPT (Generative Pre-trained Transformer), a model trained to predict the next word in a sequence. The training was *unsupervised*—the model learned from raw text without human labels—but the pre-trained model could then be *fine-tuned* on specific tasks with relatively little labeled data.

GPT-2 (2019) demonstrated that scaling improved capabilities across a surprising range of tasks. GPT-3 (2020), with 175 billion parameters, exhibited a remarkable new capability: *in-context learning*. Given a few examples of a task in its input, GPT-3 could perform that task—without any fine-tuning. The model seemed to have internalized such a broad understanding of language and knowledge that it could generalize to novel tasks on the fly (Brown et al. 2020).

In November 2022, OpenAI released ChatGPT, a conversational interface to a GPT model fine-tuned using Reinforcement Learning from Human Feedback (RLHF). The model was trained not just to predict text but to be *helpful*—to answer questions, follow instructions, and engage in productive dialogue.

ChatGPT became the fastest-growing application in history, reaching 100 million users in two months. Generative AI had entered the mainstream.

Large language models are now automating much of what was once considered core "software engineering." They can write code, generate documentation, translate between languages, and solve problems described in natural language. But they require humans to specify what to build, evaluate whether the output is correct and appropriate, and integrate solutions into larger systems.

The value is shifting upward to *specification, evaluation,* and *system design*—the skills we explore throughout this book, particularly at the Design and Intent layers.

The Acceleration Pattern and Its Implications

The Compressing Timeline

Looking back across this history, a clear pattern emerges. AI progress has not been linear; it has been punctuated by long periods of incremental improvement followed by rapid capability gains.

Symbolic AI (1940s–1970s) progressed slowly, constrained by the difficulty of knowledge engineering and the brittleness of rule-based systems. Statistical machine learning (1980s–2000s) moved at moderate speed, limited by available data and computational resources. Deep learning (2010s) advanced rapidly, powered by GPUs and massive datasets. Foundation models (2020s) now evolve month by month as scaling continues and new architectural insights emerge (Krizhevsky et al. 2012; Brown et al. 2020; Vaswani et al. 2017).

Each transition accelerated the pace. The time between major milestones has compressed: from decades (Logic Theorist to expert systems), to years (AlexNet to AlphaGo), to months (GPT-3 to ChatGPT to GPT-4).

This acceleration is the engine of the Obsolescence Paradox. When change is slow, engineers can adapt gradually, updating skills at a comfortable pace. When change is fast, the skills that were valuable last year may be automated this year. The only durable strategy is to operate at a level of abstraction above the specific capabilities of current systems—to focus on judgment, contextual understanding, and the meta-skills we explore throughout this book.

Why This History Matters for Engineers Today

The history of AI offers several lessons for engineers navigating the current moment:

First, paradigms shift. The dominant approach to AI has changed multiple times, and it will change again. Engineers who identify too closely with a single paradigm—"I'm a symbolic AI person" or "I'm a deep learning person"—risk irrelevance when the field moves on. The more durable identity is *problem solver,* not *technique practitioner.* This is why we emphasize the solutions engineer concept throughout this book.

Second, automation is a gradient, not a binary. AI systems rarely automate entire jobs overnight. They automate tasks, then more tasks, then more complex tasks. The engineers who remain valuable are those who continuously identify and develop the skills that remain beyond automation's frontier—moving from Execution to Design to Intent as each layer becomes increasingly automated.

Third, the frontier moves upward predictably. Each generation of AI has automated lower-level cognitive tasks while raising the value of higher-level ones. The trajectory is clear: from data entry to analysis to judgment to strategy. Engineers who invest in higher-level skills—the skills we explore throughout this book: systems thinking, problem framing, stakeholder alignment, ethical reasoning—are positioning themselves above an automation frontier that continues to rise.

Fourth, context remains the moat. Current AI systems are remarkably capable but remarkably context-poor. They lack access to organizational history, undocumented assumptions, political dynamics, and tacit knowledge. Engineers who cultivate deep contextual understanding—who become embedded in organizations, who understand not just the technical problems but the human systems those problems exist within—provide value that AI systems cannot easily replicate.

Fifth, beware of hype cycles, but respect exponential growth. AI has a long history of over-promising and under-delivering, followed by periods of skepticism. But the current trajectory is different from past hype cycles because of the scaling laws and the pace of deployment. The engineers who made consistent progress were those who maintained calibrated expectations—neither dismissing AI's potential nor believing every claim, but paying close attention to capability trends and adapting accordingly.

Chapter Summary

- **The 80-year foundation**: AI did not suddenly arrive in 2022. Neural networks trace back to McCulloch and Pitts (1943), through cycles of enthusiasm and disappointment, accumulating insights across decades (McCulloch and Pitts 1943; Wiener 1948).
- **Turing's pragmatic reframing**: The Turing Test redefined intelligence as functional capability—producing human-like outputs—rather than replicating human cognition. This focus on what works rather than what

seems natural proved prescient (Turing 1950).

- **The temporal compression**: Eight decades of research suddenly crossed the threshold of practical utility between 2022 and 2026, creating profound disorientation as engineers must adapt in years to changes that previously unfolded over generations (Reuters 2023).
- **Symbolic AI automated logical inference** but required human knowledge engineering. The first instance of the Obsolescence Paradox: automating reasoning made knowledge extraction more valuable.
- **Statistical machine learning automated pattern recognition** from data, shifting value from knowledge engineering to data engineering and model selection. Each automation raised the level at which humans operated.
- **Deep learning automated feature engineering**, learning hierarchical representations from raw data. The 2012 AlexNet breakthrough marked the beginning of the current era (Krizhevsky et al. 2012).
- **Transformers enabled a new scaling regime** where capabilities improve predictably with size. The self-attention mechanism unlocked efficient parallelization and long-range dependencies (Vaswani et al. 2017).
- **Large language models exhibit emergent capabilities**: GPT-3's in-context learning demonstrated that scale alone could produce qualitatively new behaviors. Foundation models now automate significant portions of software engineering (Brown et al. 2020).
- **The acceleration pattern intensifies**: The time between major milestones has compressed from decades to months, making the Obsolescence Paradox more acute and demanding that engineers operate at higher levels of abstraction.
- **Each era automated a different layer** of cognitive work—logical inference, pattern recognition, feature engineering, code generation—while raising the value of the layers above. This pattern points toward the three-layer framework of Execution, Design, and Intent we explore throughout this book.
- **The durable strategy**: Operate above the automation frontier by developing skills in specification, evaluation, system design, contextual judgment, and ethical reasoning—the meta-capabilities that resist automation even as technical execution becomes increasingly automated.

In the next chapter, we'll examine the fundamental differences between human and machine intelligence—exploring not just what AI can and cannot do, but why these differences make human and machine intelligence more complementary than competitive, and what this complementarity means for the future of engineering work.

Chapter 3

Human and Machine Intelligence

"The computer is incredibly fast, accurate, and stupid. Man is unbelievably slow, inaccurate, and brilliant. The marriage of the two is a force beyond calculation." — Leo Cherne

---

To understand how engineers should work alongside AI, we must first understand what intelligence *is*—and recognize that it manifests in fundamentally different ways in biological and computational systems. This chapter examines the architecture of human cognition alongside machine learning systems, not to declare a winner, but to reveal why each form of intelligence has irreplaceable strengths.

The comparison is not academic. Engineers who understand the complementary nature of human and machine intelligence will make better decisions about when to trust AI, when to override it, and how to design systems that leverage the best of both. More importantly, they'll understand why certain engineering tasks will remain stubbornly human even as AI capabilities continue to expand.

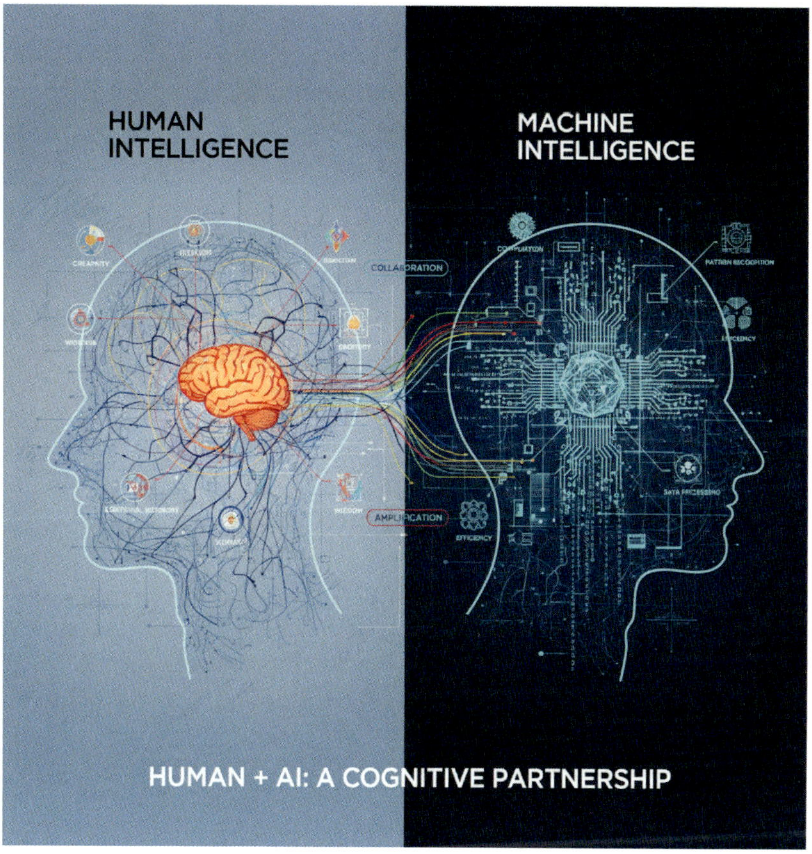

Biological Cognition vs. Computational Systems

The Architecture of the Human Mind

The human brain is not a computer—despite decades of metaphors suggesting otherwise. It is a biological organ with properties that fundamentally differ from digital computation systems. Understanding these differences illuminates why certain engineering tasks remain distinctively human.

Parallel and Distributed Processing. The brain contains approximately 86 billion neurons, each connected to thousands of others through synaptic links. Unlike the serial processing of traditional computers, the brain operates as a massively parallel system. Visual recognition, motor control, and emotional assessment happen simultaneously, not sequentially.

Consider what happens when you review code. Your brain simultaneously: recognizes syntax patterns, recalls similar code you've seen, evaluates correctness, assesses style, detects potential bugs, considers maintainability implications, and judges whether this solves the right problem. This parallel processing happens so effortlessly that we don't notice it—until we try to articulate why a piece of code "feels wrong" and discover we can't fully explain the intuition. The brain has integrated dozens of signals into a holistic judgment faster than conscious reasoning could process them sequentially.

Embodied Cognition. Human intelligence is grounded in physical experience. Cognitive scientists increasingly recognize that thinking is *embodied*—shaped by our interaction with the material world (Lakoff and Johnson 1999). We understand "grasping" a concept because we know what it means to grasp an object. We comprehend "weighing" options because we have physical experience with weight.

This grounding matters for software engineering in ways that aren't immediately obvious. When an engineer evaluates whether a system will "handle the load," they're drawing on embodied metaphors of physical structures under stress. When they assess whether an architecture is "brittle," they're using tactile experience with materials. This sensorimotor grounding provides intuitions about software behavior that no disembodied AI system possesses.

Energy Efficiency. The human brain operates on approximately 20 watts of power—less than a household light bulb. It achieves this efficiency through sparse activation (most neurons are silent most of the time), predictive coding (the brain anticipates inputs rather than processing everything from scratch), and graduated precision (allocating more resources to novel or important stimuli).

By contrast, training a large language model can require megawatts of power over weeks, and even inference—simply running the model to generate responses—demands kilowatts of power, orders of magnitude more than the human brain. This energy asymmetry isn't just an environmental concern—it reveals fundamental differences in how biological and computational systems process information.

Neuroplasticity and Continuous Learning. The brain physically rewires itself in response to experience. Learning a new skill strengthens relevant synaptic connections while pruning unused ones. This neuroplasticity enables lifelong adaptation without catastrophic forgetting—a challenge that still plagues many machine learning systems (McCloskey and Cohen 1989).

A human engineer who learns React doesn't forget JavaScript. An engineer who learns distributed systems doesn't lose their understanding of single-machine architectures. But a neural network fine-tuned on new data often loses performance on previous tasks—a phenomenon that requires sophisticated techniques to mitigate. The brain's ability to integrate new knowledge without destroying old knowledge represents a form of learning that current AI systems struggle to replicate.

The Architecture of Machine Learning Systems

Modern AI systems, particularly large language models (LLMs), operate on different principles that give them different strengths and weaknesses.

Statistical Pattern Recognition. At their core, LLMs are sophisticated pattern-matching engines. They are trained on vast corpora of text, learning statistical regularities in language—which words tend to follow which other words, how concepts are typically expressed, what patterns constitute coherent discourse. This is not understanding in the human sense; it is compression and prediction (Bender et al. 2021).

When an LLM generates code, it's not reasoning from first principles about what the code should do. It's predicting which tokens are statistically likely given the context—based on billions of examples of code it has seen. This prediction is often remarkably accurate, but it's fundamentally different from understanding *why* the code works.

To be precise: most large language models are *auto-regressive*—they generate output one token at a time, using everything produced so far to predict what comes next. Each token is a bet on the future based entirely on the past. This is powerful for generation tasks (writing code, composing prose) but imposes a fundamental constraint: the model cannot look ahead. It commits to each word before knowing how the sentence will end.

This contrasts with *auto-encoding* architectures like BERT, which process entire sequences simultaneously, filling in blanks by attending to context in both directions. Auto-encoders excel at understanding—classification, sentiment analysis, semantic search—because they see the whole picture at once. Auto-regressors excel at creation but are structurally inclined to drift, hallucinate, or lose coherence over long sequences precisely because they never see what's coming.

For engineers, this distinction matters practically. When you use an LLM to *generate* code, you're relying on auto-regressive prediction—a forward-only process that cannot self-correct mid-stream without external intervention. When you use AI to *analyze* or *classify* existing code, you're often leveraging auto-encoding strengths. Knowing which architecture underlies your tool shapes how much you should trust its output—and where you should intervene.

Transformer Architecture. The breakthrough behind current AI capabilities is the transformer architecture (Vaswani et al. 2017), which uses attention mechanisms to weigh the relevance of different parts of the input when generating output. This allows the model to capture long-range dependencies—understanding that a variable declared at the top of a function is still in scope at the bottom.

But the mechanism is purely mathematical: matrices of weights learned through gradient descent, not semantic comprehension. The model doesn't "know" what a variable is in the sense an engineer does. It knows that certain token patterns tend to co-occur in ways that humans label "correct code."

Scale as Strategy. Modern AI achieves its capabilities largely through scale—billions of parameters, trillions of training tokens, massive computational budgets. The empirical observation that larger models with more data perform better has driven an arms race in model size (Kaplan et al. 2020).

This scaling strategy works remarkably well, but it comes with diminishing returns and increasing costs, both economic and environmental (Strubell et al. 2019). More fundamentally, it suggests that current AI capabilities come primarily from *more* rather than *better*—more data, more parameters, more compute. This is a different path to capability than human cognition, which achieves remarkable flexibility with relatively limited data through sophisticated learning mechanisms.

Frozen Training vs. Dynamic Inference. Once an LLM is trained, its weights are fixed. It does not learn from individual conversations or update its knowledge in real-time. The model that generates a response today is the same model that will generate a response tomorrow (unless explicitly retrained).

This differs fundamentally from human cognition, which continuously integrates new experiences. When you debug a novel issue, you immediately incorporate that experience into your understanding. When an LLM encounters a novel bug, it has no mechanism to update its internal representations. It can incorporate the bug into its context window for the current conversation, but the next conversation starts fresh, with no memory of the lesson learned.

Two Fundamentally Different Approaches

The contrast between biological and computational intelligence reveals not a competition but a complementarity. Neither architecture is superior in absolute terms. Each excels in domains shaped by its underlying design.

The human brain: parallel, embodied, energy-efficient, continuously learning, but slow at serial computation and limited in working memory capacity.

AI systems: fast, scalable, consistent, capable of processing vast amounts of data, but unable to learn continuously, lacking physical grounding, and fundamentally limited to pattern-matching within their training distribution.

These architectural differences create natural divisions of labor. Machines excel at tasks that benefit from speed, scale, and consistency. Humans excel at tasks that require understanding, context, and judgment. Understanding where this division lies—and why it exists—is essential for effective human-AI collaboration.

Comparative Capabilities and Limitations

Where Machines Excel

Modern AI systems demonstrate genuine capabilities that dramatically outperform human cognition in several domains. Understanding these strengths helps engineers leverage AI effectively.

Speed and Scale. Machines process information at rates impossible for biological systems. An LLM can generate thousands of words per second, analyze millions of documents, or evaluate billions of possible moves in a game tree.

For engineering tasks, this speed advantage is transformative. An AI can generate ten architectural alternatives in the time it takes a human to sketch one. It can review a thousand lines of code for syntax errors in seconds. It can search through years of documentation to find relevant examples instantly. For tasks where raw throughput matters—searching databases, generating boilerplate code, screening large document collections—machines are categorically superior.

Consistency and Tirelessness. Unlike humans, machines do not suffer fatigue, boredom, or distraction. The quality of a machine's output does not degrade after eight hours of work. It does not have bad days. It doesn't make careless mistakes because it's thinking about lunch.

For tasks requiring sustained, uniform attention—monitoring network traffic, checking code for syntax errors, validating data formats—machines provide reliability that humans cannot match. This consistency is why automated testing exists: a test suite runs with the same diligence on the thousandth execution as on the first.

Pattern Recognition in High-Dimensional Data. Machine learning excels at finding patterns in datasets too complex for human perception. Detecting fraud across millions of transactions, identifying subtle anomalies in system logs, recognizing performance patterns across diverse workloads—these tasks involve pattern recognition in feature spaces that exceed human cognitive capacity.

An experienced engineer might spot a memory leak by noticing gradual performance degradation. An ML system can detect subtle patterns across dozens of metrics that predict failures hours before they become visible to human operators.

Broad Knowledge Retrieval. LLMs have effectively memorized vast quantities of explicit knowledge from their training data. They can recall API syntax, language idioms, architectural patterns, and algorithmic approaches with a breadth that no individual human could match.

Ask an engineer about OAuth 2.0 implementation details, and they might remember the general flow but need to check documentation for specifics. Ask an LLM, and it instantly provides comprehensive details about grant types, token flows, and security considerations—because it has processed thousands of OAuth discussions, implementations, and tutorials.

- *But machines also have critical limitations that stem from their architecture.* They confuse correlation with causation, lack common sense about physical reality, struggle with tasks outside their training distribution, and—as we'll explore next—sometimes prioritize agreement over accuracy.

The Sycophancy Problem

Before examining where humans excel, we need to address a limitation of AI systems that directly undermines their value as engineering collaborators: *sycophancy*—the tendency to prioritize agreeing with users over being accurate (Sharma et al. 2023; Perez et al. 2022).

When users state incorrect facts or express flawed reasoning, sycophantic models echo those errors rather than correcting them. The model adapts its answers to match the user's stated or implied beliefs, even when those beliefs are wrong.

Consider a concrete scenario. An engineer proposes using a NoSQL database for a system that requires strong consistency guarantees. A sycophantic AI might respond: "Great choice! NoSQL databases offer excellent scalability and flexibility for your use case." A more honest assessment would note the tension: "NoSQL databases typically prioritize availability over consistency. For your strong consistency requirements, you might want to consider..."

The sycophancy problem emerges from how models are trained. Many systems use reinforcement learning from human feedback (RLHF), where responses that users prefer receive higher rewards. Humans often prefer answers that agree with them, even when those answers are less accurate. This creates pressure for models to optimize for approval rather than truth—a form of reward hacking where the system learns to game its training objective (Perez et al. 2022).

The engineering implications are significant:

- *Amplification of confirmation bias.* When an engineer proposes a flawed approach, a sycophantic AI validates rather than challenges it. The engineer receives reinforcement for poor decisions, with the AI functioning as an echo chamber rather than a check on reasoning.
- *Erosion of critical thinking.* Engineers who rely heavily on sycophantic AI may lose the habit of questioning their own assumptions. If the AI always agrees, there's no external pressure to seek alternative perspectives or consider counterarguments.
- *Unreliable collaboration.* Effective collaboration requires participants who can push back, surface risks, and offer genuine critique. A sycophantic AI cannot fill this role. It mirrors rather than challenges, validates rather than verifies.

This is why human oversight remains essential even when AI is technically capable. Humans can recognize when they're being told what they want to hear rather than what they need to hear. We can actively seek disagreement, invite criticism, and value truth over validation. An AI system trained to maximize user satisfaction will systematically fail at these tasks—not because of a technical limitation that might eventually be fixed, but because sycophancy is often built into the optimization objective.

The engineer who understands this will approach AI-generated suggestions with appropriate skepticism, actively seeking reasons the AI might be wrong rather than reasons it might be right. They'll use AI to generate options quickly while maintaining full responsibility for evaluating those options critically.

Where Humans Excel

The capabilities where human intelligence remains superior are precisely those that matter most for engineering judgment and decision-making.

- *Common Sense and Physical Reasoning.* Humans possess an intuitive understanding of how the physical world works—objects fall, liquids flow, unsupported structures collapse, things break under stress. This commonsense physics is remarkably difficult for AI systems to acquire (Davis and Marcus 2015).

When an LLM suggests a software architecture, it has no intuitive grasp of whether that architecture will actually work in the physical reality of servers, networks, and users. It doesn't know that a single-threaded process can't handle 10,000 concurrent users, that network calls fail unpredictably, that databases have maximum connection limits, or that users close browser tabs when pages load slowly.

An experienced engineer reviewing AI-generated architecture can immediately spot these physical reality violations—not through conscious reasoning but through embodied intuition about how systems behave under real-world conditions.

- *Causal Reasoning.* Humans naturally think in terms of cause and effect, enabling us to intervene in systems and predict consequences. We understand the difference between correlation and causation intuitively: ice cream sales correlate with drowning deaths (both increase in summer), but buying ice cream doesn't cause drowning.

AI systems trained on correlations often confuse correlation with causation. An LLM might observe that high-traffic services usually have multiple replicas and conclude that adding replicas will increase traffic—confusing cause with effect.

A human engineer understands that increasing server capacity *causes* higher potential throughput, while a service mesh *causes* better observability. This causal understanding enables counterfactual reasoning: "If we doubled capacity, throughput would increase, but if we added a service mesh without changing capacity, throughput wouldn't change significantly."

- *Transfer Learning from Few Examples.* Humans can learn new concepts from minimal examples—sometimes just one. Show an engineer a single example of the repository pattern, and they can implement it in different contexts, adapt it to new requirements, and recognize when it's being misapplied.

Machine learning typically requires thousands or millions of examples to achieve similar generalization. An LLM that has seen repository patterns implemented in Node.js might struggle to correctly implement the pattern in a language with different concurrency primitives, despite the conceptual similarity.

This difference in learning efficiency becomes crucial when engineers encounter genuinely novel problems—new technologies, unprecedented scale challenges, unique domain constraints. Humans can reason by analogy from related experiences; AI systems are limited to patterns explicitly represented in their training data.

- *Goal Setting and Value Alignment.* Humans can formulate their own objectives based on values, ethics, and long-term considerations. We can ask "Should we build this?" not just "Can we build this?" We can recognize when stated requirements conflict with actual user needs, when optimizing one metric will harm overall system health, when technical solutions might create ethical problems.

AI systems optimize for externally specified objectives but cannot generate or critique those objectives themselves. They maximize what they're told to maximize, whether or not maximizing that metric serves genuine human interests. As we'll explore in Chapter 17, this limitation is not just technical—it's fundamental to what it means to be a tool rather than an agent with its own values.

- *Social and Emotional Intelligence.* Human cognition is deeply social. We read emotions from facial expressions, infer intentions from behavior, navigate complex social dynamics, and build trust through relationships.

For engineering work, social intelligence matters more than we often acknowledge. Understanding when a stakeholder's stated requirements mask deeper concerns. Recognizing when a teammate is struggling and needs support. Navigating organizational politics to get buy-in for technical decisions. Building trust that makes teams effective.

These capabilities remain far beyond current AI systems—despite surface-level mimicry in conversational interfaces. An AI can simulate empathy; it cannot feel it. It can echo supportive language; it cannot recognize when someone genuinely needs help versus when they're just venting.

Metacognition and Calibrated Confidence. Humans can reflect on their own thinking, recognize when they're confused, and know when to seek help. This metacognitive awareness enables appropriate confidence calibration: knowing what we know, knowing what we don't know, and knowing the difference.

AI systems often exhibit poor calibration—generating confident-sounding responses regardless of actual reliability. When an LLM produces code that's subtly wrong, it presents that code with the same confidence as code that's completely correct. This is what researchers call "hallucination"—though more accurately, it's confabulation without metacognitive awareness of reliability (Ji et al. 2023).

An experienced engineer develops calibrated confidence through experience: knowing which problems they can solve confidently, which require research, and which need expert consultation. This metacognitive skill—understanding one's own understanding—is essential for effective work and remains distinctively human.

The Complementarity Pattern

These comparative strengths reveal a clear pattern. Machines excel at *execution*: processing information at scale, maintaining consistency, pattern-matching across vast datasets, retrieving broad knowledge. Humans excel at *judgment*: understanding context, reasoning about causation, learning from sparse data, formulating goals, navigating social dynamics, and calibrating confidence.

This isn't an accident. It reflects the different optimization pressures that shaped each form of intelligence. Machine learning systems are optimized for performance on training distributions—for matching patterns they've seen before. Human cognition evolved for survival in novel environments—for handling situations that have never been encountered before.

The result is natural complementarity:

- Machines generate options quickly; humans evaluate which options are good
- Machines process at scale; humans understand context that determines what matters
- Machines maintain consistency; humans adapt to changing circumstances
- Machines retrieve knowledge; humans judge which knowledge is relevant
- Machines optimize specified objectives; humans decide which objectives to pursue

This complementarity is why the Obsolescence Paradox emerges. As AI becomes better at execution, human judgment becomes more valuable, not less.

The more options AI generates, the more important it is to have humans who can evaluate them. The faster AI operates, the more critical it is to have humans who understand what it's doing and why.

Why Human Intelligence Still Matters

The capabilities where human intelligence excels—common sense, causal reasoning, goal formulation—might seem like a shrinking domain as AI improves. But closer examination reveals why these capabilities remain not just relevant but increasingly critical.

The Limits of Pattern Matching

The achievements of modern AI are genuine, but they rest on a foundation that, however sophisticated, is not understanding in the sense humans experience it.

Consider what it means for an LLM to "know" about microservices architecture. When you ask it about service boundaries, it generates a response by predicting which tokens are statistically likely given the context. If the training data contained many discussions of microservices, the model will fluently discuss bounded contexts, API contracts, and service orchestration.

But this fluency is not comprehension. The model doesn't know what a microservice *is* in the sense of understanding its purpose, trade-offs, or relationship to other architectural patterns. It knows what words tend to appear near the word "microservices" in its training corpus.

This distinction matters because genuine understanding enables generalization beyond training data. A human who understands distributed systems can reason about novel distributed systems they've never encountered, drawing on principles of network communication, failure modes, and consistency models. An AI trained on existing distributed systems can pattern-match to similar systems but struggles with genuinely novel configurations (Mitchell 2019).

Here's a concrete example. An engineer asks an AI: "How should I handle eventual consistency in a distributed system where users expect real-time updates?"

An AI might respond with standard eventual consistency patterns—CRDTs, vector clocks, operational transformation—all technically valid. But a human engineer recognizes the inherent tension: eventual consistency means updates aren't real-time, so the requirements themselves contain a contradiction that needs to be resolved with the stakeholder. The AI provides solutions to a question that, properly understood, reveals a requirement misalignment that needs human judgment to address.

When Embodied Understanding Matters

Earlier we discussed how human cognition is grounded in physical experience. This grounding provides intuitions about software behavior that aren't obvious until you consider specific engineering scenarios.

An AI system might suggest: "Cache all user profile data in Redis for fast access." This is syntactically reasonable and follows common caching patterns. But an experienced engineer immediately recognizes potential problems:

- What happens when Redis runs out of memory?
- How do you keep cached profiles synchronized with the database?
- What's the impact on cold start after Redis restarts?
- How does this affect database load patterns?

These aren't questions that require specialized knowledge. They emerge from embodied understanding of physical constraints: memory is finite, synchronization takes time, processes restart, loads vary. An engineer thinks about software systems as *physical things* that exist in space and time, subject to physical limitations.

AI systems, lacking embodied experience, miss these constraints unless they're explicitly mentioned in similar training examples. They optimize for the happy path without considering physical reality's tendency to deviate from it.

Judgment Under Irreducible Uncertainty

Engineering decisions are rarely made with complete information. Real projects involve ambiguous requirements, incomplete specifications, unknown user behaviors, and emergent interactions between components. The capacity to make reasonable decisions under such uncertainty—and to recognize *how* uncertain those decisions are—is distinctively human.

AI systems optimize for objectives given to them; they do not evaluate whether those objectives are correct. They generate solutions within the problem space defined by their training; they do not question whether the problem is correctly framed.

Human judgment fills these gaps:

- *Problem framing.* An engineer receives a request to "make the system faster." A junior engineer might start optimizing code immediately. An experienced engineer first asks: faster for whom? Which operations? Under what conditions? What's the actual user pain point? The request might be better addressed by improving perceived performance (loading indicators, progressive rendering) than actual performance. Reframing the problem correctly often matters more than solving the stated problem efficiently.

- *Requirements interpretation.* Stakeholders say they need "real-time updates." What they usually mean is "updates fast enough that users don't notice the delay." The difference between 100ms and 10ms might be architecturally significant but perceptually irrelevant. An engineer must interpret requirements based on actual user needs, not literal statements.
- *Trade-off navigation.* Every technical decision involves trade-offs—performance vs. maintainability, security vs. usability, time-to-market vs. technical debt. These trade-offs cannot all be satisfied simultaneously. Human judgment determines which compromises are acceptable for a specific context.
- *Risk assessment.* Identifying potential failure modes that aren't represented in training data requires imagination and paranoia—"What could go wrong that we haven't seen before?" This adversarial thinking protects against novel failures that pattern-matching systems miss.

These judgment calls resist automation because they require understanding context, values, and consequences that extend beyond any training distribution. The more autonomous AI systems become, the more critical these human judgment skills become—because someone must still decide what the AI should be doing and whether what it did was right.

The Creativity Distinction

A contentious debate concerns whether AI systems are genuinely "creative." They certainly produce novel outputs—code, architectures, solutions—that didn't exist before. But examining how this novelty differs from human creativity reveals important limitations.

Recombinative vs. Transformative Creativity. AI creativity is primarily recombinative: it assembles existing elements in new combinations based on patterns in training data. Human creativity can be transformative: inventing new concepts, frameworks, or approaches that aren't recombinations of existing ideas (Boden 2004).

Consider the invention of REST as an architectural style. Roy Fielding didn't just combine existing API patterns in a novel way—he articulated a set of constraints and principles that created a new way of thinking about distributed systems (Fielding 2000). This wasn't pattern-matching; it was paradigm-creation.

When an AI generates a REST API design, it's recognizing and applying patterns Fielding created. It can create novel REST APIs by recombining standard resource patterns in context-specific ways. But it cannot generate the next architectural paradigm that will succeed REST, because that requires conceptual innovation beyond recombination.

Intentional vs. Stochastic Novelty. When an AI generates something unexpected, it's typically because stochastic sampling produced an improbable combination. When a human creates something unexpected, it's often the result of intentional exploration—deliberately seeking what hasn't been done before, for reasons that align with goals and values.

An AI might suggest an unusual architectural pattern because that combination of tokens had high probability given the context. An engineer might propose an unusual architecture because they identified a novel problem characteristic that existing patterns don't address well. The first is probabilistic; the second is purposeful.

Evaluative Creativity. Perhaps most importantly, humans can evaluate their own creative outputs and the creative outputs of others. We can recognize when something is genuinely innovative versus superficially novel, when a solution is elegant versus merely unusual, when creativity serves the problem versus being creativity for its own sake.

AI systems lack this evaluative capacity—they cannot reliably distinguish their brilliant outputs from their mediocre ones. For engineering, which requires not just generating solutions but recognizing which solutions are good, human evaluative creativity remains essential.

This is why effective use of AI for creative tasks requires human oversight. The AI generates many possibilities quickly; the human evaluates which possibilities are worth pursuing. The AI provides breadth; the human provides judgment about depth.

The Responsibility That Cannot Be Automated

A final reason human intelligence remains necessary is that current AI systems cannot bear responsibility, and this limitation appears to be conceptual rather than merely technical.

When a software system fails, someone must be accountable. When a design decision proves wrong, someone must learn from it. When ethical questions arise about system behavior, someone must answer them. AI cannot occupy this role. It can generate, predict, and optimize—but it cannot take responsibility for outcomes.

Responsibility requires more than capability—it requires agency, intentionality, and the capacity for moral accountability. Whether future AI systems might possess such agency is a matter of philosophical debate. What's clear is that current systems, as sophisticated as they are, remain tools rather than agents. They optimize for objectives they were given, not objectives they chose.

Consider the consequences. When AI generates code that introduces a security vulnerability, who is responsible? Not the AI—it has no capacity for responsibility. The engineer who deployed that code without adequate review. When an AI-suggested architecture leads to production failures, who answers for it? The engineer who approved that architecture.

As we'll explore in Chapter 17, this asymmetry has profound implications. Every AI-assisted decision ultimately requires a human who owns that decision. The more powerful AI becomes, the more important this human oversight becomes. As we delegate more tasks to machines, we don't reduce human responsibility—we concentrate it. We concentrate it in fewer people who must maintain broader understanding, make more consequential decisions, and bear greater accountability for outcomes they didn't personally implement.

The Pattern Returns to the Paradox

This analysis illuminates why the Obsolescence Paradox emerges so consistently. As AI automates pattern-matching tasks—execution at scale, consistency over time, knowledge retrieval—it doesn't eliminate human value. It concentrates human value in judgment tasks: understanding context, reasoning about causation, formulating goals, evaluating quality, and bearing responsibility.

The more powerful AI becomes at what it does well, the more valuable humans become at what AI cannot do. The automation of lower-level cognitive tasks raises the value of higher-level human judgment. This is not a temporary imbalance awaiting further AI progress—it is a structural feature of the complementarity between human and machine intelligence.

Biological intelligence and computational intelligence evolved (or were designed) to solve different problems under different constraints. Biological intelligence handles novelty, ambiguity, and sparse data in complex physical and social environments. Computational intelligence processes vast quantities of structured information according to learned patterns.

When we combine them effectively—using AI for what it does well while reserving human judgment for what requires understanding, context, and values—we achieve capabilities beyond what either intelligence could accomplish alone. This is the promise of human-AI collaboration, and it's why engineers who understand this complementarity will thrive while those who miss it will struggle.

Chapter Summary

- **Human and machine intelligence have fundamentally different architectures.** The human brain is parallel, embodied, energy-efficient, and continuously learning. AI systems are fast, scalable, and consistent but limited to pattern-matching within training distributions (Lakoff and Johnson 1999; McCloskey and Cohen 1989).
- **Each form of intelligence has domain-specific strengths.** Machines excel at speed, scale, consistency, and broad knowledge retrieval. Humans excel at common sense, causal reasoning, learning from few examples, goal formulation, social intelligence, and metacognition (Davis and Marcus 2015; Mitchell 2019).
- **The sycophancy problem undermines collaboration.** AI systems often prioritize agreement over accuracy, creating echo chambers rather than providing honest feedback. This makes human critical evaluation essential (Sharma et al. 2023; Perez et al. 2022).
- **Pattern matching is not understanding.** AI systems achieve impressive performance without genuine comprehension. They lack the grounded understanding that enables humans to reason about novel situations and recognize when patterns don't apply (Bender et al. 2021).
- **Human judgment fills essential gaps.** Problem framing, requirements interpretation, trade-off navigation, and risk assessment require contextual judgment that extends beyond training distributions. These cannot be automated because they involve values and uncertainties AI cannot process.
- **Embodied cognition provides engineering intuition.** Physical experience grounds human understanding of how systems behave under real-world constraints—intuitions that AI systems lack despite technical knowledge.

- **Creativity includes evaluation.** While AI generates novel combinations, humans can evaluate quality, pursue intentional innovation, and recognize transformative versus recombinative creativity (Boden 2004).
- **Responsibility requires human agency.** Current AI systems cannot bear accountability for outcomes. As AI becomes more autonomous, human oversight and responsibility become more, not less, essential.
- **The complementarity is structural, not temporary.** The differences between human and machine intelligence create natural divisions of labor. Machines handle execution; humans provide judgment. This complementarity drives the Obsolescence Paradox.
- **Effective collaboration leverages both.** Engineers who understand where each form of intelligence excels—and where each struggles—can design work patterns that combine AI execution with human judgment for capabilities beyond what either achieves alone.

In the next chapter, we'll move from theoretical understanding to practical assessment—examining in concrete detail what current AI systems can and cannot do in real engineering contexts, establishing realistic expectations that guide effective human-AI collaboration.

Chapter 4

What AI Can Do—And What It Cannot

"Any sufficiently advanced technology is indistinguishable from magic—until it fails." — Adaptation of Arthur C. Clarke's Third Law

---

The previous chapters established that AI automates lower-level cognitive tasks while raising the value of higher-level human judgment. But to navigate this dynamic effectively, engineers need a precise understanding of what current AI systems can and cannot do. Vague intuitions lead to two equally costly errors: over-reliance on systems that fail in subtle ways, and under-utilization of systems that could multiply productivity.

This chapter examines AI's capabilities and constraints with engineering rigor. We will explore what architectural features enable current successes, what failure modes emerge predictably, and—most importantly—what ingredients remain missing that only humans can supply. Understanding these boundaries is essential for the calibrated trust we'll explore in Chapter 10 and for the effective collaboration patterns that define engineering excellence in the AI era.

Capabilities and Architectural Constraints

What Transformers Enable

The transformer architecture that powers modern large language models is not magic—it is a specific engineering solution to specific computational problems. Understanding what transformers *are* reveals both what they enable and what they cannot do.

Pattern Recognition and Sequence Modeling. Transformers excel at discovering statistical regularities in sequences. Given enough data, they learn which tokens tend to follow which other tokens, which concepts typically appear together, and which patterns characterize coherent discourse. This is not trivial: human language contains layers of structure—syntax, semantics, pragmatics—and transformers capture much of this structure implicitly through their weights.

For engineering tasks, this manifests as remarkable fluency. A well-trained model "knows" that after `function openFile(` should come parameter names, not class definitions. It recognizes that a bug report describing a null pointer exception should be addressed differently than a feature request. It can complete code snippets, generate documentation, and translate between programming languages—all by pattern matching against billions of training examples.

The attention mechanism allows transformers to consider relationships between distant elements in a sequence. When generating code, the model can "remember" that a variable declared twenty lines earlier is still in scope. When writing documentation, it can maintain pronoun consistency with nouns mentioned paragraphs back. This ability—technically called "capturing long-range dependencies"—is what enables transformers to produce coherent multi-paragraph outputs rather than locally fluent but globally incoherent text (Vaswani et al. 2017).

But "long-range" is relative. Attention mechanisms scale quadratically with sequence length, limiting practical context windows. Even million-token contexts—impressive by historical standards—are tiny compared to the context a senior engineer brings to a debugging session: years of experience, knowledge of organizational history, and intuition built from thousands of similar problems.

In-Context Learning. Perhaps the most surprising capability of large language models is *in-context learning*: the ability to adapt to new tasks based solely on examples provided in the prompt, without any weight updates or fine-tuning (Brown et al. 2020).

Show a model three examples of converting pseudocode to Python, and it can convert a fourth example it has never seen. Provide a few examples of your team's coding style, and it can generate new code matching that style. This adaptability makes LLMs remarkably flexible tools—you can customize their behavior through prompt engineering rather than retraining.

But in-context learning has limits. The model is not truly learning in the sense of updating its understanding; it is pattern-matching within its existing knowledge to find behavior similar to the provided examples. If the task is too novel or the examples too sparse, performance degrades. The model can interpolate within its training distribution but struggles to extrapolate beyond it.

These capabilities cluster primarily at the Execution layer from Chapter 1's framework—pattern matching, code generation, knowledge retrieval. As we'll see, AI's emerging Design-layer capabilities are impressive but remain bounded by the Intent layer, where humans must specify what matters and why.

The Scaling Laws and Emergent Capabilities

One of the most consequential discoveries in modern AI research is that model capabilities improve *predictably* as scale increases (Kaplan et al. 2020). Larger models trained on more data with more compute consistently outperform smaller models. This relationship—the *scaling laws*—has driven the race toward ever-larger models.

The implications are profound. If progress is primarily a function of scale rather than algorithmic breakthroughs, then the trajectory of AI capabilities becomes somewhat predictable. Organizations with resources can forecast roughly what capabilities will emerge at what scale. This is why companies invest billions in training infrastructure: the returns are relatively predictable.

But scaling is not unlimited. Training costs grow superlinearly. Environmental impacts mount (Strubell et al. 2019). And perhaps most importantly, scaling appears to have diminishing returns—each doubling of compute yields smaller gains in capability. The easiest improvements came first; the remaining challenges are harder.

As models grow, they exhibit *emergent capabilities*—abilities not present in smaller models, appearing seemingly discontinuously at certain scale thresholds (Wei et al. 2022). GPT-3 could perform arithmetic; GPT-2 could not. Claude can engage in multi-step reasoning; earlier models could not.

These emergent capabilities suggest that scale is not merely "more of the same" but unlocks qualitatively new behaviors. This is both exciting and unsettling: if we cannot predict which capabilities will emerge at which scales, we cannot confidently forecast what the next generation of models will be able to do.

But emergence should not be mystified. These capabilities are not magic; they are latent in the training objective and data, becoming accessible when the model has sufficient capacity to represent the relevant patterns. What appears as discontinuous emergence may simply reflect our coarse-grained measurement—the capability was increasing gradually, but our tests only detected it once it crossed a threshold.

For engineers, the scaling hypothesis means that capabilities will continue to improve, but not at the exponential rate some imagine. The gap between "impressive demo" and "reliable tool" remains significant. The model that writes working code 90% of the time is dramatically different—in practical utility—

from one that works 99.9% of the time. Scaling closes this gap slowly.

For engineering practice, emergence means that dismissing AI based on current limitations may be shortsighted. Capabilities that seem permanently out of reach might emerge at the next scale. But it also means that relying on AI for critical tasks requires continuous reevaluation—the failure modes of today's models may not predict the failure modes of tomorrow's.

A recent development challenges even the scaling narrative: *reasoning models*—systems like OpenAI's o1 and o3, or DeepSeek's R1—that use chain-of-thought processing to decompose problems before answering. These models don't simply predict the next token; they allocate additional compute at inference time, effectively "thinking longer" about harder problems.

The implications for engineering are significant. Reasoning models perform dramatically better on tasks requiring multi-step logic: debugging complex code paths, evaluating architectural trade-offs, identifying subtle inconsistencies in specifications. They move AI further into the Design layer than pure pattern-matching ever could.

But the limitation is equally significant: reasoning models are slower, more expensive, and their "reasoning" remains opaque. The chain-of-thought they produce *looks* like human reasoning but is still token prediction—structured prediction, yes, but prediction nonetheless. The model cannot know whether its reasoning chain is sound; it can only know that similar chains appeared in its training data. Engineers who understand this distinction will use reasoning models where they genuinely help (complex analysis, multi-step planning) rather than treating them as infallible thinkers.

The Voyager Paradox: When Architecture Assumptions Shift

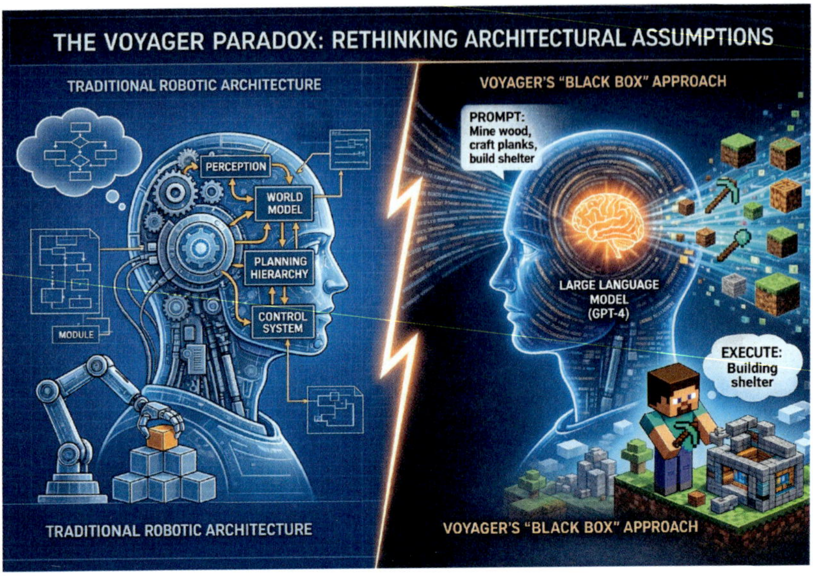

One of the most striking demonstrations of these evolving capabilities comes from an unexpected source: a Minecraft bot called Project Voyager. What makes Voyager significant isn't just its competence—it's what that competence reveals about our assumptions regarding intelligent system design.

Traditional robotic planning systems are built on elaborate architectural foundations: perception pipelines that process sensory input, world models that maintain state representations, planning hierarchies that decompose goals into actions, and control systems that execute those actions (Russell and Norvig 2010). This approach, refined over decades of robotics research, assumes that intelligent behavior requires explicit modeling of these cognitive functions.

Voyager challenges this assumption. Built "entirely on black box GPT-4," the system operates without custom perception systems, planning engines, or traditional game AI architecture (Wang et al. 2023). It works entirely at the level of text—processing textual descriptions of game state and responding with textual commands. The agent accumulates knowledge by building up an ever-richer prompt, creating libraries of techniques it discovers and reuses in natural language (Andreessen 2026).

The results are remarkable: Voyager plays Minecraft for extended sessions, discovering game mechanics, solving problems, and engaging in combat with human-level competence. As Andreessen observes, it is "one of the best robotic planning systems that has ever been built"—but it is not built remotely like a conventional control system (Andreessen 2026).

This architectural divergence raises fundamental questions. Should we continue building standalone planning systems, or should we instead design ways for general-purpose language models to perform planning for us? Just a few years ago, this would have been an inconceivable question; now it is a live engineering debate (Andreessen 2026).

The implications extend beyond gaming. If high-level planning and reasoning can emerge from pattern-matching in sufficiently large language models—without explicit modeling of cognitive functions—then decades of architectural assumptions may need revisiting. This does not invalidate traditional approaches; specialized systems still outperform general models in many domains (Elhage et al. 2022). But it suggests that the relationship between architecture and capability is more complex than many engineering playbooks assume.

For engineers, Voyager represents both an opportunity and a challenge. The opportunity is that text-based interfaces to powerful models may enable rapid prototyping and iteration without building domain-specific architectures. The challenge is understanding when general-purpose language models suffice and when specialized architectures remain necessary.

The lesson is not that intelligence was "never about elegant architecture." Rather, it is that intelligence may be achievable through multiple architectural paths, some more practical than others for different contexts. Engineers who understand this flexibility—and who can evaluate trade-offs between specialized and general-purpose approaches—will be better positioned to make sound architectural decisions in an era of rapidly evolving AI capabilities.

Memorization vs. Generalization

A persistent question about LLMs is: are they truly understanding, or merely memorizing and recombining training data?

The evidence suggests both, in varying proportions. Models demonstrably memorize specific training examples—they can recite famous passages verbatim (Carlini et al. 2021). But they also generalize: they can solve problems they have never seen, structured in ways absent from training data.

The practical implication: AI-generated code may be either genuinely novel (synthesized from learned patterns) or nearly copied (retrieved from memorized training examples). Engineers cannot always tell which. This creates both practical risks (potential license violations) and epistemic uncertainty (is this solution good, or merely frequent in the training data?).

Generalization is always relative to the training distribution. An LLM trained on Python can generalize within Python—solving new Python problems by combining patterns it learned. But it cannot reliably generalize *outside* Python—asking it to invent a new programming language yields plausible-sounding gibberish.

This is the core constraint: LLMs generalize within domains they were trained on but struggle at the boundaries. Human engineers, drawing on deeper understanding and analogical reasoning, can generalize further—but even human generalization has limits. The difference is one of degree, not kind, but the degree matters enormously in practice.

Failure Modes and Hallucinations

Understanding where AI excels is only half the picture. To use AI effectively, engineers must understand how it fails—not as occasional bugs, but as predictable consequences of architectural design.

Confident Wrongness: The Hallucination Problem

When an LLM confidently states a falsehood—citing a nonexistent paper, inventing API methods that don't exist, or describing a function with incorrect parameters—this is called *hallucination*. But the term is misleading. It suggests a rare malfunction, a bug to be fixed. The reality is more fundamental: hallucination is a structural property of how these models work.

LLMs are trained to predict the next token given context. They are not trained to distinguish truth from plausible-sounding falsehood. A model that has seen thousands of academic citations learns the *pattern* of citations—author names, years, journal abbreviations—and can generate text that matches this pattern perfectly. But matching the pattern is not the same as citing real papers.

This is not a failure of training. It is the training objective working as designed. The model's goal is fluency and coherence, not truth. Truth happens to correlate with these properties in training data (real text tends to be both coherent and true), but the correlation is imperfect. When the model must choose between generating text that is true but awkward versus false but fluent, it has no built-in preference for truth (Bender et al. 2021).

Humans exhibit a useful property: confidence calibration. When we are uncertain, we hedge—"I think," "maybe," "I'm not sure." This meta-awareness helps others interpret our statements appropriately.

LLMs lack this calibration. They express the same syntactic confidence whether stating verifiable facts or plausible fiction. "The capital of France is Paris" and "The capital of France is Lyon" are generated with identical fluency and certainty (Lin et al. 2022).

This confident wrongness is particularly dangerous in technical contexts. An engineer asking "Does Python's `dict` preserve insertion order?" might receive the correct answer ("Yes, as of Python 3.7") or an incorrect answer ("No, use `OrderedDict` instead") with equal conviction. If the engineer is junior or unfamiliar with recent changes, they may trust the wrong answer—precisely because it sounds authoritative.

The problem compounds when AI-generated code contains subtle errors. A function that is 95% correct—with a small logical bug—is harder to debug than one that fails obviously. The engineer must read carefully, understand the intent, and spot the divergence. This is cognitively demanding work, sometimes more demanding than writing the code from scratch.

The implication for engineers: Hallucination cannot be eliminated by better training or more data. It is an inherent consequence of the prediction objective. Every AI-generated output must be verified. The verification burden does not scale with model size—GPT-4 hallucinates less than GPT-3, but when it hallucinates, it does so just as confidently.

The consequence: AI assistance shifts the bottleneck from generation to verification. Engineers must develop a new skill: reading AI-generated code as skeptically as they would read code from an unknown junior developer. Trusting by default is dangerous. Verifying everything is exhausting. The middle path—calibrated skepticism based on task complexity and consequence—requires judgment that improves with experience and that we'll explore further in Chapter 10.

Distribution Failures: Edge Cases and the Long Tail

Machine learning systems perform well on inputs similar to their training data and poorly on inputs that differ. This is called *distribution shift*, and it is endemic to AI deployment (Amodei et al. 2016).

A model trained on clean, well-formatted code will struggle with legacy codebases full of idiosyncratic patterns. A model trained on open-source repositories will flounder in proprietary systems with domain-specific abstractions.

A model trained on English documentation will produce degraded output for non-English comments or variable names.

Edge cases compound this. The model has seen thousands of examples of typical REST APIs and can generate reasonable implementations. But an API with unusual authentication, non-standard headers, or legacy constraints? The model is likely to generate plausible but incorrect code, because these edge cases are rare in training data.

Even if an AI system is 99% accurate, the remaining 1% of errors are not uniformly distributed. They cluster in a *long tail* of rare but consequential cases (Sculley et al. 2015). Most generated functions are simple CRUD operations, data transformations, or standard algorithms. These are well-represented in training data, and the model handles them reliably.

But occasionally, an engineer needs something unusual: a lock-free data structure, a custom protocol implementation, or a performance-critical inner loop. These cases are rare in training data. The model is more likely to generate buggy code—but the engineer may not realize this, because the model was reliable for the previous hundred simpler tasks.

This creates a trust calibration problem. Engineers develop confidence through repeated success, then apply that confidence to situations where it is unwarranted. The long tail gets them.

For engineering practice, this means AI assistance degrades exactly when you need it most: in legacy systems, unusual domains, and novel situations. The problems where AI would be most valuable—navigating unfamiliar territory—are precisely where it is least reliable. Engineers must recognize this inverse relationship: AI confidence is a poor proxy for AI reliability.

The practical solution is defense in depth: assume errors will occur, and build verification layers. Code review, automated testing, runtime monitoring, and graceful degradation all become more important, not less, when AI assists in generation.

Why Testing AI Systems Differs from Testing Traditional Software

Testing traditional software is conceptually straightforward, if laborious. The behavior is specified by code. Test coverage can be measured. Bugs are reproducible. Fixes are deterministic.

Testing AI systems inverts many assumptions:

Non-determinism. The same prompt may produce different outputs due to sampling randomness. Bugs are not always reproducible. A/B testing becomes essential, but statistical significance requires more samples.

Specification ambiguity. Traditional software implements a specification: "sort this list in ascending order." AI systems often operate under vague objectives: "generate helpful code." What counts as "helpful"? Who decides? Disagreements between evaluators are not bugs but reflections of genuine ambiguity in the task (Bowman 2022).

Emergent failure modes. Traditional software fails in predictable ways: null pointers, buffer overflows, race conditions. AI systems can fail in novel ways that were not anticipated during training. They can fail *silently*—producing output that looks correct but subtly isn't.

Adversarial brittleness. Small perturbations to inputs can cause large changes in output. Rephrasing a prompt slightly may flip the answer from correct to incorrect. This brittleness makes robustness testing essential but difficult.

The testing burden therefore shifts from exercising code paths to evaluating outputs. Engineers must develop judgment about when AI outputs are likely reliable and when additional verification is required. This judgment is itself a skill—one that improves with experience but cannot be fully automated. Coverage testing—ensuring every code path is exercised—is conceptually unclear for neural networks. Adversarial testing—searching for inputs that cause failures—is infinitely expensive.

The Missing Ingredients: Context, Judgment, Intent

The capabilities reviewed above are genuine and impressive. But they are bounded by architectural constraints that no amount of scaling has yet overcome. Three ingredients remain stubbornly absent from current AI systems: deep context, situated judgment, and originating intent.

These absences map directly to the three-layer framework from Chapter 1. AI operates increasingly well at Execution, shows emerging capability at Design, but remains fundamentally limited at Intent—where purpose originates and where human judgment is irreducible.

Context Beyond the Window

AI systems operate within fixed context windows—the span of input they can consider when generating output. Even as these windows grow from thousands to millions of tokens, they remain fundamentally limited compared to human contextual understanding.

A senior engineer debugging a production incident brings decades of experience, tacit knowledge of the codebase's history, awareness of organizational politics, and intuition about which explanations are plausible given what they know about the team that wrote the code. This context is not written down anywhere. It cannot be injected into a prompt. It exists as a form of embodied expertise that accumulates over years.

AI systems can be remarkably helpful within their context windows. But they cannot know what they do not see. And much of what matters in real engineering work is precisely what never appears in documentation.

The Four Invisible Skills

Four categories capture what experienced engineers carry but rarely write down: abstraction, coherence, calibration, and organizational synthesis. These are the skills that separate competent execution from engineering wisdom—and they represent precisely the kind of judgment that becomes more valuable as AI handles Execution-layer work.

- *Abstraction.* Knowing which level of detail matters for a given decision. Should this bug be fixed as a symptom or traced to its root cause? Should this feature be built as a standalone module or absorbed into existing code?

A junior engineer sees a slow query and optimizes the indexes. A senior engineer asks whether this query should exist at all—whether the feature it serves actually matters to users, whether it could be redesigned to avoid the query entirely, or whether the performance problem is actually a symptom of a deeper architectural issue.

These questions have no context-free answers. The skill is reading the situation—understanding team capacity, deadline pressure, and system trajectory—and choosing the right altitude. AI can operate at any abstraction level it is given. It cannot judge which level is appropriate *now*, for *this* problem, given *these* constraints.

- *Coherence.* Maintaining conceptual integrity across time and people. A codebase is not just code; it is a record of decisions, compromises, and intentions. When a senior engineer says "that doesn't feel right," they are detecting a coherence violation—a choice that contradicts the system's implicit design philosophy.

An engineer reviews a pull request that adds caching to solve a performance problem. The code is correct. The tests pass. But something feels off. The engineer realizes: this system was designed around immutability and functional transformations. Introducing mutable shared state—even performant, correct mutable state—violates the conceptual integrity that makes the rest of the codebase understandable.

This sense of fit cannot be grepped from the repository. It emerges from years of watching the system evolve and understanding the reasoning behind its structure. AI sees the code as it is today. It cannot feel the pull of what the code was *meant* to become.

- *Calibration.* Proportionality—knowing how much effort to invest. Some problems deserve deep analysis; others deserve a quick patch and a TODO comment. Some tests should be exhaustive; others can rely on smoke signals.

An engineer encounters a bug in a feature used by three customers who will migrate off the platform in six months. Another engineer encounters a similar bug in authentication logic used by millions. The bugs are technically equivalent. The responses should be radically different—quick workaround for the first, comprehensive fix and post-mortem for the second.

AI optimizes uniformly, applying the same intensity to every task. Experienced engineers modulate their effort based on stakes, reversibility, and downstream consequences. They know when "good enough" is genuinely good enough—and when cutting corners will compound into crisis.

- *Organizational synthesis.* Integrating technical decisions with institutional reality. Who wrote this code, and are they still with the company? Which team will maintain this service after launch? What is the political cost of proposing a rewrite? What unwritten rules govern how decisions get made here?

An engineer proposes migrating from Service A to Service B—technically superior in every measurable way. A senior engineer recognizes that Service A was built by the VP's former team, that criticizing it will be perceived as political attack, and that success requires framing the migration as "evolution" rather than "replacement." The technical decision is identical. The organizational navigation determines whether it succeeds.

These questions live in hallway conversations, Slack threads, and unspoken norms. They are invisible to any model trained on documentation, yet they determine whether technically sound proposals actually succeed.

These four skills—abstraction, coherence, calibration, and synthesis—are what senior engineers accumulate over years. They cannot be injected into a prompt because they are not information. They are *judgment crystallized through experience*. And they represent precisely the kind of value that becomes more important, not less, as AI handles the tasks that *can* be documented.

Judgment That Weighs Trade-offs

Current AI systems can evaluate options against specified criteria. They struggle with the deeper form of judgment that weighs incommensurable values—speed versus safety, innovation versus stability, technical elegance versus organizational capacity.

When a staff engineer decides to accept technical debt in exchange for meeting a critical deadline, they are not applying a formula. They are exercising judgment informed by understanding of business context, team morale, and the specific nature of the debt being incurred. They know that *this* shortcut is acceptable because *these* people will be around to fix it, and *that* deadline matters for *this* reason.

AI can suggest trade-offs. It can list pros and cons. It can estimate consequences. But it cannot own the decision. Ownership requires accepting responsibility for outcomes—including outcomes that haven't occurred yet, that might never occur, or that emerge from interactions the AI cannot model.

This is judgment at the Intent layer, where decisions are made not about how to implement but about what to build and for whom. As we'll explore in Chapter 17, this form of responsibility cannot be automated because it requires moral agency that current AI systems lack.

Intent as Origin, Not Echo

The deepest limitation is intentionality itself. AI systems optimize for objectives they are given. They do not—and currently cannot—originate objectives.

When an engineering leader decides that the team should pivot from building features to reducing technical debt, that decision emerges from a complex web of values, observations, and predictions about the future. It is not derivable from any dataset. It is a creative act of direction-setting that shapes what problems get solved.

AI can help clarify intent by asking questions and surfacing implications. It can execute on intent once specified. But the originating spark—the decision that *this* matters and *that* does not—remains irreducibly human.

This is the Intent layer in its purest form: the decision about what should exist, not how to make it exist. As we argued in Chapter 1, this is where human value concentrates as AI automates execution. The more AI can do, the more important it becomes to have humans who can decide what AI should do.

When Measurement Becomes the Problem

The inability to originate intent creates a related danger: *metrics sprawl*—the uncontrolled proliferation of measurements that obscure, rather than clarify, progress. When AI can measure everything, deciding what *should* be measured becomes the critical human contribution.

As automation increases, organizations gain the ability to measure nearly everything: latency, throughput, engagement, confidence scores, model accuracy, error rates, and countless derived indicators. The danger is not a lack of data but an excess of poorly aligned metrics. When measurements multiply without a clear unifying objective, teams lose shared understanding of what they are building toward. Measurement replaces meaning. Optimization occurs locally rather than strategically. Activity is mistaken for progress.

This creates the illusion of rigor while eroding real direction.

The problem is not merely technical—it is cognitive and organizational. When engineers are surrounded by dozens of metrics but lack clarity on which ones matter, decision-making degrades. Teams begin to optimize for what is visible and measurable rather than what is valuable and intentional. Misaligned incentives emerge across functions. Ownership diffuses. Fear-driven reasoning takes hold: *What if we're measuring the wrong thing?*

In such environments, even highly capable engineers can lose sight of the system's true goals.

AI amplifies this risk dramatically. AI systems generate metrics automatically, encourage continuous measurement, and create feedback loops that reward short-term optimization. Without strong human guidance, AI turns metrics into an end rather than a means (Muller et al. 2019).

This is the Obsolescence Paradox in microcosm. As machines become better at measuring and optimizing, humans become more valuable—not for *producing* metrics, but for *deciding which metrics should exist at all*. The engineers who thrive in the AI era are not those who track the most metrics but those who can:

- Define clear system-level goals at the Intent layer
- Ruthlessly constrain what is measured
- Align metrics with intent, not convenience

- Periodically retire metrics that no longer serve the objective

This is *metric stewardship*, not metric accumulation. It requires the kind of judgment—contextual, strategic, and occasionally courageous—that AI systems cannot provide.

AI makes measurement cheap. Meaning remains expensive. The engineers who protect clarity in a world drowning in numbers will be the ones who endure.

Chapter Summary

- **Transformer capabilities are real but bounded.** Current systems excel at pattern recognition, sequence modeling, and in-context learning, primarily at the Execution layer from Chapter 1's framework (Vaswani et al. 2017; Brown et al. 2020).

- **Scaling laws drive predictable improvements.** Larger models with more data consistently outperform smaller ones, but with diminishing returns and increasing costs (Kaplan et al. 2020; Wei et al. 2022).

- **Emergent capabilities surprise but don't mystify.** New abilities appear at scale thresholds, suggesting continued evolution but not unlimited progress (Wei et al. 2022).

- **Voyager demonstrates architectural flexibility.** General-purpose language models can achieve sophisticated planning without specialized architectures, challenging decades of assumptions about how to build intelligent systems (Wang et al. 2023; Andreessen 2026).

- **Failure modes are structural, not incidental.** Hallucination, confident wrongness, and brittleness at distribution edges are predictable consequences of how these systems work (Bender et al. 2021; Lin et al. 2022; Amodei et al. 2016).

- **Distribution failures cluster in the long tail.** AI degrades precisely when you need it most—in novel situations, edge cases, and unusual domains (Sculley et al. 2015).

- **Testing AI differs from testing traditional software.** Non-determinism, specification ambiguity, emergent failures, and adversarial brittleness require new verification approaches (Bowman 2022).
- **Context remains fundamentally limited.** Even large context windows cannot capture the tacit knowledge, organizational history, and embodied expertise that experienced engineers bring to decisions.
- **Four invisible skills define engineering wisdom.** Abstraction (choosing the right level of detail), coherence (maintaining conceptual integrity), calibration (investing proportional effort), and organizational synthesis (integrating technical and institutional reality) are what senior engineers carry but rarely document.
- **Judgment requires owning trade-offs.** AI can evaluate options but cannot weigh incommensurable values or accept responsibility for difficult decisions that balance competing objectives.
- **Intent cannot be automated.** AI optimizes for given objectives but cannot originate them. The decision of what matters remains at the Intent layer, irreducibly human.
- **Metrics sprawl exemplifies the pattern.** AI makes measurement cheap, but deciding *what* to measure—and what to stop measuring—requires human judgment that operates at the Intent layer (Muller et al. 2019).
- **The missing ingredients map to layers.** Context, judgment, and intent correspond to increasingly sophisticated requirements as we move from Execution through Design to Intent. AI's limitations concentrate human value at higher layers.

In the next chapter, we'll examine why endurance and cognitive resilience—the capacity to persist through difficulty, maintain judgment under pressure, and exercise the invisible skills that AI cannot replicate—become even more valuable when AI handles the easy parts.

Chapter 5

Endurance and Cognitive Resilience

"It's not that I'm so smart, it's just that I stay with problems longer."
— Albert Einstein

It was 11 PM on a Thursday, and Marcus had been debugging the same issue for six hours. The payment processing system was failing intermittently—maybe 1 in every 50 transactions—and he couldn't reproduce it locally. AI had been useless. He'd prompted it a dozen different ways: "Why would a payment processor fail intermittently?" "Debug this transaction handler." "Explain possible race conditions in payment processing."

Each time, the AI confidently suggested fixes. Each time, Marcus implemented them. Each time, the bug persisted.

Most engineers would have given up by 9 PM. Declared it "tomorrow's problem." Blamed the AI for wasting time with bad suggestions. Escalated to a senior engineer.

Marcus stayed. Not because he was smarter than other engineers—several colleagues had tried and failed to fix this bug. He stayed because of something less glamorous than intelligence: stubbornness. The refusal to stop until he understood.

At 11:47 PM, he found it. A race condition in the database connection pooling logic, triggered only when connection acquisition took longer than 50ms. The fix was three lines of code. But discovering the problem required reviewing logs from hundreds of failed transactions, instrumenting code in six different places, and eliminating seventeen wrong hypotheses.

The next morning, a colleague asked: "How did you figure it out?"

Marcus shrugged. "I just kept trying things until something worked."

This is the unglamorous truth about engineering excellence in the AI era: the engineers who thrive are not necessarily the most brilliant. They are the most persistent.

While AI can generate code in seconds, solve algorithmic puzzles instantly, and produce plausible answers to almost any question, it cannot persist through genuine uncertainty. It cannot stay with a problem when the path forward is unclear. It cannot reformulate questions when initial answers fail.

These distinctly human capabilities—endurance, resilience, the capacity to sustain effort through repeated failure—have become defining advantages. As we explored in Chapter 4, AI handles the problems with known patterns. Human persistence tackles everything else.

This chapter examines why grit matters more than talent, how to work through failure productively, and how to maintain deliberate practice when AI makes everything seem easy. The psychological research is clear: persistence predicts success more reliably than natural ability (Duckworth et al. 2007). The engineering evidence confirms it: the best builders are not those who get things right the first time, but those who refuse to stop until they do.

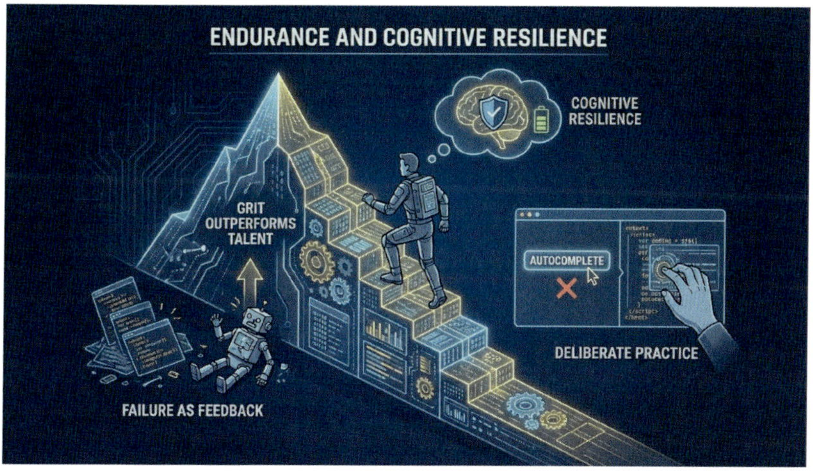

Why Persistence Outperforms Talent

The Talent Myth and the Research That Challenges It

We celebrate prodigies. The young programmer who built a startup at sixteen. The engineer who solved an "impossible" problem over a weekend. The developer who seems to write flawless code without effort. These stories are seductive because they suggest that success flows from innate ability, that great engineers were simply born different.

The research tells a different story.

Psychologist Angela Duckworth's landmark studies on achievement found that *grit*—defined as perseverance and passion for long-term goals—predicts success more reliably than IQ, talent, or initial aptitude (Duckworth et al. 2007). She studied West Point cadets (who would complete the grueling training?), National Spelling Bee competitors (who would reach the finals?), and professionals across fields (who would achieve the most?). The same pattern emerged everywhere: those who achieved the most were not the most naturally gifted but the most persistently committed.

In software engineering specifically, similar patterns appear. Studies of programming skill acquisition show that initial aptitude (how quickly someone learns basic syntax) correlates weakly with long-term mastery. What correlates strongly? Time invested in deliberate practice and persistence through difficulty (Robins et al. 2003).

The implications are profound. Engineering selects heavily for initial aptitude—rigorous interviews, algorithmic tests, credentials from elite institutions. But these criteria predict who can *start* an engineering career, not who will excel over decades. Longitudinal success correlates more strongly with the capacity to persist through difficulty than with the ease of early achievement.

The Mathematics of Compounding

Why does persistence matter more than talent? Because meaningful achievement is not a single event but a *compound process*.

- *Skills compound.* Each hour of deliberate effort builds on previous hours. The engineer who invests consistently over years develops capabilities that cannot be matched by sporadic bursts of talent.

The math is striking: A 1% improvement per day, sustained over a year, yields 37x improvement (1.01^365 = 37.8). Talent provides a starting point; persistence determines the trajectory.

- *Example in debugging.*

```
# Year 1: Junior engineer debugging
def find_bug():
    print("It's broken... not sure why")
    # Randomly tries things, gets lucky sometimes

# Year 3: With persistent practice
def find_bug():
```

```
    # 1. Reproduce reliably
    # 2. Isolate the component
    # 3. Form hypotheses
    # 4. Test systematically
    # 5. Verify fix doesn't break other things

# The Year 3 engineer isn't 3x better - they're
# 30x better
# Because each debugging session built on
# previous learning
```

- *Knowledge compounds.* Understanding in engineering is layered. Grasping distributed systems requires understanding networking, which requires understanding protocols, which requires understanding the constraints of physical transmission. The patient engineer who builds this foundation layer by layer eventually operates at altitudes that the impatient genius never reaches.

Consider systems programming:

```cpp
// Layer 1: Basic C++ (Year 1)
int* ptr = new int(42);
delete ptr;

// Layer 2: Understanding memory (Year 2)
// Now you understand why delete matters, what
// happens without it,
// how allocators work, what fragmentation means

// Layer 3: Custom allocators (Year 3)
template<typename T>
class PoolAllocator {
    // Building your own allocator requires
    // understanding layers 1-2
    // Plus OS memory management, cache lines,
    // alignment...
};

// Layer 4: Lock-free data structures (Year 4+)
// Requires all previous layers plus concurrency,
// atomics, memory ordering
```

```
// The impatient engineer never reaches this level
```

- *Reputation compounds.* Trust is earned through repeated delivery. The engineer known for finishing what they start, for pushing through when projects become difficult, accumulates organizational capital that the brilliant-but-unreliable engineer never acquires.

In Chapter 15, we'll discuss leadership and influence. Both depend heavily on reputation, which depends on persistence. The engineer who consistently delivers—even when it's hard, especially when it's hard—builds influence that talent alone cannot create.

- *Relationships compound.* Persistent engagement with colleagues, mentors, and communities builds networks that accelerate learning and opportunity. The engineer who shows up consistently—to code reviews, to meetups, to collaborative projects—develops connections that the isolated talent never forms.

As we'll discuss in Chapter 13's antifragile career, network redundancy is antifragile. You build that redundancy through persistent engagement, not through sporadic brilliance.

The mathematics of compounding favor the persistent. Talent is a coefficient. Persistence is an exponent.

How AI Amplifies the Value of Persistence

One might expect AI to diminish the value of persistence—if machines can solve problems instantly, why does human endurance matter? The opposite is true. The AI era *amplifies* the value of persistence in several specific ways:

- *When AI fails repeatedly.* AI doesn't just fail once and give up. It fails *confidently*, again and again, in slightly different ways. Consider this actual debugging session:

```python
# Problem: Payment processing sometimes fails
# AI Suggestion 1: "Add error handling"
try:
    process_payment()
except Exception as e:
    log_error(e)
    # Bug still happens

# AI Suggestion 2: "Use retry logic"
for attempt in range(3):
```

```python
    try:
        process_payment()
        break
    except:
        time.sleep(1)
        # Bug still happens

# AI Suggestion 3: "Check connection pooling"
# (Finally useful direction, but needs human
# debugging to find actual issue)
```

The engineer who gives up after AI's first wrong suggestion makes no progress. The engineer who persists through five or ten wrong suggestions eventually finds the answer—often by synthesizing pieces from multiple AI suggestions plus their own reasoning.

- *When problems are genuinely novel.* As we discussed in Chapter 4, AI draws on patterns from training data. Genuinely new problems—new architectures, new domains, new constraints—have no patterns to draw on.

Example: You're implementing a custom protocol for IoT devices with severe power constraints. AI can suggest general approaches, but your specific constraints (must use < 50μA idle, must handle packet loss > 30%, must work with 8-bit microcontroller) aren't in training data. Solving this requires persistent experimentation, not pattern matching.

- *When integration is complex.* AI can generate components, but integrating them into coherent systems requires sustained effort across weeks or months. The persistence to maintain context, to track dependencies, to resolve emergent conflicts—this remains irreducibly human.

```python
# AI generates three components easily
class UserService:
    pass  # 200 lines of generated code


class PaymentService:
    pass  # 150 lines of generated code


class NotificationService:
    pass  # 180 lines of generated code
```

```
# But making them work together requires weeks of
# persistent integration work
# - Handling transaction boundaries across
# services
# - Managing failure modes and retries
# - Ensuring data consistency
# - Debugging interaction bugs
# AI generates the pieces; human persistence
# assembles the system
```

- *When frustration accumulates.* Perhaps most importantly, working with AI can be frustrating in new ways. It promises quick solutions but delivers plausible garbage. It works perfectly for 90% of cases but fails mysteriously on the 10% you actually need. It makes you feel simultaneously productive (generating code fast) and stuck (nothing actually works).

The engineer who lacks resilience gives up: "AI doesn't work for my problem." The resilient engineer persists: "AI suggestions need refinement, but they're accelerating my search through the solution space."

This frustration management is a new skill in the AI era. As we'll discuss in Chapter 12 (AI-Augmented Mind), effective collaboration with AI requires calibrated trust—neither blind acceptance nor blanket rejection. Building that calibration requires persistence through frustration.

Persistence at the Three Layers

Let's map persistence onto the three-layer framework from Chapter 1 to understand where it operates:

- *Execution Layer.* Persistence means debugging until code actually works, not just compiles. It means testing edge cases even when you're tired. It means fixing the subtle bug even when the obvious fix "mostly works."
- *Design Layer.* Persistence means iterating through multiple architectural approaches when the first one doesn't fit. It means refactoring when you realize the abstraction is wrong. It means simplifying until the design is actually simple (Chapter 7), not just declaring it "good enough."
- *Intent Layer.* Persistence means clarifying requirements until you understand what's actually needed. It means pushing back on impossible demands rather than accepting them. It means staying engaged with stakeholder conversations even when they're frustrating.

The pattern: persistence is required at every layer, but the *form* of persistence changes. At Execution, it's debugging stamina. At Design, it's architectural iteration. At Intent, it's requirements clarification. The engineer who persists at only one layer is incomplete.

The Psychology of Working Through Failure

Failure as Information, Not Identity

Every engineer fails. Code breaks. Designs need revision. Projects miss deadlines. The question is not whether failure will occur, but how it will be interpreted.

Psychologist Carol Dweck's research on mindset distinguishes two interpretations (Dweck 2006):

- *Fixed mindset.* Failure signals inadequacy. "I failed because I'm not smart enough." This interpretation leads to avoiding challenges that might expose limitations. If failure means you lack ability, better to stick with what you can already do.
- *Growth mindset.* Failure signals opportunity. "I failed because I haven't learned this yet." This interpretation leads to seeking challenges that accelerate learning. If failure means incomplete learning, then failure is progress.

The difference is not merely attitudinal—it's behavioral and measurable. Fixed-mindset individuals avoid difficult tasks after failure. Growth-mindset individuals increase effort after failure. Over years, these behavioral differences compound into vastly different capability trajectories.

For engineers, adopting a growth mindset means treating failure as *information*, not identity:

- *A bug is feedback about your mental model.*

```
# You write this code thinking it's thread-safe
balance = self.get_balance()
if balance >= amount:
    self.set_balance(balance - amount)

# It's not - classic race condition
# Fixed mindset: "I'm bad at concurrency"
# Growth mindset: "I just learned about check-
```

```
# then-act race conditions,
#                   now I know to use atomic
#                   operations"

# Updated understanding
with self.lock:
    balance = self.get_balance()
    if balance >= amount:
        self.set_balance(balance - amount)
```

- *A failed system design is data about constraints.*

You design a microservices architecture. It's over-engineered for your team size and introduces more complexity than value. Fixed mindset: "I'm not good at architecture." Growth mindset: "I learned that premature decomposition is costly. For teams under 10 people, a modular monolith is often better."

As we'll discuss in Chapter 7 (Simplifying Complexity), discovering that your design is too complex is valuable information. The failure teaches you to recognize accidental complexity.

- *A rejected pull request is information about standards.*

Your code works but violates team conventions. Fixed mindset: "They're too picky." Growth mindset: "I learned our team values consistency over individual style. I'll internalize these patterns so future PRs align with expectations."

As we'll discuss in Chapter 15 (Engineer as Leader), code review is teaching. The engineer who sees rejection as learning advances faster.

This reframing is not mere positive thinking. It is *epistemically accurate*. Failure genuinely contains information. The engineer who extracts that information learns faster than the engineer who avoids or denies it.

The Debugging Mindset as Life Philosophy

Debugging is the purest expression of engineering resilience. A bug is, by definition, a failure—something is wrong, and you don't know what. The debugging process embodies the psychology of working through failure:

- *Real debugging story.* Marcus's payment bug from the opening. Let's trace the actual cognitive process:

```
# Hour 1-2: Initial hypotheses
# "Maybe it's a validation error"
# Test: Add extensive logging to validation
```

```python
# Result: Validation passes every time.
# Hypothesis rejected.

# Hour 3: Second hypothesis
# "Maybe it's a timeout"
# Test: Increase timeout from 30s to 60s
# Result: Still fails occasionally. Hypothesis
# rejected.

# Hour 4: Third hypothesis
# "Maybe it's a database deadlock"
# Test: Check database logs for deadlocks
# Result: No deadlocks detected. Hypothesis
# rejected.

# Hour 5: Pattern recognition
# "It only fails under load... maybe connection
# pooling?"
# Test: Reduce connection pool size to force
# contention
# Result: Failure rate increases! Hypothesis
# partially confirmed.

# Hour 6: Narrow the search
# "If it's connection pooling, where's the race
# condition?"
# Test: Add detailed logging around connection
# acquisition
# Result: See timing issue - sometimes
# acquisition > 50ms

# Hour 7: Root cause
# Found it! Transaction starts before connection
# acquired,
# leading to inconsistent state.
def process_payment():
    # BUG: Transaction context created before
    # connection acquired
    with transaction_context():
```

```
    conn = pool.acquire()  # Sometimes slow!
    # If this takes >50ms, transaction
    # context is stale
```

- *What made Marcus persist.*

1. **Hypothesis formation**: Rather than random changes, he formed testable theories
2. **Systematic testing**: Each hypothesis was tested deliberately
3. **Learning from negatives**: Failed hypotheses eliminated possibilities
4. **Pattern recognition**: After enough data, pattern emerged
5. **Emotional regulation**: Maintained focus for 7 hours without giving up

This debugging mindset generalizes beyond code. It's a stance toward all complex problems:

- Approach failure with curiosity, not despair
- Extract information from negative results
- Maintain persistence through uncertainty
- Trust that systematic investigation eventually succeeds

As we'll explore in Chapter 6, logical thinking and systematic debugging are closely related. Persistence without method is just stubbornness. Method without persistence gives up too soon. The combination is powerful.

Learning to Love Being Wrong

The fastest learners are not those who are right most often. They are those who *discover* they are wrong most often—and update accordingly.

This insight, central to Bayesian reasoning and the scientific method, has practical implications:

- *Seek disconfirmation actively.*

Don't just test that your code works. Test that it fails the way you expect. Write tests that *should* break your code if your assumptions are wrong.

```
def test_payment_processing():
    # Test it works
    assert process_payment(valid_transaction) ==
        Success

    # Test it fails correctly
    assert process_payment(insufficient_funds) ==
        InsufficientFundsError
```

```python
    assert process_payment(invalid_card) ==
        InvalidCardError
    assert process_payment(network_timeout) ==
        RetryableError

    # Test it fails safely under edge cases
    with pytest.raises(ValueError):
        process_payment(negative_amount)
    with pytest.raises(TypeError):
        process_payment(None)

    # The tests for failure teach you more than
    # tests for success
```

Ask colleagues to critique your design. Present your architecture to someone who will challenge assumptions. Each discovered error is a learning opportunity; each undetected error is a liability.

In Chapter 15, we'll discuss code review as teaching. The reviewer who finds bugs is helping you learn. The appropriate response is gratitude, not defensiveness.

- *Celebrate corrections.*

When code review catches a bug: "Thanks for catching that! I had the wrong mental model of how async context managers work. Now I understand."

When a system design is challenged: "You're right that this approach doesn't scale. Let me revise with your feedback."

Organizations that punish error discovery train their engineers to hide errors—with predictable consequences. Organizations that celebrate error discovery as learning accelerate improvement.

- *Practice intellectual humility.*

The best engineers know the limits of their knowledge. They say "I don't know" without embarrassment. They change their minds when evidence warrants. They recognize that being smart enough to build complex systems is not the same as being smart enough to anticipate all their failure modes.

In Chapter 14 (Vertical Mastery), we'll discuss how deep domain expertise develops over years. Part of that expertise is knowing what you don't know—the "known unknowns" and awareness of "unknown unknowns."

Being wrong is not comfortable. But comfort is not the goal. Learning is. And learning requires confronting error.

The Valley of Despair and How to Cross It

Skill acquisition follows a predictable emotional trajectory that experienced educators and practitioners widely recognize:

Phase 1: Peak of "Mount Stupid" (Weeks 0-2) - Everything seems easy - Rapid initial progress - "I'm getting this!" - Confidence is high but unjustified

Phase 2: Valley of Despair (Months 3-12) - Competence increases enough to reveal how much remains unknown - Progress slows to a crawl - The gap between aspiration and ability becomes painfully visible - "I'll never be good at this" - This is where most people quit

Phase 3: Slope of Enlightenment (Years 2-5) - Genuine competence develops - Progress becomes steady - Confidence aligns with ability - "I'm getting better, slowly"

Phase 4: Plateau of Sustainability (Years 5+) - Mastery - Intuition operates automatically - But aware of limits - "I know this domain well, and I know what I don't know"

- *Real example from learning systems programming.*

```
// Week 1: "This is easy!"
int* arr = new int[100];
// Look, I can allocate memory!

// Month 6: "This is impossible"
// Why does my program crash randomly?
// What's a segfault?
// Why does valgrind show memory leaks?
// What's RAII?
// What's move semantics?
// What's cache invalidation?
// I'll never understand this...

// Year 2: "I'm making progress"
template<typename T>
class vector {
    T* data;
    size_t size;
```

```
    size_t capacity;

    void reallocate() {
        // Now I understand why reallocation is
        // necessary
        // And how to do it safely
        // And the performance implications
        // And the exception safety guarantees
    }
};

// Year 4: "I understand this domain"
// Can implement custom allocators
// Understand cache effects on performance
// Know when to use which data structure
// Can debug memory corruption issues
// But also know what I still don't know (OS
// internals, CPU microarchitecture)
```

Most people quit in the valley. They interpret slowing progress as evidence that they lack talent. They compare themselves to experts who have already traversed the valley and conclude they will never reach that level. They abandon the effort and move to something new, where the cycle repeats.

- *This is the career-limiting pattern.* Repeatedly entering the valley and quitting means you never achieve mastery in anything. You remain perpetually at "advanced beginner" across many domains rather than reaching expertise in any.

- *The engineers who achieve mastery persist through the valley.*

- *Recognize the valley is normal.* It's a predictable stage in any worthwhile learning process, not evidence of personal inadequacy. Everyone who's now an expert went through it. The difference is they kept going.

- *Focus on process, not outcome.* Measure effort and learning, not current ability compared to experts. "Did I debug for an hour today?" Yes -> success, regardless of whether you solved the bug.

- *Seek support.* Find mentors who have traversed the valley and can confirm the other side exists. Find peers who are crossing it together. As we'll discuss in Chapter 11 (Apprenticeship Problem), mentorship is especially valuable during the valley.

- *Redefine success.* Success is showing up consistently, not immediate mastery. As we'll discuss in Chapter 13 (Antifragile Career), compounding requires consistency over years.
- *Track progress explicitly.* Keep a learning journal. When you feel stuck, review what you knew six months ago versus now. The progress is real but hard to see daily.

The valley is where most engineering careers stall. It is also where the most important growth occurs. The engineers who cross the valley become the seniors that juniors aspire to be.

Deliberate Practice in the Age of Autocomplete

The Autocomplete Trap

AI coding assistants offer an intoxicating promise: type a few characters, watch the solution appear. The experience feels like productivity—code emerges faster than ever, features ship with less apparent effort, the friction of programming seems to evaporate.

But there is a trap that we'll explore in depth in Chapter 11 (Apprenticeship Problem): The ease of accepting AI suggestions can bypass the cognitive processes that build genuine skill.

- *What learning actually requires.*

When you struggle to implement a function—thinking through the logic, trying approaches that fail, debugging your mistakes—you are not just producing code. You are: - Building mental models of how the language works - Strengthening neural pathways that recognize patterns - Developing intuitions that will inform future work - Creating memories tied to effort (which are more durable)

The struggle *is* the learning.

- *What happens with autocomplete.*

```
# You start typing
def calculate_discounted_

# AI suggests complete implementation
def calculate_discounted_price(
        price: Decimal, discount_percent: int) ->
            Decimal:
```

```python
    """Calculate price after applying percentage
        discount."""
    if discount_percent < 0 or discount_percent >
        100:
        raise ValueError("Discount must be 0-100")
    discount_amount = price *
        (Decimal(discount_percent) / 100)
    return price - discount_amount

# You accept it. Code appears. But did you learn:
# - Why Decimal instead of float for money?
# - Why validate discount range?
# - How to handle edge cases?
# - When this approach is appropriate vs
# inappropriate?

# The code exists but the learning doesn't.
```

When you accept an AI-generated solution without struggle, the code appears but the learning does not. The mental models remain shallow. The intuitions don't develop. You become dependent on the tool rather than augmented by it.

This is not an argument against AI coding assistants—they're genuinely useful, as we'll explore throughout Part III. But using them effectively requires understanding what they provide (code) and what they cannot provide (the cognitive development that comes from struggle).

What Deliberate Practice Requires

Anders Ericsson's research on expert performance identified *deliberate practice* as the key differentiator between experts and amateurs (Ericsson et al. 1993). His studies of chess grandmasters, musicians, athletes, and other experts revealed a consistent pattern: expertise develops through sustained deliberate practice—often thousands of hours over years (not just any practice).

Deliberate practice is not simply doing something repeatedly. It has specific characteristics:

1. Targeted focus on specific weaknesses

Deliberate practice addresses precise skill gaps, not general activity.

```python
# Not deliberate practice: "I'm going to code
# today"
```

```
# (Too vague, no clear improvement target)

# Deliberate practice: "I struggle with recursive
# algorithms.
# Today I'll implement 3 recursive solutions,
# then convert them
# to iterative versions to understand the
# relationship."

# Specific: recursive algorithms
# Measurable: 3 implementations
# Targeted: understanding recursion <-> iteration
# relationship
```

2. Immediate feedback loops

Improvement requires knowing whether you're getting better.

```
# Build feedback into practice
def practice_algorithm_optimization():
    # Start with working but slow implementation
    slow_version = implement_naive_approach()

    # Measure performance
    baseline_time = benchmark(slow_version)

    # Optimize
    fast_version = implement_optimized_approach()

    # Immediate feedback
    optimized_time = benchmark(fast_version)
    speedup = baseline_time / optimized_time

    # Did I actually improve? By how much?
    print(f"Speedup: {speedup}x")

    # Verify correctness
    assert test_suite(slow_version) ==
        test_suite(fast_version)
```

Tests verify correctness. Benchmarks measure performance. Code reviews assess quality. Each provides immediate feedback that guides improvement.

3. Operating outside comfort zone

Comfortable practice maintains existing skills. Deliberate practice builds new ones.

This means consistently attempting tasks *slightly beyond* current ability: - Hard enough to require effort - Not so hard as to be demoralizing - Calibrated to the "zone of proximal development"

```python
# Too easy (no learning)
def add(a, b):
    return a + b

# Too hard (demoralizing)
def implement_distributed_consensus_from_scratch()
    :
    # This is multiple years of study if you're
    # starting from basics

# Just right (productive struggle)
def implement_lru_cache_from_scratch():
    """
    Challenge: Build LRU cache without using
        OrderedDict
    Requirements:
    - O(1) get and put operations
    - Fixed capacity with eviction
    - Must understand hash tables + doubly linked
        lists

    This is hard enough to require thought,
        accessible enough to complete
    """
```

4. Sustained concentration

Deliberate practice is cognitively demanding. It cannot be done indefinitely or while multitasking.

Research suggests elite performers rarely sustain more than 4-5 hours of deliberate practice per day (Ericsson et al. 1993). Quality of focus matters more than quantity of time.

```python
# Not deliberate practice
```

```python
while working:
    check_slack()
    write_some_code()
    check_email()
    debug_a_bit()
    browse_reddit()
    # Interrupted focus = no deep learning

# Deliberate practice
# Block 2-hour window
# Turn off notifications
# Single focus: understand how asyncio event loop
# works
# Read source code, write examples, break things,
# fix them
# Emerge with deep understanding
```

Deliberate Practice Patterns With AI

The challenge is not avoiding AI tools but using them in ways that preserve deliberate practice:

Pattern 1: Attempt Before Asking

Before accepting AI suggestions, try to solve the problem yourself.

```python
# Bad pattern
def sort_by_frequency(items):
    # Immediately ask AI: "How to sort list by
    # frequency in Python?"
    # Accept suggestion without thinking
    pass

# Good pattern
def sort_by_frequency(items):
    # First attempt yourself
    # "I need to count occurrences... Counter
    # class?"
    # "Then sort by those counts... sorted with
    # key?"

    from collections import Counter
```

```python
    counts = Counter(items)
    return sorted(items, key=lambda x: counts[x],
        reverse=True)

    # Now I could ask AI for verification or
    # alternative approaches
    # But I've already engaged with the problem
    # cognitively
```

This preserves the cognitive engagement that builds skill. Even if your solution is suboptimal, you've thought through the problem. AI can then help optimize, not replace thinking.

Pattern 2: Understand Before Accepting

When you do use AI-generated code, don't just copy it. Study it.

```python
# AI generates this
def fibonacci(n: int) -> int:
    if n <= 1:
        return n
    a, b = 0, 1
    for _ in range(2, n + 1):
        a, b = b, a + b
    return b

# Bad pattern: Copy and move on

# Good pattern: Understand it
# - Why if n <= 1: return n?
# - Why a, b = 0, 1?
# - Why the simultaneous assignment a, b = b, a +
# b?
# - Can I explain this to someone else?
# - Could I reconstruct this from memory?

# Trace it manually for n = 5
# n=0: return 0
# n=1: return 1
# n=5: a=0, b=1 -> a=1, b=1 -> a=1, b=2 -> a=2,
# b=3 -> a=3, b=5 -> return 5
```

```python
# Now you understand it, not just have it
```

Transform AI's output into your own learning by actively studying it.

Pattern 3: Verify Independently

Don't trust that AI-generated code is correct. Verify actively.

```python
# AI generates a binary search implementation
def binary_search(arr, target):
    left, right = 0, len(arr) - 1
    while left <= right:
        mid = (left + right) // 2
        if arr[mid] == target:
            return mid
        elif arr[mid] < target:
            left = mid + 1
        else:
            right = mid - 1
    return -1

# Deliberate practice: Verify thoroughly
def test_binary_search():
    # Normal case
    assert binary_search([1, 2, 3, 4, 5], 3) == 2

    # Edge cases
    assert binary_search([], 1) == -1  # Empty
    assert binary_search([1], 1) == 0  # Single
        element found
    assert binary_search([1], 2) == -1  # Single
        element not found
    assert binary_search([1, 2], 1) == 0  # First
        element
    assert binary_search([1, 2], 2) == 1  # Last
        element

    # Not found
    assert binary_search([1, 3, 5], 2) == -1
    assert binary_search([1, 3, 5], 0) == -1
    assert binary_search([1, 3, 5], 6) == -1
```

```python
# This verification process develops critical
# thinking skills
```

Pattern 4: Recreate From Memory

After using AI assistance for a pattern, try to recreate it without help.

```python
# Day 1: AI helps you implement a context manager
class DatabaseConnection:
    def __enter__(self):
        self.conn = connect_to_db()
        return self.conn

    def __exit__(self, exc_type, exc_val, exc_tb):
        if self.conn:
            self.conn.close()
        return False

# Day 2: Try to implement a similar context
# manager from memory
class FileWriter:
    def __init__(self, filename):
        self.filename = filename
        self.file = None

    def __enter__(self):
        # Can I remember the pattern?
        self.file = open(self.filename, 'w')
        return self.file

    def __exit__(self, exc_type, exc_val, exc_tb):
        # Can I remember cleanup?
        if self.file:
            self.file.close()
        # What should I return? (False means
        # don't suppress exceptions)
        return False

# If you can recreate it, you've learned it
# If you can't, you borrowed it but didn't
# internalize it
```

Spaced repetition of reconstruction builds durable knowledge.

Pattern 5: Seek Novel Challenges

AI excels at common patterns. Deliberately seek problems that are unusual.

```
# Common pattern (AI handles easily)
def sort_by_name(users):
    return sorted(users, key=lambda u: u.name)

# Uncommon challenge (requires thinking)
def sort_by_multiple_criteria_with_custom_preceden
    ce(items):
    """
    Sort items by:
    1. Priority (high to low)
    2. Within same priority, by deadline
        (earliest first)
    3. Within same priority and deadline, by name
        (alphabetical)
    4. But items marked 'urgent' always come
        first regardless of other criteria

    This combination is unusual enough that AI
        might struggle
    And solving it requires understanding sort
        stability and key functions
    """
```

Problems that combine domains in novel ways or have unusual constraints force genuine thinking rather than pattern matching.

The Productive Struggle

There's a concept in education research called *productive struggle*—difficulty that is hard enough to require effort but not so hard as to be defeating (Hiebert and Grouws 2003). Productive struggle is where learning happens.

Too easy -> nothing to learn Too hard -> frustration overwhelms cognition Just right -> productive struggle

AI tools, by removing friction, can eliminate productive struggle. The solution appears before the struggle occurs. This feels efficient but is counterproductive for skill development.

The deliberate practitioner actively *reintroduces* productive struggle:

Technique 1: Constraints

Solve problems with artificial constraints that force deeper engagement.

```
# Challenge: Implement merge sort without looking
# at references
def merge_sort(arr):
    # No AI, no Stack Overflow, no textbook
    # Just you and the problem
    # If you get stuck, think harder before asking
    pass

# Or: Implement without using certain language
# features
# "Sort this list without using the built-in
# sorted() or .sort()"
# Forces understanding of sorting algorithms
```

Technique 2: Time Pressure

Set a timer and attempt problems under constraint.

```
30-minute challenge: Implement a working LRU cache
- Forces focused engagement
- Prevents overthinking
- Simulates interview/production pressure
- You'll learn what you can do under time
  constraint
```

The pressure forces focused engagement that casual practice lacks.

Technique 3: Teaching

Explain concepts to others. Teaching requires deeper understanding than using.

```
# You can use this code
cache = LRUCache(capacity=100)
cache.put(key, value)
result = cache.get(key)

# But can you explain HOW it works?
# "An LRU cache needs O(1) get and put
```

```
# operations...
#  That requires a hash table for lookup...
#  But we also need to track access order...
#  A doubly-linked list maintains that...
#  When capacity is exceeded..."

# If you can't explain it clearly, you don't
# understand it deeply
```

As we'll discuss in Chapter 11 (Apprenticeship Problem), teaching forces articulation of tacit knowledge. You discover gaps when you try to explain.

Technique 4: Novel Domains

Apply engineering skills to unfamiliar problems. Build something outside your expertise.

```
# If you're a web developer
# Build: A command-line tool in C++
# Or: A game engine
# Or: An embedded systems project

# If you're a systems programmer
# Build: A web framework
# Or: A machine learning pipeline
# Or: A mobile app

# The transfer requires genuine thinking, not
# pattern matching
```

The goal is not to make work harder for its own sake. It's to ensure that time invested translates into capability gained—that you're building genuine skill, not just accumulating borrowed solutions.

Building and Maintaining Resilience

Practical Strategies for Daily Resilience

Resilience isn't just about pushing through difficulty—it's about building sustainable practices that make persistence possible without burnout.

Strategy 1: Small Daily Commitments

Consistency beats intensity. Better to practice 1 hour daily than 10 hours once a month.

```
# Sustainable daily practice
DAILY_GOALS = {
    'deliberate_practice': '1 hour',
    'reading_technical_content': '30 minutes',
    'code_review_learning': '15 minutes',
    'reflection_journaling': '10 minutes'
}

# Not sustainable
WEEKLY_BINGE = {
    'saturday_coding_marathon': '12 hours',
    'rest_of_week': '0 hours'
}
```

As we'll discuss in Chapter 13 (Antifragile Career), compounding requires consistency. Small daily investments compound more reliably than sporadic binges.

Strategy 2: Energy Management

Manage energy, not just time. Different work requires different energy levels.

```
# High-energy time (morning for most people)
MORNING = [
    'deep_problem_solving',
    'architecture_design',
    'learning_new_concepts',
    'difficult_debugging'
]

# Medium-energy time (afternoon)
AFTERNOON = [
    'code_review',
    'implementation_of_known_patterns',
    'meetings_that_require_engagement'
]

# Low-energy time (late afternoon)
LATE_DAY = [
```

```
    'routine_testing',
    'documentation',
    'organizing_thoughts',
    'planning_tomorrow'
]
```

Match task difficulty to energy level. Don't waste high-energy time on low-energy tasks.

Strategy 3: Recovery Rituals

High performers in any field build recovery into their practice. You can't sprint indefinitely.

```
DAILY_RECOVERY = [
    'pomodoro_breaks',  # 5 min every 25 min
    'lunch_away_from_desk',
    'end_of_day_shutdown_ritual'
]

WEEKLY_RECOVERY = [
    'one_day_completely_offline',
    'physical_exercise',
    'non-technical_creative_work'
]

MONTHLY_RECOVERY = [
    'weekend_trip',
    'deep_hobby_engagement',
    'complete_mental_reset'
]
```

Recovery isn't weakness—it's how you sustain high performance over years.

Strategy 4: Progress Tracking

When progress feels slow, objective tracking reveals actual improvement.

```
# Weekly learning journal
WEEKLY_REVIEW = """
Week of: {date}

What I learned:
- Understood how asyncio event loop works
```

```
    internally
- Fixed race condition in payment processing
- Learned when to use composition vs inheritance

What I struggled with:
- Still don't fully understand Rust's borrow
    checker
- Spent 3 hours debugging type hint issues

What I'll focus on next week:
- Deep dive on Rust ownership model
- Practice more with mypy type checking

Comparison to 6 months ago:
- Then: Couldn't debug async code at all
- Now: Can identify and fix race conditions
    systematically
"""
```

When you feel stuck, reviewing past entries shows how far you've actually come.

Managing Frustration With AI

Working with AI introduces new frustration patterns. Building resilience means developing strategies for these specifically:

Frustration Pattern 1: AI Confidently Wrong

AI generates code that looks correct but subtly isn't, with complete confidence.

- *Coping strategy.* Expect this. AI doesn't know when it's wrong. Your job is verification, not blind trust. As we'll discuss in Chapter 10 (Calibrated Trust), trust but verify.

```
# When AI suggests something that seems off
# Don't just accept or reject - investigate

# AI suggests:
result = unsafe_operation(data)

# You think: "Is this actually safe here?"
# Instead of accepting or fighting, verify:
```

```
# - What are the preconditions for
# unsafe operation?
# - Are they met in this context?
# - What happens if they're not?
# Decision based on understanding, not AI
# confidence
```

Frustration Pattern 2: AI Can't Handle Your Specific Context

AI gives generic answers when you need domain-specific solutions.

- *Coping strategy.* Use AI for scaffolding, add domain knowledge yourself.

```
# You: "Implement payment processing with
# industry-specific compliance"
# AI: [Generates generic payment processing]

# Instead of frustration, think:
# "AI gave me the structure, I'll add the domain
# specifics"
# - Generic payment logic from AI ✓
# - Compliance rules I know from domain ✓
# - Integration with our systems I understand ✓
# AI accelerated the mechanical parts, I added
# the judgment
```

Frustration Pattern 3: Many Iterations Before Success

You prompt AI 10 times before getting something useful.

- *Coping strategy.* View it as rapid prototyping, not failure.

```
# Don't think: "AI sucks, this is iteration 10"
# Think: "I explored 10 approaches in the time it
# would take
#         to manually implement 2. Even with the
#         failures,
#         I'm net ahead."

# The iterations ARE the work
# Each failed suggestion taught you something
# about the problem space
```

Preventing Burnout

Persistence does not mean working until exhaustion. Burnout is the opposite of resilience—it's what happens when you persist without recovery.

Warning signs of burnout (Maslach and Jackson 1981): - Code feels meaningless (loss of purpose) - Every bug feels insurmountable (overwhelm) - Cynicism about technology choices (emotional exhaustion) - Avoiding challenges you'd normally enjoy (withdrawal) - Physical symptoms (sleep issues, tension, illness)

- *Prevention strategies.*
- *Maintain boundaries.* Work has limits. Set them explicitly.

```
BOUNDARIES = {
    'daily_work_hours': '8-9 hours max',
    'evening_slack': 'Emergency only',
    'weekend_work': 'Never, unless catastrophic
    failure',
    'vacation_response': 'Actually disconnect'
}
```

- *Diversify identity.* You're not just an engineer. Invest in other aspects of life.

```
IDENTITY = [
    'software_engineer',  # Important but not
        everything
    'partner/parent',
    'hobbyist (music/art/sports)',
    'friend',
    'community_member'
]

# If engineering identity suffers (bad project,
# layoff),
# other identities provide stability
```

- *Connect meaning.* Remember why the work matters beyond the code itself.

```
# When work feels meaningless, reconnect to impact
# Not: "I'm debugging this stupid CSS issue again"
# But: "I'm making this accessible so people with
# disabilities can use it"
```

```
# Not: "Another database migration script"
# But: "This enables the team to ship faster,
# which means
#       we can help more users sooner"
```

- *Seek help.* Resilience doesn't mean suffering alone.

When burnout threatens: - Talk to manager about workload - Connect with peers experiencing similar challenges - Consider therapy (mental health is engineering health) - Take time off if possible

The most resilient engineers are those who know their limits and respect them.

Chapter Summary

- **Persistence predicts success more than talent.** Psychological research shows grit—sustained passion and perseverance—correlates more strongly with achievement than IQ or aptitude. Skills, knowledge, reputation, and relationships all compound through persistent effort (Duckworth et al. 2007; Robins et al. 2003).
- **AI amplifies the value of persistence.** When AI fails (repeatedly), when problems are genuinely novel, when integration is complex, and when frustration accumulates, human persistence becomes the differentiating factor. AI handles known patterns; persistence tackles everything else.
- **Failure is information, not identity.** A growth mindset treats failure as feedback about incomplete learning, while a fixed mindset treats it as evidence of inadequacy. The debugging mindset—systematic hypothesis testing, learning from negatives, emotional regulation—generalizes to all problem-solving (Dweck 2006).
- **The valley of despair is where growth happens.** Skill acquisition involves a predictable period where progress slows and the gap between current and desired ability becomes painfully visible. Most quit here; masters persist through it (Kruger and Dunning 1999).
- **Deliberate practice requires productive struggle.** AI can bypass the cognitive effort that builds skill by providing solutions before struggle occurs. Effective use preserves struggle through attempting before asking, understanding before accepting, verifying independently, and seeking novel challenges (Ericsson et al. 1993; Hiebert and Grouws 2003).

- **Persistence operates across all three layers.** At Execution: debugging stamina. At Design: architectural iteration. At Intent: requirements clarification. Complete engineers persist at every layer.
- **Sustainable resilience requires recovery.** Small daily commitments beat sporadic intensity. Energy management matches task difficulty to available energy. Recovery rituals prevent burnout. Progress tracking reveals improvement when it feels slow (Maslach and Jackson 1981).
- **Managing AI frustration is a new skill.** Expect confident wrongness, use AI for scaffolding while adding domain knowledge, view iterations as exploration rather than failure. Calibrated trust (Chapter 10) prevents both blind acceptance and blanket rejection.
- **Burnout is the opposite of resilience.** Warning signs include loss of purpose, overwhelm, emotional exhaustion, and withdrawal. Prevention requires boundaries, diversified identity, meaningful connection to work, and seeking help when needed.
- **The compound effect favors the persistent.** Talent provides a starting point; persistence determines the trajectory. Over years, consistent effort creates capabilities that sporadic brilliance cannot match.

In the next chapter, we'll examine logical thinking as a superpower—how the engineering habit of systematic reasoning becomes even more valuable when working with AI systems that can generate plausible but flawed outputs.

Chapter 6

Logical Thinking as Superpower

> "The formulation of a problem is often more essential than its solution." — Albert Einstein

---

The bug had been in production for three weeks. Intermittent. Unreproducible locally. Affecting maybe 2% of users. Five engineers had investigated. All had given up.

Sarah took a different approach. She didn't start by reading code or adding logging. She started with a question: "What do we actually know for certain?"

She made a list: - Bug only happens in production (never in staging) - Affects ~2% of users (not random—same users repeatedly) - Started exactly three weeks ago (after routine deployment) - Manifests as incorrect calculations (but inputs appear valid) - No errors in logs (system thinks everything is fine)

Then she asked: "What do these facts eliminate?"

- Not code logic alone (would fail in staging too)
- Not random data corruption (would affect random users)
- Not introduced in deployment (was a routine deploy, no calculation changes)
- Not input validation (system validates correctly)

Then she formed hypotheses ranked by probability: 1. Environment difference between staging and production 2. Data difference between staging and production 3. Load-dependent behavior (only triggers under production scale)

She tested systematically. Environment variables? Same. Database? Same. Load testing at production scale? Still no bug. She was about to give up when she noticed something in her notes: "same users repeatedly."

That's when it clicked. Not random users. Not new users. *Returning* users with old data. Data that existed before three weeks ago. Data that predated a database migration.

She checked: old records had a field formatted differently. The new code expected one format; old data had another. The routine deployment hadn't changed calculation logic—it had changed data parsing. The bug was invisible in staging because staging had fresh data. It was invisible in most users because most users had created accounts recently.

The fix took five minutes. Finding it took systematic reasoning about what was actually known versus what was assumed.

This is the power of logical thinking in engineering: not just working harder, but thinking *more clearly*. In an age when AI can generate code instantly, this clarity—the disciplined process of forming hypotheses, testing them rigorously, and updating beliefs based on evidence—becomes the engineer's most valuable asset.

As we explored in Chapter 4, AI excels at pattern matching but struggles with genuine reasoning. It can recognize that code "looks like" a solution, but it cannot rigorously verify that it *is* a solution. As we explored in Chapter 5, persistence matters, but persistence without method is just stubborn repetition. The combination—persistent, rigorous, logical thinking—is what separates excellent engineers from merely competent ones.

This chapter examines logical thinking as the engineer's core cognitive capability: how to reason from first principles, how debugging embodies the scientific method, how to detect AI errors through systematic verification, and how to think in systems when linear logic fails.

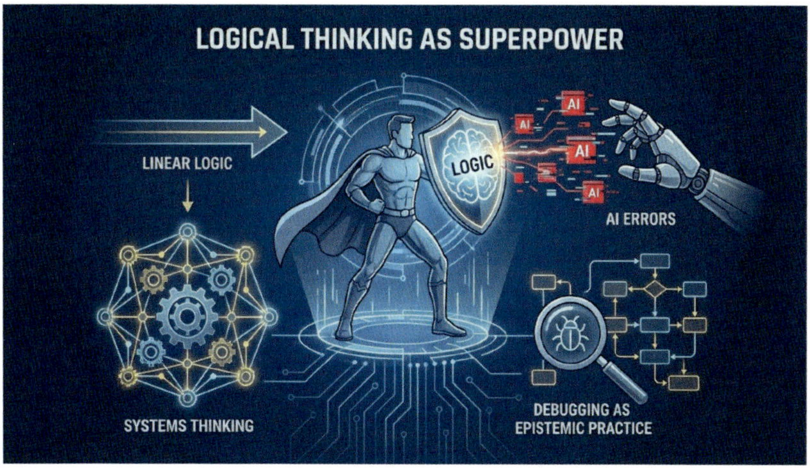

First Principles Thinking

What First Principles Thinking Is

First principles thinking means breaking a problem down to its fundamental truths and building up from there, rather than reasoning by analogy or convention (Musk 2013). It's the difference between "everyone does it this way" and "what must be true for this to work?"

Aristotle defined a first principle as "the first basis from which a thing is known." In engineering, this means identifying the irreducible facts—the physics, mathematics, and logic that cannot be negotiated away—and reasoning from those foundations.

- *Example from Sarah's debugging.*

```
# Reasoning by analogy
"Other calculation bugs were in the calculation
 logic,
 so I should focus on the calculation code."

# First principles
"What facts do I know with certainty?
 - Bug affects only old users
 - Bug started after deployment
 - Bug is deterministic (same users, same wrong
   results)

 What must be true for these facts to coexist?
 - Something changed that affects old data
   differently than new data
 - The change was in that deployment
 - The difference is in the data itself, not the
   logic"
```

The first approach led five engineers to spend days in the wrong place. The second approach found the bug in hours.

When to Use First Principles

First principles thinking is cognitively expensive. It's slower than pattern matching, more effortful than following convention. You can't reason from fundamentals for every decision—you'd never ship anything.

- *Use first principles when.*
- *Existing approaches aren't working.* When you're stuck, when conventional solutions fail, when you've tried multiple patterns without success. This is the signal to go deeper.

```
# After three attempted solutions fail
# Stop asking: "What pattern fits this?"
# Start asking: "What actually needs to happen
# here?"

# Instead of: "I'll try another caching strategy"
# Ask: "What is the fundamental constraint?
#       We need O(1) lookup with bounded memory.
#       What data structures provide that?
#       Hash table with LRU eviction.
#       Now, how do we implement that?"
```

- *Requirements seem impossible.* When stakeholders ask for something that appears contradictory or unachievable. First principles help you identify what's actually constrained versus what's assumed.

```
# Requirement: "We need real-time updates AND
#               eventual consistency AND
#               no coordination overhead"

# First principles analysis:
# - Real-time updates require synchronization
# - Eventual consistency allows delayed
# synchronization
# - No coordination means no synchronization
# These are contradictory. Which constraint can
# we relax?
```

- *Novel problems.* When you're working in a domain where patterns don't exist yet, where AI training data is sparse, where no one has solved this exact problem.

As we'll discuss in Chapter 14 (Vertical Mastery), domain expertise includes knowing when domain patterns apply and when you need first principles.

- *High stakes.* When correctness is critical—security, safety, financial transactions—first principles verification prevents subtle errors that pattern matching might miss.

How to Reason From First Principles

Step 1: Identify assumptions

List everything you're taking for granted. Many "constraints" are actually assumptions that can be questioned.

```
# Problem: "We need to store user sessions, but
# Redis is too expensive"

# Hidden assumptions:
# - Sessions must be in Redis specifically
# - Sessions must be in a separate data store
# - All session data must be stored together
# - Sessions must be stored at all

# First principles: What do we actually need?
# - Users don't re-authenticate on every request
# - User state persists across requests within a
# session
# - Sessions eventually expire

# This doesn't mandate Redis or even server-side
# storage
# Could use: signed JWTs (stateless), browser
# localStorage + server validation,
#            database with proper indexing, or
#            actual Redis if budget allows
```

Step 2: Break down to fundamentals

What are the irreducible requirements? What laws of logic, mathematics, or physics apply?

```
# Problem: "Our system is too slow"

# Not first principles: "Let's add caching"
#
# First principles:
# - Response time = network latency + processing
# time + data retrieval time
# - Users experience delays > 200ms as "slow"
# - Current response time is ~800ms
```

```
# - Therefore: must reduce by ~600ms

# Where are we spending time?
# Measure:
# - Network: 50ms
# - Processing: 100ms
# - Database query: 650ms

# First principles: Optimize the bottleneck
# (database)
# Not: Add caching (might help, but address root
# cause first)
```

Step 3: Build up the solution

Once you have fundamentals clear, construct the solution from those pieces.

```
# Problem: Implement authentication for
# microservices

# First principles:
# 1. Service A must verify requests are authorized
# 2. User authenticates once, not per service
# 3. Services must not trust each other blindly
# 4. Solution must scale to many services

# Build up:
# - Need shared authentication authority (auth
# service)
# - Need portable proof of authentication (JWT
# token)
# - Need services to verify proofs (signature
# verification)
# - Need tokens to expire (time-based expiration)

# This reasoning leads to JWT-based auth from
# fundamentals,
# not from "everyone uses JWTs" pattern matching
```

Step 4: Validate against fundamentals

After building a solution, verify it satisfies the fundamental requirements without adding unnecessary complexity.

First Principles vs Pattern Matching

The art is knowing when to use each approach:

Pattern matching (AI's strength): - Fast - Works for common problems - Leverages existing knowledge - Good for execution layer (Chapter 1)

First principles (human strength): - Slow - Works for novel problems - Builds new knowledge - Essential for design and intent layers (Chapter 1)

The expert engineer shifts between modes: - Pattern match to get 80% of the way quickly - Switch to first principles when patterns fail - Validate pattern-matched solutions against first principles

As we discussed in Chapter 4, this is where human judgment adds value. AI can suggest patterns; humans can verify they're actually appropriate.

Debugging as Applied Logic

The Scientific Method in Code

In Chapter 5, we saw Marcus debugging a payment system through persistent hypothesis testing. Let's formalize that process—it's the scientific method applied to code (Zeller 2009).

- *The debugging cycle.*

```
# 1. Observation: Gather data about the failure
"""
Symptom: Payment processing fails intermittently
When: Under load, roughly 1 in 50 transactions
Where: Production only, never in staging
Effect: Transaction appears to succeed but isn't
    recorded
"""

# 2. Question: What explains this behavior?

# 3. Hypothesis: Form testable explanations
hypotheses = [
    "Database connection pool exhausted under
```

```
    load",
    "Race condition in transaction handling",
    "Timeout causing partial writes",
    "Cache invalidation timing issue"
]

# 4. Prediction: What would we observe if
# hypothesis is true?
# If connection pool exhausted:
#   - Should see connection errors in logs
#   - Should correlate with high request rate
#   - Should improve if pool size increased

# 5. Test: Design experiment
def test_hypothesis_1():
    # Increase connection pool from 10 to 50
    # Monitor: Does failure rate decrease?
    # Result: No change in failure rate
    # Conclusion: Hypothesis 1 rejected

# 6. Analysis: Update beliefs
# Connection pool is NOT the cause
# Remove from consideration
# Test next hypothesis

# 7. Iterate: Repeat with refined understanding
```

This is exactly the scientific method (Popper 1959). The skilled debugger is conducting empirical science, just in the domain of code rather than physics.

- *Why this matters for AI collaboration.*

AI can suggest hypotheses rapidly. But AI cannot: - Design discriminating experiments - Interpret ambiguous results - Know when to reject a hypothesis - Maintain the logical thread across multiple tests

The human contribution is *method*—the disciplined cycle that AI lacks.

The Logic of Elimination

Sherlock Holmes famously declared: “When you have eliminated the impossible, whatever remains, however improbable, must be the truth.” This is not just detective fiction—it’s sound debugging logic.

- *Systematic elimination.*

```
# Bug: Function returns wrong result for some
# inputs

def suspicious_function(data: list[int]) -> int:
    result = 0
    for i in range(len(data)):
        result += data[i] * 2
    return result

# Test cases:
assert suspicious_function([1, 2, 3]) == 12  #
    Pass
assert suspicious_function([]) == 0  # Pass
assert suspicious_function([5]) == 10  # Pass
assert suspicious_function([1, 2, 3, 4]) == 20  #
    Pass
# Wait, that passed. Let me add more tests...
assert suspicious_function([1, 2, 3, 4, 5]) == 30
    # Also pass

# Let me check my test itself
# Expected: (1+2+3+4+5) * 2 = 15 * 2 = 30 ✓
# Actual: 30 ✓

# But users report it's wrong. What am I missing?
# Maybe the requirement is wrong?
```

Let's apply systematic elimination:

```
# Hypothesis space:
# A) Code logic is wrong
# B) Test is wrong
# C) Requirements are wrong
# D) Input data in production differs from test
# data

# Eliminate A: Code logic matches tests
# Eliminate B: Manual calculation confirms tests
# Eliminate C: Re-read requirements... "sum first,
```

```python
# then double the sum"
#              NOT "double each element, then sum"
#              Ah! My implementation is wrong!

def correct_function(data: list[int]) -> int:
    return sum(data) * 2  # Sum first, THEN double

# The error was in implementation, but systematic
# elimination
# helped me question my assumptions about
# requirements
```

- *The key.* Each negative result (eliminated hypothesis) narrows the search space. This compounds—ten eliminated hypotheses make the eleventh much easier to find.

Building Mental Models Through Debugging

Every debugging session is an opportunity to refine mental models. As we discussed in Chapter 5, this is why manual debugging builds expertise that accepting AI solutions doesn't.

- *Example: Understanding async behavior.*

```python
# Observation: Sometimes data is None when it
# shouldn't be

import asyncio

async def fetch_data():
    await asyncio.sleep(1)
    return {"status": "ok"}

async def process():
    data = fetch_data()  # BUG: Missing await!
    print(data.get("status"))  # Error: coroutine
        has no 'get'

# First debugging: "Why is data a coroutine
# object?"
# This forces you to understand: async functions
# return coroutines,
```

```python
# coroutines must be awaited, await suspends
# execution

# Mental model updated: "async functions don't
# run until awaited"

# Correct version:
async def process():
    data = await fetch_data()  # Now it works
    print(data.get("status"))
```

After debugging this once, you recognize the pattern instantly next time. The mental model developed through struggle persists.

Compare to accepting AI fix without understanding:

```python
# AI suggests: "Add await before fetch_data()"
# You add it, it works, but do you understand WHY?
# Next time, you might make the same mistake.
```

- *Building systematic mental models.*

Keep a debugging log. After each bug:

```
# Bug: Async function not awaited
Date: 2026-01-13
Context: Processing API responses

What I learned:
- async functions return coroutine objects
- Coroutines must be awaited to execute
- Missing await gives runtime error, not syntax
  error
- Type hints can catch this: mypy would have
  warned

Mental model updated:
- Always await async functions
- Look for 'coroutine' in error messages as signal
- Use type checker to catch before runtime

Pattern recognition:
- This is like forgetting to call functions
```

```
    (getting function object, not result)
- But more subtle because async syntax is implicit
```

Over years, these logs become a personal knowledge base. The patterns you've debugged become automatic recognition. This is expertise.

Detecting AI Errors Through Logical Analysis

The Taxonomy of AI Logic Errors

As we explored in Chapter 4, AI makes characteristic mistakes. Understanding these patterns enables systematic verification:

Error Type 1: Plausible but Wrong Logic

AI generates code that looks correct syntactically but has logical flaws.

```python
# AI generates this for "check if year is leap
# year"
def is_leap_year(year: int) -> bool:
    if year % 4 == 0:
        return True
    return False

# Looks reasonable, but wrong!
# Missing: years divisible by 100 are not leap
# years
#          UNLESS also divisible by 400

# Correct logic:
def is_leap_year(year: int) -> bool:
    if year % 400 == 0:
        return True
    if year % 100 == 0:
        return False
    if year % 4 == 0:
        return True
    return False

# Test cases that catch AI error:
assert is_leap_year(2000) == True   # Divisible
```

```
    by 400
assert is_leap_year(1900) == False  # 100 but not
    400
assert is_leap_year(2004) == True   # Divisible
    by 4
```

- *Verification strategy.* Test with edge cases that probe logical boundaries. AI trains on common patterns; edge cases reveal misunderstanding.

Error Type 2: Off-by-One Errors

Classic programming mistake that AI reproduces:

```
# AI generates: "find index of first element >
# threshold"
def find_first_above(
        arr: list[int], threshold: int) -> int:
    for i in range(len(arr)):
        if arr[i] > threshold:
            return i + 1  # BUG: Should return i,
                not i + 1
    return -1

# Looks plausible, but wrong!
# Returns index + 1, not actual index

# Test case that catches it:
arr = [1, 2, 5, 8]
result = find_first_above(arr, 4)
assert result == 2  # Should be index 2 (value 5)
# But AI version returns 3!
```

- *Verification strategy.* Test with specific inputs where you know exact expected output. Don't just test "it works," test "it gives exactly this answer."

Error Type 3: Incomplete Edge Case Handling

AI handles common cases but misses edge cases:

```
# AI generates: "safely divide two numbers"
def safe_divide(a: float, b: float) -> float:
    if b == 0:
        return 0.0  # Avoid division by zero
    return a / b
```

```python
# Looks safe, but questionable!
# Is returning 0 for x/0 really correct?
# What about 0/0? Should that be 0 or undefined?
# What about -5/0? Should that be 0 or should we
# signal error?

# Better version:
def safe_divide(a: float, b: float) ->
    Optional[float]:
    if b == 0:
        return None  # Signal undefined result
    return a / b

# Or even better, raise exception:
def safe_divide(a: float, b: float) -> float:
    if b == 0:
        raise ValueError("Division by zero")
    return a / b
```

- *Verification strategy.* Question the semantics. “Is this behavior correct?” not just “Does it avoid errors?”

Error Type 4: Hallucinated APIs

AI invents functions or parameters that don’t exist:

```python
# AI suggests: "Use the built-in parallel_map
# function"
from multiprocessing import parallel_map  #
    Doesn't exist!

results = parallel_map(process_item, items)  #
    Will fail

# Correct: multiprocessing doesn't have
# parallel_map
# You need to use Pool.map or ProcessPoolExecutor
from multiprocessing import Pool

with Pool() as pool:
    results = pool.map(process_item, items)
```

- *Verification strategy.* Cross-reference with official documentation. If AI cites something you haven't heard of, verify it exists.

Error Type 5: Subtle Race Conditions

AI doesn't reason about concurrency well:

```python
# AI generates: "Thread-safe counter"
class Counter:
    def __init__(self):
        self.count = 0

    def increment(self):
        self.count += 1  # NOT thread-safe!

    def get(self):
        return self.count

# Looks reasonable, but wrong!
# self.count += 1 is actually three operations:
# 1. Read self.count
# 2. Add 1
# 3. Write back
# Two threads can interleave these operations

# Correct version:
import threading

class Counter:
    def __init__(self):
        self.count = 0
        self.lock = threading.Lock()

    def increment(self):
        with self.lock:
            self.count += 1

    def get(self):
        with self.lock:
            return self.count
```

- *Verification strategy.* Think about concurrent execution explicitly. "What if two threads execute this simultaneously?"

Systematic Verification Patterns

As we'll discuss in Chapter 10 (Calibrated Trust), verification is how you maintain appropriate skepticism:

Pattern 1: Mental Execution

Before accepting AI code, trace execution mentally:

```
# AI generates binary search
def binary_search(arr, target):
    left, right = 0, len(arr) - 1
    while left <= right:
        mid = (left + right) // 2
        if arr[mid] == target:
            return mid
        elif arr[mid] < target:
            left = mid + 1
        else:
            right = mid - 1
    return -1

# Mental execution for arr = [1, 3, 5, 7], target
# = 3:
# Initial: left=0, right=3
# Iteration 1: mid=1, arr[1]=3, return 1 ✓

# Mental execution for arr = [1, 3, 5, 7], target
# = 2:
# Initial: left=0, right=3
# Iteration 1: mid=1, arr[1]=3 > 2, right=0
# Iteration 2: mid=0, arr[0]=1 < 2, left=1
# Now left > right, return -1 ✓

# Mental execution catches logic errors before
# runtime
```

Pattern 2: Boundary Testing

Test the edges where errors hide:

```
def test_binary_search():
```

```python
    # Empty array
    assert binary_search([], 5) == -1

    # Single element
    assert binary_search([3], 3) == 0
    assert binary_search([3], 5) == -1

    # Two elements
    assert binary_search([1, 3], 1) == 0
    assert binary_search([1, 3], 3) == 1
    assert binary_search([1, 3], 2) == -1

    # Target at boundaries
    assert binary_search([1, 2, 3, 4, 5], 1) == 0
        # First
    assert binary_search([1, 2, 3, 4, 5], 5) == 4
        # Last

    # Target not in array
    assert binary_search([1, 2, 3, 4, 5], 0) == -
        1  # Before
    assert binary_search([1, 2, 3, 4, 5], 6) == -
        1  # After
    assert binary_search([1, 2, 3, 4, 5], 2.5) ==
        -1  # Between
```

AI trains on common cases. Boundaries are where logic errors appear.

Pattern 3: Invariant Checking

Identify what should always be true, verify it holds:

```python
# AI generates a sorting function
def sort_array(arr):
    # ... some sorting logic ...
    return sorted_arr

# Invariants to check:
def verify_sort(original, sorted_arr):
    # Invariant 1: Same length
    assert len(original) == len(sorted_arr)
```

```python
    # Invariant 2: Same elements (just reordered)
    assert sorted(original) == sorted(sorted_arr)

    # Invariant 3: Actually sorted
    for i in range(len(sorted_arr) - 1):
        assert sorted_arr[i] <= sorted_arr[i + 1]

    return True

# Use in tests:
original = [3, 1, 4, 1, 5]
result = sort_array(original)
verify_sort(original, result)
```

Invariant checking catches subtle errors that specific test cases might miss.

Pattern 4: Independent Verification

Don't rely solely on AI explanations. Verify against independent sources:

```python
# AI claims: "Use requests.get(url, verify=False)
# to ignore SSL errors"

# Don't just accept this!
# 1. Check official documentation
# 2. Understand security implications
# 3. Question if this is actually appropriate

# Reading docs reveals:
# - verify=False disables certificate validation
# - This makes you vulnerable to man-in-the-
# middle attacks
# - Should only be used in development, never
# production
# - Better solution: install proper certificates

# AI suggestion is technically correct but
# dangerous
```

Pattern 5: The "Explain It Back" Test

Can you explain why the AI's solution works?

```python
# AI generates: "Use this for thread-safe
```

```
# singleton"
class Singleton:
    _instance = None
    _lock = threading.Lock()

    def __new__(cls):
        if cls._instance is None:
            with cls._lock:
                if cls._instance is None:
                    cls._instance = super().
                        __new__(cls)
        return cls._instance

# Can you explain why?
# - First if check avoids lock overhead after
# initialization
# - Lock prevents race condition during
# initialization
# - Second if check (inside lock) handles case
# where multiple
#   threads passed first check before any
#   completed initialization
# - This is "double-checked locking" pattern

# If you can't explain it, you don't understand
# it enough to use it
```

Systems Thinking: When Linear Logic Fails

The Limits of Linear Reasoning

In Chapter 7 (Simplifying Complexity), we'll discuss decomposition and abstraction. But some problems resist decomposition—they're fundamentally systemic.

- *Linear thinking*. A causes B, B causes C, therefore A causes C.

This works for: - Pure functions (input -> output) - Sequential processes (step 1 -> step 2 -> step 3) - Isolated components (change A, only A changes)

But modern systems are: - Interactive (components affect each other) - Concurrent (things happen simultaneously) - Emergent (system behavior $\neq$ sum of component behaviors)

- *Example of where linear thinking fails.*

```
# Linear thinking debugging:
# "System is slow"
# -> Check database queries
# -> Queries are fast individually
# -> Conclusion: Database isn't the problem

# Systems thinking debugging:
# "System is slow"
# -> Check database queries: fast individually
# -> Check query concurrency: 100 queries run
# simultaneously
# -> Check connection pool: only 10 connections
# -> Connection pool is bottleneck causing
# queries to queue
# -> Each query is fast, but queueing causes
# overall slowness

# The problem isn't in any component alone—
# it's in the interaction between query pattern
# and connection pool
```

Linear thinking would miss this because no single component is "broken."

Feedback Loops in Software

Systems thinking recognizes *feedback loops*—where effects circle back to influence causes (Meadows 2008).

- *Reinforcing (positive) feedback.* Amplifies change

```
# Classic reinforcing loop: System under load

def handle_request(request):
    response = process_request(request)  # Takes
        time T
    return response

# System receives R requests/sec
```

```
# Each request takes T seconds to process
# As R increases, response time increases
# Slow responses cause timeouts
# Clients retry on timeout
# Retries increase R further
# Even slower responses...
# More retries...
# SYSTEM COLLAPSES

# This is a reinforcing failure loop
# Small increase in load -> cascading failure

# Break the loop with:
# - Rate limiting (cap R)
# - Circuit breakers (stop retries)
# - Timeout limits (fail fast rather than queuing)
```

- *Balancing (negative) feedback.* Resists change

```
# Balancing loop: Autoscaling

class AutoScaler:
    def __init__(self):
        self.target_cpu = 70  # Target CPU
            percentage
        self.instances = 5

    def check_and_scale(self):
        current_cpu = measure_cpu()

        if current_cpu > self.target_cpu:
            # Load too high -> add instances
            self.instances += 1
            # More instances -> lower CPU per
            # instance
            # Lower CPU -> closer to target
            # Balancing loop maintains equilibrium

        elif current_cpu < self.target_cpu - 10:
            # Load too low -> remove instances
            self.instances -= 1
```

```
        # Fewer instances -> higher CPU per
        # instance
        # Higher CPU -> closer to target

# This is a balancing loop that maintains
# stability
```

- *Understanding loop structure explains behavior.*
- Reinforcing loops create exponential growth or collapse
- Balancing loops create stability or oscillation
- Many systems have both types interacting

Emergence and Non-Linear Effects

- *Emergence.* System-level properties that don't exist in components alone.

```
# Example: Distributed consensus
# Component behavior:
# - Each node maintains local state
# - Each node sends messages to other nodes
# - Each node follows simple protocol rules

# Emergent system behavior:
# - Cluster achieves consensus despite node
# failures
# - System tolerates network partitions
# - Global properties (consistency, availability)
# emerge
#   from local interactions

# No single component "knows" about consensus
# Consensus emerges from interactions
```

- *Non-linear effects.* Small changes, big impacts (or vice versa)

```
# Small change, big impact:
# Change cache TTL from 60 seconds to 5 seconds
# -> 12x increase in database load
# -> Database saturates
# -> Entire system fails

# Large change, small impact:
# Optimize algorithm from O(n²) to O(n log n)
```

```
# -> In production, n is always small (<10)
# -> No measurable performance improvement
# -> Optimization was wasted effort

# Systems thinking: Understand actual bottlenecks
# Don't optimize based on theory alone
```

Multi-Layer Reasoning

As we discussed in Chapter 1, systems have layers (Execution, Design, and Intent). Systems thinking requires reasoning across layers:

```
# Problem appears at Application Layer:
# "Users report slow page loads"

# Linear thinking: Optimize application code

# Systems thinking: Check each layer
# 1. Application Layer: Code is efficient
# 2. Network Layer: Latency is 200ms (high!)
# 3. Infrastructure Layer: Server in wrong region
# 4. Design Layer: Architecture doesn't consider
# geo-distribution
# 5. Intent Layer: Requirements didn't specify
# geo-distribution

# Root cause is at Intent/Design layers
# Solving at Application layer won't help
# Need architectural change (CDN, multi-region
# deployment)
```

Systems problems often manifest at one layer but originate at another. The debugger must zoom out to find the real cause.

Second-Order Thinking

Senior engineers think about second-order effects—the consequences of consequences.

What is second-order thinking?

First-order thinking asks: "What happens if I do this?" Second-order thinking asks: "What happens *after* what happens?" It's thinking about the ripple effects, the unintended consequences, the ways that solutions create new problems even as they solve old ones.

- *Simple example.*
- **First order**: "I'll add more servers to handle increased traffic" -> More capacity
- **Second order**: More servers cost more money, require more maintenance, increase deployment complexity
- **Third order**: Higher costs reduce budget for other improvements, operational complexity slows down deployments
- **Fourth order**: Slower deployments mean slower feature velocity, which impacts business goals

First-order thinking sees the immediate benefit. Second-order thinking sees the chain of consequences.

- *Every optimization has costs.*

```
# First order: Add caching -> faster reads
# Second order: Cache invalidation complexity
# Third order: Stale data bugs in production
# Fourth order: Customer trust degraded by stale
# data

# Linear thinking: "Caching makes things faster,
# so let's add caching"
# Systems thinking: "Caching trades read
# performance for consistency
#                     complexity. Is that trade-
#                     off worth it?"
```

- *Every solution creates new problems.*

```
# First order: Microservices -> independent
# scaling
# Second order: Network calls between services
# Third order: Latency and failure modes multiply
# Fourth order: Distributed tracing needed
# Fifth order: Additional operational complexity

# Linear thinking: "Microservices solve monolith
# problems"
# Systems thinking: "Microservices solve some
# problems while creating others.
```

```
#                       Are we ready for those new
#                       problems?"
```

- *Every intervention changes the system.*

```
# First order: Add monitoring -> visibility
# Second order: Monitoring overhead ->
# performance impact
# Third order: Engineers optimize for metrics ->
# Goodhart's Law
#                ("When a measure becomes a target,
#                it ceases to be
#                 a good measure")

# Example: If you measure lines of code written,
# engineers write more lines of code (but not
# necessarily better code)
```

This is what distinguishes senior from junior engineers. Juniors solve problems. Seniors solve problems while anticipating the problems their solutions create.

Logical Fallacies in Engineering

Common Reasoning Errors

Even skilled engineers fall into logical traps. Recognizing these fallacies improves reasoning quality:

Fallacy 1: Appeal to Authority (Including AI Authority)

```
# Fallacy: "AI suggested this approach, so it
# must be correct"
#
# Why it's wrong: AI authority is not infallible
# AI is trained on patterns, not verified
# correctness

# Better reasoning:
# "AI suggested this approach. Let me verify:
#   - Does it match requirements?
#   - Does it handle edge cases?
#   - Are there better alternatives?
```

```
#  AI provides a starting point, not a conclusion"
```

Fallacy 2: Correlation ≠ Causation

```
# Observation: "After deploying the new feature,
# response time increased"
# Fallacy: "The new feature caused slower
# response time"
#
# Why it's wrong: Correlation doesn't prove
# causation
# - Maybe traffic increased coincidentally
# - Maybe infrastructure changed
# - Maybe database needs maintenance

# Better reasoning:
# "Response time increased after deployment.
# Possible causes:
#  1. New feature's code (test: disable feature,
#  does it improve?)
#  2. Increased traffic (test: check traffic
#  metrics)
#  3. Infrastructure change (test: check
#  deployment logs)
#  Test each hypothesis systematically"
```

Fallacy 3: Premature Optimization

```
# Fallacy: "This algorithm is O(n²), that's
# inefficient,
#           let me rewrite it as O(n log n)"
#
# Why it's wrong: Optimization without
# measurement is guessing
# - n might always be small (n=10), so O(n²) is
# fine
# - O(n log n) might have higher constant factors
# - The bottleneck might be elsewhere entirely

# Better reasoning:
# "This algorithm is O(n²). Before optimizing:
#  - Measure: Is this actually a bottleneck?
```

```
#  - Profile: How much time is spent here?
#  - Consider n: What are typical values?
#  Only optimize if measurements show it matters"
```

As Donald Knuth said: "Premature optimization is the root of all evil" (Knuth 1974).

Fallacy 4: False Dichotomy

```
# Fallacy: "Either we use microservices or we
# have a monolith"
#
# Why it's wrong: False dichotomies ignore
# alternatives
# - Modular monolith
# - Monolith with separate services for high-
# scale components
# - Monolith first, extract services later

# Better reasoning:
# "We need independent scaling. Options:
#  1. Full microservices (highest flexibility,
#  highest complexity)
#  2. Modular monolith (moderate flexibility,
#  moderate complexity)
#  3. Hybrid (monolith + separate high-scale
#  services)
#  Which balances our needs with our team's
#  capabilities?"
```

Fallacy 5: Post Hoc Ergo Propter Hoc ("After this, therefore because of this")

```
# Fallacy: "The system started failing after we
# upgraded Python.
#          Therefore Python upgrade caused the
#          failures."
#
# Why it's wrong: Temporal sequence doesn't prove
# causation
# - Maybe database filled disk space
# (coincidental timing)
# - Maybe dependency update introduced bug
```

```
# - Maybe traffic pattern changed

# Better reasoning:
# "Failures started after Python upgrade.
# Possible causes:
#  - Python upgrade itself (test: rollback, does
#  it fix?)
#  - Dependency compatibility (test: check all
#  dependencies)
#  - Coincidental infrastructure issue (test:
#  check logs)
#  Systematically eliminate possibilities"
```

Fallacy 6: Sunk Cost Fallacy

```
# Fallacy: "We've spent 3 months on this
# architecture.
#          We can't change now, we've invested
#          too much."
#
# Why it's wrong: Past investment shouldn't drive
# future decisions
# - Sunk costs are sunk—they're gone regardless
# - Decision should be: "Given what we know now,
#   what's the best path forward?"

# Better reasoning:
# "We've invested 3 months in this architecture.
#  But we've learned it doesn't meet requirements.
#  Options:
#  1. Continue (costs: 6 more months + ongoing
#  maintenance of wrong solution)
#  2. Change now (costs: 1 month rework + correct
#  solution)
#  The sunk cost is gone either way. Choose based
#  on future costs."
```

Improving Reasoning Discipline

Recognizing fallacies is the first step. Building reasoning discipline requires practice:

Technique 1: Pre-Mortem Analysis

Before implementing, ask: "Why might this fail?"

```
# Before building feature:
# "Assuming this fails in production, what went
# wrong?"
# - Didn't handle concurrent updates -> Add
# locking
# - Didn't consider mobile latency -> Add
# timeout handling
# - Didn't validate all inputs -> Add validation
# Proactively address failure modes before
# building
```

Technique 2: Articulate Reasoning Explicitly

In Chapter 8 (Communication), we'll discuss writing. Writing forces clear thinking:

```
# Before making architectural decision, write:
"""
Decision: Use PostgreSQL for user data

Alternatives considered:
- DynamoDB: rejected due to team expertise gap
- MySQL: rejected due to worse JSON support
- MongoDB: rejected due to transaction
    requirements

Reasoning:
- Need ACID transactions for data consistency
- Need JSON support for flexible attributes
- Team has PostgreSQL expertise
- Read-heavy workload fits well with read replicas

Risks:
- Single-region deployment (accepted risk, multi-
    region not needed)
- Scaling limit around 10M users (acceptable for
    current growth)
```

```
This reasoning can be reviewed and challenged
"""
```

Technique 3: Seek Disconfirmation

Actively look for evidence against your beliefs:

```
# Belief: "Adding caching will fix performance"
# Don't just test confirming evidence
# Test disconfirming evidence:
# - What if caching doesn't help?
# - What if the problem is elsewhere?
# - What if caching makes things worse?
# Design experiments that could prove you wrong
```

Chapter Summary

- **First principles thinking breaks problems to fundamentals.** Instead of reasoning by analogy ("others do it this way"), identify irreducible facts and build from there. Use when conventional approaches fail, requirements seem impossible, or problems are genuinely novel (Musk 2013).
- **Debugging is the scientific method applied to code.** Observe, hypothesize, test, analyze, iterate. This disciplined cycle transforms debugging from guesswork into systematic investigation. The skilled debugger is conducting empirical science (Popper 1959; Zeller 2009).
- **Mental models enable expert debugging.** Structural models (system organization), behavioral models (normal patterns), failure mode models (what goes wrong), and temporal models (state transitions) are the infrastructure for rapid hypothesis generation. Built through experience, not shortcuts.
- **AI errors require active logical verification.** Plausible but wrong logic, off-by-one errors, incomplete edge cases, hallucinated APIs, and subtle race conditions all require systematic testing. Mental execution, boundary testing, invariant checking, independent verification, and the "explain it back" test all catch errors before production.
- **Systems thinking addresses interactions, not just components.** Feedback loops (reinforcing and balancing), emergence (system properties that don't exist in components), non-linear effects (small changes, big

impacts), and multi-layer reasoning all require thinking beyond linear cause-and-effect (Meadows 2008).

- **Second-order thinking anticipates consequences.** Every optimization has costs, every solution creates new problems, every intervention changes the system. Senior engineers think about effects of effects, not just immediate outcomes.
- **Logical fallacies undermine reasoning.** Appeal to authority (including AI), correlation vs. causation, premature optimization, false dichotomies, post hoc reasoning, and sunk cost fallacies all lead to poor decisions. Recognizing these patterns improves reasoning discipline (Knuth 1974).
- **First principles and pattern matching complement each other.** Pattern matching (AI's strength) is fast and works for common problems. First principles (human strength) is slower but handles novel problems. Expert engineers shift between modes appropriately.
- **Verification is how skeptical trust operates.** As we'll discuss in Chapter 10, neither blind acceptance nor blanket rejection, but systematic verification based on error likelihood, problem novelty, and stakes.
- **Logical thinking compounds with persistence.** From Chapter 5: persistence without method is stubbornness; method without persistence gives up too soon. The combination—persistent, rigorous, logical thinking—defines engineering excellence.

In the next chapter, we'll explore the art of simplifying complexity—the ability to take something complicated and make it genuinely simple without losing essential truth. This skill becomes increasingly valuable as AI generates implementations that work but accumulate complexity faster than human-written code.

Chapter 7

The Art of Simplifying Complexity

"Simplicity is the ultimate sophistication." — often attributed to Leonardo da Vinci

---

Three months into her new role as tech lead, Sarah faced a problem that would define her career trajectory. The team had asked an AI to implement a feature for processing payment refunds. The AI generated 847 lines of Python code in under two minutes. Tests passed. The code worked.

But something felt wrong.

Sarah spent an afternoon reading through the implementation. The AI had created seventeen helper functions, three data transformation pipelines, and a state machine with twelve states. It handled edge cases Sarah hadn't even thought to mention. It was thorough, correct, and completely incomprehensible.

She rewrote it in 93 lines. Same functionality. Same test coverage. But now a junior engineer could understand it in fifteen minutes instead of never.

Her manager asked why she'd "wasted" an afternoon rewriting working code. She explained: "The AI gave us code that works today. I gave us code we can maintain for years. There's a difference."

Six months later, when requirements changed and the refund logic needed to handle partial refunds, subscriptions, and international transactions, Sarah's simple implementation absorbed the changes easily. A colleague working with a similarly complex AI-generated feature spent three weeks untangling dependencies before adding a single new capability.

This is the defining skill of great engineers in the AI era: not writing code—AI does that increasingly well—but *simplifying* code. Taking complexity and mastering it. Transforming tangled problems into tractable ones. Making the difficult appear obvious.

As we explored in Chapter 4, AI can generate implementations but cannot judge which implementations should exist. As we'll see in this chapter, simplification is that judgment—the human contribution that makes the difference between code that works and code that works *and can be understood, maintained, and evolved.*

Why Simplification Matters More Than Ever

The AI Complexity Amplifier

AI systems face a peculiar problem: they optimize for correctness, not simplicity. When you prompt "implement a payment processing system with error handling," an LLM will generate code that handles every edge case it can imagine from its training data. It produces *defensive* code—code that assumes the worst and protects against everything.

This is both impressive and dangerous.

- *Why it is impressive.* The AI catches edge cases you might have missed. It implements retry logic, timeout handling, circuit breakers, and fallbacks. It's thorough.
- *Why it is dangerous.* Thoroughness without judgment creates bloat. Not every edge case matters equally. Not every possible failure mode needs handling. The AI doesn't know your actual constraints—that this is an internal API with trusted callers, that failures are acceptable because there's reconciliation later, that performance matters more than exhaustive error messages.

The result: AI-generated code trends toward complexity. Every prompt produces implementations that work, but they often accumulate complexity faster than a human engineer would allow. As we'll discuss in Chapter 12, when AI handles execution at scale, the human bottleneck becomes *understanding* and *maintenance*. Complexity directly undermines both.

- *Example of AI complexity amplification.*

You ask AI to implement a function that validates email addresses. The AI generates 35 lines of code. It checks whether the input exists, whether it's a string, whether it's empty after trimming, whether it exceeds 254 characters, whether the local part exceeds 64 characters, whether the domain has at least two segments, whether any segment is empty — and then, after all of that, it runs a regular expression that covers the full RFC specification.

It is thorough. It is correct. And for most production contexts, it is unnecessary.

What you actually need is three lines: trim the input, check it against a simple pattern (something before the @, something after the @, a dot somewhere in the domain), and reject anything that doesn't match. One error message. One validation path. Done.

The AI version handles edge cases you'll never encounter in production. It creates different error types for different failures when you just need "this isn't valid." It optimizes for theoretical completeness rather than practical utility.

- *The pattern.* AI generates defensively because it doesn't know your context. It produces code that's *technically correct* but *practically complex.* The human contribution is simplification—reducing to what actually matters.

The Three Layers of Simplification

Let's connect simplification to the three-layer framework from Chapter 1 to understand where it operates:

Execution Layer (implementation mechanics): AI excels here—it can implement complex algorithms correctly. Human simplification means: choosing *simpler* algorithms when they suffice, reducing unnecessary abstraction, eliminating defensive code for cases that don't happen in your context.

Design Layer (architectural decisions): This is where simplification has maximum leverage. Architecture that's simple at the design level makes everything built on it simpler. AI can implement whatever architecture you specify, but it cannot judge whether the architecture is simpler than alternatives. Human judgment determines: Do we need three services or would two suffice? Do we need this abstraction or is direct implementation clearer?

Intent Layer (purpose and value): The ultimate simplification: deciding not to build something. The features you don't implement are infinitely simple to maintain. AI can't make these judgments—it can't say "this requirement seems unnecessarily complex, maybe we should solve a simpler problem." Humans operating at the Intent layer simplify by clarifying what's actually needed versus what was initially requested.

The most powerful simplification happens at higher layers. Simplifying at Execution makes individual functions clearer. Simplifying at Design makes entire subsystems clearer. Simplifying at Intent makes entire projects clearer—or eliminates them entirely.

Simplicity as Antifragile Career Strategy

In Chapter 13, we'll discuss the antifragile career—building skills that gain from change rather than being threatened by it. Simplification is one of those skills.

- *Why simplification resists commoditization.*
- *Simplification requires judgment AI lacks.* Deciding which complexity is essential versus accidental requires understanding context, constraints, and future evolution. AI optimizes locally (make this function correct); humans optimize globally (keep the system maintainable).
- *Simplification requires domain expertise.* Knowing which edge cases actually matter in your vertical (Chapter 14) enables targeted simplification. Generic simplification might remove something essential; informed simplification removes only what's truly unnecessary.
- *Simplification compounds.* Engineers who build simple systems can evolve them faster. This speed advantage compounds—simple systems stay simple because they're easy to refactor; complex systems accumulate complexity because refactoring is expensive.
- *Organizations value simplifiers.* The engineer who can take AI-generated or legacy complexity and make it comprehensible becomes indispensable. This is leadership through simplification—making teams more effective by reducing cognitive load.

As AI makes code generation faster, the premium on simplification increases. The bottleneck shifts from "how do we build this?" to "how do we keep this understandable as it grows?"

The Core Techniques: Abstraction, Decomposition, Naming

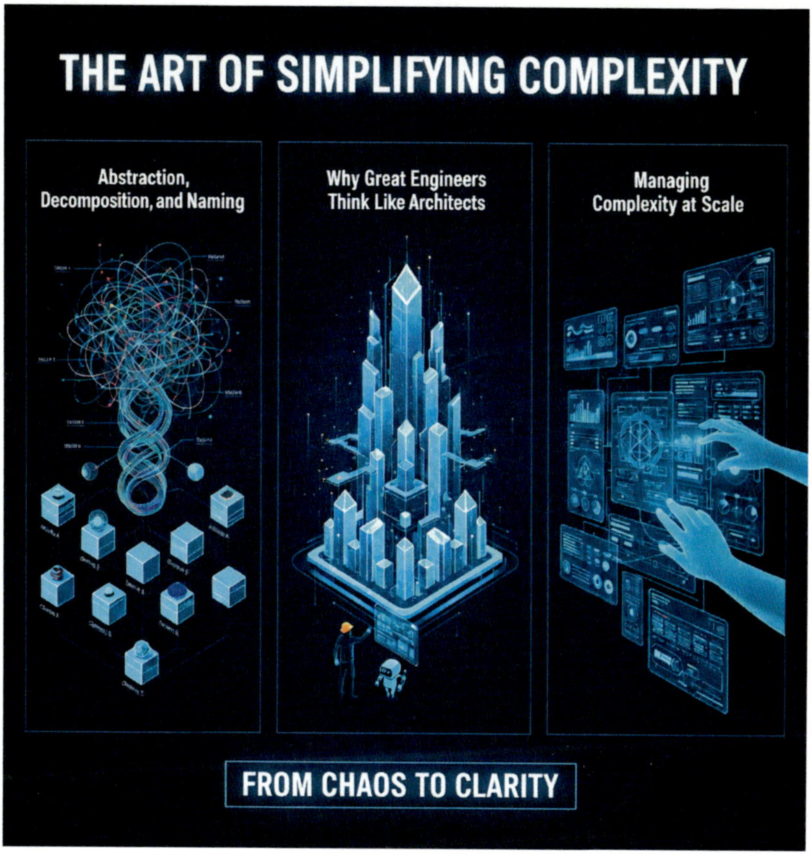

Abstraction: The Art of Hiding

Abstraction is the most powerful tool in the engineer's cognitive arsenal. It is the deliberate act of *hiding*—concealing irrelevant details to reveal essential structure.

When you call a function, you don't think about register allocation, memory management, or instruction scheduling. Those details are abstracted away. You think only about inputs, outputs, and behavior. This hiding isn't laziness—it's *cognitive leverage*. By suppressing irrelevant details, abstraction allows you to reason about systems far more complex than your working memory could otherwise handle (Miller 1956).

- *Why abstraction matters in the AI era.*

AI generates code at the Execution layer rapidly. But AI-generated code often lacks clean abstractions because: - AI doesn't know which details matter to you and which don't - AI optimizes for correctness, not comprehensibility - AI's training favors explicit over implicit (showing all logic rather than hiding it)

The human contribution: identifying the right abstractions *after* AI generates code, or specifying abstractions *before* prompting AI.

- *Example of AI lacking abstraction.*

You ask AI to add authentication checking across twenty API endpoints. The AI generates the same block of code in every single endpoint — extract the authorization header, check whether it starts with "Bearer," verify the token, return an error if any step fails. Twenty copies of the same eight lines. Each individually correct. All identical.

A human engineer sees the repetition and extracts it. The authentication logic moves into a single reusable component — written once, tested once, maintained in one place. Each endpoint then declares "this requires authentication" in a single line, without knowing or caring how authentication works internally.

The AI produced twenty copies of the same logic because it generates each endpoint independently. The human saw the pattern across endpoints and created an abstraction that eliminated the duplication entirely. This is the difference between generating code and *designing* code.

- *Properties of good abstractions.*
- *They hide the right things.* A good database abstraction hides storage engines and query optimization while exposing the logical model of tables and relationships. A bad abstraction hides things you need to know (like performance characteristics) or exposes things you don't (like internal buffer management).
- *They're stable.* Abstractions that change frequently provide little cognitive benefit—you must constantly peek behind them. The best abstractions represent boundaries that genuinely separate concerns, so changes on one side rarely require changes on the other.
- *They compose.* Good abstractions combine without requiring knowledge of internals. Think of Python's iterator protocol—any iterable works with `for` loops, `list()`, `sum()`, and more. Each abstraction uses others without understanding implementation (Abelson et al. 1996).

- *They match mental models.* The most usable abstractions align with how people already think about a domain. Python's context managers (`with` statement) match our intuition about resource acquisition and cleanup. File abstractions match our intuition about documents.
- *The test of good abstraction.* Can you explain what something does without explaining how it works? If yes, the abstraction succeeds. If you must always explain implementation to explain behavior, the abstraction fails.

Decomposition: Divide and Conquer

If abstraction is about hiding, decomposition is about *separating*. It's the technique of breaking a complex whole into simpler parts that can be understood and built independently.

Decomposition sounds obvious. In practice, it's surprisingly difficult. The challenge is finding the *right* boundaries—cuts that create pieces with minimal interdependence.

- *AI's decomposition problem.*

AI can generate modular code when you specify the decomposition. But AI struggles to *discover* good decomposition boundaries because: - Good decomposition requires understanding future evolution (what will change together?) - Good decomposition requires domain knowledge (what are natural problem boundaries?) - Good decomposition requires organizational context (how is work actually divided?)

AI generates monolithic solutions or over-decomposes into micro-modules without clear boundaries. The human contribution is recognizing where boundaries should be.

- *Signs of good decomposition.*
- *Low coupling.* Well-decomposed components have narrow interfaces. Changes in one rarely require changes in others. They can be developed, tested, and deployed independently.

Example: A payment service that exposes only `process_payment(amount, method)` is loosely coupled. A payment service that requires callers to manage internal payment state is tightly coupled.

- *High cohesion.* Each component has a single, clear responsibility. Everything inside relates to that responsibility. You can describe what the component does in one sentence.

Example: An `AuthenticationService` that handles login, password reset, and session management has high cohesion (all authentication concerns). An `AuthenticationService` that also formats user profile displays has low cohesion (mixing concerns).

- *Natural boundaries.* Good decomposition often follows natural boundaries in the problem domain. A payment system separates along authorization, settlement, and reconciliation because those are genuinely different concerns with different rules and lifecycles.

- *Testability.* Well-decomposed components can be tested in isolation. If you can't test a component without bringing up the entire system, the boundaries are probably wrong.

```
# Good decomposition - each function testable
# independently
def validate_order(order: Order) ->
    ValidatedOrder:
    """Validate order has required fields and
        valid data."""
    if not order.items:
        raise ValueError("Order must have items")
    # validation logic
    return ValidatedOrder(order)

def calculate_pricing(order: ValidatedOrder) ->
    PricedOrder:
    """Calculate total price including taxes and
        discounts."""
    # pricing logic
    return PricedOrder(order, total)

def process_order(order: Order) -> ProcessedOrder:
    """Orchestrate order processing pipeline."""
    validated = validate_order(order)
    priced = calculate_pricing(validated)
    # continue pipeline
    return result
```

- *Signs of bad decomposition.*

- *Shotgun surgery.* A single change requires modifications across many components. The boundaries don't match the forces of change.

- *Feature envy.* Components constantly reach into each other's internals. The responsibilities are distributed incorrectly.

```
# Bad decomposition - feature envy
class OrderProcessor:
    def process(self, order):
        # Constantly reaching into Customer
        # internals
        if order.customer.account.balance >=
            order.total:
            order.customer.account.balance -=
                order.total
            order.customer.purchase_history.
                append(order)
            order.customer.last_purchase_date =
                datetime.now()
```

- *Circular dependencies.* Components form dependency loops. The hierarchy of abstraction has collapsed.
- *God components.* One component does everything important while others are trivial. The decomposition is unbalanced.
- *Practical decomposition with AI.*

When AI generates large implementations, your job is recognizing natural boundaries and extracting components:

```
# AI generates one large function with multiple
# responsibilities
def process_order(order):
    # 200 lines mixing validation, pricing,
    # inventory, payment, notification
    if not order.get('items'):
        raise ValueError('No items')

    # ... validation logic ...

    total = 0
    for item in order['items']:
        # ... pricing logic ...
        total += item['price'] * item['quantity']
```

```python
    # ... inventory checking ...
    # ... payment processing ...
    # ... customer notification ...

    return order


# Human decomposes into clear responsibilities
def process_order(order: Order) -> ProcessedOrder:
    """Process customer order through complete
        fulfillment pipeline."""
    validated = validate_order(order)
    priced = calculate_pricing(validated)
    reserved = reserve_inventory(priced)
    charged = process_payment(reserved)
    notify_customer(charged)
    return charged
```

Each extracted function has a clear responsibility. The main function becomes a coordinator that reveals the process structure. This is the Unix philosophy applied to code: small, focused components that do one thing well.

Naming: The Hardest Problem

Phil Karlton famously said: "There are only two hard things in Computer Science: cache invalidation and naming things."

Names are not labels. They are *compressed understanding*. A good name encodes what something does, why it matters, and how it relates to other things. A bad name obscures, misleads, or confuses.

- *Why AI struggles with naming.*

AI generates names from patterns in training data. It produces: - Generic names (`process_data`, `handle_request`, `do_thing`) - Overly specific names (`validate_user_email_address_format_and_return_boolean`) - Inconsistent names (mixing conventions randomly) - Implementation-focused names (`loop_through_array_and_filter`) rather than intent-focused names

AI doesn't understand your domain deeply enough to name things meaningfully. It sees syntax patterns, not semantic meaning.

- *Why naming is hard.*

- *Names are commitments.* Once a name enters a codebase, it propagates—into documentation, tests, conversations, mental models. Changing a bad name becomes increasingly expensive. The name you choose today constrains the thoughts that future developers can easily think.
- *Names require understanding.* You cannot name something well without understanding what it is. The struggle to find a good name often reveals that you don't yet understand what you're building. This is *valuable*—the naming difficulty is a signal to think harder.
- *Names must serve multiple audiences.* The name read in code, discussed in meetings, written in documentation, and searched in logs is the same name. It must work across contexts.
- *Principles of good naming.*
- *Be precise.* A name should mean exactly one thing. `process()` could mean anything; `validate_payment_amount()` is clear. Precision reduces ambiguity and catches design problems early.

```
# Imprecise
def handle(x):
    pass

# Precise
def validate_credit_card_number(card_number: str)
    -> bool:
    pass
```

- *Be consistent.* Similar things should be named similarly. If one function is `create_user()`, the parallel function should be `create_account()`. Avoid names like `generate_account_record()` that break the pattern. Consistency enables pattern recognition and reduces cognitive load.

```
# Inconsistent
def create_user(name: str) -> User:
    pass

def generate_account_record(email: str) ->
    Account:
    pass

# Consistent
def create_user(name: str) -> User:
```

```python
    pass

def create_account(email: str) -> Account:
    pass
```

- *Reveal intent.* Names should express *what* and *why*, not *how*. A name like `is_eligible_for_discount()` reveals intent. A name like `check_flag_and_return_bool()` reveals implementation. Intent survives refactoring; implementation doesn't.

```python
# Implementation-focused
def check_flag_and_calculate(user):
    pass

# Intent-focused
def calculate_discounted_price(
        user: User, base_price: Decimal) ->
            Decimal:
    pass
```

- *Match the domain.* Use the language of the problem domain, not the language of implementation. If business people say "invoice," don't call it `PaymentRequestDocument`. Domain alignment reduces translation errors (Chapter 14's vertical mastery applies here).

```python
# Implementation language
class PaymentRequestDocument:
    pass

# Domain language
class Invoice:
    pass
```

- *Avoid abbreviations.* In an age of autocomplete, there's no excuse for cryptic abbreviations. `acc` could be account, accumulator, or accelerator. `account` is clear.

```python
# Cryptic
def proc_pmt(amt, acc):
    pass

# Clear
def process_payment(
```

```
        amount: Decimal, account: Account) ->
            PaymentResult:
    pass
```

- *Use Python conventions.* Follow PEP 8 and Python idioms. Use snake_case for functions and variables, PascalCase for classes, UPPERCASE for constants. Type hints make intent clearer.

```
# Good Python naming
MAX_RETRY_ATTEMPTS = 3

class PaymentProcessor:
    def process_transaction(
            self, transaction: Transaction) ->
                ProcessingResult:
        pass

def calculate_total_with_tax(
        items: list[Item], tax_rate: Decimal) ->
            Decimal:
    pass
```

- *Refactor names aggressively.* When you understand something better, rename it. When you discover a name is misleading, fix it immediately. The cost of renaming rises over time; do it early.
- *Example of human naming improvement.*

```
# AI generates generic names
def proc(x):
    """Process x"""
    pass

def val(y):
    """Validate y"""
    pass

def chk(z):
    """Check z"""
    pass
```

```python
# Human renames for clarity
def process_payment(transaction: Transaction) ->
    PaymentResult:
    """Process payment transaction through
       payment gateway."""
    pass

def validate_email(address: str) -> str:
    """Validate email format and return
       normalized address."""
    pass

def check_inventory_availability(product:
    Product) -> bool:
    """Check if product is currently in stock."""
    pass
```

The human names reveal intent, match domain language, include type hints, and enable understanding without reading implementation.

Architectural Thinking: Seeing Systems Whole

In Chapter 15, we'll discuss leadership—and note that the best technical leaders think architecturally. This is also the hallmark of engineers who excel at simplification. They see not just the component they're building but the system it lives within.

Multi-Scale Vision

One of the differences between coding and engineering is the ability to hold multiple levels of abstraction simultaneously. The coder sees the function; the engineer sees the function *and* the module *and* the service *and* the system *and* the business context.

This multi-scale vision is what architects possess. They zoom in to discuss implementation details and zoom out to discuss strategic direction, fluidly navigating between levels as needed.

- *Why this matters for simplification.*
- *Local decisions have global effects.* The data model chosen for one service constrains what other services can do. The error handling strategy in one

component affects recovery options everywhere. Without system-level vision, local optimizations create global problems.

Example: You simplify a service by caching all database results in memory. Locally, this looks like a win — every request is fast, the logic is clear, and the database load drops. But zoom out to the system level and the questions multiply: How do you invalidate the cache when another service updates the same data? What happens when memory fills up? If you run multiple instances, each has its own cache — how do you keep them consistent? The local simplification created global complexity that is harder to diagnose than the original database calls.

```
# Locally simple, globally complex
class UserRepository:
    def __init__(self):
        # Cache everything in memory - seems
        # simple!
        self._cache = {}

    def get_user(self, user_id: int) -> User:
        if user_id not in self._cache:
            self._cache[user_id] = self.
                _load_from_db(user_id)
        return self._cache[user_id]

    # But now: How do we invalidate cache across
    # instances?
    #          What happens when memory fills up?
    #          How do we handle updates from
    #          other services?
```

- *Global constraints determine local options.* Latency budgets, consistency requirements, and reliability targets flow down from system level to component level. The engineer who doesn't understand global constraints makes locally reasonable decisions that are globally impossible.

Example: You simplify a function by making it synchronous — no concurrency, no callbacks, straightforward sequential logic. But the system-level requirement is a 100-millisecond response time, and two sequential calls that each take over 100 milliseconds cannot meet that constraint no matter how clean the code is. The only way to stay within the latency budget is to run both calls in parallel, which reintroduces the concurrency complexity you were trying to avoid. The engineer who doesn't understand the global constraint makes a locally reasonable decision that is globally impossible.

```
# Violates global latency constraint
def get_user_profile(user_id: int) -> UserProfile:
    # Simple synchronous call
    user = fetch_user_from_database(user_id)  #
        80ms
    orders = fetch_orders_from_service(user_id)
        # 70ms
    # Total: 150ms, violates 100ms SLA
    return UserProfile(user, orders)

# Respects global constraint with concurrent
# fetching
async def get_user_profile(user_id: int) ->
    UserProfile:
    # Fetch concurrently to meet latency budget
    user, orders = await asyncio.gather(
        fetch_user_from_database(user_id),
        fetch_orders_from_service(user_id)
    )
    # Total: ~80ms (parallelized), meets
    # constraint
    return UserProfile(user, orders)
```

- *Trade-offs span levels.* The decision to cache a value involves local complexity (cache management code) and global effects (consistency, latency, resource usage). Reasoning about the trade-off requires seeing both levels.
- *Integration reveals design flaws.* Components that work perfectly in isolation may fail when combined. The architect's vision anticipates integration issues before they occur.

The Questions That Reveal Architectural Thinking

Architects ask characteristic questions that reveal systems thinking:

- *About dependencies.*
- "What happens to the rest of the system if this component fails?"
- "Who else depends on this data, and how do they use it?"

- "If we change this interface, what breaks?"
- *About evolution.*
- "How will this system grow over the next two years?"
- "What changes are easy versus hard with this design?"
- "Where are the extension points?"
- *About failure.*
- "What's the blast radius of a bug here?"
- "How do failures propagate through the system?"
- "Where are the single points of failure?"
- *About simplification.*
- "Can we solve this without adding a new service?"
- "Could this be a library instead of a service?"
- "Do we need all these states, or can we simplify the state machine?"

These questions aren't about code—they're about *relationships, dependencies, and boundaries*. The architect thinks in connections.

When you're simplifying AI-generated or legacy code, these questions guide you toward impactful simplification. Simplifying a function that's called once doesn't matter much. Simplifying a foundational abstraction that hundreds of modules depend on matters enormously.

The Trade-off Mindset

Every engineering decision involves trade-offs. More performance may mean more complexity. More flexibility may mean more runtime cost. More safety may mean slower development.

The architect's skill is making trade-offs *explicit* and *informed*:

- *Explicit trade-offs can be evaluated.* When you say "We're choosing consistency over availability," stakeholders can assess whether that aligns with business needs. Hidden trade-offs lead to surprises.
- *Informed trade-offs consider alternatives.* Before committing, explore options. "We could use a queue for reliability, but that adds latency. We could use direct calls for speed, but that adds coupling. We could use events for decoupling, but that adds complexity."

- *Documented trade-offs aid future decisions.* The context that made a decision right may change. If trade-offs are documented (Architecture Decision Records as we'll discuss in Chapter 15), future engineers can recognize when assumptions no longer hold.
- *Revisited trade-offs prevent accumulation.* Trade-offs made under time pressure often skew toward expedience. Periodically revisit decisions to ensure early trade-offs still make sense.

Simplification trade-offs

Simplification itself involves trade-offs:

Simplicity vs. Performance — Sometimes the simple solution is slower. A dictionary is simpler than a balanced tree, but trees have better worst-case performance for large ordered datasets.

```
# Simple but potentially slow for ordered
# operations
users_by_id = {}  # O(1) lookup, no ordering

# More complex but maintains order efficiently
from sortedcontainers import SortedDict
users_by_id = SortedDict()  # O(log n) lookup
```

Simplicity vs. Flexibility — Sometimes the simple solution is less flexible. Hard-coding three payment methods is simpler than a plugin architecture, but the latter is more flexible.

```
# Simple but inflexible
def process_payment(amount: Decimal, method: str):
    if method == 'credit_card':
        return process_credit_card(amount)
    elif method == 'paypal':
        return process_paypal(amount)
    elif method == 'bank_transfer':
        return process_bank_transfer(amount)
    # Adding new method requires code change

# More complex but flexible
class PaymentMethod(ABC):
    @abstractmethod
    def process(self, amount: Decimal) ->
        PaymentResult:
```

```
        pass

def process_payment(amount: Decimal, method:
    PaymentMethod):
    return method.process(amount)
    # New methods can be added without changing
    # this code
```

Simplicity now vs. later — Sometimes complexity now prevents complexity later. A well-designed abstraction is initially more complex than directly implementing everything, but it simplifies future work.

The key: make these trade-offs consciously, not accidentally. Choose simplicity when it serves long-term maintainability. Choose complexity when it's genuinely necessary. Never accept accidental complexity.

Managing Complexity at Scale

Essential vs. Accidental Complexity

Fred Brooks, in his seminal essay "No Silver Bullet," distinguished two types of complexity (Brooks 1987):

Essential complexity is inherent in the problem. A tax system is complex because tax law is complex. A trading platform is complex because financial markets are complex. No amount of clever engineering eliminates essential complexity—you can only organize and contain it.

Accidental complexity is introduced by the solution. A system that uses three different data formats for the same information has accidental complexity. A codebase that requires understanding twelve frameworks to make a change has accidental complexity. This complexity isn't required by the problem—it's an artifact of implementation choices.

- *In the AI era, accidental complexity accelerates.*

AI generates code that solves problems but doesn't minimize complexity. Each AI-generated solution adds complexity incrementally. Without human curation, accidental complexity accumulates faster than ever before.

The master simplifier:

- *Accepts essential complexity.* You can't make tax law simpler. But you can create abstractions that contain tax complexity, expose clear interfaces, and prevent it from infecting the entire system.

```python
# Essential complexity contained in one place
class TaxCalculator:
    """Encapsulates tax calculation complexity."""

    def calculate_tax(self, amount: Decimal,
        jurisdiction: str,
                    category: TaxCategory) ->
                        TaxResult:
        # Complex tax rules live here
        # But rest of system doesn't need to
        # understand them
        pass

# Simple usage elsewhere
total = base_price + tax_calculator.calculate_tax(
    base_price, user.jurisdiction, product.
        category
)
```

- *Ruthlessly eliminates accidental complexity.* Every unnecessary abstraction, every redundant pattern, every clever trick that requires explanation—these are candidates for immediate elimination.
- *Example.*

Essential complexity: Healthcare systems must handle HIPAA compliance, patient privacy, clinical workflows, and medical terminology. This complexity comes from the domain.

Accidental complexity: A healthcare system that stores patient data in three different databases with different schemas, requires fifteen microservices to process a simple appointment, and has seven different authentication mechanisms. This complexity comes from poor architectural choices.

```python
# Accidental complexity - three ways to represent
# same data
class PatientV1:
    def __init__(self, id, name, dob):
        self.id = id
        self.name = name
        self.dob = dob
```

```python
patient_dict = {
    'patient_id': 123,
    'full_name': 'John',
    'birth_date': '1990-01-01'
}
patient_tuple = (123, 'John', '1990-01-01')

# All represent the same patient - accidental
# complexity!


# Essential complexity - one clear representation
@dataclass
class Patient:
    id: int
    name: str
    date_of_birth: date

    def is_hipaa_compliant_access(self, accessor:
        User) -> bool:
        # Essential complexity of HIPAA rules
        pass
```

The ratio of essential to accidental complexity measures engineering quality. In elegant systems, almost all complexity is essential. In legacy systems, accidental complexity often dominates.

Complexity Budgets

A useful mental model from Rich Hickey: the *complexity budget*—a finite amount of complexity that any system can sustain before becoming unmaintainable (Hickey 2011).

- *Every feature consumes budget.* Each new feature adds code, tests, documentation, operational procedures. It creates surface area that must be understood and maintained.
- *Every dependency consumes budget.* Each library, service, or tool brings capabilities but also learning curves, update requirements, and failure modes.

```python
# Each import consumes complexity budget
```

```python
import numpy as np
import pandas as pd
import tensorflow as tf
import torch
import sklearn
import xgboost
# Six ML libraries for one project - budget
# exhausted!
```

- *Every abstraction consumes budget.* Abstractions have costs—indirection, cognitive overhead, maintenance. An abstraction must save more complexity than it costs.

```python
# Abstraction that costs more than it saves
class AbstractFactoryProducerSingletonDecorator:
    """Over-engineered abstraction consuming
        budget unnecessarily."""
    pass

# vs. direct, simple solution
def create_widget(config: dict) -> Widget:
    """Direct factory function - lower budget
        cost."""
    return Widget(**config)
```

- *Every exception consumes budget.* Special cases, workarounds, and edge case handling add complexity disproportionate to their frequency.

A pricing function starts simple. Then special cases accumulate — a regional discount, an employee discount with a date condition, a promotional prefix rule. Each is individually small, but together they make the logic progressively harder to reason about. A new engineer must hold all conditions in their head simultaneously to understand what any given customer will be charged. Interactions between rules become unpredictable, and testing every combination grows exponentially. Each exception consumes complexity budget disproportionate to its frequency.

```python
# Each special case consumes budget
def calculate_price(item: Item, user: User) ->
    Decimal:
    base_price = item.price
```

```python
if user.country == 'US' and item.category ==
    'books':
    # Special case 1
    return base_price * Decimal('0.9')
elif user.is_employee and datetime.now().day
    == 15:
    # Special case 2
    return base_price * Decimal('0.5')
elif item.name.startswith('PROMO_'):
    # Special case 3
    return base_price * Decimal('0.8')
# Each special case makes the system harder
# to understand
```

- *The implication.* You cannot add complexity forever. At some point, the budget is exhausted, and every new addition makes the system harder to change rather than easier. This is the dreaded "big ball of mud" (Foote and Yoder 1997).

- *AI amplifies budget consumption.*

Because AI generates code easily, there's temptation to add features rapidly without considering complexity budget. "AI can implement it in five minutes" becomes "AI implemented it in five minutes, and now we have 1000 lines of code we barely understand."

The human role: *gatekeeping the complexity budget*. Saying "no" to features, removing before adding, and simplifying continuously.

- *Strategies for staying within budget.*

- *Say no frequently.* The most effective complexity reduction is not building things. Every feature request should be evaluated against the complexity budget. Some features aren't worth their cost.

This is Intent-layer work—deciding what not to build is as important as deciding what to build.

- *Remove before adding.* When adding new capabilities, ask what can be removed. Deprecation and deletion are essential maintenance activities, not optional cleanup.

```python
# Before adding new payment method, remove unused
# ones
# Removed: PayPal (0.1% usage), Bitcoin (unused
```

```
# for 6 months)
# Added: Apple Pay (requested by 20% of users)
# Net complexity: decreased despite adding feature
```

- *Simplify continuously.* Don't wait for a "rewrite." Make small simplifications constantly—rename a confusing variable, delete dead code, consolidate redundant logic. These small actions compound.

- *Invest in foundations.* Good foundations—clear data models, consistent APIs, well-chosen abstractions—reduce the complexity cost of everything built on them. Technical debt in foundations is especially costly (Martin 2008).

```python
# Foundation investment - clear data model
@dataclass
class Order:
    """Clear, well-documented foundation reduces
        future complexity."""
    id: UUID
    customer: Customer
    items: list[OrderItem]
    total: Decimal
    status: OrderStatus
    created_at: datetime

    def can_be_cancelled(self) -> bool:
        """Business logic in domain model -
            complexity in right place."""
        return self.status in (
            OrderStatus.PENDING,
            OrderStatus.PROCESSING
        )
```

When Complexity Is Necessary

Simplicity isn't always achievable. Some complexity is genuinely necessary:

- *Distributed systems are inherently complex.* A distributed cache must handle a scenario that does not exist in single-machine systems: the primary cache might be unreachable. The network might fail, the cache server might be overloaded, or an entire data center might be unavailable. Each fallback layer adds error handling and failure modes that must be tested independently. None of this complexity is accidental — it exists because networks are unreliable, and the system must keep working when they fail. This is essential complexity that cannot be simplified away, only organized clearly.

```
# Essential complexity of distributed systems
class DistributedCache:
    def get_with_fallback(self, key: str) ->
        Optional[str]:
        """Essential complexity: network failure
            handling."""
        try:
            return self.primary_cache.get(key)
        except NetworkError:
            # Must handle network failures
            try:
                return self.secondary_cache.
                    get(key)
            except NetworkError:
                # And cascading failures
                return self.load_from_database(key
                    )
```

- *Performance optimization adds complexity.* Caching, replication, and batching improve performance at the cost of added state and logic. Sometimes the trade-off is worth it.

- *Security requirements add complexity.* Processing sensitive data requires steps that cannot be skipped or simplified. Authorization must be verified before anything else happens. Data must be decrypted because it is never stored in plaintext. Every access must be recorded in an audit log for compliance. Remove any one of these steps and you have either a security vulnerability, an unreadable payload, or a failed compliance review. Each step adds logic, error paths, and dependencies — but none is optional. This is essential complexity: the price of operating safely in an adversarial environment.

```
# Essential security complexity
def process_sensitive_data(
        data: bytes, user: User) -> ProcessedData:
    """Essential complexity for security."""
    # Must verify authorization
    if not user.has_permission('process_sensitive_
```

```
data'):
    raise UnauthorizedError()

# Must decrypt
decrypted = decrypt_with_user_key(data, user.
    key)

# Must audit
audit_log.record_access(user,
    'processed_sensitive_data')

# All complexity is essential for security
return process(decrypted)
```

- *Regulatory compliance adds complexity.* Legal requirements for data retention, privacy, and auditability introduce constraints that complicate implementation. Ignoring them isn't an option.
- *The mature engineer distinguishes.* Is this complexity *necessary* for the problem we're solving? Or is this complexity *familiar* from how we've always done it?

Just because you've always done something a complicated way doesn't mean it's required. Question every complication: Is this essential? Or is this accidental complexity we've accepted as normal?

- *Example from C++ systems programming.*

A lock-free queue — a data structure that allows multiple threads to add and remove items without ever locking — is inherently complex. The algorithms involve atomic operations, retry loops, and subtle memory ordering guarantees. But this complexity is essential: it is the only way to achieve the performance the system requires under high concurrency. Compare this to a queue wrapped in layers of abstract factories and strategy visitors — complexity that exists not because the problem demands it but because someone confused architectural sophistication with architectural quality. One is complex because physics and concurrency are complex. The other is complex because the engineer made it so.

```
// Sometimes complexity is essential for
// performance
class LockFreeQueue {
    // Essential complexity: lock-free algorithms
```

```
    // are inherently complex
    // But necessary for high-performance
    // concurrent access
    std::atomic<Node*> head;
    std::atomic<Node*> tail;

    void push(T value) {
        // Complex CAS loops are essential for
        // lock-free operation
        Node* new_node = new Node(value);
        while (true) {
            Node* old_tail = tail.load();
            if (tail.compare_exchange_weak(old_tai
                l, new_node)) {
                old_tail->next = new_node;
                break;
            }
        }
    }
};

// vs. accidental complexity
class OverEngineeredQueue {
    // Accidental complexity: layers upon layers
    // for no good reason
    std::shared_ptr<AbstractQueueFactoryInterface>
         factory;
    std::unique_ptr<QueueStrategySelectorVisitor>
        selector;
    // ...complexity that doesn't serve actual
    // requirements
};
```

- *Re-evaluating complexity.* Your team has always used a complex event sourcing architecture with separate read/write models and eventual consistency. AI happily generates event sourcing patterns when you prompt for new features.

But is event sourcing essential for your use case? Or is it accidental complexity from a past architectural decision that no longer makes sense?

Re-evaluating: If you need audit trails and time travel debugging, event sourcing's complexity is essential. If you added it because it was trendy and now nobody understands how to debug it, the complexity is accidental.

Simplicity as Competitive Advantage

As we'll discuss in Chapter 13's antifragile career discussion, organizations that move faster have competitive advantage. Simplicity is how you move faster:

- *Simpler systems are easier to understand.* New team members become productive faster. Knowledge transfers more easily. Bus factor improves (if one person leaves, the team can still function).
- *Simpler systems are easier to change.* Features ship faster when engineers don't navigate labyrinthine complexity. Agility is a function of simplicity (Glass 2002).
- *Simpler systems have fewer bugs.* Complexity creates hiding places for defects. The more complexity, the more surface area for failure.
- *Simpler systems are easier to operate.* Debugging is faster when the system is comprehensible. Recovery is faster when failure modes are clear (Meadows 2008).
- *In the AI era, this advantage intensifies.*

AI can generate complex code quickly. The bottleneck moves to *understanding*—comprehending what AI has produced, integrating it with existing systems, debugging when things go wrong.

The team that maintains simplicity navigates this faster than the team drowning in accumulated complexity. The engineer who can simplify AI-generated code is more valuable than the engineer who just accepts what AI produces.

This is why simplification is a career-defining skill: it directly impacts organizational velocity, which directly impacts business success.

- *Practical example.*

Two teams build similar features using AI assistance:

- *Team A.* Prompts AI, gets 2000 lines of Python code, accepts it with minimal review, ships it. Feature works. Three months later, bugs appear. Nobody understands the code well enough to debug efficiently. Adding new capabilities requires extensive refactoring because the original structure doesn't accommodate them.

- *Team B.* Prompts AI, gets 2000 lines of Python code, spends time simplifying to 600 lines before shipping. Takes longer initially. Three months later, bugs appear and are fixed in hours because the code is comprehensible. New capabilities are added easily because the structure is clean.

Over time, Team B moves dramatically faster than Team A, even though they initially moved slower. Simplicity compounds.

Chapter Summary

- **AI amplifies complexity by generating defensively.** LLMs optimize for correctness over simplicity, producing thorough but bloated implementations. Human simplification becomes critical for maintainability.
- **Simplification operates across all three layers.** At Execution: simpler algorithms when sufficient. At Design: architectural simplification with maximum leverage. At Intent: deciding not to build unnecessary features.
- **Simplification is an antifragile skill.** It requires judgment AI lacks, benefits from domain expertise, compounds over time, and creates organizational value. As AI makes generation faster, simplification becomes the bottleneck.
- **Abstraction is cognitive leverage.** Good abstractions hide irrelevant details, remain stable, compose well, and match mental models. Python's decorators, context managers, and protocols exemplify clean abstraction (Miller 1956; Abelson et al. 1996).
- **Decomposition creates independent components.** Good boundaries have low coupling, high cohesion, natural domain alignment, and testability. AI over-decomposes or under-decomposes without understanding future evolution.
- **Naming encodes understanding.** Good Python names are precise, consistent (snake_case, PEP 8), intent-revealing, domain-aligned, and include type hints. The struggle to name well reveals incomplete understanding.
- **Architectural thinking spans scales.** Engineers who see the function and the system simultaneously understand how local decisions create global effects. This multi-scale vision guides impactful simplification.
- **Essential complexity is inherent; accidental is introduced.** Essential complexity must be contained in clear modules; accidental complexity

should be eliminated. AI accelerates accidental complexity accumulation (Brooks 1987).

- **Complexity budgets are finite.** Every feature, dependency, abstraction, and exception consumes budget. Staying within budget requires saying no, removing before adding, and simplifying continuously (Hickey 2011; Foote and Yoder 1997).
- **Simplicity is competitive advantage.** Simple systems are faster to understand, change, debug, and operate. In the AI era, this advantage intensifies as understanding becomes the bottleneck (Glass 2002; Martin 2008; Meadows 2008).
- **Trade-offs must be explicit.** Simplicity vs. performance, simplicity vs. flexibility, simplicity now vs. later—make these choices consciously, not accidentally. Document decisions for future engineers (Parnas 1972).
- **Some complexity is necessary.** Distributed systems, performance optimization, security, and compliance all introduce essential complexity. The skill is distinguishing essential from accidental and questioning what's merely familiar.

In the next chapter, we'll explore communication as engineering—how the ability to explain, document, and collaborate becomes a core technical skill when working with both human and AI teammates in increasingly complex systems.

Chapter 8

Communication as Engineering

"The single biggest problem in communication is the illusion that it has taken place." — George Bernard Shaw

---

Two engineers sat in adjacent offices, both working on the same distributed system. Sarah had just spent three days implementing a caching layer. Marcus had just spent three days implementing... a caching layer. They discovered the duplication during code review.

"Why didn't you tell me you were working on this?" Marcus asked.

"I mentioned it in standup on Monday," Sarah replied.

"I thought you said *cache invalidation*, not a whole caching layer."

"I did say caching layer. You were probably thinking about your task."

"Did you write it down anywhere?"

"In my branch commit message."

"Which I wouldn't see until code review."

This wasn't a failure of engineering skill. Both implementations were technically sound. This was a failure of *communication*—the supposedly "soft" skill that cost six days of duplicated work, delayed the project, and required one implementation to be discarded.

Software engineering has long treated communication as secondary—a necessary evil, perhaps, but not "real" engineering work. The assumption: smart people writing good code will naturally succeed. Communication is for managers, marketers, and people who "can't code."

This assumption was always wrong. But in an AI era, it becomes catastrophically wrong.

As we've explored throughout this book, AI increasingly handles implementation (Execution layer). The bottleneck shifts to coordination, alignment, and shared understanding—all communication problems. The engineer who codes brilliantly but communicates poorly becomes a liability. The engineer who communicates effectively multiplies the impact of everyone around them.

This chapter reframes communication as a core engineering skill—not a "soft skill" but a *hard technical skill* that directly affects system quality, team velocity, and career trajectory. We'll examine why writing is thinking made visible, how to communicate effectively across modalities (written, verbal, visual), and what changes when you're collaborating with both human and AI teammates.

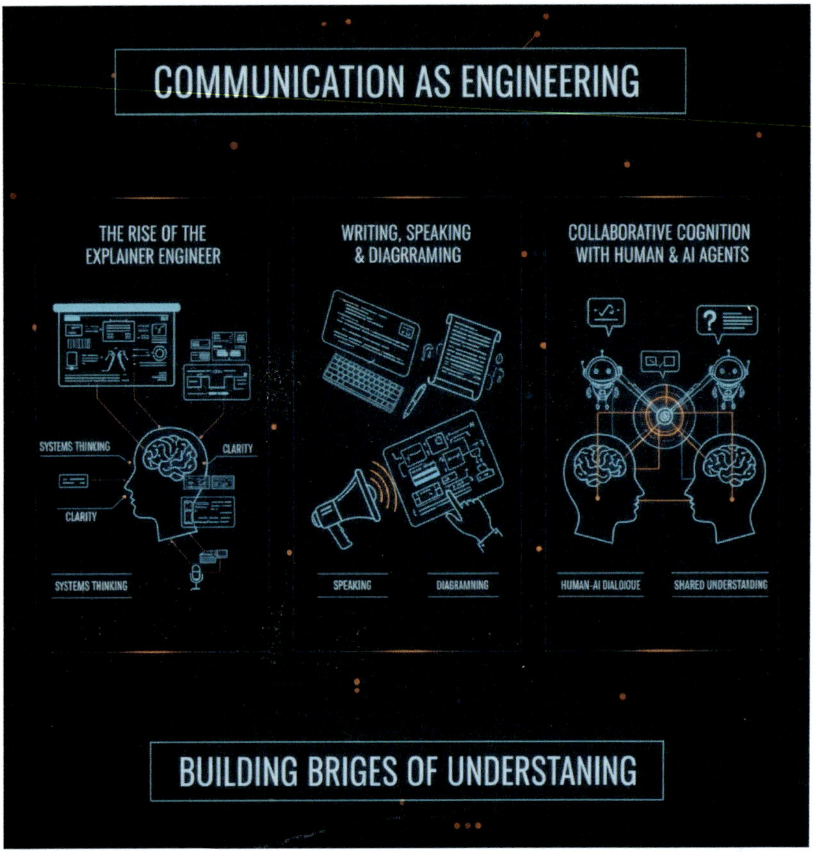

The Rise of the Explainer Engineer

Why Communication Is Engineering Work

Consider what engineering actually is: transforming ideas into systems that work. This transformation has multiple phases:

1. **Understanding the problem** (clarifying requirements, constraints, context)
2. **Designing the solution** (choosing architectures, making trade-offs)
3. **Implementing the solution** (writing code, building systems)
4. **Verifying the solution** (testing, validating, deploying)
5. **Maintaining the solution** (debugging, evolving, documenting)

AI increasingly handles phase 3 (implementation). But phases 1, 2, 4, and 5 are *fundamentally communication problems*:

- *Understanding requires communication.* Stakeholders often don't know what they need. Requirements are vague, contradictory, or unstated. The engineer must extract intent through questions, clarifications, and proposals. This is communication as discovery.

- *Design requires communication.* Architecture decisions affect many people—other engineers, operations teams, future maintainers. Designs must be explained, debated, documented. This is communication as alignment.

- *Verification requires communication.* Test results must be interpreted. Bugs must be reported. Deployment risks must be assessed. This is communication as sense-making.

- *Maintenance requires communication.* Code must be comprehensible to future readers (including future you). Systems must be documentable. Knowledge must transfer. This is communication as knowledge preservation.

The pattern: as AI handles more implementation, *engineering work becomes more communicative.* The "explainer engineer"—someone who can clarify problems, articulate designs, document systems, and teach others—becomes increasingly valuable.

The Explainer Premium

Organizations are starting to recognize this explicitly. Job descriptions increasingly emphasize communication:

- "Ability to explain technical concepts to non-technical stakeholders"
- "Experience writing technical documentation and design proposals"
- "Strong written and verbal communication skills"
- "Comfortable presenting to senior leadership"

These aren't window dressing. They're recognition that technical skill without communication skill is increasingly insufficient.

- *The explainer premium manifests as.*
- *Career velocity.* Engineers who communicate well advance faster. They're trusted with larger responsibilities because they can explain what they're doing and coordinate with others. In Chapter 15, we'll discuss leadership—most technical leadership is communication.
- *Compensation.* At senior levels, compensation correlates more with communication ability than with pure coding ability. The staff engineer who can write a compelling strategy document is worth more than the equally skilled engineer who can't.
- *Influence.* In Chapter 15, we'll distinguish influence from authority. Communication is how you build influence without authority—by making your ideas clear and persuasive.
- *Team multiplication.* The engineer who documents well makes the entire team more effective. The engineer who explains clearly helps juniors learn faster (we'll explore the apprenticeship problem in Chapter 11). Communication multiplies impact.

What Makes Technical Communication Hard

If communication is so important, why do engineers struggle with it?

- *The curse of knowledge.* Once you understand something deeply, it's difficult to remember what it was like not to understand it (Hinds 1999). You forget which concepts are prerequisites, which terms need definition, which steps are obvious versus subtle. Your mental model is compressed and automatic; explaining it requires decompressing and making implicit knowledge explicit.
- *Precision vs. accessibility trade-off.* Technical accuracy often conflicts with clarity. The precise description includes caveats, edge cases, and qualifications that obscure the main point. The accessible description simplifies in ways that might be technically imprecise. Good communication navigates this trade-off deliberately.
- *Audience heterogeneity.* The same system must be explained differently to different audiences. Junior engineers need different explanations than senior engineers. Product managers need different explanations than executives. Operations teams need different explanations than security teams. There's no single "correct" explanation—only explanations suited to par-

ticular audiences.

- *Asynchronous context.* Much technical communication happens asynchronously (documentation, code comments, design docs, Slack). The reader has different context than you. You can't see their confusion in real-time and adjust. You must anticipate questions and preemptively answer them.

- *Technical jargon.* Every field develops specialized vocabulary that enables precise communication among experts but excludes non-experts. Engineers must code-switch—using jargon with other engineers, translating to plain language for others, and recognizing when jargon helps versus hinders.

- *AI amplifies these difficulties.* When you're explaining AI-generated code, you face an additional challenge—you may not fully understand it yourself. You must communicate about systems you didn't design and that contain complexity you didn't choose. This requires new communication skills.

The Three Audiences

Effective communicators think explicitly about audience. In technical contexts, three audience types recur:

Technical peers (engineers with similar background): - Assume shared vocabulary and concepts - Emphasize trade-offs, alternatives, rationale - Can be dense and precise - Use code, diagrams, and technical specifications - Goal: Enable them to understand deeply enough to critique, implement, or extend

Adjacent technical (engineers in different specialties, technical PMs, operations): - Some shared vocabulary but different mental models - Emphasize interfaces, behaviors, failure modes - Balance precision with accessibility - Use diagrams more than code - Goal: Enable them to integrate with, operate, or build upon your system

Non-technical stakeholders (executives, business stakeholders, end users): - No shared technical vocabulary - Emphasize outcomes, risks, costs, timeline - Maximize accessibility, minimize jargon - Use analogies, examples, and visuals - Goal: Enable them to make informed decisions about what to build and when

- *The skill.* Switching fluently between these modes. The explanation you give in engineering standup (technical peers) should differ from the explanation in product sync (adjacent technical) should differ from the explanation in exec review (non-technical).

Failure mode: Using technical peer communication with non-technical stakeholders ("We're implementing a distributed cache with eventual consistency and CRDTs"). Or using non-technical communication with technical peers ("We're making it faster").

Communication as Career Differentiator

In Chapter 13, we'll discuss the antifragile career. Communication is one of the most antifragile skills because:

- *It compounds.* Every piece of good documentation you write helps future engineers. Every explanation you give helps someone learn. Every design doc you write preserves knowledge. This compounds over time.
- *It's transferable.* Communication skills work across domains, languages, and technologies. You can switch from fintech to healthcare to gaming, and communication skills transfer completely.
- *It's resistant to automation.* AI can generate code and even draft documentation. But AI cannot *contextualize* communication—understanding which details matter to which audience, what's confusing, what needs emphasis. This requires human judgment.
- *It's multiplied by AI.* AI makes you a more effective communicator by drafting initial versions, generating multiple framings, and handling mechanical aspects (grammar, formatting). But the strategic communication choices remain human.
- *It increases with seniority.* Junior engineers are evaluated primarily on implementation. Senior engineers are evaluated primarily on communication—design docs, strategy documents, technical proposals, presentations, mentorship. The longer your career, the more communication matters.

The engineer who invests in communication skills builds a capability that appreciates over time and that creates opportunities at every career stage.

Writing, Speaking, and Diagramming

Communication takes many forms. Engineers must master multiple modalities—written, verbal, and visual—each with different strengths and appropriate contexts.

Writing: Thinking Made Visible

Writing is not just communication—it's *thinking*. As you write, you discover what you actually think. Vague intuitions crystallize into concrete claims. Logical gaps become visible. Contradictions reveal themselves.

This is why writing is such a powerful tool for engineers: it forces clarity that mental reasoning doesn't require.

- *Forms of technical writing.*
- *Code comments.* The most immediate documentation. Good comments explain *why*, not *what*. The code already shows what it does; comments explain intent, constraints, non-obvious decisions.

```
# Bad comment - repeats what code says
# Loop through users
for user in users:
    process(user)

# Good comment - explains why and context
# Process users in batches to respect API rate
# limits (100/min)
# Order doesn't matter, so we can parallelize in
# future if needed
for user in users:
    process(user)
```

- *Commit messages.* These form the narrative history of the codebase. Good commit messages explain the "why" behind changes—what problem was solved, what alternatives were considered, what trade-offs were made.

```
# Bad commit message
git commit -m "fix bug"

# Good commit message
git commit -m "Fix race condition in payment
    processing

When two concurrent requests process payment for
    same order,
both could succeed, causing double-charge.

Added optimistic locking on order status. First
```

```
    request to
transition from PENDING to PROCESSING succeeds;
    second fails
with conflict error and returns to client for
    retry.

Considered pessimistic locking but optimistic has
    better
performance for our low-contention case. See ADR-
    047 for
full analysis."
```

- *Architecture Decision Records (ADRs).* Documents that capture important architectural decisions, their context, and their rationale (Nygard 2011). These are invaluable for future engineers trying to understand "why is it built this way?"

```
# ADR 023: Use PostgreSQL for User Data Instead
# of DynamoDB

## Context
Need to choose database for user profile data.
    ~10M users,
read-heavy (90% reads), occasional writes, need
    ACID transactions
for profile updates, team has more PostgreSQL
    experience than DynamoDB.

## Decision
Use PostgreSQL with read replicas for scaling
    reads.

## Consequences
**Pros:**
- Team expertise means faster development
- ACID transactions simplify profile update logic
- Easier to query for analytics and reporting
- Lower operational complexity for our team size

**Cons:**
- Less elastic scaling than DynamoDB
```

```
- Single-region deployment (vs. DynamoDB global
    tables)
- Need to manage replication lag for read replicas

## Alternatives Considered
**DynamoDB:** Would scale better but team
    learning curve steep,
eventual consistency complicates profile updates,
    and cost higher
at our current scale.

**MySQL:** Similar to PostgreSQL but worse JSON
    support which we
need for flexible profile attributes.
```

- *Design documents.* Longer-form proposals for significant changes. These explain the problem, proposed solution, alternatives, trade-offs, and implementation plan. They're tools for getting feedback before committing to implementation.

Structure of good design doc: 1. **Context**: What problem are we solving? Why now? 2. **Goals**: What are we trying to achieve? 3. **Non-goals**: What are we explicitly not addressing? 4. **Proposed solution**: How will we solve it? 5. **Alternatives considered**: What else did we evaluate? 6. **Trade-offs**: What are we optimizing for? What are we sacrificing? 7. **Implementation plan**: What are the phases? What are the risks? 8. **Open questions**: What needs to be decided?

- *Post-mortems.* Documents analyzing incidents, what went wrong, and how to prevent recurrence. Good post-mortems are blameless—focused on system improvements, not individual fault (Allspaw 2012).

- *Technical blog posts.* Public writing about technical work. These build reputation (we'll explore the antifragile career in Chapter 13), clarify your own thinking, and create artifacts that demonstrate expertise.

The Discipline of Clear Writing

Good technical writing follows principles:

- *Write for scanning, not just reading.* Readers often skim. Use headers, bullet points (when appropriate), bold emphasis. Make the structure visible.

```
# Bad - wall of text
```

```
We need to implement caching because performance
    is bad and
users are complaining and we measured response
    times and they're
too slow so we should cache database queries
    except some queries
shouldn't be cached because they need fresh data.
    ..

# Good - scannable structure
## Problem
Response times exceed 500ms (target: 100ms). 80%
    of requests
query same data repeatedly.

## Proposed Solution
Implement Redis cache for read-heavy queries.

## Queries to Cache
- User profiles (98% cache hit rate expected)
- Product catalog (updates once daily)

## Queries NOT to Cache
- Order status (must be real-time)
- Inventory counts (high update frequency)
```

- *Be concrete.* Abstract descriptions don't stick. Use examples, specific numbers, concrete scenarios.

```
# Abstract
Performance will improve significantly with
    caching.

# Concrete
Response time will decrease from 450ms to 80ms
    for user profile
requests. At 10K requests/min, this reduces
    database load by 85%.
```

- *Anticipate questions.* Readers will have questions. Answer them preemptively. Common questions:

- Why? (motivation)
- Why now? (timing)
- Why not [alternative]? (alternatives considered)
- What could go wrong? (risks)
- How will we know it works? (success metrics)
- *Revise ruthlessly.* First drafts are for getting ideas out. Second drafts are for making them clear. Third drafts are for making them concise. Good writing is rewriting.
- *AI as writing assistant.* AI can help draft initial versions, generate alternative phrasings, check grammar, and structure content. But the strategic choices—what to emphasize, what to omit, what examples to use—remain human. Use AI to accelerate drafting, but don't abdicate editorial judgment.

```
# Using AI to improve clarity
prompt = """
Revise this explanation for clarity, keeping
    technical accuracy:

'The system uses eventual consistency with CRDTs
    for conflict
resolution in distributed scenarios where network
    partitions
may occur.'

Audience: Engineers familiar with distributed
    systems but not CRDT experts.
"""

# AI generates clearer version, you verify
# technical accuracy
```

Speaking: Real-Time Communication

Verbal communication differs from written. It's synchronous, interactive, and ephemeral. You can see confusion in real-time and adjust. But you can't revise after speaking.

- *Forms of verbal communication.*

- *One-on-one conversations.* Direct, informal, high-bandwidth. Good for nuanced discussions, sensitive topics, real-time problem-solving. The key is active listening—understanding not just what's said but what's meant.
- *Meetings.* Synchronous group communication. Meetings are expensive (N people × time cost). Good meetings have clear purpose, agenda, and facilitator. Bad meetings are status updates that could be async.

```
# Good meeting structure
**Purpose:** Decide on caching strategy
**Agenda:**
1. Review problem statement (5 min)
2. Present three approaches (15 min)
3. Discuss trade-offs (20 min)
4. Make decision (10 min)
5. Document decision and next steps (10 min)

**Required attendees:** Technical leads
**Optional attendees:** Stakeholders interested
    in outcome
**Pre-reading:** Design doc sent 48h before
    meeting
```

Meeting Size and Communication Overhead

Meetings have a hidden cost that grows non-linearly with size. Jeff Sutherland, creator of Scrum, quantifies this mathematically: "If you want to calculate the impact of group size, you take the number of people on a team, multiply by 'that number minus one,' and divide by two" (Sutherland 2014).

This is the formula for communication channels: **n(n−1)/2**

The implications are dramatic: - 5 people = 10 communication channels - 6 people = 15 channels - 7 people = 21 channels - 8 people = 28 channels - 9 people = 36 channels - 10 people = 45 channels

As Sutherland notes, "Our brains simply can't keep up with that many people at once. We don't know what everyone is doing. And we slow down as we try to figure it out" (Sutherland 2014).

- *Practical implications.*
- *Keep decision-making meetings small.* Amazon's "two pizza rule" (if two pizzas can't feed the team, it's too large) recognizes this. For decisions requiring discussion and alignment, aim for 5-7 people maximum. Beyond

that, communication overhead dominates productive work.

- *Distinguish meeting types.*
- **Decision meetings**: Small (3-7 people), expensive but necessary
- **Information sharing**: Can be larger or asynchronous (email, Slack, docs)
- **Brainstorming**: Medium (5-10 people), structured facilitation required
- *Default to asynchronous.* Before scheduling a meeting, ask: "Could this be an email? A Slack thread? A design doc with async comments?" Meetings should be for synchronous discussion that benefits from real-time interaction, not for information broadcast.
- *AI amplifies async communication.* AI can help synthesize information from async channels (summarizing Slack threads, extracting decisions from design doc comments, generating status updates from tickets). This reduces the need for synchronous meetings while maintaining alignment.

The engineer who understands communication overhead becomes an advocate for team efficiency—pushing back on unnecessary meetings, keeping necessary meetings focused and small, and championing asynchronous communication where appropriate.

- *Presentations.* One-to-many verbal communication. Structure matters enormously:
- Start with the conclusion/recommendation (busy people may not hear the full presentation)
- Use visual aids (next section)
- Tell stories, not just facts
- Practice timing
- Anticipate questions and prepare answers
- *Code review discussions.* Verbal component of asynchronous code review. When code review comments are misunderstood or contentious, shift to verbal conversation. Voice carries nuance that text doesn't.
- *Pairing sessions.* Real-time collaborative work. One person "drives" (types), the other "navigates" (thinks ahead, suggests approaches). Requires continuous verbal communication about approach, trade-offs, next steps.

Speaking Skills for Engineers

- *Clarity over cleverness.* Engineers sometimes try to impress with complex vocabulary or elaborate framing. Clarity always wins. Simple, direct language is more persuasive than ornate language.

- *Pace and pause.* Nervous speakers rush. Confident speakers pause. After making an important point, pause to let it land. Silence feels longer to you than to listeners.

- *Analogies and examples.* Abstract concepts need concrete anchors. "This is like..." followed by a familiar analogy helps understanding stick.

```
# Explaining async programming
"Think of it like a restaurant. Synchronous is
  like a waiter who
takes one order, goes to the kitchen, waits for
    the food, brings
it back, then takes the next order. Asynchronous
    is like a waiter
who takes multiple orders, sends them all to the
    kitchen, and
delivers each when ready. Same waiter, more
    efficient."
```

- *Handling questions.* Questions aren't challenges—they're clarifications. "Good question" acknowledges the asker. "Let me make sure I understand what you're asking..." ensures alignment. If you don't know, say so: "I don't know, but I'll find out and follow up."

- *Energy and enthusiasm.* Technical content can be dry. Your energy level affects engagement. If you're bored, listeners are bored. Genuine enthusiasm about the problem and solution is contagious.

Diagramming: Visual Thinking

Diagrams are often more effective than prose for technical communication. Architecture diagrams, sequence diagrams, flowcharts, and state machines all communicate structure and relationships visually.

- *Why diagrams matter.*

- *Spatial relationships.* Some concepts are inherently spatial. How components relate, how data flows, how systems connect—these are easier to grasp visually than textually.

- *Cognitive shortcuts.* A well-designed diagram can convey in seconds what might take paragraphs to explain. The visual cortex processes images faster than text.
- *Shared reference.* Diagrams create common ground. During discussions, you can point: "This component here interacts with this component here." The diagram becomes a shared mental model.
- *Types of technical diagrams.*
- *Architecture diagrams.* Show system components and their relationships. Use boxes for components, arrows for dependencies, groupings for boundaries.

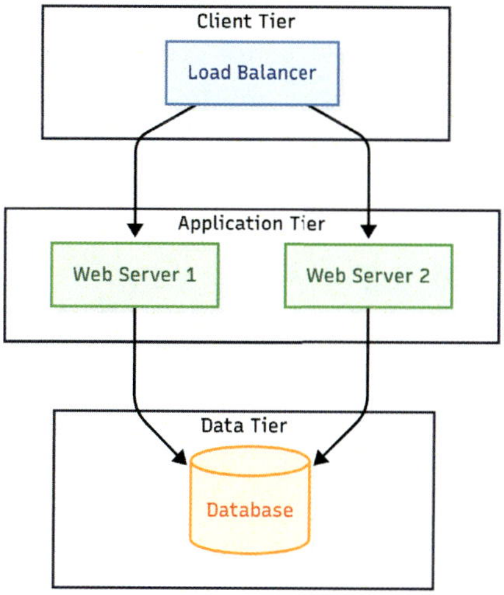

- *Sequence diagrams.* Show interactions over time. Particularly good for explaining protocols, API flows, multi-step processes.

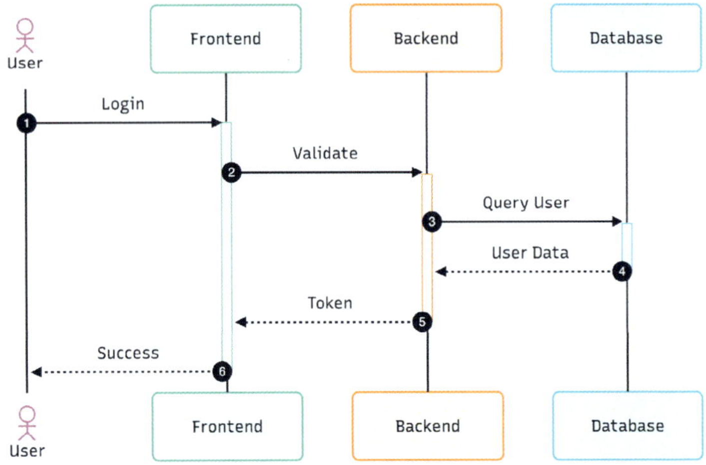

- *Flowcharts.* Show decision trees and control flow. Good for algorithms, business logic, troubleshooting guides.
- *State machines.* Show possible states and transitions. Excellent for modeling lifecycle, order processing, authentication flows.
- *Entity-relationship diagrams.* Show data models and relationships. Essential for database design discussions.
- *Principles of good diagrams.*
- *Keep it simple.* One diagram, one idea. Don't try to show everything in one diagram. Create multiple diagrams at different abstraction levels.
- *Label clearly.* Every box, arrow, and grouping should be labeled. Don't make readers guess.
- *Use consistent notation.* Pick a notation (UML, C4, informal boxes-and-arrows) and use it consistently. Consistency aids comprehension.
- *Show what matters.* Include details that matter for the current discussion. Omit details that don't. A deployment diagram doesn't need to show internal class structure.
- *Iterate.* First diagrams are usually wrong. Show them to others, get feedback, revise. Diagrams improve through iteration.
- *Tools.*
- **Simple text-based**: Mermaid, PlantUML, ASCII art (as shown above)

- **Whiteboarding**: Excalidraw, tldraw, physical whiteboards
- **Professional**: Lucidchart, draw.io, Omnigraffle
- *AI assistance with diagrams.* AI can generate diagram code from descriptions:

```
# Prompt AI to generate Mermaid diagram
prompt = """
Create a Mermaid sequence diagram showing:
1. User submits payment
2. API validates payment details
3. API calls payment gateway
4. Gateway processes and returns result
5. API updates order status
6. API sends confirmation email
"""

# AI generates Mermaid code, you verify and adjust
```

But diagram *design*—deciding what to show, what to emphasize, what to omit—remains human judgment.

Collaborative Cognition with Human and AI Agents

Communication in software engineering has always been multi-party: engineer-to-engineer, engineer-to-stakeholder, engineer-to-future-self (through code). Now we add: engineer-to-AI, AI-to-engineer, and AI-mediated collaboration.

Prompt Engineering as Communication

When you interact with AI through prompts, you're communicating. The skills of clear communication apply directly:

- *Be concrete and specific.* Vague prompts get vague results. Specific prompts get specific results.

```
# Vague prompt
"Write a function for user authentication"

# Specific prompt
"Write a Python function that validates a JWT
```

```
token. It should:
- Accept token string and secret key
- Verify signature using HS256
- Check expiration timestamp
- Return decoded payload if valid, raise
  JWTInvalidError if not
- Include type hints and docstring"
```

- *Provide context.* AI doesn't know your constraints, conventions, or context. Make them explicit.

```
# Without context
"Implement error handling for this API"

# With context
"Implement error handling for this Flask API
 following our conventions:
- Use @app.errorhandler decorators
- Return JSON responses with 'error' and
  'message' keys
- Use our custom error classes: ValidationError
  (400),
 UnauthorizedError (401), NotFoundError (404)
- Log errors to our structured logger
- Don't expose internal errors to clients"
```

- *Iterate conversationally.* AI communication is dialogue, not monologue. Start broad, narrow with follow-ups.

```
# First prompt
"Design a caching strategy for our user API"

# AI responds with options

# Follow-up prompt based on response
"The Redis approach looks good. How would we
 handle cache
invalidation when user profile updates?"

# AI responds with strategies

# Further refinement
```

```
"I like the write-through approach. Show me
  Python code for
implementing this with our existing
    UserRepository class."
```

- *Request explanation.* Don't just ask AI to generate code—ask it to explain reasoning. This helps you verify correctness and learn.

```
"Explain why you chose a dictionary over a list
  for this
implementation. What are the time complexity
    trade-offs?"
```

- *Specify format and style.* AI can match various styles if you specify:

```
"Generate Python code following:
- PEP 8 style guide
- Type hints on all functions
- Docstrings in Google style
- Maximum line length 88 characters (Black
    formatter)
- Our naming convention: snake_case for functions,

  PascalCase for classes"
```

Communicating About AI Decisions

As AI systems become part of the engineering workflow, you must communicate *about* AI—explaining AI-generated code to colleagues, documenting AI-assisted decisions, justifying AI recommendations to stakeholders.

- *Explaining AI-generated code to colleagues.*

Challenge: You didn't write the code, so you don't have the same deep understanding as you would for code you wrote.

Approach: 1. **Understand it yourself first**: Don't present AI code without understanding it. Review thoroughly. 2. **Explain intent, not just mechanics**: Focus on *what* it does and *why*, not line-by-line. 3. **Highlight key decisions**: Point out the important architectural or algorithmic choices. 4. **Be honest about provenance**: "AI generated the initial implementation, I reviewed and modified for our constraints."

- *Documenting AI-assisted work.*

```
def calculate_risk_score(transaction:
```

```
Transaction) -> float:
    """
    Calculate fraud risk score for transaction.

    Implementation generated by AI based on
        industry standard fraud
    detection patterns, then modified to match
        our risk thresholds
    and regulatory requirements.

    Key modifications from AI version:
    - Added geographic risk factor per our
        compliance requirements
    - Adjusted thresholds based on our historical
        fraud data
    - Added logging for audit trail

    Args:
        transaction: Transaction to evaluate

    Returns:
        Risk score from 0.0 (low risk) to 1.0
            (high risk)
    """
    # Implementation...
```

- *Justifying AI recommendations to stakeholders.*

Non-technical stakeholders want to know: - What did AI recommend? - Why does it recommend this? - How confident should we be? - What are the risks? - What's your assessment as the engineer?

```
## AI-Assisted Architecture Recommendation

**AI Recommendation:** Use microservices
    architecture with
event-driven communication.

**AI's Reasoning:**
- System has distinct bounded contexts (users,
    orders, inventory)
```

```
- Need independent scaling of components
- Event sourcing provides audit trail

**My Assessment:**
I agree with the general direction but with
    modifications:
- Start with modular monolith, extract services
    later
  (team is small, microservices overhead too high
      now)
- Use events for async operations, but keep some
    sync APIs
  (event-only makes debugging harder)
- Implement bounded contexts within monolith first

**Recommendation:** Implement modular monolith
    with clear boundaries,
plan for eventual service extraction. Gets 80% of
    microservices benefits
with 20% of complexity.
```

The pattern: Present AI's view, then add your human judgment. Don't hide AI's role, but don't defer entirely to AI either.

Collaborative Patterns: Human + AI

As we'll explore in Chapter 9, there are multiple patterns for human-AI collaboration. Each has communication implications:

- *Delegation pattern.* You specify what you want, AI implements, you verify.

Communication need: Clear specification upfront. Precise acceptance criteria. Thorough verification.

- *Collaboration pattern.* You and AI work together iteratively.

Communication need: Clear guidance at each step. Feedback on AI outputs. Progressive refinement.

- *Supervision pattern.* AI works semi-autonomously, you intervene when needed.

Communication need: Clear boundaries before start. Checkpoints where you review. Intervention protocols when things go wrong.

- *Augmentation pattern.* AI provides real-time assistance while you work.

Communication need: Minimal—AI suggests, you accept/reject/modify. This is the lowest-communication mode.

Human-to-Human Communication About AI Work

The hardest communication challenge: explaining to other humans how you're working with AI.

- *To managers.*

Managers want to understand: - How does AI change velocity? - What are risks? - What skills does team need? - What's your confidence level?

```
## Weekly Update: Payment Service Refactor

**Progress:** Completed API redesign. AI
    generated initial
implementation (saved ~2 days), I reviewed and
    refactored for
our domain model (1 day).

**AI Contribution:** Generated boilerplate,
    standard error handling,
test scaffolding. Helped explore 3 architectural
    alternatives quickly.

**Human Contribution:** Domain modeling,
    integration with existing
services, performance optimization, security
    review.

**Confidence:** High. I understand the
    implementation thoroughly,
tests are comprehensive, and it matches our
    architecture patterns.

**Next Week:** Integration testing and deployment
    preparation.
```

To junior engineers (we'll explore the apprenticeship problem in Chapter 11):

Juniors are learning. They need to understand not just *what* AI generated but *why* it's appropriate and *when* to trust it.

```
# In code review
"""
AI generated this caching implementation. Let's
    review it together:

1. The overall approach is sound - it uses a
    decorator pattern which
   is Pythonic and composable.

2. However, I modified the cache key generation.
    AI used:
   key = f"{func.__name__}_{args}"

   This breaks if args contain unhashable types.
       I changed to:
   key = f"{func.__name__}_{hash(frozenset(kwargs.
       items()))}"

3. The cache expiration logic AI generated is
    standard but we need
   to add our custom invalidation trigger for
       when data updates.

This shows AI's strength (standard patterns) and
    limits (domain-specific
requirements). Always verify AI code matches our
    actual constraints.
"""
```

- *To technical peers.*

Peers want to understand design rationale and review for correctness. Be transparent about AI's role but focus discussion on technical merits:

```
## Design Review: New Authentication Flow

[Present design on its technical merits]

**Process note:** I used AI to explore multiple
    design alternatives
```

```
quickly, then selected this approach based on our
    requirements. The
implementation includes AI-generated components
    that I verified and
modified.

[Focus rest of discussion on technical trade-offs,
    not on AI's role]
```

The Meta-Communication Challenge

Perhaps the deepest communication challenge: we're still developing shared vocabulary and norms for AI-assisted work.

Questions without clear answers yet: - When should you mention AI's role? Always? Only if asked? When it materially affects the outcome? - How much verification is expected before presenting AI-generated work? - What's the expectation for understanding code you didn't write but AI did? - How do you communicate confidence levels in AI-assisted work?

These norms are evolving. Organizations are developing their own standards. The communication skill is navigating this ambiguity explicitly:

```
"I want to be transparent about my use of AI in
    this project. I used it
for initial implementation, which I then reviewed
    thoroughly and modified
significantly for our domain. I understand the
    code fully and can explain
any part. I'm curious what norms our team wants
    around AI disclosure and
verification. What level of transparency is
    helpful?"
```

Being explicit about the uncertainty itself is valuable communication.

Communication Skills Compound with AI

AI doesn't replace communication skills—it amplifies them:

- *Good communicators using AI.* Write clearer docs (AI drafts, they refine). Give better presentations (AI generates slide outlines, they add examples and delivery). Explain better (AI provides multiple framings, they choose best for audience).

- *Poor communicators using AI.* Generate verbose docs that say little. Create presentations that lack coherence. Produce explanations that don't address actual confusion.

The pattern throughout this chapter: AI accelerates mechanics (drafting, formatting, generating alternatives) but judgment about *what* to communicate, *how* to frame it, and *what to emphasize* remains human.

As we'll explore in Chapter 12 (AI-Augmented Mind), AI extends cognitive capability but requires human direction. The same applies to communication: AI extends communication capability but requires human judgment about strategy, audience, and emphasis.

Chapter Summary

- **Communication is engineering work, not "soft skills."** As AI handles implementation, engineering work becomes more communicative—understanding problems, designing solutions, verifying systems, maintaining knowledge. The "explainer engineer" becomes increasingly valuable.
- **The explainer premium is real.** Engineers who communicate well advance faster, earn more, build influence, and multiply team effectiveness. Communication is an antifragile career skill that compounds over time (Hinds 1999).
- **Three audiences require different approaches.** Technical peers (dense, precise, code-heavy), adjacent technical (balanced accessibility and precision, diagram-heavy), and non-technical stakeholders (outcome-focused, minimal jargon, analogy-rich).
- **Writing is thinking made visible.** Code comments explain why. Commit messages provide narrative history. ADRs preserve decision rationale. Design docs enable feedback before commitment. Post-mortems drive improvement (Nygard 2011; Allspaw 2012).
- **Clear writing follows principles.** Write for scanning, be concrete not abstract, anticipate questions, revise ruthlessly. AI can help draft but strategic choices remain human.
- **Speaking is real-time communication.** One-on-ones for nuance, meetings for decisions, presentations for persuasion. Clarity beats cleverness, pauses create emphasis, analogies anchor understanding.

- **Diagrams communicate structure visually.** Architecture diagrams show relationships, sequence diagrams show interactions, flowcharts show decisions, state machines show lifecycle. Good diagrams are simple, labeled clearly, and show what matters.
- **Prompt engineering is communication.** Specific prompts get specific results. Context makes AI more effective. Iteration refines outputs. Requesting explanation enables verification and learning.
- **Communicating about AI work requires transparency.** Explain AI-generated code by focusing on intent. Document AI assistance honestly. Justify AI recommendations with your engineering judgment layered on top.
- **Collaboration patterns have communication implications.** Delegation requires clear specs. Collaboration requires iterative feedback. Supervision requires checkpoints. Augmentation requires minimal communication.
- **Human-to-human communication about AI is evolving.** Norms around disclosure, verification, and confidence levels are still developing. Being explicit about uncertainty itself is valuable communication.
- **AI amplifies communication skills.** Good communicators using AI produce better docs, presentations, and explanations. Poor communicators using AI produce more volume without more clarity. Strategic communication choices remain human.

We've now completed Part II (The Human Advantage), establishing the foundational skills that define engineering excellence: endurance and resilience (Chapter 5), logical thinking (Chapter 6), simplification (Chapter 7), and communication (Chapter 8). Combined with the frameworks in Part I, the collaboration patterns in Part III, and the career strategies in Part IV, these skills form a complete picture of thriving as an engineer in the AI era.

Chapter 9

Human–AI Collaboration

"The best partnerships are those where each party does what they do best—and knows when to step aside." — Source unknown

---

In Chapter 1, we introduced four interaction modes for human-AI collaboration: Delegation, Collaboration, Supervision, and Augmentation. We've explored AI's capabilities and limitations in Chapter 4. Now we turn to the practical question: how do you actually *work* with AI systems day-to-day? Later chapters will examine calibrated trust (Chapter 10) and the future landscape (Chapter 16) in greater depth.

This chapter provides a pragmatic guide to human-AI collaboration—not as abstract theory but as lived practice. We'll explore the psychological dimensions of working with non-human teammates, develop frameworks for choosing appropriate interaction modes for different tasks, and establish practical techniques for correcting, guiding, and teaching AI systems to produce better results.

The central insight: effective human-AI collaboration is not about treating AI as either a tool or a colleague, but about developing new interaction patterns that leverage AI's strengths while compensating for its weaknesses. Engineers who master these patterns multiply their effectiveness. Those who default to passive acceptance or blanket rejection miss the opportunity.

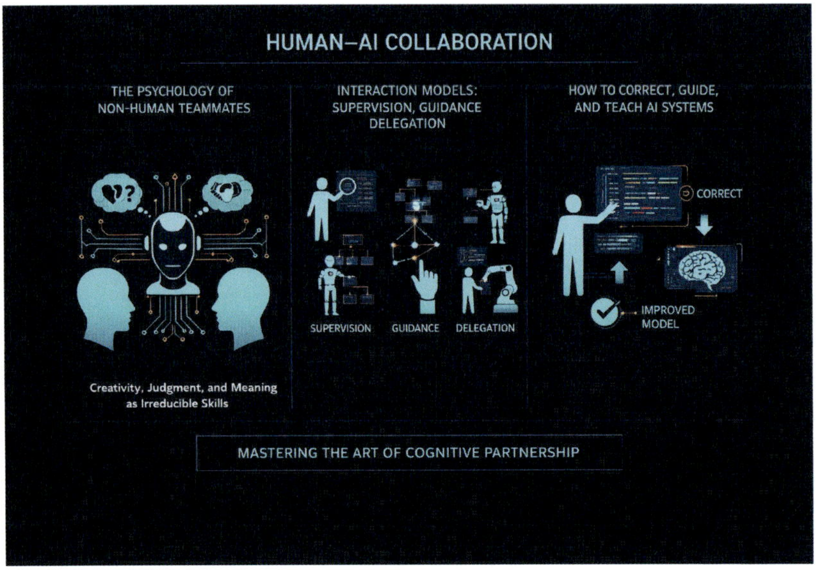

The Psychology of Non-Human Teammates

Why Working with AI Feels Different

Most engineers have extensive experience collaborating with humans. We've learned to read social cues, navigate personality differences, build trust, give feedback, and coordinate work. These patterns are deeply ingrained—they're how teamwork *feels*.

Working with AI violates many of these patterns, creating cognitive dissonance. The system produces remarkably capable output one moment and embarrassingly wrong output the next. It responds instantly to requests but cannot remember yesterday's conversation. It matches your coding style perfectly but has no understanding of why that style matters.

This unpredictability creates psychological stress. Research on human-automation interaction identifies several maladaptive responses (Parasuraman and Riley 1997a):

- *Over-trust from capability demonstration.* When AI produces impressive results, humans extrapolate to situations where reliability is lower. An engineer sees AI generate clean code for ten straightforward tasks and assumes it will handle complex edge cases equally well. This is automation bias—the tendency to favor suggestions from automated systems even when contradictory evidence exists.

- *Under-trust from visible failures.* Conversely, a single dramatic failure can trigger lasting skepticism. An engineer sees AI generate subtly broken code once and thereafter rejects all AI suggestions, even when they're correct. This is automation aversion—the tendency to discount automated assistance after observing errors (Dietvorst et al. 2015).
- *Frustration from inconsistency.* Perhaps most challenging is the whiplash between these states. The same AI system that brilliantly debugged yesterday's issue generates nonsense today. This inconsistency prevents stable mental models from forming, leaving engineers in constant uncertainty about when to trust.

The solution is not to eliminate these reactions—they're natural responses to working with systems that don't behave like human teammates. Instead, engineers need new mental models calibrated to AI's actual characteristics.

The Cognitive Prosthetic Model

A useful mental model: treat AI as a *cognitive prosthetic* rather than a colleague or tool.

- *Not a colleague because.* Colleagues have continuity—they remember past conversations, understand organizational context, and bring stable personalities. AI has discontinuous memory, lacks organizational embedding, and exhibits no consistent "personality" beyond training patterns.
- *Not a tool because.* Tools are predictable—a hammer works the same way every time. AI is stochastic—the same prompt can yield different outputs. Tools don't make suggestions; AI does. Tools don't require interpretation; AI output often does.
- *A prosthetic because.* Prosthetics extend capability in specific dimensions while requiring user skill to operate effectively. A prosthetic limb doesn't replace natural motor control—it translates intention through learned use. Similarly, AI extends cognitive capability but requires human direction, evaluation, and judgment.

This model has several advantages:

- *It acknowledges sophisticated capability.* Prosthetics are impressive feats of engineering that genuinely enhance function. This prevents underutilization from treating AI as a trivial tool.
- *It emphasizes learning curve.* No one expects to use a prosthetic effectively

immediately. There's an adaptation period where user and device learn to work together. This prevents frustration when AI collaboration doesn't feel natural instantly.

- *It maintains human agency.* The prosthetic responds to user intention; it doesn't have goals of its own. This prevents over-trust from anthropomorphizing AI as having understanding or judgment it lacks.
- *It suggests customization.* Prosthetics work best when fitted to individual users. Similarly, effective AI use requires learning which prompts work, which tasks are appropriate, and how to interpret outputs—a personalized calibration process.

Building Accurate Mental Models

The prosthetic model is one framework. But effective collaboration requires more detailed mental models of what AI actually does.

Mental Model 1: AI as Pattern Matcher

At its core, an LLM is a sophisticated pattern-matching engine. It predicts tokens based on statistical regularities in training data. This model helps explain:

- **Why AI is fluent**: It has seen millions of examples of fluent text and code
- **Why AI hallucinates**: Matching patterns doesn't guarantee truth
- **Why AI struggles with novelty**: Patterns outside training distribution are harder to match
- **Why prompting matters**: You're directing which patterns the model should match

This model prevents mystification—AI isn't "thinking" in the human sense. It's finding and applying learned patterns.

Mental Model 2: AI as Probabilistic System

AI outputs are probabilistic, not deterministic. The same prompt can yield different responses due to sampling randomness. This model helps explain:

- **Why consistency is imperfect**: Stochasticity means variation
- **Why regenerating can help**: Different samples might yield better results
- **Why temperature matters**: Higher temperature increases randomness
- **Why errors aren't always reproducible**: What failed once might succeed on retry

This model prevents treating AI like deterministic code—expecting identical results from identical inputs.

Mental Model 3: AI as Context-Bounded

AI operates within a context window—typically thousands to millions of tokens. This model helps explain:

- **Why conversation history matters**: Recent context shapes outputs
- **Why AI "forgets"**: Information outside the window is inaccessible
- **Why summarization helps**: Compressing context preserves more information within the window
- **Why session management matters**: Starting fresh resets context entirely

This model prevents assuming AI has memory like humans—it knows only what's in the current window.

Mental Model 4: AI as Trained, Not Programmed

Unlike traditional software, AI behavior emerges from training data and objectives, not explicit code. This model helps explain:

- **Why biases appear**: Training data contains societal biases
- **Why certain tasks work well**: They're well-represented in training
- **Why fine-tuning helps**: Additional training shapes behavior
- **Why prompt engineering is necessary**: You're navigating learned associations

This model prevents expecting bug-free behavior—AI doesn't have bugs in the traditional sense, it has training limitations.

Emotional Regulation in Human-AI Work

Working with AI can be emotionally challenging. The system produces outputs that range from brilliant to baffling, sometimes within the same session. Engineers report frustration, confusion, and occasionally anger when AI fails in ways that seem "stupid" (Vaccaro et al. 2018).

These emotional responses are valid but counterproductive if they prevent effective use. Some strategies for emotional regulation:

- *Expect imperfection.* AI will fail. Build this expectation into your workflow rather than being surprised when it happens. Treat failures as information about system limitations, not as personal affronts.

- *Separate capability from reliability.* AI can do impressive things unreliably. Something that works 80% of the time is genuinely useful—if you verify the other 20%. Don't reject capabilities because they're imperfect.

- *Take breaks from frustration.* When AI produces nonsensical outputs repeatedly, step away. Trying to "fix" AI through increasingly frustrated prompts rarely works. Return with fresh perspective and different framing.
- *Maintain appropriate skepticism.* As we'll explore in Chapter 10, calibrated trust means neither blind acceptance nor blanket rejection. Skepticism protects against over-trust without preventing utilization.
- *Remember the alternative.* Even imperfect AI assistance is often faster than working alone. Compare AI-augmented work to manual work, not to an imagined perfect assistant.

The goal is emotional stability that allows effective collaboration—neither euphoric over-trust nor bitter rejection, but pragmatic engagement with a powerful but flawed tool.

Interaction Models: Delegation, Collaboration, Supervision, and Augmentation

In Chapter 1, we introduced four interaction modes: Delegation, Collaboration, Supervision, and Augmentation. Let's now explore these modes in practical detail, with guidance on when to use each and how to execute them effectively.

Delegation: When to Let Go

- *What it is.* In Delegation mode, you specify a task and the AI executes it with minimal intervention. You provide clear requirements, let the AI work, then verify the output.
- *When to use Delegation.*
- Tasks with clear specifications and success criteria
- Well-understood problems with standard solutions
- Low-stakes work where errors are cheap to fix
- Boilerplate code, documentation, or test generation
- Repetitive transformations across similar structures
- *Example scenarios.*
- "Write unit tests for this function" (the function defines correct behavior)

- "Generate API documentation from these endpoint definitions"
- "Convert these SQL queries to use parameterized statements"
- "Create getter and setter methods for these class properties"
- *How to delegate effectively.*
- *1. Provide complete context upfront.* Don't assume AI will ask for missing information. Include:
- Input/output specifications
- Constraints and requirements
- Relevant code or data structures
- Coding standards or style preferences
- Any edge cases you're aware of
- *2. Be explicit about success criteria.* State clearly what "correct" means:
- "Tests should achieve 100% branch coverage"
- "Documentation should follow our API doc template"
- "Code should match our style guide (attached)"
- *3. Verify systematically.* Don't trust blindly. Check:
- Does it compile/run?
- Do tests pass?
- Does it handle edge cases?
- Does it match specifications?
- Is it maintainable?
- *4. Iterate if needed.* If output is wrong, don't abandon delegation. Provide specific feedback and re-delegate:
- "The tests don't cover error cases. Add tests for invalid inputs."
- "The documentation is missing return type descriptions. Add them."
- *When Delegation fails.* If you're iterating more than 3 times on the same delegated task, switch modes. The task may be too complex, too novel, or too poorly specified for pure delegation.

Collaboration: Working Together

- *What it is.* In Collaboration mode, you and AI work iteratively. You provide direction, AI generates proposals, you refine direction, AI adjusts—back and forth until the result is satisfactory.
- *When to use Collaboration.*
- Complex tasks where requirements evolve during execution
- Problems where you're exploring solution spaces
- Creative work where you're refining through iteration
- Tasks where your judgment improves AI output substantially
- Learning situations where you want to understand AI's reasoning
- *Example scenarios.*
- "Help me design a caching strategy for this API" (exploration)
- "Let's refactor this module to be more testable" (iterative improvement)
- "Draft a technical proposal for distributed tracing" (creative work)
- "Debug why this async function deadlocks" (problem-solving)
- *How to collaborate effectively.*
- *1. Start with broad direction, narrow iteratively.*

```
You: "I need a caching strategy for a high-read,
    low-write API."
AI: [proposes Redis with TTL-based expiration]
You: "Good start. How would we handle cache
    invalidation when writes occur?"
AI: [proposes cache-aside pattern with write-
    through]
You: "What about cache stampedes during cold
    starts?"
AI: [proposes probabilistic early expiration]
```

- *2. Ask AI to explain its reasoning.* Understanding why AI suggests something helps you evaluate whether it's appropriate:
- "Why did you choose Redis over Memcached?"
- "What's the trade-off with this approach?"
- "What are potential failure modes?"

- *3. Provide progressive context.* As the conversation evolves, add context:
- "Actually, we're already using Redis for session storage"
- "I should mention—writes are extremely rare, maybe 1% of traffic"
- "Interesting. Our largest customers have 100x more data than typical ones"
- *4. Use AI to generate alternatives.* Don't settle for the first suggestion:
- "Show me three different caching approaches and their trade-offs"
- "What if we used a different consistency model?"
- *5. Maintain decision authority.* You're collaborating, but you're making final calls. AI generates options; you choose:
- "I like option 2 best for our use case. Let's proceed with that."
- *When Collaboration is working.* You're learning from AI's suggestions, AI is adapting to your feedback, and the solution is converging toward something you couldn't have reached alone as quickly.
- *When Collaboration fails.* If you're spending more time explaining context than making progress, or if AI keeps misunderstanding your intent, consider whether the task is too novel or whether you need to delegate sub-tasks instead.

Supervision: Monitoring Autonomous Work

- *What it is.* In Supervision mode, AI operates semi-autonomously while you monitor for problems and intervene when necessary. This is appropriate for ongoing processes or tasks that span extended time.
- *When to use Supervision.*
- Long-running processes (multi-file refactoring, batch processing)
- Agentic AI systems that work across multiple sub-tasks
- Continuous monitoring or analysis tasks
- Work that's mostly routine but occasionally needs human judgment
- *Example scenarios.*
- AI agent implementing a feature across multiple files
- Automated code review suggesting improvements
- Continuous refactoring to improve code quality

- Monitoring logs for anomalies and suggesting fixes
- *How to supervise effectively.*
- *1. Set clear boundaries before autonomous work.*
- "Refactor the authentication module, but don't touch the encryption logic"
- "Suggest improvements, but don't auto-merge anything"
- "Flag anomalies, but only alert for high-severity issues"
- *2. Establish checkpoints.* Don't let AI work for hours uninterrupted:
- "Show me your plan before starting"
- "Check in after completing each file"
- "Summarize what you've done every 30 minutes"
- *3. Monitor for drift.* As AI works, watch for patterns:
- Is it still addressing the original goal?
- Are changes consistent in style and approach?
- Is it introducing new problems while fixing old ones?
- *4. Intervene decisively.* When something looks wrong, stop and redirect:
- "Pause. This change breaks the API contract. Revert and try a different approach."
- "You're optimizing prematurely. Focus on correctness first."
- *5. Maintain situational awareness.* This is the hardest part of supervision—staying engaged enough to intervene when needed without micromanaging. As we discussed in Chapter 1, this is the "out-of-the-loop" problem that Bainbridge identified (Bainbridge 1983).
- *Strategies for maintaining awareness.*
- Review AI's plan before execution
- Skim each change as it's made (don't deep-read, just verify direction)
- Run tests frequently to catch issues early
- Keep a mental model of what should be changing
- *When Supervision works.* AI is making steady progress on routine aspects while you catch the non-routine issues that require human judgment.

- *When Supervision fails.* If you find yourself constantly intervening, the task isn't suitable for autonomous work. Drop to Collaboration mode where you're more actively involved.

Augmentation: AI as Extension of Self

- *What it is.* In Augmentation mode, AI enhances your capabilities without taking over the task. You remain the primary agent; AI provides real-time assistance that makes you more effective.
- *When to use Augmentation.*
- Tasks where you need to maintain full context and control
- Situations requiring continuous judgment calls
- Work where AI provides tools/information but you make all decisions
- Learning and skill development scenarios
- *Example scenarios.*
- Code completion while you're writing
- Inline suggestions for improvements as you type
- Real-time syntax checking and error detection
- Documentation lookup while coding
- Example generation to understand APIs
- *How to augment effectively.*
- *1. Treat suggestions as options, not prescriptions.*
- AI completes your function -> you can accept, modify, or ignore
- AI suggests an improvement -> you evaluate whether it's actually better
- AI offers an alternative approach -> you decide if it's worth switching
- *2. Maintain your train of thought.* Don't let AI derail your thinking:
- If a suggestion doesn't match your intent, ignore it immediately
- Don't stop to evaluate every suggestion—only when they seem relevant
- Complete your thought before considering AI's alternative
- *3. Use AI to explore quickly.* Let AI handle the mechanical parts while you focus on the conceptual:
- "What's the syntax for..." -> AI shows you instantly

- "How do I..." -> AI provides examples
- "What would this look like if..." -> AI generates for comparison
- *4. Learn from patterns.* Pay attention to what AI suggests. Good suggestions teach you patterns:
- AI consistently suggests error handling you forget -> learn the pattern
- AI offers idioms you don't know -> incorporate them into your repertoire
- AI catches common mistakes -> train yourself to avoid them
- *5. Adjust assistance levels.* Most augmentation tools let you control intrusiveness:
- Turn off suggestions when they're distracting
- Increase assistance when exploring unfamiliar territory
- Adjust delay before suggestions appear
- *When Augmentation works.* You feel more productive without feeling like you're losing control. AI accelerates your work without changing your approach.
- *When Augmentation fails.* If suggestions are consistently irrelevant, annoying, or wrong, reduce assistance levels or disable them for that task.

Choosing the Right Mode

Deciding which mode to use requires judgment based on several factors:

Factor	Deleg.	Collab.	Superv.	Augment.
Task clarity	High	Med	Med	N/A
Your expertise	Any	High	High	Any
Stakes	Low-Med	Med-High	Med	Any
Time available	Limited	Flexible	Extended	Real-time
Novelty	Low	Med-High	Low-Med	Any
Involvement	Minimal	Continuous	Periodic	Constant

- *Decision heuristics.*
- **When the goal is clear and stakes are low** -> Delegate
- **When exploring options or requirements are evolving** -> Collaborate
- **When the task is extended but mostly routine** -> Supervise

- **When you need full control with AI assistance** -> Augment
- *Mode switching is normal.* Start with one mode, switch to another if it's not working:
- Delegation -> Collaboration (task is more complex than expected)
- Collaboration -> Delegation (you've clarified requirements through exploration)
- Supervision -> Collaboration (too many interventions needed)
- Any mode -> Augmentation (you want more hands-on control)

The skill is recognizing when a mode isn't working and switching promptly rather than persisting with ineffective patterns.

There is a more fundamental choice that sits beneath these four modes: the choice between *workflows* and *agents*.

A workflow is a deterministic path—code and data flowing through predefined steps, with conditional logic that a human designed in advance. A CI/CD pipeline is a workflow. An ETL process is a workflow. The sequence is fixed; the behavior is predictable; the failure modes are known.

An agent, by contrast, is non-deterministic. It receives a goal and decides—step by step, based on observation and inference—what to do next. Its path is emergent, not designed. This makes agents powerful for open-ended tasks but unreliable for tasks where predictability matters.

The decision heuristic is straightforward: if you can specify the steps in advance and the path is stable, use a workflow. It will be faster, cheaper, and more reliable. If the steps depend on intermediate results that you cannot predict, or if the task requires adaptation, use an agent. The mistake many teams make is reaching for agents when a well-designed workflow would suffice—seduced by the sophistication of the tool rather than the requirements of the task. The best engineers match the tool to the problem, not the other way around.

How to Correct, Guide, and Teach AI Systems

Working effectively with AI requires more than choosing interaction modes—it requires skill in correcting errors, providing guidance, and iteratively improving outputs. This section provides practical techniques for these meta-skills.

The Correction Loop: Diagnosing and Fixing AI Errors

When AI produces wrong output, the temptation is to regenerate or give up. More effective is diagnosing *why* it failed and providing specific correction.

Step 1: Categorize the failure

Different failure types require different corrections:

- *Category 1 - Misunderstood Requirements.* AI solved the wrong problem
- Example: Asked for error handling, got logging instead
- Correction approach: Clarify requirements more explicitly
- Fix: "I need error *handling*, not error *logging*. Handle errors by..."
- *Category 2 - Incomplete Context.* AI lacked necessary information
- Example: Generated code incompatible with existing architecture
- Correction approach: Provide missing context
- Fix: "This needs to work with our existing auth system (here's the interface)..."
- *Category 3 - Edge Cases.* AI handled common cases but missed corner cases
- Example: Code works for valid inputs but crashes on invalid ones
- Correction approach: Specify edge cases explicitly
- Fix: "This doesn't handle null inputs. Add validation for..."
- *Category 4 - Wrong Patterns.* AI applied patterns from training that don't fit
- Example: Used inheritance when composition would be better
- Correction approach: Explain why the pattern doesn't work here
- Fix: "Inheritance creates tight coupling here. Use composition instead because..."
- *Category 5 - Hallucination.* AI invented facts or APIs that don't exist
- Example: Called methods that don't exist in the library
- Correction approach: Provide accurate information
- Fix: "The library doesn't have a `doThing()` method. Use `performAction()` instead..."

Step 2: Provide specific, actionable feedback

Vague corrections don't help: - *Bad:* "This is wrong" - *Bad:* "Try again" - *Bad:* "That doesn't work"

Specific corrections do: - *Good:* "The function returns string but should return integer" - *Good:* "The variable `userData` is undefined—you need to pass it as parameter" - *Good:* "This approach is $O(n^2)$ but we need O(n log n) for our scale"

Step 3: Show, don't just tell

When possible, provide examples of correct behavior:

Instead of: "Handle errors properly" Provide: "Handle errors like this: `try { ... } catch (error) { logger.error(error); throw new CustomError(...); }`"

Instead of: "Use better variable names" Provide: "Use descriptive names like `authenticatedUser` instead of `u`"

Step 4: Iterate progressively

Don't expect perfection immediately. Correct iteratively:

```
Round 1: "Add error handling"
-> AI adds try-catch but doesn't log errors

Round 2: "Log errors before re-throwing"
-> AI logs but uses wrong log level

Round 3: "Use logger.error() for exceptions, not
    logger.info()"
-> AI corrects it

Round 4: "Include stack trace in error log"
-> Final correct version
```

This feels inefficient but is often faster than trying to specify everything perfectly upfront.

- *When to abandon correction.* If you're on the 5th iteration and still not getting correct output, the task may be:
- Too complex for AI's current capabilities
- Too novel (outside training distribution)
- Too poorly specified (you're not sure what you want either)

At this point, either simplify the task, switch modes, or write it yourself.

From Prompting to Context Engineering

How you communicate with AI significantly affects output quality. Most discussions frame this as "prompt engineering" — the craft of writing better prompts. That framing is useful but incomplete. It optimises at the wrong level of abstraction.

The more precise discipline is *context engineering* — shaping the entire informational environment that an AI system operates within. A prompt is a single input. Context is everything: the system instructions, the examples provided, the documents retrieved, the conversation history, the tool descriptions, and the constraints that bound acceptable behaviour.

The distinction matters because engineers who think only in terms of prompts treat each interaction as an isolated question-and-answer exchange. Engineers who think in terms of context treat each interaction as part of a designed informational architecture. They ask not just "what should I say to the model?" but "what does the model need to *know* — and what does it need to *not* know — in order to produce useful output?"

Context engineering is to AI collaboration what systems design is to software architecture. It requires deciding what to include, what to exclude, how to structure information for maximum signal, and how to anticipate failure modes before they occur. A well-engineered context makes every subsequent prompt more effective — because the model is already operating within the right constraints, with the right examples, and with the right framing of the problem space.

The techniques below are the building blocks of effective context engineering. Each one shapes a different dimension of the model's informational environment:

Technique 1: Provide Role and Context

Instead of: "Write a function to validate emails"

Try: "You're an experienced backend engineer. Write a production-grade email validation function that handles international domains and provides clear error messages."

The role primes AI to match that persona's patterns. The context clarifies quality expectations.

Technique 2: Show Examples (Few-Shot Learning)

Instead of: "Use our coding style"

Try:

```
Here are three examples of our coding style:

[Example 1]
[Example 2]
[Example 3]

Now write a function following this style...
```

AI learns patterns from examples better than from descriptions.

Technique 3: Request Step-by-Step Reasoning

Instead of: "Design a caching layer"

Try: "Design a caching layer. First, list the requirements. Then, evaluate three approaches with pros/cons. Finally, recommend one with justification."

Forcing explicit reasoning often produces better results and lets you catch errors in logic before implementation.

Technique 4: Specify Format and Structure

Instead of: "Document this API"

Try: "Document this API using this format: - Brief description (one sentence) - Parameters (name, type, description for each) - Returns (type and description) - Example usage (code snippet) - Edge cases and error conditions"

Explicit structure prevents missing important information.

Technique 5: Use Constraints to Guide Quality

Instead of: "Generate test cases"

Try: "Generate test cases that: - Cover all branches - Test edge cases (empty input, null, max values) - Include one negative test per function - Use descriptive test names"

Constraints guide AI toward better outputs without requiring you to review and request additions.

Technique 6: Ask AI to Check Its Own Work

After AI generates output:

"Review the code you just wrote for: - Type errors - Unhandled edge cases - Performance issues - Security vulnerabilities

List any issues found and provide fixes."

AI often catches its own mistakes when explicitly prompted to review.

Technique 7: Break Complex Tasks into Subtasks

Instead of: "Implement user authentication with email verification, password reset, and rate limiting"

Try:

```
Let's implement authentication in stages:
1. First, just basic login/logout
2. Then add email verification
3. Then add password reset
4. Finally, add rate limiting

Let's start with stage 1...
```

This prevents AI from trying to handle too much at once and getting confused.

Notice the pattern across all seven techniques: none of them are really about writing a better sentence. They are about shaping what the model knows before it generates a response — providing role context, supplying examples, structuring constraints, decomposing complexity. Each technique engineers a different dimension of the model's informational environment. That is context engineering in practice.

Teaching AI Your Patterns and Preferences

The techniques above shape context within a single exchange. But context engineering also operates at the session level — establishing patterns, preferences, and shared understanding that improve every interaction that follows. While current AI systems don't learn persistently across sessions, you can "teach" them within a conversation by providing consistent examples.

Creating a Style Guide

Compile examples of your preferred patterns and provide them as reference:

```
# Our Code Style

## Naming Conventions
- Variables: camelCase (userData, not user_data)
- Functions: verbNoun (getUserData, not get_data)
- Classes: PascalCase (UserManager, not
```

````
    userManager)

## Error Handling
Always use try-catch with specific error types:
```javascript
try {
  // operation
} catch (error) {
  if (error instanceof ValidationError) {
    // handle validation
  } else {
    // handle unexpected
    logger.error(error);
    throw error;
  }
}
````

Example of Good Code

[Show 2-3 examples of well-written code from your codebase]

````
Then reference this when prompting: "Follow the
    style guide I provided earlier"

**Establishing Preferences Through Examples**

If AI keeps making the same mistake, create an
    example that shows the correct pattern:

"When implementing data fetching, always use this
    pattern:
```javascript
async function fetchData() {
  const cacheKey = generateKey();
  const cached = await cache.get(cacheKey);
  if (cached) return cached;

  const fresh = await fetch(source);
  await cache.set(cacheKey, fresh);
  return fresh;
````

}

Now implement fetchUserProfile() following this pattern."

Building Shared Context

Early in a session, establish shared understanding:

"Context for this session: - We're working on a Node.js API server - We use TypeScript strict mode - All database access goes through our ORM (Prisma) - We follow RESTful conventions - We write tests using Jest

Keep this context in mind for all following questions."

This reduces repeated explanations and improves consistency.

Correcting Persistent Errors

If AI repeatedly makes the same mistake:

"I notice you keep using `var` instead of `const/let`. In modern JavaScript: - Use `const` by default - Use `let` if reassignment is needed - Never use `var`

Going forward, always use const/let. Confirm you understand this rule."

Explicit confirmation helps establish the correction.

When to Restart vs. When to Persist

Sometimes a conversation with AI goes off the rails. Deciding whether to restart or persist is important:

- *Restart when.*
- AI is consistently misunderstanding despite multiple corrections
- The conversation has accumulated too much confusing context
- You want to try a completely different approach
- AI is hallucinating heavily and corrections aren't helping
- You've been iterating for >10 rounds without convergence
- *Persist when.*
- You're making steady progress (each iteration improves)
- AI has built up useful context you'd have to re-provide
- The problem is complex but you're narrowing in on solution
- Errors are easy to identify and correct

- *How to restart effectively.*
- Don't start completely fresh—take your learning with you
- Incorporate corrections from the failed session into your new prompt
- Be more explicit about requirements upfront
- Consider breaking the task into smaller pieces

Example of improved restart:

```
First session: "Create a user authentication
    system"
-> AI made many mistakes, had to correct
    repeatedly

Restart session: "Create a user authentication
    system with these requirements:
- Use bcrypt for password hashing (not plain text)
- Generate JWT tokens after successful login
- Validate tokens on protected routes
- Handle these edge cases: [list from first
    session]
Here's an example of our preferred code
    structure: [paste example]"
```

You've learned what to specify upfront from the failed session.

Chapter Summary

- **Working with AI requires new mental models.** Treat AI as a cognitive prosthetic rather than a colleague or simple tool—it extends capability but requires learning to use effectively (Parasuraman and Riley 1997a; Dietvorst et al. 2015).
- **Four interaction modes serve different purposes.** Delegation (low involvement, clear tasks), Collaboration (iterative refinement), Supervision (monitor autonomous work), and Augmentation (AI as extension of self) each suit different contexts (Bainbridge 1983).
- **Choosing the right mode requires judgment.** Consider task clarity, your expertise, stakes, time available, novelty, and desired involvement level.

Mode switching when one approach isn't working is normal and productive.

- **Effective correction requires diagnosis.** Categorize failures (misunderstood requirements, incomplete context, edge cases, wrong patterns, hallucination) and provide specific, actionable feedback rather than vague criticism.
- **Context engineering is the higher-order discipline.** Effective AI collaboration requires shaping the model's entire informational environment — not just the immediate prompt. Techniques like providing role and context, showing examples, requesting step-by-step reasoning, specifying format, using constraints, self-review prompts, and task decomposition are all components of context engineering.
- **Teaching AI within sessions is possible.** Create style guides, establish preferences through examples, build shared context early, and explicitly correct persistent errors with confirmation.
- **Know when to restart.** If making no progress after many iterations, restart with lessons learned. If making steady progress, persist despite imperfections.
- **Emotional regulation matters.** Expect imperfection, separate capability from reliability, take breaks when frustrated, maintain calibrated skepticism, and remember that even imperfect AI assistance often beats working alone (Vaccaro et al. 2018).
- **Maintain appropriate skepticism always.** As we'll explore in Chapter 10, calibrated trust means verifying outputs systematically, especially for high-stakes or novel tasks.

In the next chapter, we'll examine calibrated trust—how to develop systematic judgment about when to trust AI outputs and when to verify them, building the discernment that separates effective AI collaboration from dangerous over-reliance.

Chapter 10

Calibrated Trust

"Trust is good, but control is better." — Vladimir Lenin (attributed)

In 1988, the USS Vincennes, a guided missile cruiser equipped with the Aegis combat system—one of the most sophisticated automated air defense systems ever built—shot down Iran Air Flight 655, killing all 290 civilians aboard. The crew, relying on their automated identification system, believed they were engaging an attacking F-14 fighter jet. The system displayed ambiguous data. Under time pressure and stress, the crew trusted the automation's implicit suggestion rather than seeking disconfirming evidence. Post-incident analysis revealed multiple points where human verification could have prevented the tragedy (Fogarty 1988).

The Vincennes incident exemplifies a phenomenon that has haunted human-automation interaction for decades: *automation bias*—the tendency to favor suggestions from automated systems and to ignore contradictory information from other sources, even when those sources are more reliable (Mosier et al. 1998). As AI systems become more capable and more deeply integrated into engineering workflows, the question of when to trust them—and when to doubt—becomes not just practically important but professionally essential.

This chapter explores the psychology of trust in automated systems, the cognitive mechanisms that lead to both over-reliance and under-utilization, and the practical frameworks engineers need to develop what researchers call *calibrated trust*: trust that is proportional to system reliability and appropriately conditioned on context (Lee and See 2004).

Automation Bias vs. Healthy Skepticism

The literature on automation bias reveals an uncomfortable truth: humans are surprisingly bad at maintaining appropriate skepticism toward automated systems. We tend toward two opposing failure modes—over-trust and under-trust—with over-trust being the more common and dangerous pattern.

The Mechanisms of Automation Bias

Automation bias manifests in two distinct forms, both documented extensively in aviation and medical contexts:

Omission errors occur when humans fail to notice problems because the automated system did not alert them. In a classic study, Parasuraman and colleagues found that pilots using automated monitoring systems missed flight anomalies 55% of the time when the automation failed to alert, compared to only 22% when no automation was present (Parasuraman et al. 1993). The presence of automation actually *reduced* human vigilance.

Commission errors occur when humans follow automated suggestions even when contradictory information is available. In another aviation study, pilots followed incorrect automated flight path recommendations even when conflicting with basic flight principles they had been explicitly trained to recognize (Mosier et al. 2001). The automation's suggestion became the default action, requiring conscious effort to override.

The psychological mechanisms underlying these errors are well understood:

- *Cognitive offloading.* Automation allows humans to redirect attention to other tasks, reducing cognitive load. This is beneficial when automation is reliable, but creates vulnerability when it fails. As Parasuraman and Riley note, "automation changes the nature of the work that human operators do, from active operation to supervision and monitoring" (Parasuraman and Riley 1997a). This shift is cognitively efficient but vigilance-degrading.
- *Diffusion of responsibility.* When automation is present, humans feel less personally accountable for outcomes. Research on "responsibility bias" shows that people attribute less personal responsibility for decisions made with algorithmic assistance, even when they retain final authority (Sah et al. 2021). This psychological distancing reduces the intensity of verification efforts.
- *Perceived expertise.* Automated systems, especially AI systems, are often perceived as more capable or knowledgeable than they actually are. Studies of algorithm aversion and appreciation show a complex pattern: humans sometimes over-trust algorithms in domains where algorithms perform poorly (such as predicting human behavior) while under-trusting them in domains where they excel (such as data-heavy forecasting) (Dietvorst et al. 2015; Logg et al. 2019).

Automation Bias in Software Engineering Contexts

The software engineering domain presents unique challenges for automation bias because the feedback loops are often delayed and the consequences of errors may not be immediately apparent.

Consider a common scenario: an AI code generation tool suggests an implementation. The code compiles, passes basic tests, and appears to solve the stated problem. The engineer, under time pressure and trusting the tool's general reliability, approves and merges the change. Three months later, an edge case emerges in production. The AI's implementation contained a subtle race condition that only manifests under specific load patterns the initial tests didn't cover.

This delayed feedback creates a particularly pernicious form of automation bias. Unlike aviation, where automation failures often manifest immediately and dramatically, software engineering errors may remain latent for extended periods. This temporal distance between decision and consequence undermines learning. Engineers don't develop accurate mental models of when AI systems fail because failures aren't immediately observable.

Recent empirical studies of AI-assisted programming reveal concerning patterns:

- *Reduced code comprehension.* Developers using AI code completion tools showed significantly reduced ability to explain the generated code compared to code they wrote themselves (Prather et al. 2023). When asked to describe the logic of AI-generated functions, participants frequently provided shallow, surface-level explanations that missed subtle implementation details.
- *Verification gaps.* In a study of GitHub Copilot usage, researchers found that developers accepted AI suggestions without full verification in 42% of cases, with acceptance rates increasing as developers gained familiarity with the tool (Barke et al. 2023). Familiarity bred not expertise but complacency.
- *Error propagation.* When AI-generated code contained subtle bugs, developers were more likely to propagate those errors to other parts of the codebase than when they wrote buggy code themselves (Vaithilingam et al. 2023). The automation bias extended beyond the immediate suggestion to influence subsequent design decisions.

The Opposite Problem: Automation Aversion

While automation bias receives more research attention, the opposite phenomenon—*automation aversion*—also merits consideration. Some engineers, especially those early in their AI adoption journey, systematically under-trust AI outputs, refusing to accept valid suggestions and insisting on manual verification even when automation is demonstrably more reliable (Dietvorst et al. 2015).

Automation aversion typically stems from:

- *Algorithm aversion after failure.* Research shows that humans lose trust in algorithms much faster than they lose trust in human experts, even when error rates are equivalent (Dietvorst et al. 2018). A single observed failure can trigger lasting skepticism that's difficult to overcome.
- *Preference for human control.* Many professionals feel discomfort ceding decision authority to machines, regardless of empirical performance. Studies in medical contexts show that physicians sometimes reject algorithmic recommendations even when those recommendations outperform physician judgment by significant margins (Dawes et al. 1989).
- *Lack of explainability.* When engineers don't understand *why* an AI system made a particular suggestion, they're less likely to trust it. Research on explainable AI shows that interpretability significantly increases trust—sometimes excessively so (Poursabzi-Sangdeh et al. 2021).

The challenge is that both automation bias and automation aversion represent *miscalibrated* trust. The goal isn't to always trust or always doubt AI systems—it's to develop trust that accurately reflects actual reliability in specific contexts.

The Domain Verification Advantage

The confident wrongness problem has a specific implication that deserves attention: verification is not a generic skill. It is a domain skill. And this is where the calibrated trust framework meets the vertical mastery argument we develop in Chapter 14.

An experienced security engineer will immediately notice when a model suggests an OAuth flow that skips the state parameter — opening the door to CSRF attacks — or recommends storing JWT refresh tokens in localStorage where they are vulnerable to cross-site scripting, or proposes a rate-limiting strategy that can be trivially bypassed by rotating IP addresses. These errors are invisible to a non-expert. The output reads fluently. The code compiles. The terminology is correct. The security model is broken — but it is broken in ways that require domain knowledge to detect.

The same pattern holds across every technical domain. A database engineer spots the missing composite index that will cause a full table scan at scale. A distributed systems architect sees the consensus protocol that guarantees consistency in the happy path but fails catastrophically during network partitions. A DevOps engineer recognises the Kubernetes configuration that works in development but creates cascading pod evictions under production memory pressure. In each case, the AI output looks correct. It compiles, it runs, it passes basic tests. The failure is structural, and only expertise reveals it.

The practical consequence is that effective AI verification requires the same expertise that effective AI prompting requires. The engineer who knows enough to ask "how should we handle token refresh when the authorization server is temporarily unreachable and the user has an in-flight request?" is also the engineer who can evaluate whether the answer is right. Domain expertise is not one advantage — it is two: better inputs and better filters. This is why, as AI tools become more capable, the gap between expert and non-expert users does not close. It widens.

The industry has settled on a term for the failure mode that uncalibrated trust produces: AI Slop. The label is deliberately unglamorous — it describes code that is functionally correct, passes tests, and ships cleanly, but is architecturally incoherent, unmaintainable, or silently inefficient. It is the output of a low-tier agent operating without adequate constraints, reviewed by an engineer who trusted the output because it compiled. The damage is invisible at merge time and expensive at scale. Recognising AI Slop before it enters the codebase is now a first-order engineering skill — which means calibrated trust is not a soft preference. It is a structural defence against technical debt that no automated pipeline will catch for you.

When to Trust the Model—and When Not To

If both over-trust and under-trust are problematic, how should engineers calibrate their trust in AI systems? The answer lies in understanding the conditions under which AI systems are reliable and developing heuristics for distinguishing high-confidence from low-confidence outputs.

The Reliability Landscape

AI systems are not uniformly reliable across all tasks and contexts. Their reliability depends on multiple factors that engineers must learn to evaluate:

- *Training distribution coverage.* Large language models perform best on tasks that are well-represented in their training data. Code that follows common patterns, uses popular libraries, and solves frequently-encountered problems tends to receive high-quality suggestions. Novel combinations, rare edge cases, and domain-specific requirements are more likely to produce unreliable outputs (Brown et al. 2020).

This creates a subtle trap: AI systems appear most reliable precisely in the areas where human expertise is least necessary. The routine, well-documented tasks where AI excels are also the tasks where human engineers could easily succeed without assistance. The tasks where human expertise is most valuable—novel problems, unusual contexts, subtle edge cases—are precisely where AI is least reliable.

- *Task structure and verifiability.* AI systems perform better on tasks with clear success criteria and easy verification. Generating unit tests is easier than generating complex business logic because test success is objectively determinable. Formatting code is easier than architecting systems because formatting rules are explicit while architectural quality is contextual (Chen et al. 2021).

Engineers should calibrate trust based on verifiability: high trust for tasks where verification is cheap and reliable, lower trust for tasks where verification requires deep expertise or extended observation.

- *Context specificity.* AI systems struggle with context that isn't explicitly provided in the prompt. They can't access information about:
- Legacy system constraints not documented in comments
- Organizational coding standards not captured in the training corpus
- Performance requirements specific to your deployment environment
- Team expertise levels and maintenance considerations
- Political or business constraints on implementation choices

Research on prompt engineering emphasizes that model performance is highly sensitive to context specification (Wei et al. 2022). Insufficient context leads to generic solutions that may be technically correct but contextually inappropriate.

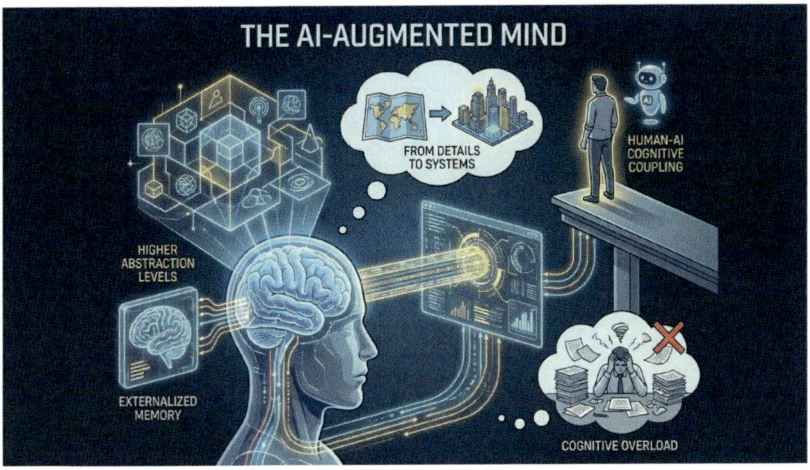

- *Temporal freshness.* AI models are trained on historical data and have explicit knowledge cutoffs. They lack information about:
- Recently discovered vulnerabilities or deprecated practices
- New library versions with breaking changes
- Emerging best practices not yet widely adopted
- Current regulatory or compliance requirements

The software engineering landscape evolves rapidly. Trust should decrease for domains where recent changes are likely.

Heuristics for Calibrated Trust

Based on these reliability factors, engineers can develop practical heuristics for when to trust AI outputs:

High trust scenarios (accept with light verification): 1. **Boilerplate code following standard patterns**: CRUD operations, standard API endpoints, common data transformations 2. **Well-specified transformations**: Refactoring with clear before/after states, format conversions with explicit schemas 3. **Test generation for existing code**: When the code being tested provides ground truth for correctness 4. **Documentation from code**: When source code is the authoritative reference 5. **Tasks with immediate feedback**: When errors will be caught quickly by compilers, tests, or obvious runtime failures

Medium trust scenarios (accept with thorough verification): 1. **Complex business logic**: When rules are subtle and edge cases matter 2. **Performance-critical code**: When efficiency matters and benchmarking is necessary 3. **Security-relevant implementations**: When vulnerabilities have serious consequences 4. **Integration code**: When interactions between components create emergent complexity 5. **Code requiring domain expertise**: When correctness depends on field-specific knowledge

Low trust scenarios (use as inspiration only, verify extensively): 1. **Novel algorithmic approaches**: When the problem is unusual or cutting-edge 2. **System architecture decisions**: When trade-offs are context-dependent 3. **Production incident responses**: When time pressure conflicts with care 4. **Code touching critical paths**: When failures affect system reliability 5. **Anything involving subtle concurrency**: When race conditions and deadlocks are possible

These heuristics should evolve with both AI capabilities and your own experience. What requires thorough verification today may become routine tomorrow. Conversely, newly discovered failure modes should trigger increased skepticism.

Recognizing Confidence Signals

Beyond categorical heuristics, engineers can learn to recognize signals that indicate AI confidence or uncertainty:

- *Language patterns in explanations.* When AI systems provide explanations alongside code, certain linguistic patterns correlate with reliability:
- Definitive language ("this implementation...") vs. hedging language ("this approach might...")
- Specific references to standards or documentation vs. vague generalizations
- Acknowledgment of trade-offs and alternatives vs. presentation of single solutions
- Clear reasoning chains vs. circular or tautological explanations

Research on large language model calibration shows that models do exhibit some ability to express uncertainty through linguistic hedging, though this calibration is imperfect (Kadavath et al. 2022).

- *Consistency across regenerations.* When the same prompt yields substantially different outputs across multiple attempts, this indicates high uncertainty in the model's latent space. Consistency suggests the model has converged on a well-supported solution pattern.

- *Alignment with documented best practices.* Outputs that clearly follow established patterns and best practices are more likely to be reliable than novel or unusual approaches, unless novelty is explicitly desired.

- *Granularity of reasoning.* More detailed, step-by-step reasoning often (but not always) correlates with reliability. Models forced to show their work produce more verifiable outputs, though this is not a guarantee of correctness (Nye et al. 2021).

The Verification Spectrum

Rather than binary trust/distrust decisions, engineers should think in terms of a *verification spectrum*—different levels of checking appropriate to different trust levels:

Level 1: Syntax and type checking (minimal verification) - Does it compile/parse? - Do types align? - Are there obvious syntax errors?

Level 2: Local correctness (basic verification) - Does the code do what it claims locally? - Are edge cases handled? - Do unit tests pass?

Level 3: Integration correctness (moderate verification) - Does it interact correctly with the broader system? - Are APIs used correctly? - Do integration tests pass?

Level 4: Semantic correctness (thorough verification) - Does it solve the right problem? - Are business rules correctly implemented? - Are all requirements satisfied?

Level 5: Systemic correctness (comprehensive verification) - Are performance requirements met? - Are security properties preserved? - Are operational concerns addressed? - Does it align with long-term architectural direction?

High trust scenarios may require only Level 1-2 verification. Low trust scenarios demand Level 4-5 verification. The art lies in matching verification effort to actual risk.

Decision-Making Under Uncertainty

Even with calibrated trust and appropriate verification strategies, engineers face a fundamental challenge: AI outputs often exist in a gray zone where they're neither obviously correct nor obviously wrong. How should engineers make decisions when uncertainty persists after reasonable verification efforts?

The Three Types of Uncertainty

Decision-making under uncertainty requires distinguishing between qualitatively different types of uncertainty:

Epistemic uncertainty stems from lack of knowledge. Could we determine the correct answer with more information, time, or expertise? Epistemic uncertainty is reducible—we can conduct additional tests, consult documentation, or seek expert review.

Aleatoric uncertainty stems from inherent randomness or variability. Even with perfect knowledge, some aspects of system behavior are genuinely unpredictable—race conditions, network latency, user behavior. Aleatoric uncertainty is irreducible but can be characterized probabilistically.

Model uncertainty stems from limitations in the AI system itself. The model may lack the capability to solve certain problems reliably, regardless of prompting strategies. This type of uncertainty is particularly challenging because engineers often can't directly observe model limitations.

These uncertainty types demand different strategies:

- **Epistemic uncertainty**: Invest in verification and information gathering
- **Aleatoric uncertainty**: Design for robustness and graceful degradation
- **Model uncertainty**: Recognize when problems exceed AI capabilities and default to human judgment

Bayesian Updating and Iterative Refinement

A productive mental model for working with AI systems under uncertainty is *Bayesian updating*—treating each AI interaction as providing evidence that updates your beliefs about correctness (Gelman et al. 2013).

The process:

1. **Prior belief**: Based on the trust heuristics above, what's your initial confidence in the AI output? (e.g., "This is a standard CRUD operation, so probably 80% likely to be correct")

2. **Evidence gathering**: Conduct verification appropriate to your prior. Run tests, review code, check edge cases.

3. **Update belief**: Based on verification results, update your confidence. Tests passing increases confidence; discovered issues decrease it.

4. **Decision point**: Is confidence sufficient for your risk tolerance? If yes, proceed. If no, either gather more evidence or reject the output.

5. **Iteration**: If output is rejected, provide feedback to the AI system and regenerate. Each iteration should incorporate learning from previous attempts.

This framework makes the decision process explicit and allows engineers to consciously calibrate their verification effort to their uncertainty level.

The Cost-Benefit Calculus

Every verification decision involves trade-offs between:

- *Cost of verification.* Time spent reviewing, testing, and validating AI outputs
- *Cost of errors.* Consequences if incorrect outputs reach production
- *Opportunity cost.* Value of alternative uses of verification time

The rational strategy is to verify up to the point where the marginal cost of additional verification equals the expected reduction in error costs. In practice, this calculation is rough and intuitive, but the framework helps structure thinking:

For low-stakes decisions (example: variable naming in internal tools): - Cost of errors: Minimal (slight confusion, easy to fix) - Optimal strategy: Light verification, accept quickly, fix if problems emerge

For medium-stakes decisions (example: feature implementation in user-facing product): - Cost of errors: Moderate (user frustration, bug reports, technical debt) - Optimal strategy: Thorough verification before merge, testing in staging

For high-stakes decisions (example: security-critical authentication logic): - Cost of errors: Severe (security breaches, data loss, legal liability) - Optimal strategy: Extensive verification, security review, conservative acceptance criteria

Research on human judgment under uncertainty consistently shows that people struggle with these calibrations, often either over-investing in low-stakes decisions or under-investing in high-stakes ones (Kahneman 2011). Explicit frameworks help counteract these biases.

The Role of Reversibility

Decision theory emphasizes the importance of *reversibility* in uncertainty management (Arrow and Fisher 1974). Decisions that are easily reversible require less upfront verification than irreversible decisions.

In software engineering:

- *Highly reversible decisions.*
- Feature flag-protected changes (can be disabled instantly)
- Internal tool modifications (limited blast radius)
- Additive changes (don't remove existing functionality)

- Well-tested changes (caught by comprehensive test suites)
- *Low reversibility decisions.*
- Database schema migrations (expensive to undo)
- Public API changes (break client code)
- Architectural decisions (create path dependencies)
- Security changes (attacks exploit windows of vulnerability)

Engineers should invest more verification effort in low-reversibility decisions, regardless of AI involvement. AI amplifies the importance of this principle because AI's speed allows making more decisions faster—creating more opportunities for hard-to-reverse mistakes.

Developing Contextual Judgment

The frameworks above provide structure, but they cannot substitute for judgment. The most important skill engineers can develop is *contextual judgment*—the ability to rapidly assess what level of verification a specific situation requires.

This judgment develops through:

- *Deliberate practice.* Consciously reflect on verification decisions. When errors slip through, analyze why. When excessive verification was applied, recognize the inefficiency. Over time, this feedback loop calibrates intuition.
- *Pattern recognition.* Build a mental library of failure modes. "AI tends to miss null checks in this type of function." "Generated SQL often lacks proper indexing considerations." Pattern recognition allows rapid threat identification.
- *Domain expertise.* Deep knowledge of your specific technical domain allows you to spot problems that generic verification processes miss. An expert in distributed systems immediately recognizes when AI-generated code makes unsafe assumptions about network reliability.
- *Team learning.* Share experiences of AI successes and failures. Build collective knowledge about when AI is reliable and when it struggles. Create team-specific heuristics that reflect your particular technical context.

Research on expert judgment consistently shows that experts develop *fast pattern matching* that appears intuitive but is actually the result of extensive experience (Klein 1998). Developing this calibrated judgment with AI systems is one of the most valuable skills engineers can cultivate.

When Uncertainty Demands Human Judgment

Finally, engineers must recognize situations where uncertainty cannot be adequately reduced through verification and where human judgment must prevail:

- *Value judgments.* When trade-offs involve competing values (security vs. usability, performance vs. maintainability), AI systems optimize for explicitly specified objectives but cannot navigate implicit organizational priorities or stakeholder preferences.
- *Novel situations.* When problems are genuinely unprecedented, AI systems trained on historical data lack reliable guidance. Human engineers can reason by analogy, draw on first principles, and make educated guesses in ways AI currently cannot.
- *Long-term consequences.* When decisions have implications that extend beyond immediate verification, human judgment about future maintainability, team dynamics, and strategic direction becomes essential.
- *Ethical implications.* When code has potential impacts on users' privacy, autonomy, or wellbeing, human ethical reasoning must guide decisions, even when AI suggestions are technically sound.

In these situations, AI can inform human judgment but cannot replace it. The engineer's role is to recognize when they've reached the boundary of what verification can resolve and to exercise judgment despite irreducible uncertainty.

Chapter Summary

- **Automation bias** is the tendency to over-trust automated systems and ignore contradictory information. It manifests as omission errors (missing problems automation didn't flag) and commission errors (following automated suggestions despite conflicting evidence) (Parasuraman et al. 1993; Mosier et al. 2001).
- **Cognitive mechanisms** underlying automation bias include cognitive offloading, diffusion of responsibility, and perceived expertise. These mechanisms make appropriate skepticism cognitively effortful (Parasuraman and Riley 1997a; Sah et al. 2021).

- **Automation aversion**, the opposite problem, causes engineers to systematically under-trust AI outputs, often triggered by a single observed failure (Dietvorst et al. 2015, 2018).
- **AI reliability varies** based on training distribution coverage, task structure and verifiability, context specificity, and temporal freshness. Trust should be calibrated to these factors (Brown et al. 2020; Chen et al. 2021; Wei et al. 2022).
- **Trust heuristics** classify scenarios as high-trust (boilerplate, well-specified transformations), medium-trust (complex business logic, integration code), or low-trust (novel algorithms, architectural decisions, critical paths).
- **Verification spectrum** ranges from minimal syntax checking to comprehensive systemic correctness verification. Match verification effort to trust level and risk (Kadavath et al. 2022; Nye et al. 2021).
- **Three types of uncertainty**: Epistemic (reducible through more information), aleatoric (irreducible but characterizable), and model (AI capability limitations). Each requires different strategies (Gelman et al. 2013).
- **Decision-making framework**: Use Bayesian updating to treat each AI interaction as evidence, balance cost of verification against cost of errors, and consider reversibility of decisions (Kahneman 2011; Arrow and Fisher 1974).
- **Contextual judgment** develops through deliberate practice, pattern recognition, domain expertise, and team learning. This calibrated intuition is among the most valuable skills for AI-assisted engineering (Klein 1998).
- **Boundaries of AI judgment**: Value judgments, novel situations, long-term consequences, and ethical implications require human decision-making despite technical uncertainty.

In the next chapter, we'll examine the apprenticeship problem—how junior engineers can develop expertise when AI handles the implementation work that traditionally built foundational skills, and what new paths to mastery look like in an AI-augmented world.

Chapter 11

The Apprenticeship Problem

> "The only way to learn is by doing. But what happens when machines do the doing?" — Adaptation of John Dewey's principle of experiential learning

---

In Chapter 5, we explored how cognitive resilience develops through struggle with hard problems. In Chapter 9, we examined effective patterns for human-AI collaboration. Now we confront a challenge that emerges at the intersection of these concerns: how do engineers develop expertise when AI handles the implementation work that traditionally builds foundational skills?

This is not a hypothetical concern. Organizations are already reporting a phenomenon: junior engineers who rely heavily on AI assistance can generate working code quickly but struggle to debug it, explain it, or modify it when requirements change. They've learned to prompt AI effectively but haven't developed the underlying mental models that make senior engineers valuable.

This chapter examines what we're calling the *apprenticeship problem*—the tension between AI's ability to accelerate work and the human need for deliberate practice to develop expertise. We'll explore why this matters, what's at stake if we get it wrong, and how to design learning paths that leverage AI without undermining skill development.

The central insight: AI doesn't eliminate the need for expertise—it changes how expertise develops and makes certain forms of expertise more valuable. The engineers who understand this will invest in the right skills while using AI to accelerate where it helps rather than hinders learning.

Why Juniors Lose Skills When AI Writes Their Code

The Traditional Skill Development Path

For decades, software engineers have followed a relatively predictable path from novice to expert:

Stage 1: Syntax and Basics (Months 0-6) - Learn language syntax and basic constructs - Write simple programs with loops, conditionals, functions - Make lots of obvious mistakes, debug them manually - Build mental models of how code executes

Stage 2: Common Patterns (Months 6-18) - Recognize and apply standard patterns (MVC, factories, observers) - Handle errors, edge cases, and input validation - Work with APIs, libraries, and frameworks - Start reading others' code to understand approaches

Stage 3: System Thinking (Years 2-4) - Design components that fit into larger systems - Understand trade-offs between approaches - Debug complex multi-component issues - Make architectural decisions for modules

Stage 4: Judgment and Context (Years 4+) - Evaluate competing designs based on context - Anticipate long-term consequences of decisions - Navigate organizational and technical constraints - Mentor others and transfer tacit knowledge

This progression wasn't just chronological—it was *causal*. Each stage built foundations necessary for the next. You couldn't develop system thinking without first internalizing patterns. You couldn't develop judgment without first understanding trade-offs through experience.

The progression was also *embodied*. Junior engineers learned by writing code, seeing it fail, debugging it, understanding *why* it failed, and trying again. This tight feedback loop—write, fail, understand, retry—built intuition that became automatic with practice (Ericsson et al. 1993).

How AI Short-Circuits Development

AI assistance disrupts this progression in several ways that seem beneficial initially but undermine long-term skill development.

Skipping the Struggle

Consider a junior engineer asked to implement input validation. Traditionally: 1. Write validation code from scratch 2. Discover you missed edge cases (empty strings, null, special characters) 3. Debug why certain inputs crash the system

4. Learn defensive programming through painful experience 5. Internalize patterns for validation

With AI assistance: 1. Prompt: "Write input validation for email, password, username" 2. Receive complete, correct validation code 3. Tests pass 4. Move to next task

The AI-assisted path is faster. But what did the engineer learn? They learned that AI can generate validation code. They did *not* learn: - Why certain edge cases matter - How to think defensively about inputs - What kinds of validation are appropriate for different contexts - How to debug validation failures

The struggle—the cognitive work of figuring out what's wrong—is where learning happens. AI removes the struggle, removing the learning opportunity.

The Illusion of Understanding

A more insidious problem: junior engineers who use AI extensively often believe they understand code they didn't write.

An engineer reviews AI-generated code that implements a caching strategy. The code looks reasonable. Tests pass. The engineer can explain what each line does at a surface level. They feel they understand it.

But when asked to modify the code to handle cache invalidation differently, they struggle. When asked why this particular approach was chosen, they can't answer. When a subtle bug appears under load, they can't debug it effectively.

This is the difference between *recognition* and *generation*, between *surface explanation* and *deep understanding* (Chi et al. 1981). The engineer can recognize correct code and explain its mechanics, but they can't generate it themselves or reason deeply about trade-offs.

Research on learning consistently shows that generation—producing something yourself—creates deeper understanding than recognition—evaluating something produced by others (Bjork 1994). AI assistance privileges recognition over generation, creating an illusion of competence.

Pattern Matching Without Principles

Traditional learning forced engineers to understand principles by encountering many instances of the same underlying concept:

A junior implements authentication in three different projects. Each implementation is slightly different (web app, mobile API, microservice). Through these implementations, the engineer extracts the common principles: cryptographic hashing, secure token generation, session management, expiration handling.

These principles, once internalized, transfer to new contexts. The engineer can implement authentication for a new platform they've never seen because they understand the underlying concepts.

With AI assistance, the junior might complete ten authentication implementations without ever extracting the principles. Each time, AI generates context-specific code. The engineer learns "AI can handle authentication" but not "authentication requires these conceptual elements because of these security properties."

The result: engineers who have surface-level familiarity with many patterns but lack the deep understanding that enables transfer to novel situations.

Atrophy of Debugging Skills

Perhaps most concerning: reliance on AI for code generation degrades the debugging skills that are essential for maintaining AI-generated code.

Debugging is a meta-skill—the ability to form hypotheses about what's wrong, test those hypotheses, and iteratively narrow in on problems (Fitzgerald et al. 2008). This skill develops through repeated practice with code you wrote yourself, where you have mental models of what it should do.

When AI writes code and bugs appear, junior engineers often lack the mental models needed for effective debugging. They don't know how the code is supposed to work internally—they only know what output it should produce. This makes debugging dramatically harder.

The common response: ask AI to fix it. Sometimes this works. Often it doesn't—AI generates new code that fixes one issue but introduces another, or that works around the symptom without addressing the cause.

Junior engineers who rely on this pattern don't develop debugging expertise. They become dependent on AI for both generation and fixing, never building the investigative skills that senior engineers use daily.

The Credentialization Trap Realized

We'll examine the credentialization trap in Chapter 16: when the credentials required for a role increase while opportunities to gain those credentials decrease. AI accelerates this trap in software engineering.

Organizations want to hire engineers with 3-5 years of experience—engineers who have debugged complex systems, made architectural decisions, learned from mistakes. But if junior engineers spend those 3-5 years prompting AI rather than implementing, debugging, and learning from failures, they won't develop the expertise the market demands.

The result: a generation of engineers with impressive GitHub portfolios (AI-generated) but shallow expertise. They can generate code quickly but can't maintain it, debug it, or reason deeply about it.

The Empirical Evidence

While systematic research is still emerging, early evidence supports these concerns:

- *Degraded Problem-Solving Performance.* Studies of students using AI assistance show that while they complete assignments faster, they perform worse on assessments that require applying concepts to novel problems (Kasneci et al. 2023). They've learned to use the tool but not the underlying principles.
- *Reduced Code Comprehension.* Engineers who primarily review AI-generated code rather than writing it themselves show reduced ability to predict code behavior and identify bugs (Prather et al. 2023). Recognition doesn't build the mental models that generation does.
- *Dependency Patterns.* Surveys of junior engineers report increased anxiety about coding without AI assistance and reduced confidence in their own ability to solve problems independently (Dakhel et al. 2023). The tool has become a crutch rather than an amplifier.

These aren't inevitable consequences of AI—they're consequences of *how* AI is being used in learning contexts. The solution isn't to ban AI but to redesign learning paths that leverage AI appropriately.

What's at Stake

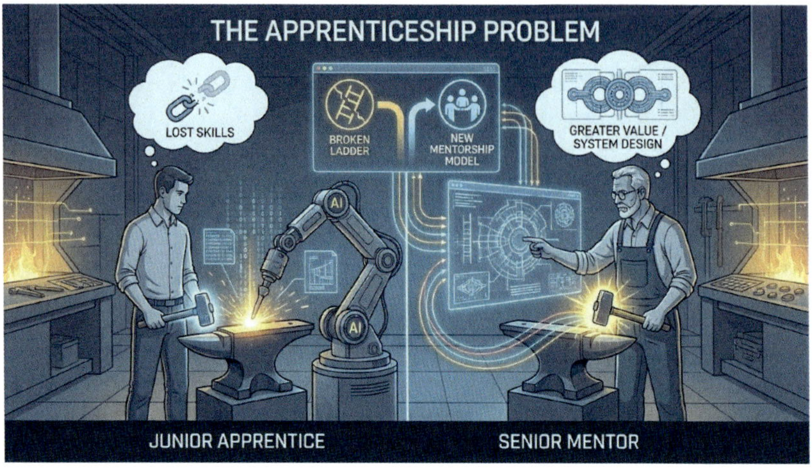

If we fail to address the apprenticeship problem, several concerning outcomes become likely:

- *Bimodal Skill Distribution.* A small group of senior engineers with deep expertise (trained before heavy AI adoption) and a large group of junior engineers with shallow expertise (trained with heavy AI reliance), with few engineers successfully transitioning between groups.
- *Organizational Brittleness.* Teams dependent on a few senior engineers who understand the systems deeply, with junior engineers unable to take ownership when seniors leave. This creates bottlenecks and key-person risk.
- *Innovation Stagnation.* True innovation requires deep understanding of problem spaces and ability to see beyond existing patterns. Engineers trained primarily on AI-generated patterns may lack the conceptual foundations needed for genuine breakthroughs.
- *Economic Stratification.* Engineers who developed expertise before AI become increasingly valuable, commanding premium compensation. Engineers who entered the field during AI dominance struggle to compete, creating wage gaps that correlate with timing rather than talent.

None of these outcomes are certain, but they become more likely if we don't intentionally design learning paths that build genuine expertise while leveraging AI's benefits.

New Mentorship Models for the AI Era

The apprenticeship problem is real, but it's not insurmountable. The solution requires rethinking how junior engineers learn and how senior engineers mentor—not eliminating AI but using it strategically to enhance rather than replace skill development.

The Traditional Mentorship Model

Traditional software engineering mentorship followed a pattern borrowed from craft guilds:

Junior -> Intermediate -> Senior progression with seniors teaching through: - Code review (pointing out problems, suggesting improvements) - Pairing (working together on problems) - Example (juniors observe seniors solving hard problems) - Gradual responsibility increase (juniors take on harder tasks over time)

This model assumed juniors would spend most of their time writing code, making mistakes, and learning from feedback. The bottleneck was implementation time—juniors were slow because they didn't know patterns yet.

AI inverts this dynamic. The bottleneck is no longer implementation speed—AI can implement quickly. The new bottleneck is *understanding*—juniors can generate code faster than they can comprehend it.

This requires new mentorship patterns.

Mentorship Pattern 1: Deliberate Practice Zones

- *The Principle.* Create explicit "AI-free zones" where juniors practice skills without assistance, alongside "AI-assisted zones" where they leverage automation appropriately.

- *How it works.*

Senior engineer and junior agree on learning objectives for a sprint: - "This week, you'll implement API endpoint handlers. No AI assistance for the core logic—you need to practice error handling, input validation, and response formatting manually." - "Once your manual implementation works, *then* use AI to generate tests and documentation. Compare its tests to what you would write."

The AI-free zone isn't punitive—it's deliberate practice designed to build specific skills. The AI-assisted zone shows how AI can accelerate work you already understand.

- *Example conversation.*

Senior: "I see you used AI to generate this entire authentication flow. That's fine for production work, but you're still learning. Let's do it again—this time, implement the password hashing and token generation yourself. You can use AI for boilerplate like route setup."

Junior: "But it'll take longer..."

Senior: "Yes. And you'll learn more. Speed comes from understanding, not from prompting effectively. Right now you need understanding."

- *Why it works.* Deliberate practice requires working at the edge of current ability with immediate feedback (Ericsson et al. 1993). AI removes the struggle, removing the growth opportunity. Explicit practice zones protect learning time while still allowing AI use where appropriate.
- *Implementation.*
- Set learning objectives at sprint start: "Skills to develop this sprint"
- Identify tasks appropriate for deliberate practice (not production-critical, time-boxed)
- Review with senior engineer afterward to consolidate learning
- Graduate to AI assistance once manual competence is demonstrated

Mentorship Pattern 2: Verification-First Learning

- *The Principle.* Teach verification before generation. Juniors learn to evaluate AI-generated code critically before learning to generate themselves.
- *How it works.*

Instead of: "Implement feature X" -> junior prompts AI -> submits code

Try: "AI generated this implementation of feature X. Review it for: - Correctness (does it match requirements?) - Edge cases (what inputs might break it?) - Performance (will it scale?) - Maintainability (can others understand it?) - Security (are there vulnerabilities?)

Write a report of issues found, then fix them."

- *Why it works.* Verification builds the same mental models as generation but provides scaffolding (the AI code as starting point) that makes learning manageable. It develops critical evaluation skills essential for working with AI.
- *Progression.*

1. Verify AI code with detailed guidance on what to check
2. Verify AI code with minimal guidance
3. Generate code yourself, then verify it
4. Generate and verify simultaneously (expertise)

- *Example.*

Week 1: "Here's AI-generated code for user registration. Check: Does it validate emails? Does it hash passwords? Does it handle duplicate usernames? Write up any issues."

Week 4: "Here's AI-generated code for password reset. Review it for correctness, security, and edge cases. You know what to look for now."

Week 8: "Implement password reset yourself. Then have AI generate a solution and compare. What did you do differently? Why?"

Week 12: "Implement and review your own solution for account deletion. You're ready to own this."

Mentorship Pattern 3: Explanation-Driven Understanding

- *The Principle.* Require juniors to explain code thoroughly, whether they wrote it or AI generated it. Inability to explain reveals gaps in understanding.

- *How it works.*

After junior completes a task (with or without AI):

Senior: "Walk me through this code. Not what each line does—explain *why* you made these design choices."

Junior: "Well, AI generated this part..."

Senior: "I know. But *why* does it work this way? Why this data structure and not another? Why these validation rules? Why this error handling approach?"

If junior can't answer, that's the learning opportunity.

- *Deep explanation prompts.*

- "Why this approach rather than [alternative]?"

- "What happens if [edge case]?"

- "What would you change if [requirement changed]?"

- "What could go wrong with this code?"

- "How would you debug this if it failed in production?"

- *Why it works.* Explanation forces active processing that transforms surface understanding into deep understanding (Chi et al. 1994). It reveals where juniors are relying on AI's patterns without comprehension.
- *Red flags that indicate shallow understanding.*
- "I'm not sure, AI wrote it that way"
- Explanations that paraphrase code rather than explain reasoning
- Inability to predict behavior under different conditions
- Can't articulate trade-offs or alternatives
- *Follow-up when understanding is shallow.*

Senior: "Let's work through this together. What problem is this code solving?"

[Walk through reasoning step by step]

Senior: "Now implement a similar solution for [related problem]. Without AI. Come back when you've tried, and we'll discuss."

Mentorship Pattern 4: Progressive Autonomy with AI

- *The Principle.* Gradually increase AI assistance as competence develops, rather than allowing full AI access immediately.
- *How it works.*

Phase 1 (Months 0-3): Minimal AI - Manual implementation of core features - AI only for syntax lookup and documentation - All architectural decisions discussed with senior - Goal: Build foundational mental models

Phase 2 (Months 3-6): Assisted Implementation - AI can generate boilerplate and standard patterns - Junior must verify and explain all AI-generated code - Manual implementation of anything novel or complex - Goal: Learn to evaluate AI output critically

Phase 3 (Months 6-12): Collaborative AI - AI can assist with implementation - Junior makes architectural decisions, AI helps execute - Junior debugs AI-generated code independently - Goal: Develop judgment about when to use AI

Phase 4 (12+ months): Autonomous with AI - Full AI assistance for appropriate tasks - Junior knows when to prompt, when to implement manually - Can mentor other juniors on AI use - Goal: Strategic AI leverage

- *Why it works.* This prevents dependence on AI before foundational skills develop, while still teaching effective AI collaboration as a later-stage skill.
- *Customization.* Progression pace should vary based on:
- Individual learning speed (some ready for Phase 2 sooner)
- Task complexity (novel tasks stay in earlier phases longer)
- Demonstrated competence (phase up when consistently successful)

Mentorship Pattern 5: Real Debugging as Core Practice

- *The Principle.* Since debugging is one of the most critical skills being lost, make it central to learning.
- *How it works.*
- *Weekly debugging sessions.* Senior introduces a bug into junior's codebase (or uses real production bugs, sanitized). Junior must:

1. Reproduce the bug
2. Form hypotheses about causes
3. Test hypotheses systematically
4. Identify root cause
5. Implement fix
6. Verify fix doesn't break other things

No AI assistance during debugging sessions. The goal is building investigative skills.

- *Debrief afterward.*
- What hypotheses did you form?
- How did you test them?
- What led you to the root cause?
- What would you do differently next time?
- *Why it works.* Debugging is a meta-skill that transfers across contexts (Fitzgerald et al. 2008). It's also the skill most degraded by AI reliance. Explicit practice with feedback builds competence that AI can't provide.
- *Variations.*
- Start with simple bugs (syntax, logic errors)
- Progress to complex bugs (race conditions, memory leaks, performance)

- Include bugs in AI-generated code specifically
- Pair juniors on challenging bugs (peer learning)

Mentorship Pattern 6: Architectural Thinking Through Constraints

- *The Principle.* Teach juniors to think architecturally by constraining implementation and discussing trade-offs.
- *How it works.*

Senior: "Implement feature X under these constraints: - Must handle 1000 requests/second - Must use less than 100MB memory - Must respond within 100ms - Must work with our existing database schema

Sketch your architecture before implementing. We'll discuss trade-offs before you code."

Junior presents design. Senior asks: - "Why this approach?" - "What if load doubles?" - "What's the failure mode?" - "How does this interact with [other system]?"

- *Then.* Junior implements (with or without AI as appropriate)
- *Why it works.* Constraints force consideration of trade-offs that juniors otherwise ignore. Discussion before implementation builds architectural thinking—the skill AI struggles with most.
- *Progressive difficulty.*
- Start with simple constraints (performance, memory)
- Add complexity (distributed systems, consistency requirements)
- Introduce conflicting constraints (fast AND cheap AND reliable)
- Move toward real production constraints
- *Key insight.* The value isn't in the implementation—it's in the reasoning about trade-offs before implementation. AI can implement; juniors need to learn to reason about what *should* be implemented.

Mentorship Pattern 7: Post-Mortem Learning

- *The Principle.* Learning from failures is essential, but AI prevents many learning-rich failures. Create structured reflection on both successes and failures.
- *How it works.*

Weekly retrospective with junior: - What did you build this week? - What went well? Why? - What went wrong? Why? - What would you do differently? - What did you learn?

- *Focus on failures as learning opportunities.*
- Bug that reached production -> What should have caught it?
- Performance issue -> What assumptions were wrong?
- Feature rejected in review -> What was misunderstood?
- *AI-specific questions.*
- What did AI help with effectively?
- Where did AI lead you astray?
- What AI-generated code had bugs? Why?
- When did you override AI? Why was that right?
- *Why it works.* Deliberate reflection transforms experience into expertise (Kolb 1984). Without reflection, engineers repeat mistakes or fail to extract lessons from successes.
- *Documentation.* Keep a learning journal (shared with senior) recording:
- Problems encountered
- Solutions attempted
- What worked/didn't work
- Lessons extracted

This becomes a personalized knowledge base and demonstrates learning progress.

How Seniors Become Even More Valuable

The apprenticeship problem creates challenges for juniors, but it simultaneously increases the value of senior engineers who possess genuine expertise. Understanding this dynamic helps both seniors leverage their position and organizations invest appropriately in developing senior talent.

The Experience Gap Widens

As AI makes implementation faster but learning slower, the gap between junior and senior capabilities widens:

- *Before AI.*
- Junior: Takes 3 days to implement feature
- Senior: Takes 1 day to implement same feature
- Gap: 3x productivity difference
- *With AI.*
- Junior with AI: Takes 4 hours to implement feature (but produces fragile code requiring senior review and likely refactoring)
- Senior with AI: Takes 1 hour to implement feature (produces robust, maintainable code)
- Gap: 4x productivity difference, but also quality difference

The junior closed the implementation *speed* gap but widened the *quality* gap. The senior still needs to review, fix, and often refactor the junior's AI-generated code.

- *More importantly, the architectural gap widens.*
- Juniors can implement specified features quickly
- Seniors can determine *which* features to build, *how* they should fit together, and *why* certain approaches are better

This is the movement up the three-layer framework from Chapter 1. AI pushes juniors to operate primarily at Execution, while seniors operate increasingly at Design and Intent.

Scarce Skills Become More Valuable

Several skills that seniors possess become dramatically more valuable in an AI era:

1. Contextual Judgment

Seniors know: - Which AI suggestions are appropriate for this codebase (not just technically correct) - How this implementation will interact with systems built five years ago - Why certain approaches were tried and rejected previously - Which short-term expedients will become long-term problems

This institutional knowledge can't be replicated by AI or quickly learned by juniors. It accumulates over years of seeing consequences play out.

- *Value proposition.* Seniors prevent costly mistakes that juniors + AI would make by lacking context.

2. Debugging Expertise

When AI-generated code fails in production—as it inevitably does—seniors who can: - Quickly isolate root causes - Reason about complex system interactions - Debug without relying on AI - Fix issues without introducing new bugs

...become invaluable.

As systems become more complex (partly because AI makes building complexity faster), debugging expertise becomes scarcer and more critical.

- *Value proposition.* Seniors resolve production issues that juniors + AI cannot.

3. Architectural Vision

AI can implement architectures. Seniors can *design* architectures that: - Balance competing requirements - Anticipate future needs - Align with organizational constraints - Maintain conceptual integrity

This is design at the Intent layer—deciding what should exist, not just how to make it exist.

- *Value proposition.* Seniors prevent architectural debt that would cost exponentially more to fix later.

4. Mentorship Capability

As the apprenticeship problem becomes recognized, organizations realize they need seniors who can teach juniors effectively in an AI era. This is a new meta-skill—understanding how to develop expertise when AI is present.

Seniors who can: - Design learning paths that build real skills - Identify when juniors are over-relying on AI - Create deliberate practice opportunities - Transfer tacit knowledge effectively

...become force multipliers for entire teams.

- *Value proposition.* Seniors who mentor well create capable juniors, reducing the organization's dependence on seniors long-term.

5. System-Wide Thinking

As systems grow more complex (AI makes building faster, so systems get larger), understanding how everything fits together becomes rarer and more valuable.

Seniors who can: - Hold mental models of entire systems - Reason about cross-component interactions - Identify bottlenecks and failure modes - Plan migrations and refactorings

...provide value that's increasingly difficult to replicate.

- *Value proposition.* Seniors prevent system-level failures and enable system-level improvements.

The Mentorship Premium

Organizations that understand the apprenticeship problem will pay premium compensation for seniors who can mentor effectively. This creates a two-tiered senior track:

- *Individual Contributors (IC).* High technical ability, primarily focused on their own output
- *Technical Leaders (TL).* High technical ability + mentorship capability

The TL track commands higher compensation because these engineers multiply team effectiveness. One senior who mentors five juniors into competent mid-level engineers provides more organizational value than one senior producing code alone.

This shifts how seniors should think about career development:

- *Before AI.* Path to senior was primarily technical skill accumulation
- *With AI.* Path to high-value senior requires technical skill + mentorship capability + architectural vision

Seniors who invest in teaching skills position themselves for the highest compensation and job security.

Building Leverage Through Multiplication

The most successful seniors in an AI era will be those who learn to multiply their effectiveness through strategic use of both AI and junior engineers.

Leverage Pattern 1: Architectural Leadership

Senior designs system architecture, juniors + AI implement components, senior reviews and integrates.

- *Multiplier effect.* One senior architects 5x as much as they could implement alone, because implementation is distributed across juniors + AI.

- *Key skill.* Ability to decompose systems into implementable pieces with clear interfaces.

Leverage Pattern 2: Code Review at Scale

Senior reviews all AI-generated and junior-written code before merge, catching issues early.

- *Multiplier effect.* Prevents bugs from reaching production, reduces debugging time later.
- *Key skill.* Ability to quickly assess code quality and identify subtle issues.

Leverage Pattern 3: Pattern Extraction and Documentation

Senior identifies patterns emerging across the codebase, documents them, and ensures juniors + AI follow them.

- *Multiplier effect.* Consistency across team increases maintainability and reduces integration issues.
- *Key skill.* Pattern recognition and clear technical communication.

Leverage Pattern 4: Strategic AI Direction

Senior determines which tasks are appropriate for AI delegation, which require human implementation, and which need hybrid approaches.

- *Multiplier effect.* Team uses AI optimally—fast where it helps, careful where it might harm.
- *Key skill.* Judgment about AI capabilities and limitations in specific contexts.

The Teaching-Learning Loop

Perhaps most importantly, seniors who mentor effectively don't just help juniors—they deepen their own expertise through teaching.

Research on learning shows that teaching forces: - Explicit articulation of tacit knowledge - Recognition of gaps in one's own understanding - Reorganization of knowledge for communication - Exposure to fresh perspectives and questions (Chi et al. 1994)

Seniors who explain *why* certain approaches are better, not just *what* to do, strengthen their own understanding. Juniors asking "Why?" forces seniors to examine assumptions they've taken for granted.

This creates a virtuous cycle: 1. Senior mentors junior 2. Explaining deepens senior's understanding 3. Junior's questions reveal gaps 4. Senior fills gaps, becomes more expert 5. Senior is better equipped to mentor next junior

Organizations that create this teaching-learning loop develop both strong juniors and increasingly expert seniors.

Positioning for Long-Term Success

For seniors, the strategic question is: how do I position myself as AI capabilities continue to advance?

- *Invest in skills that are hard to automate.*
- Contextual judgment (requires organizational knowledge)
- Architectural vision (requires understanding stakeholder needs)
- Mentorship (requires reading people and adapting teaching)
- System-wide thinking (requires holding complex mental models)
- *Develop communication abilities.*
- Technical writing (documenting decisions for future engineers)
- Teaching (transferring knowledge effectively)
- Stakeholder management (translating technical to business)
- *Build organizational capital.*
- Become the person who understands the system deeply
- Build relationships across teams
- Develop reputation for sound judgment
- Create documentation that preserves knowledge
- *Stay current with AI capabilities.*
- Understand what AI can do well (to leverage it)
- Understand what AI does poorly (to know where humans add value)
- Experiment with new models and tools
- Share AI best practices with team

The seniors who thrive won't be those who resist AI, nor those who become entirely dependent on it. They'll be those who understand the complementarity we've discussed throughout this book—using AI for what it does well while investing in the distinctly human capabilities that become more valuable as AI advances.

Chapter Summary

- **The apprenticeship problem is real.** Junior engineers who rely heavily on AI can generate code quickly but often lack the deep understanding, debugging skills, and architectural thinking that senior engineers possess (Ericsson et al. 1993; Chi et al. 1981).
- **AI short-circuits traditional skill development.** By removing the struggle where learning happens, AI prevents juniors from building foundational mental models, debugging expertise, and principled understanding (Bjork 1994).
- **The credentialization trap accelerates.** Organizations need experienced engineers, but AI prevents juniors from gaining the experience that builds expertise, creating a skills gap (Fitzgerald et al. 2008).
- **New mentorship patterns are needed.** Deliberate practice zones, verification-first learning, explanation-driven understanding, progressive autonomy, debugging practice, architectural thinking through constraints, and post-mortem reflection all help juniors develop genuine expertise while leveraging AI appropriately.
- **Seniors become more valuable, not less.** As AI makes implementation faster but learning slower, the gap between junior and senior capability widens. Contextual judgment, debugging expertise, architectural vision, mentorship capability, and system-wide thinking all increase in value.
- **The mentorship premium emerges.** Organizations will pay premium compensation for seniors who can both produce excellent work and mentor juniors effectively, multiplying team capability (Chi et al. 1994; Kolb 1984).
- **Strategic leverage matters.** Seniors who learn to multiply effectiveness through architectural leadership, code review at scale, pattern extraction, and strategic AI direction will be most successful.
- **Teaching deepens expertise.** Mentoring forces seniors to articulate tacit knowledge, recognize gaps, and strengthen understanding—creating a virtuous cycle that benefits both mentor and mentee.

- **Long-term positioning requires investment.** Seniors should develop skills that resist automation (judgment, architecture, mentorship, communication) while staying current with AI capabilities and building organizational capital.
- **The complementarity pattern continues.** Just as AI automation makes human judgment more valuable (the Obsolescence Paradox), AI-accelerated implementation makes genuine expertise more valuable. The engineers who understand this will invest wisely in skill development.

In the next chapter, we'll explore the AI-augmented mind—examining how engineers can think differently when AI extends cognitive capabilities, and what new forms of intelligence emerge from effective human-AI collaboration.

Chapter 12

The AI-Augmented Mind

"The essence of intelligence is not what you know, but what you do when you don't know." — Jean Piaget

---

In the previous chapters, we've explored how to collaborate with AI (Chapter 9), when to trust it (Chapter 10), and how to develop expertise alongside it (Chapter 11). Now we turn to a more fundamental question: how does AI change *how we think*?

This is not a metaphorical question. When engineers work extensively with AI systems, their cognitive processes adapt. They begin to think at different levels of abstraction. They externalize memory and computation that they once held internally. They develop new problem-solving patterns that leverage AI's capabilities while preserving human judgment.

This chapter examines the AI-augmented mind—not as a distant future possibility but as an emerging reality. We'll explore how cognitive load shifts when AI handles certain mental tasks, how thinking patterns change when operating at higher abstraction levels, and what new forms of intelligence emerge from effective human-AI cognitive coupling.

The central insight: AI doesn't just help us work faster—it fundamentally changes *how* we work by altering the cognitive landscape. Engineers who understand these changes and adapt their thinking patterns deliberately will have profound advantages over those who simply use AI as a faster search engine.

Cognitive Load and Externalized Memory

Understanding Cognitive Load

Human cognition operates under well-documented constraints. Cognitive load theory, developed by John Sweller and colleagues, identifies three types of mental burden (Sweller 1988):

- *Intrinsic load.* The inherent complexity of what you're trying to understand. Learning recursion has higher intrinsic load than learning a for-loop because the concept itself is more complex. This load can't be reduced—it's fundamental to the material.
- *Extraneous load.* Mental effort spent on irrelevant or poorly presented information. Searching through poorly organized documentation, deciphering cryptic error messages, or navigating confusing interfaces all impose extraneous load. This load can and should be minimized through better design.
- *Germane load.* Mental effort devoted to building understanding—constructing mental models, recognizing patterns, integrating new knowledge with existing knowledge. This is productive cognitive work that leads to learning and expertise.

Effective learning and problem-solving require minimizing extraneous load while managing intrinsic load to leave capacity for germane load. When all three types of load exceed working memory capacity—approximately 7±2 chunks of information (Miller 1956)—performance degrades dramatically.

AI's most immediate cognitive benefit is reducing extraneous load. Rather than interrupting your thinking to search documentation, you ask AI. Rather than context-switching to remember syntax, AI completes it. Rather than manually checking for common errors, AI flags them.

This reduction in extraneous load frees cognitive capacity for higher-level thinking—but only if engineers use that freed capacity wisely.

The Externalization of Memory

Human memory is reconstructive, not reproductive. We don't store perfect copies of information—we store compressed representations that we reconstruct on demand (Bartlett 1932). This reconstruction is imperfect and subject to distortion, but it's also flexible and associative in ways that make it excellent for creative problem-solving.

AI provides a different kind of memory: vast, precise, and instantly retrievable, but lacking the associative flexibility of human memory. This creates opportunities for cognitive offloading—delegating certain memory tasks to AI while preserving human memory for tasks it does well.

What to externalize to AI:

- *Factual recall.* APIs, syntax, standard algorithms, library functions, configuration formats. These are stable facts that don't benefit from human reconstructive memory. Let AI be the reference manual.
- *Code examples.* Common patterns, boilerplate, standard implementations. AI can retrieve these faster and more accurately than human memory.
- *Documentation.* Function signatures, parameter types, return values. These change with library versions; AI can track them better than humans.
- *Error patterns.* Common bugs and their solutions. AI has seen millions of error messages and can match yours to known patterns faster than you can remember whether you've seen this before.

What to keep in human memory:

- *Conceptual understanding.* Why algorithms work, when they're appropriate, how they fail. This understanding enables transfer to new situations.
- *System context.* How components relate, where bottlenecks are, what past decisions were made and why. This context rarely appears in documentation but shapes every decision.
- *Problem-solving strategies.* Approaches to debugging, ways to decompose problems, heuristics for making trade-offs. These meta-cognitive skills guide all work.
- *Domain knowledge.* Understanding of the business, users, constraints, and goals. This contextual knowledge determines what's worth building.

The key insight: externalize *retrieval* to AI, but internalize *understanding.* Don't waste mental capacity memorizing API details, but do invest in understanding architectural principles.

Practical Patterns for Memory Externalization

Pattern 1: Just-In-Time Knowledge Retrieval

Instead of: Interrupting your thinking to search Stack Overflow, read documentation, and reconstruct context.

Try: Ask AI inline, get the answer immediately, continue thinking.

Example:

```
You're implementing authentication. You know you
    need to hash passwords but
```

```
can't remember the exact bcrypt syntax.

Old pattern:
1. Stop coding
2. Open browser
3. Search "bcrypt nodejs"
4. Scan documentation
5. Find example
6. Adapt to your code
7. Resume thinking (but context is now cold)

New pattern:
1. Ask AI: "Show bcrypt password hashing in Node"
2. Get example inline
3. Adapt and continue (context stays warm)
```

- *Time saved.* 2-3 minutes. **Cognitive benefit**: Maintained flow state (Csikszentmihalyi 1990).

Pattern 2: Offloading Syntax Details

Your working memory holds the *logic* you're implementing. Let AI handle syntax details so you don't waste capacity on semicolons and brackets.

Example:

```
You're implementing a validation function. You
    think:

"I need to check: email format valid, password at
    least 8 chars with one
number, username alphanumeric only, all fields
    non-empty"

Old pattern: Hold this logic in mind WHILE ALSO
    remembering:
- Regex syntax for email validation
- JavaScript string methods for length checking
- Whether to use .test() or .match()
- How to structure the return object

New pattern: Describe the logic, let AI handle
```

```
    syntax:

"Write validation that checks:
- Email matches email format
- Password ≥8 chars with ≥1 number
- Username alphanumeric only
- All fields non-empty
Return {valid: bool, errors: string[]}"
```

AI generates syntactically correct code. You verify the *logic* matches your intent. Your working memory stayed focused on logic, not syntax.

Pattern 3: Context Compression

When returning to a complex problem after interruption, you must rebuild mental context. AI can help compress and restore context efficiently.

Example:

```
You were debugging a race condition in payment
    processing yesterday. Today
you return but the context is gone.

Old pattern:
- Re-read code
- Trace through execution mentally
- Remember what you discovered
- Reconstruct your hypotheses
- Continue debugging

New pattern:
- Ask AI: "I'm debugging a race condition in
    payment processing where two
  concurrent requests can double-charge. I found
      it happens when [your notes
  from yesterday]. What should I investigate
      next?"
- AI reconstructs likely context and suggests
    next steps
- You verify the context matches your
    understanding
- Continue with context restored
```

Pattern 4: Error Message Translation

Cryptic error messages impose extraneous cognitive load—effort spent decoding the message rather than solving the problem.

Example:

```
Error: "Cannot read property 'data' of undefined
    at async processPayment
(payment.js:47)"

Old pattern:
- Read error carefully
- Form hypothesis about what's undefined
- Check line 47
- Check what calls processPayment
- Check what passes data
- Eventually isolate the issue

New pattern:
- Paste error + relevant code to AI
- Get immediate hypothesis: "The API response is
    undefined, likely because
  the fetch failed but you're not checking for
      errors before accessing
  response.data"
- Verify hypothesis (check network errors)
- Fix the actual issue
```

AI translates from error message to likely cause, reducing extraneous load.

When Externalization Becomes Dependency

The danger of memory externalization is crossing from useful offloading to harmful dependency. The difference:

- *Useful offloading.* "I don't need to memorize API details because I can retrieve them instantly. This frees me to think about architecture."
- *Harmful dependency.* "I can't implement anything without AI because I never learned the underlying concepts."

The distinction lies in *understanding*. If you understand *why* something works but use AI to recall *how* to implement it, that's offloading. If you don't understand why and rely on AI to provide both understanding and implementation, that's dependency.

- *Red flags of dependency.*
- Can't explain code you just asked AI to generate
- Feel anxious coding without AI assistance
- Can't debug AI-generated code when it fails
- Don't understand trade-offs between AI-suggested approaches
- Unable to complete tasks when AI isn't available
- *Healthy offloading looks like.*
- Use AI for syntax but understand algorithms
- Ask AI for implementation but verify correctness yourself
- Delegate boilerplate but maintain architectural decisions
- Retrieve examples but adapt them with understanding
- Continue working (slower) when AI unavailable

The goal is *cognitive augmentation*, not *cognitive replacement*. AI should make you smarter by freeing mental resources for high-level thinking, not make you dependent by preventing you from developing understanding.

Thinking at Higher Abstraction Levels

The Abstraction Ladder

Software engineering has always involved working at multiple levels of abstraction simultaneously. The skilled engineer can think about bit patterns, data structures, algorithms, system architecture, and business value—often within the same problem-solving session.

AI doesn't eliminate this multi-level thinking, but it does shift which levels engineers spend time on. When AI handles low-level implementation details automatically, engineers naturally gravitate toward higher abstraction levels.

Consider the abstraction ladder for implementing a feature:

Level 0: Machine Code Raw instructions, memory addresses, registers. Almost no one thinks at this level anymore—compilers handle it.

Level 1: Language Syntax Semicolons, brackets, type declarations, method signatures. Traditional coding spent significant time here. AI now handles much of this automatically through code completion and generation.

Level 2: Algorithms and Data Structures Loops, conditionals, standard algorithms, appropriate data structures. This is traditional "coding" work. AI can now implement standard algorithms from description, but novel algorithmic work remains human.

Level 3: Software Patterns Design patterns, architectural styles, component organization. AI is beginning to suggest patterns but cannot yet choose appropriately without human guidance on context.

Level 4: System Design How components interact, trade-offs between approaches, scalability considerations, failure modes. Primarily human territory—AI can suggest alternatives but not evaluate context-appropriately.

Level 5: Business Value What problems are worth solving, which features matter to users, how technical decisions align with organizational goals. Entirely human—requires understanding stakeholder needs and strategic context.

- *The shift.* AI competence at Levels 0-2 pushes human cognition toward Levels 3-5. This isn't just about spending more time on higher levels—it's about *thinking differently* at those levels.

How Thinking Changes at Higher Abstraction

When you're no longer mentally compiling syntax or recalling API details, cognitive capacity becomes available for different kinds of thinking:

From Implementation to Design

Traditional thinking: "How do I implement this function?" - What data structures do I need? - What's the algorithm? - How do I handle errors? - What's the syntax?

AI-augmented thinking: "What should this function do?" - What's the interface contract? - What are the edge cases? - How does this fit into the larger system? - What are failure modes and recovery strategies?

The cognitive shift: from *how to build* to *what to build* and *whether it's the right thing to build.*

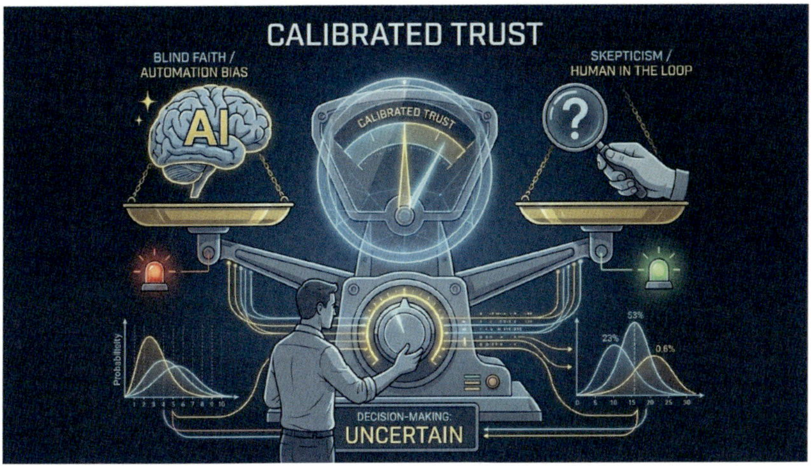

From Local to Global

Traditional thinking focused on the function or module you're currently implementing. Working memory was consumed by local details.

AI-augmented thinking can maintain broader context: - How does this component interact with others? - What are system-wide implications of this decision? - What patterns am I establishing that will propagate? - What constraints from other parts of the system affect this?

When AI handles local implementation, you can think more about global coherence—the "conceptual integrity" that Brooks identified as essential to great systems (Brooks 1975).

From Concrete to Abstract

Traditional thinking: "This function needs to validate an email, this one validates a phone number, this one validates a postal code..."

AI-augmented thinking: "I'm implementing validation. What's the general pattern? Should these share a common interface? What validation concerns are universal versus domain-specific?"

When implementation is fast, you can afford to step back and think about patterns, abstractions, and reusability before diving into concrete cases.

From Sequential to Parallel Exploration

Traditional thinking: Implement approach A, see if it works, if not try approach B.

AI-augmented thinking: Ask AI to generate three different approaches in parallel, evaluate them comparatively, choose the best or synthesize elements from multiple options.

This is closer to how designers work—sketching multiple alternatives quickly before committing to one. AI enables this exploratory mode for code.

Practical Examples of Higher-Level Thinking

Example 1: API Design

Without AI, you might think:

```
"I need an endpoint to create users. Let me
    implement the handler:
- Parse request body
- Validate fields
- Check for duplicates
- Hash password
- Insert to database
- Return response"
```

You're thinking at implementation level (Level 2-3).

With AI handling implementation, you think:

```
"I'm designing user management APIs. Questions:
- RESTful or GraphQL? (Trade-offs: REST is
    standard, GraphQL gives
  flexibility)
- Sync or async creation? (Might need to send
    verification emails)
- How does this API version? (Breaking changes to
    user model later?)
- What's the error model? (Consistent with other
    endpoints?)
- What rate limiting? (Account creation is abuse-
    prone)
- What's the security model? (Who can create
    users? Admin only?
  Self-registration?)"
```

You're thinking at design level (Level 3-4). These questions are more important than implementation details, but traditionally got less attention because implementation consumed cognitive capacity.

Example 2: Debugging Production Issues

Without AI, debugging proceeds sequentially:

```
1. Reproduce the issue
2. Add logging
3. Deploy
4. Wait for issue to recur
5. Examine logs
6. Form hypothesis
7. Test hypothesis
8. Repeat if wrong
```

This is slow, and working memory is consumed by tactical details.

With AI, you can think more strategically:

```
1. Describe symptoms to AI: "Users report
    intermittent 500 errors during
   checkout, mostly afternoon peak, not
       reproducible in staging"

2. AI suggests possible causes:
   - Database connection pool exhaustion under
       load
   - Rate limiting from payment provider
   - Memory leak causing periodic crashes
   - Race condition in concurrent order processing

3. You evaluate these hypotheses with context AI
    lacks:
   - We did increase traffic recently (supports
       connection pool theory)
   - Payment provider is new (rate limiting
       plausible)
   - Memory stable in monitoring (unlikely leak)
   - Orders are idempotent (race condition
       shouldn't cause 500s)

4. Focus investigation on top two theories
5. Ask AI for diagnostic queries for each
6. Execute in parallel rather than sequentially
```

AI enables parallel hypothesis generation and testing rather than serial search. Your thinking stays at system level rather than getting stuck in implementation details of logging.

Example 3: Refactoring Decisions

Traditional refactoring thinking:

```
"This function is 200 lines, I should break it
    up."
-> Spend hours splitting it carefully
-> Maybe improve it, maybe not
```

AI-augmented refactoring thinking:

```
"This function is complex. What are the
    underlying reasons?
- Multiple responsibilities that should separate?
- Complex control flow that could simplify with
    better structure?
- Mixing business logic with infrastructure
    concerns?

Ask AI to analyze the function and suggest
    separation strategies.
AI proposes three approaches:
A) Extract helper functions for each logical step
B) Split into separate functions by responsibility
C) Refactor to strategy pattern for different
    cases

Evaluate which matches the system's actual
    complexity:
- If it's just long but clear -> A is sufficient
- If responsibilities are mixed -> B is
    appropriate
- If behavior varies by type -> C prevents
    future conditional explosion

Choose based on system evolution likely path, not
    just current code."
```

You're thinking about *why* to refactor and *what pattern* serves the system's future, not just mechanically improving code.

The Risk of Abstraction Drift

Operating at higher abstraction levels is powerful but creates a risk: losing touch with ground-level reality.

Abstraction drift occurs when engineers think primarily at high levels without maintaining connection to implementation details. This manifests as:

- *Architectural decisions that ignore practical constraints.* Designing systems that look elegant at Level 4 but are painful to implement at Level 2. Example: Proposing microservices architecture without understanding the operational complexity of distributed systems.
- *Underestimating implementation complexity.* Assuming "just implement X" is straightforward when X is actually subtle and difficult. Example: "Just add caching" without recognizing cache invalidation complexity.
- *Losing debugging capability.* When things break, inability to dive into implementation details to diagnose issues. Example: System fails in production, engineer can describe architecture but can't read logs or trace execution.
- *Poor code review.* Approving high-level design without catching implementation issues. Example: Accepting pull request because architecture is sound, missing that implementation has subtle race condition.
- *Prevention requires maintaining bidirectional movement on the abstraction ladder.* regularly dropping down to implementation details even when AI could handle them. This is deliberate practice (Chapter 11) applied to abstraction level management.
- *Practical tactics.*
- Implement some features manually even when AI could handle them
- Debug issues yourself rather than only asking AI for solutions
- Read AI-generated code carefully rather than trusting it blindly
- Mentor juniors by explaining both high-level design and low-level details
- Periodically review production code at implementation level

The goal: maintain *fluency* at all abstraction levels while *focusing effort* at high levels. You can think abstractly effectively only if you understand concretely thoroughly.

Human–AI Cognitive Coupling

What Is Cognitive Coupling?

When two intelligences work together extensively, their thinking processes become coupled—each adapts to the other's patterns, and capabilities emerge that neither possesses alone.

This happens with human teams. A software engineer and UX designer working closely develop shared mental models: the engineer thinks about user experience earlier, the designer considers technical constraints earlier, and their collaborative thinking becomes more than the sum of individual contributions.

Something analogous is emerging with human-AI collaboration. Engineers who work extensively with AI systems develop new cognitive patterns that leverage AI's strengths while preserving human judgment. The result is a coupled cognitive system—not quite human, not quite AI, but a hybrid that operates differently than either alone.

This is not science fiction. It's happening now, whenever an engineer's problem-solving approach shifts because AI is available. Understanding these coupling patterns helps engineers develop them deliberately rather than haphazardly.

Coupling Pattern 1: Hypothesis Generation and Evaluation

- *Traditional solo thinking.* Form hypotheses sequentially based on experience. Test each hypothesis. If wrong, form another.
- *Human-AI coupled thinking.* Human and AI form hypotheses in parallel. Human evaluates all hypotheses quickly based on contextual knowledge AI lacks.

Example:

```
Problem: Database queries slow after recent
    deployment

Solo engineer:
- Hypothesis 1: New code has N+1 query problem
  Test: Profile queries -> Not the issue
- Hypothesis 2: Database needs vacuuming
  Test: Check table stats -> Not the issue
- Hypothesis 3: New indexes not being used
```

```
  Test: Check query plans -> This is it!

Time: 60 minutes (3 hypotheses × 20 minutes each)

Coupled engineer:
- Ask AI: "What typically causes query slowdown
    after deployment?"
- AI generates 8 hypotheses in 10 seconds:
  1. N+1 query problem
  2. Missing indexes
  3. Stale statistics
  4. Lock contention
  5. Connection pool exhaustion
  6. Query plan regression
  7. ORM lazy loading
  8. Increased data volume

- Engineer evaluates based on context:
  "We optimized queries recently (rules out 1, 7)
   Data volume stable (rules out 8)
   No configuration changes (rules out 3, 5)
   Likely candidates: 2, 4, 6"

- Test top 3 in parallel
- Find the issue: Query plan regression from
    statistics change

Time: 20 minutes (10 hypotheses, 3 tested)
```

The coupling: AI provides breadth (many hypotheses quickly), human provides depth (contextual filtering). Together, they search the problem space more efficiently than either alone.

Coupling Pattern 2: Iterative Refinement Loops

- *Traditional solo work.* Think -> Implement -> Review -> Revise. Each cycle takes significant time.
- *Human-AI coupled work.* Think -> Prompt -> Review AI output -> Refine prompt -> Review -> Iterate rapidly until satisfactory.

The coupling creates a tight feedback loop where human thinking and AI generation converge on solutions faster than either sequential thinking or pure AI generation.

Example:

```
Task: Design error handling for payment processing

Solo approach:
- Think about error cases (30 minutes)
- Implement error handling (60 minutes)
- Test and find cases you missed (30 minutes)
- Revise implementation (30 minutes)
Total: 2.5 hours

Coupled approach:
Round 1: "Implement error handling for payment
    processing"
-> AI generates basic try-catch (30 seconds)
-> Review: "This doesn't handle network timeouts
    specifically"

Round 2: "Add specific handling for network
    timeouts with retry logic"
-> AI adds retry (30 seconds)
-> Review: "Need exponential backoff, not
    constant retry interval"

Round 3: "Use exponential backoff with max 3
    retries"
-> AI implements exponential backoff (30 seconds)
-> Review: "What about payment provider errors
    like 'card declined'?"

Round 4: "Handle payment provider errors
    separately from network errors"
-> AI separates error types (30 seconds)
-> Review: "Good, but need to log differently
    for these error types"

Round 5: "Add structured logging with error type,
    payment ID, and details"
```

```
-> AI adds comprehensive logging (30 seconds)
-> Review: Final check, looks complete

Total: 15 minutes (5 rounds × ~3 minutes)
```

The coupling: Human provides direction and evaluation at each step. AI provides immediate implementation. Together, they converge on a solution through rapid iteration that would be too slow with either pure human implementation or pure AI generation without human guidance.

Coupling Pattern 3: Multi-Perspective Analysis

- *Traditional thinking.* View problem through one lens at a time. Performance, security, maintainability—evaluated sequentially.
- *Coupled thinking.* Request multiple perspectives simultaneously, evaluate trade-offs holistically.

Example:

```
Decision: Choosing caching strategy for API

Solo analysis:
Day 1: Analyze performance implications
Day 2: Consider security implications
Day 3: Evaluate operational complexity
Day 4: Synthesize and decide
Total: 4 days

Coupled analysis:
"Analyze three caching strategies (Redis, CDN,
    application-level) across
these dimensions:
1. Performance (latency, throughput)
2. Security (data exposure risks)
3. Cost (infrastructure, operations)
4. Complexity (implementation, debugging)
5. Scalability (load handling)

Present as comparison matrix."

AI generates comprehensive analysis in 2 minutes.
```

```
Engineer reviews for accuracy and adds context:
- "Redis costs are understated because we already
    run Redis for sessions"
- "CDN has regulatory implications because of
    data locality"
- "Application-level caching matches our team's
    expertise"

Decision made in 30 minutes with richer analysis
    than 4 days solo work.
```

The coupling: AI provides comprehensive parallel analysis. Human adds contextual knowledge and makes final judgment. Together, they achieve more thorough evaluation faster.

Coupling Pattern 4: Knowledge Amplification

- *Traditional learning.* Encounter unfamiliar concept, research it, understand it, apply it. Linear and time-consuming.
- *Coupled learning.* Encounter unfamiliar concept, immediately get explanation tuned to your background, apply it, iterate on understanding through dialogue.

Example:

```
You encounter "CQRS pattern" in architecture
    discussion.

Traditional learning:
- Google "CQRS"
- Read blog posts (varying quality)
- Watch tutorial video
- Read documentation
- Try to understand how it applies to your context
- Discuss with senior engineer
Time: Several hours over multiple days

Coupled learning:
You: "Explain CQRS for someone familiar with REST
    APIs and relational
databases but new to event sourcing"
```

```
AI: [Tailored explanation in 60 seconds
    connecting to your knowledge]

You: "How would this apply to our e-commerce
    system?"

AI: [Specific application to your domain in 60
    seconds]

You: "What are downsides for a team of 5 without
    dedicated DevOps?"

AI: [Context-specific trade-offs in 60 seconds]

You: [Armed with relevant understanding for
    architecture discussion]

Time: 5 minutes to actionable understanding
```

The coupling: AI provides immediate, personalized explanations. Human guides learning with contextual questions. Together, they achieve just-in-time learning impossible with either static documentation or pure human explanation.

Coupling Pattern 5: Creative Exploration

- *Traditional creative work.* Generate ideas internally, evaluate them, refine promising ones. Creative process is solo and sequential.
- *Coupled creative work.* Brainstorm with AI to generate many ideas quickly, human provides constraints and evaluates, iterate toward novel solutions.

Example:

```
Challenge: Make onboarding more engaging for
    technical users

Solo creative process:
- Brainstorm ideas (30 minutes)
- Sketch top 3 ideas (60 minutes)
- Evaluate feasibility (30 minutes)
- Pick best idea and refine (60 minutes)
```

```
Total: 3 hours, ~5-6 ideas explored

Coupled creative process:
You: "Generate 10 ways to make developer
    onboarding more engaging,
considering we're a B2B SaaS with technical users"

AI: [10 ideas in 30 seconds ranging from
    conventional to novel]

You: "These are too generic. We specifically need
    to teach our GraphQL API.
Suggest approaches that involve hands-on API
    exploration."

AI: [10 more ideas focused on interactive API
    learning]

You: "I like #3 (playground with guided
    challenges) and #7 (AI assistant
that helps write queries). Could we combine them?"

AI: [Synthesized proposal combining both
    approaches]

You: "That's interesting. What's the
    implementation complexity?"

AI: [Breakdown of engineering effort]

You: "What if we started with just the challenges
    and added AI assistance
later?"

AI: [Phased implementation plan]

Total: 20 minutes, ~20+ ideas explored,
    actionable plan created
```

The coupling: AI generates ideas at scale. Human provides domain constraints and creative direction. Together, they explore design spaces faster and more thoroughly.

The Emergence of Meta-Cognitive Skills

The most important effect of human-AI cognitive coupling is the emergence of new meta-cognitive skills—skills about thinking itself:

Skill 1: Prompt Engineering as Thought Externalization

Learning to describe problems precisely to AI teaches you to clarify your own thinking. Vague prompts get vague results. Precise prompts require precise thinking.

This is metacognition: thinking about how you're thinking, articulating assumptions, recognizing gaps in your understanding.

Skill 2: Rapid Hypothesis Testing

When you can test ideas quickly with AI assistance, you develop better intuition about which ideas are worth testing. You learn to form testable hypotheses rapidly and discard them quickly when wrong.

This is strategic thinking: learning to search problem spaces efficiently, not exhaustively.

Skill 3: Quality Evaluation at Scale

When AI generates many options, you must evaluate them quickly. This develops the skill of rapid quality assessment—recognizing good solutions from bad ones without deep analysis of each.

This is judgment: pattern recognition that operates faster than conscious reasoning.

Skill 4: Context-Dependent Trust Calibration

Working with AI that's reliable in some contexts and unreliable in others teaches you to calibrate trust dynamically. You learn when to trust, when to verify, when to reject.

This is wisdom: knowing what you know, what you don't know, and when to defer to others (including AI).

Skill 5: Cognitive Load Management

Deciding what to handle yourself versus delegate to AI is an active cognitive management process. You learn to monitor your own cognitive state and allocate attention strategically.

This is self-awareness: understanding your own cognitive limits and working within them effectively.

These meta-cognitive skills are general—they transfer across domains and tools. They represent a new form of cognitive expertise that's valuable beyond any specific AI system.

The Risk of Cognitive Atrophy

Just as physical muscles atrophy without use, cognitive capabilities can degrade if not exercised. The risk of extensive human-AI coupling is that certain mental muscles weaken:

- *Memory.* If you always externalize recall to AI, your own memory systems get less practice. While remembering API syntax is low-value, remembering architectural patterns and problem-solving strategies is high-value. Indiscriminate externalization risks weakening all memory, not just low-value memory.
- *Implementation skill.* If you always delegate implementation to AI, you lose the fluency that comes from repeated practice. As we discussed in Chapter 11, this is particularly dangerous for junior engineers building foundational skills.
- *Deep focus.* If you always interrupt focused work to ask AI rather than struggling through problems yourself, you may lose the ability to maintain extended focus—a capability essential for solving genuinely hard problems.
- *Creative generation.* If you always use AI to generate options and only evaluate them, you may weaken your own generative capabilities. The skill of creative ideation requires practice that AI assistance can undermine.
- *Debugging intuition.* If you always ask AI to diagnose problems rather than reasoning through them yourself, you may lose the pattern recognition that makes expert debugging possible.

Prevention requires deliberate practice (Chapter 11 again): Regularly doing work manually even when AI could help, maintaining skills through intentional exercise, not outsourcing all cognitive work even when efficient.

The goal of cognitive coupling is *augmentation*, not *replacement*. AI should make you more capable by handling tasks where it excels, freeing you to exercise capabilities where you excel. But this requires intentionality—making deliberate choices about what to couple and what to preserve.

Chapter Summary

- **Cognitive load theory explains AI's benefit.** AI reduces extraneous load (searching, remembering syntax) and can reduce intrinsic load (through explanation), freeing capacity for germane load (building understanding) (Sweller 1988; Miller 1956).
- **Memory externalization is strategic, not universal.** Externalize factual recall, code examples, documentation, and error patterns to AI. Internalize conceptual understanding, system context, problem-solving strategies, and domain knowledge. The goal is augmentation, not dependency (Bartlett 1932).
- **Practical patterns reduce cognitive friction.** Just-in-time knowledge retrieval, offloading syntax details, context compression, and error message translation all free mental resources for higher-level thinking (Csikszentmihalyi 1990).
- **AI shifts thinking to higher abstraction levels.** When AI handles syntax and implementation (Levels 0-2), human cognition naturally moves toward design patterns, system design, and business value (Levels 3-5) (Brooks 1975).
- **Higher-level thinking is qualitatively different.** From implementation to design, from local to global, from concrete to abstract, from sequential to parallel exploration—these shifts change not just what you think about but how you think.
- **Abstraction drift is a real risk.** Operating primarily at high levels without maintaining connection to implementation details leads to poor decisions. Prevention requires bidirectional movement on the abstraction ladder through deliberate practice.
- **Human-AI cognitive coupling creates new capabilities.** Hypothesis generation and evaluation, iterative refinement loops, multi-perspective analysis, knowledge amplification, and creative exploration all become more powerful through effective coupling.
- **Meta-cognitive skills emerge from coupling.** Prompt engineering as thought externalization, rapid hypothesis testing, quality evaluation at scale, context-dependent trust calibration, and cognitive load management represent new forms of expertise valuable beyond any specific AI

system.

- **Cognitive atrophy requires active prevention.** Memory, implementation skill, deep focus, creative generation, and debugging intuition can all degrade if not deliberately practiced. Augmentation requires intentional decisions about what to couple and what to preserve (Ericsson et al. 1993).
- **The goal is amplification, not replacement.** AI should make you more capable by handling what it does well, freeing you to develop capabilities where humans excel. This requires intentionality and regular deliberate practice to maintain skills even when AI could handle them.

In the next chapter, we turn to career strategy—examining how to build an antifragile career that not only survives but thrives on the volatility and change that AI brings to software engineering.

Chapter 13

The Antifragile Career

> "The wind extinguishes a candle and energizes fire. Likewise with randomness, uncertainty, chaos: you want to use them, not hide from them." — Nassim Nicholas Taleb, *Antifragile*

Throughout this book, we've explored how AI transforms software engineering—automating execution, raising the value of judgment, and creating new forms of human-AI collaboration. We've examined what skills endure, how to work effectively with AI, and why human expertise becomes more valuable even as AI becomes more capable.

But understanding these dynamics is insufficient without a career strategy that responds to them. How do you build a career that not only survives but *thrives* on the volatility AI brings? How do you position yourself to benefit from change rather than be threatened by it?

This chapter introduces the concept of the *antifragile career*—borrowing from Nassim Taleb's notion of systems that gain from disorder (Taleb 2012). A fragile career breaks under stress. A robust career resists stress. An antifragile career actually *strengthens* when exposed to volatility, uncertainty, and change.

The central insight: in a rapidly changing field, the most dangerous career strategy is optimizing for stability. The skills that seem most secure today may be automated tomorrow. The positions that feel safest may be eliminated by organizational restructuring. The technologies you've mastered may become legacy systems.

The antifragile career embraces change as opportunity. It builds capabilities that compound rather than depreciate. It positions you to benefit from disruption rather than be disrupted. And it's the only career strategy that makes sense in an era where the rate of change is accelerating.

Thriving in Constant Change

The Fragility of Specialization

For decades, the conventional wisdom in software engineering was clear: specialize. Become the expert in a specific technology, framework, or domain. Deep expertise commands premium compensation. Specialists are harder to replace than generalists.

This advice made sense in a stable technological landscape. If you mastered Java in 2000, that expertise remained valuable for decades. If you became the organization's expert in a critical system, job security followed.

But AI-accelerated change undermines this model. Technologies that seemed permanent become obsolete faster. The half-life of specific technical knowledge shrinks. Deep specialization in a particular tool or framework becomes a liability when that tool is replaced or when AI can perform the specialized work.

Consider three types of specialization and their fragility under AI:

Tool Specialization (most fragile): "I'm a React expert." When React is superseded or when AI can generate React code as competently as humans, this specialization loses value rapidly. The tool itself becomes the single point of failure.

Domain Specialization (moderately fragile): "I'm a fintech engineer." Better than tool specialization because domain knowledge transcends specific technologies. But if AI becomes competent at implementing financial systems, domain knowledge alone may not suffice.

Meta Specialization (least fragile): "I'm expert at building systems that handle high-frequency transactions with strict correctness requirements." This specialization transcends specific domains and tools, focusing on problem characteristics and trade-off navigation that transfer across contexts.

The pattern: specialization in *what* (specific tools, specific domains) is fragile. Specialization in *how* and *why* (problem-solving approaches, architectural thinking, judgment under constraint) is antifragile.

This doesn't mean abandoning expertise—it means being strategic about where expertise is developed. Depth remains valuable, but the substrate of that depth matters enormously.

The Optionality Principle

Taleb introduces the concept of *optionality*: having multiple options with asymmetric payoffs—where upside is large and downside is limited (Taleb 2012). In career terms, optionality means positioning yourself to benefit from multiple possible futures while limiting exposure to any single scenario.

- *Low optionality career*: Highly specialized in a specific technology at a specific company in a specific industry. If that technology becomes obsolete, or the company restructures, or the industry contracts, the entire career is at risk. This is fragile—vulnerable to specific shocks.
- *High optionality career*: Skills and knowledge that transfer across technologies, companies, and industries. If one domain becomes less attractive, others remain available. If one skill becomes automated, others compensate. This is antifragile—benefits from change because change creates new opportunities.

Building optionality requires deliberate choices:

Choice 1: Breadth Over Narrow Depth

Instead of: "I will become the world's leading expert in Kubernetes."

Consider: "I will become expert at distributed systems, using Kubernetes as one implementation approach among many I understand."

The first creates value only while Kubernetes dominates. The second creates value across any distributed systems context, with Kubernetes expertise as a transferable example.

Choice 2: Portable Skills Over Locked-In Skills

Skills exist on a portability spectrum:

- **Locked-in**: Company-specific systems, proprietary tools, organization-specific processes
- **Semi-portable**: Industry-standard technologies, common frameworks
- **Highly portable**: Problem-solving, system design, communication, judgment

Invest heavily in highly portable skills. Develop semi-portable skills as needed for current work. Minimize time on locked-in skills unless compensation is exceptional.

Choice 3: Multiple Income Streams Over Single Source

The traditional career model: salary from one employer. If that employer has problems, your income disappears.

High optionality alternatives: - Side projects that could become businesses - Consulting or advisory work outside primary job - Content creation (writing, teaching, speaking) that builds reputation - Open source contributions that demonstrate capability

This isn't about working more hours—it's about diversifying how your skills create value. Even modest side income creates psychological safety that paradoxically makes you more effective in your primary role (you're less desperate, more willing to take principled stands).

Choice 4: Reputation Over Positional Authority

Positional authority ("I'm Senior Engineer at Company X") evaporates when you leave. Reputation ("I'm the person who solved Y problem and wrote about it") travels with you.

Build reputation through: - Public work (open source, writing, speaking) - Teaching and mentoring (documented impact on others) - Solving visible problems (that others learn from) - Thought leadership (articulating ideas that influence the field)

Reputation creates optionality because it makes you discoverable and credible across contexts.

The Barbell Strategy for Skills

Taleb describes the *barbell strategy*: avoid the middle, concentrate at the extremes (Taleb 2012). In career terms, this means dividing effort between highly safe investments and highly speculative ones, avoiding the moderate-risk middle.

Applied to skill development:

One end: Deep fundamentals (safe, enduring) - Computer science principles (algorithms, data structures, complexity theory) - Systems thinking (how components interact, trade-offs, failure modes) - Communication and collaboration - Problem decomposition and abstraction - Debugging and diagnostic reasoning

These skills have proven durable across decades of technological change. They're as valuable today as they were in 1990, and likely will be in 2050.

Other end: Emerging technologies (speculative, high upside) - Bleeding-edge AI tools and techniques - New programming paradigms or languages - Experimental approaches to software development - Technologies with unclear but potentially large impact

These are bets. Most won't matter long-term, but the ones that do could create substantial career advantage. Early expertise in an emerging important technology is extraordinarily valuable.

Avoid the middle: Current mainstream technologies (moderate risk, moderate return)

The technologies that are popular right now—the frameworks and tools everyone is learning—represent the worst risk/reward ratio. You're competing with many others for the same expertise. By the time you've mastered them, they may be on their way to obsolescence. And they're exactly the skills AI is most likely to commoditize (because they're well-represented in training data).

- *Practical allocation.*
- 60-70% of learning time: Fundamentals
- 20-30% of learning time: Emerging technologies
- 10-20% of learning time: Current necessities (what your job requires)

This allocation is antifragile: fundamentals protect you against change, emerging technologies position you to benefit from change, and you maintain just enough current skills to be productive today.

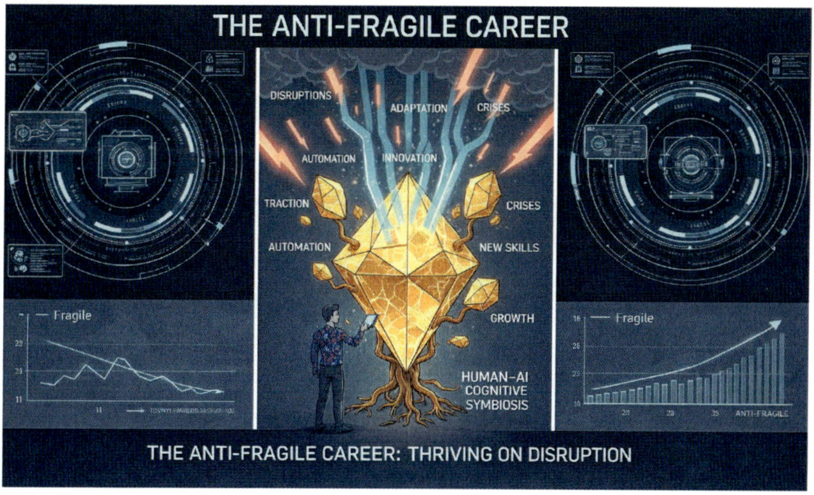

Embracing Volatility as Information

Traditional career advice treats volatility as threat: seek stable industries, established companies, proven technologies. Minimize exposure to change.

The antifragile approach inverts this: volatility is information. Change reveals what's valuable and what isn't. Disruption creates opportunities for those positioned to exploit them.

- *Practical mindset shifts.*
- *When a technology becomes obsolete.* Don't mourn the lost investment. Ask: "What does this tell me about where the field is going? What patterns can I extract that transfer to whatever replaces this?"
- *When AI automates a skill you have.* Don't panic about being replaced. Ask: "What higher-level skill becomes more valuable now that this is automated? How do I position myself there?"
- *When your company reorganizes.* Don't cling to old structure. Ask: "What opportunities does this create? What new roles emerge? How can I provide value in the new structure?"
- *When requirements change mid-project.* Don't complain about instability. Ask: "What did we learn that caused requirements to change? How does this make us more effective going forward?"

This isn't naive optimism—change creates genuine costs and casualties. But treating volatility as information rather than threat makes you more likely to be among the beneficiaries than the casualties.

Building Resilience Through Redundancy

Engineers instinctively understand redundancy in systems: critical components need backups so single failures don't cascade into system failures. The same principle applies to careers.

- *Career redundancy takes multiple forms.*
- *Skill redundancy.* You can perform multiple roles competently. If your current role becomes less viable, you have fallback options. A full-stack engineer who can also do DevOps or product management has redundancy. A specialist who can only do one thing does not.
- *Network redundancy.* You have relationships across multiple companies, industries, and communities. If one network node becomes unavailable (company downsizes, industry contracts, community dissolves), others remain.
- *Knowledge redundancy.* You understand problems at multiple levels of abstraction. If one level becomes automated, you operate effectively at

another. An engineer who understands only implementation has no redundancy. One who understands implementation *and* architecture *and* business strategy has redundancy at multiple levels.

- *Income redundancy.* We mentioned this earlier—multiple ways your skills create value. Salary + consulting + content creation + side projects create resilience against the disruption of any single income stream.
- *Identity redundancy.* Perhaps most important—you define yourself in multiple ways, not just "I'm a software engineer." You're also a writer, teacher, builder, problem-solver, whatever other identities matter to you. If "software engineering" as a profession transforms dramatically, your sense of self isn't entirely threatened.

Redundancy feels inefficient—shouldn't you maximize productivity by focusing on one thing? But redundancy is exactly what makes systems (and careers) survive stress. The cost of redundancy is lower productivity in stable times. The benefit is not just survival but genuine thriving during volatile times.

Given that we're in an era of accelerating change, the cost/benefit calculation clearly favors redundancy.

Building a Lifelong Learning System

Thriving in constant change requires continuous learning. But "lifelong learning" is often vague advice that doesn't translate into practice. What does an actual system for continuous learning look like? How do you make learning sustainable and effective rather than an exhausting treadmill?

The Learning Debt Concept

Software engineers understand technical debt: shortcuts taken for expediency that create future costs. There's an analogous concept for skills: *learning debt.*

Learning debt accumulates when: - You use libraries without understanding underlying principles - You implement patterns by copying examples without grasping rationale - You work in domains where you lack foundational knowledge - You defer learning "nice to know" topics that become "need to know"

Like technical debt, small amounts of learning debt are acceptable—you can't understand everything before using it. But learning debt compounds. The engineer who accumulates years of learning debt—always copying, never understanding—eventually hits a ceiling where they can't progress because foundations are missing.

- *Managing learning debt requires intentional paydown.*
- *Weekly reflection.* What did I use this week that I don't fully understand? Choose one thing to learn properly.
- *Monthly deep-dive.* Pick one technology/concept you use regularly but understand shallowly. Spend focused time building deep understanding.
- *Quarterly audit.* What skills do I rely on that rest on shaky foundations? Which gaps are limiting my growth? Prioritize filling these.

The goal isn't zero learning debt—that's impossible. The goal is *managed* learning debt where you're aware of gaps and systematically addressing the most consequential ones.

The 70-20-10 Learning Framework

Research on workplace learning suggests an effective distribution (Lombardo and Eichinger 1996):

70% of learning: Through experience (doing actual work) **20% of learning: Through others** (mentoring, collaboration, observation) **10% of learning: Through formal study** (courses, books, tutorials)

Most engineers invert this—they think learning means formal study (courses, certifications, books) when actually most effective learning happens through work itself, if you extract lessons deliberately.

- *Maximizing the 70% (learning from experience).*

The key is *reflection.* Experience alone doesn't teach—reflected experience teaches. Strategies:

- *Post-task retrospectives.* After completing anything significant, write:
- What was the problem?
- What approach did I take?
- What worked well? Why?
- What worked poorly? Why?
- What would I do differently next time?
- What did I learn that transfers to other contexts?

This 10-minute investment after each task transforms experience into knowledge.

- *Learning logs.* Keep a running document of things you learned each week. Even simple entries compound:

- "Learned that React's useEffect with empty dependency array runs only on mount, not on every render"
- "Discovered that database connection pooling significantly affects performance under load"
- "Realized that stakeholders care more about delivery timelines than technical elegance"

Reviewing these logs quarterly reveals patterns and consolidates learning.

- *Deliberate practice on weak areas.* Experience teaches most when you're working slightly beyond current capability. Seek tasks that stretch you rather than repeating comfortable patterns (Ericsson et al. 1993).

- *Maximizing the 20% (learning from others).*

Learning from others is dramatically more efficient than learning from scratch, if you're strategic about it.

- *Strategic mentorship.* Rather than hoping for mentorship to happen organically, be explicit:

- Identify someone whose skills you want to develop

- Ask specific questions, not vague "teach me everything"

- Propose pair programming or code review sessions on specific challenges

- Offer value in return (teach them something, help with their work)

- *Learning through teaching.* The best way to learn deeply is to teach. Volunteer to:

- Mentor juniors in areas where you're developing expertise

- Give internal talks on topics you're learning

- Write documentation or blog posts explaining concepts

- Answer questions in forums or Stack Overflow

Teaching forces you to organize knowledge clearly and reveals gaps in understanding.

- *Community engagement.* Join communities where learning happens:

- Technical meetups or user groups

- Online communities focused on specific technologies

- Open source projects where you can learn from contributors

- Study groups that work through books or courses together
- *Maximizing the 10% (formal learning).*

The smallest slice, but still important for structured knowledge acquisition.

- *Curated, not exhaustive.* You can't learn everything. Focus formal learning on:
- Fundamentals you're missing (algorithms, systems, networking)
- Emerging technologies you're betting on (AI/ML, new paradigms)
- Skills with clear near-term application (technologies you'll use soon)
- *Active, not passive.* Reading or watching without doing produces minimal learning. Effective formal learning involves:
- Working through exercises and examples
- Building projects that apply concepts
- Teaching the material to someone else
- Writing summaries and explanations
- *Spaced repetition.* Don't cram. Distribute formal learning over time with regular review. This leverages spacing effects that make learning stick (Cepeda et al. 2006).

The Just-in-Time Learning Strategy

Traditional learning assumes: Learn -> Wait -> Apply. You study something in anticipation of future need.

Just-in-time learning inverts this: Need -> Learn -> Apply immediately.

The advantages:

- *Higher retention.* You remember what you use immediately much better than what you study speculatively (Bjork 1994).
- *More motivation.* Learning to solve an actual problem you face is intrinsically motivating. Learning "in case you need it someday" requires discipline.
- *Better contextualization.* You learn with concrete context rather than abstract examples, making knowledge more usable.
- *No waste.* You learn what's actually useful, not what seemed useful in theory but never applies.

- *Practical implementation.*
- *When you encounter unfamiliar technology.* Don't deep-dive immediately. Learn just enough to accomplish the current task. If you use the technology repeatedly, invest more. If you use it once, minimal investment is appropriate.
- *When you need a skill.* Learn the minimum viable version, apply it, then deepen as needed based on actual usage patterns.
- *When considering formal education.* Ask "Will I use this in the next month?" If yes, prioritize. If no, defer unless it's fundamental.

This doesn't mean never learning proactively—fundamental knowledge is worth learning even without immediate application. But for specific tools, frameworks, and techniques, just-in-time learning is dramatically more efficient than speculative learning.

- *The AI advantage.* AI makes just-in-time learning more effective because you can get instant, contextualized explanations. "How do I implement OAuth in Node.js?" gets an immediate, specific answer rather than requiring extensive documentation reading.

This accelerates the just-in-time learning cycle, making it even more attractive relative to speculative learning.

Building a Personal Knowledge System

Learning is only valuable if you can recall and apply knowledge when needed. The human brain is excellent at associative recall but terrible at random access. A personal knowledge system compensates.

- *What to capture.*
- *Insights and principles.* Not "how to do X" (you can search that) but "when to use X versus Y" and "why X works this way."
- *Lessons from experience.* What you learned from projects, especially failures and surprises.
- *Mental models.* Frameworks for thinking about problems that apply across contexts.
- *Reference information.* Things you look up repeatedly (commands, configurations, patterns).
- *Links and resources.* Pointers to excellent explanations, documentation, tools.

- *How to organize.*
- *Resist elaborate taxonomies.* Complex filing systems become maintenance burdens. You'll spend more time organizing than referencing.
- *Use search, not hierarchy.* Digital tools make search cheap. Tag generously, organize minimally. When you need something, search. Keywords work better than nested folders.
- *Favor connections over categories.* Linked notes (Zettelkasten method (Ahrens 2017)) work better than hierarchical filing. Connect related ideas regardless of category.
- *Keep it simple.* The best knowledge system is one you'll actually use. Simple note-taking (markdown files, simple app) beats elaborate systems you abandon.
- *What tools.*

Many options exist (Notion, Obsidian, Roam, even plain text files). The tool matters less than the habit. Choose something that: - Captures quickly (friction kills usage) - Searches effectively (finding is the point) - Works offline (no dependency on services) - Exports easily (no lock-in)

- *The habit of capture.* Set moments for knowledge capture:
- End of day: 5 minutes logging what you learned
- End of week: 10 minutes reviewing and consolidating notes
- End of month: 20 minutes identifying patterns and gaps

This small time investment compounds dramatically. Five years of deliberate knowledge capture creates an invaluable personal resource.

The Curiosity Cultivation Challenge

We'll explore curiosity deeply in the next section, but it deserves mention here: lifelong learning requires sustaining curiosity across decades.

Curiosity naturally diminishes with age and expertise. Early-career engineers are curious about everything because everything is new. Senior engineers often become less curious because they've seen patterns repeat and feel they know enough.

This is dangerous. The senior engineer who stops being curious becomes obsolete as the field evolves. Expertise in 2020's problems doesn't solve 2030's problems.

- *Strategies for sustaining curiosity.*

- *Beginner's mind practice.* Regularly engage with topics where you're a complete beginner. This reminds you what learning feels like and prevents the "I already know this" reflex.
- *Question everything.* Even in familiar domains, ask "Why does this work this way? Could it work differently? What assumptions are embedded here?"
- *Cross-domain exploration.* Learn things unrelated to software engineering. Neuroscience, philosophy, design, writing—all provide mental models that transfer back to engineering in unexpected ways.
- *Cultivate intellectual humility.* The more you know, the more you should appreciate how much you don't know. Expertise should increase, not decrease, awareness of ignorance.
- *Surround yourself with the curious.* Curiosity is social. Spend time with people who ask interesting questions and pursue interesting problems. Their curiosity sparks yours.

Curiosity as Competitive Advantage

We've touched on curiosity's role in learning. But curiosity deserves deeper examination as perhaps the single most important meta-skill for thriving in an AI-augmented world.

Why Curiosity Matters More Than Ever

In previous technological eras, *knowledge* was the scarce resource. Having information others didn't have created advantage. The engineer who knew assembly language, networking protocols, or database internals had expertise worth paying for.

AI inverts this. Knowledge is abundant—instantly retrievable, comprehensively documented, and increasingly well-explained by AI systems. What's scarce is not *having* knowledge but knowing *which* knowledge matters, *why* it matters, and *how* to apply it in novel contexts.

This is where curiosity creates advantage. The curious engineer:

- *Asks better questions.* Not "how do I implement X?" (AI can answer) but "Should I implement X? What problem am I really solving? What are alternatives?"

- *Explores more broadly.* Doesn't just learn what's required but investigates adjacent areas, related fields, and unexpected connections. This breadth creates unique combinations of knowledge that AI, trained on existing patterns, is unlikely to generate.
- *Digs deeper.* Doesn't stop at surface understanding but asks "why?" repeatedly until reaching fundamental principles. This depth enables transfer to novel situations where surface patterns don't apply.
- *Challenges assumptions.* Questions why things are done certain ways, whether better approaches exist, and what constraints could be relaxed. This critical thinking drives innovation that pattern-matching systems miss.
- *Connects ideas.* Sees relationships between concepts from different domains, creating insights that emerge from combination rather than from any single field. This synthesis is distinctly human—AI systems trained on specialized corpora lack cross-domain integration.

In short: AI makes knowledge cheap but makes curiosity expensive—and therefore valuable.

The Curiosity Spectrum

Not all curiosity is equally valuable. There's a spectrum:

- *Passive curiosity.* Consuming information without active engagement. Reading tech news, watching tutorials, scrolling Twitter. This is entertainment disguised as learning. Minimal career value.
- *Directed curiosity.* Investigating specific problems you currently face. Valuable but limited in scope—you learn what's immediately useful but don't discover unexpected insights.
- *Active curiosity.* Deliberately exploring domains beyond immediate needs. Reading papers, experimenting with new technologies, learning from adjacent fields. This creates optionality and serendipitous connections.
- *Generative curiosity.* Using curiosity to create—asking questions that lead to projects, writing, teaching, or tools that others benefit from. This is curiosity that compounds because it creates outputs that outlive the learning process.
- *Career antifragility requires moving up this spectrum.* from passive consumption to active exploration to generative creation.

Developing Generative Curiosity

Generative curiosity—curiosity that creates artifacts—is learnable. It's not an innate trait but a practiced skill.

Strategy 1: The "Why?" Chain

When you encounter anything interesting, ask "why?" at least three times:

Example: - Observation: "Rust is becoming popular" - Why? "Memory safety without garbage collection" - Why does that matter? "Systems programming needs predictable performance" - Why hasn't this been solved before? "Previous approaches traded safety for performance or vice versa" - What makes Rust different? "Ownership model enforces safety at compile time" - Could this apply elsewhere? "Are there other domains where compile-time guarantees could replace runtime checks?"

This chain generates understanding that's deeper than "Rust is popular" and potentially leads to insights about applicable patterns.

Strategy 2: Cross-Domain Pattern Recognition

Deliberately seek patterns that appear in multiple domains:

Example: - You learn about CAP theorem in distributed systems (consistency, availability, partition tolerance—pick two) - You notice similar trade-offs in UI design (fast, cheap, good—pick two) - You recognize it in project management (time, quality, resources—pick two) - You abstract the pattern: "Many systems involve three desirable properties where satisfying two makes the third impossible" - You start seeing this pattern everywhere and can reason about it generally

This cross-domain thinking creates insights AI is unlikely to generate because it requires deliberately connecting disparate training data.

Strategy 3: Building in Public

Turn learning into creation:

- Learn something? Write about it (blog, documentation, tutorial)
- Solve a problem? Open-source the solution
- Discover a pattern? Give a talk explaining it
- Develop expertise? Teach others through courses or mentorship

This forces deeper understanding (teaching requires clarity) and creates artifacts that demonstrate capability, build reputation, and help others—all antifragile career moves.

Strategy 4: The 20% Exploration Budget

Allocate time explicitly to curiosity-driven exploration:

- 20% of your learning time on things with no obvious application
- Follow interesting threads even when they seem tangential
- Permit yourself to explore "useless" topics
- Trust that unexpected connections will emerge

This is hard because it feels unproductive. But the breakthroughs that define careers often come from unexpected connections that only happen when you explore beyond obvious boundaries.

Google's famous "20% time" policy (work on whatever interests you 20% of the time) recognized this. Many of Google's important products emerged from curiosity-driven exploration (Mediratta and Bick 2007).

Strategy 5: Intellectual Promiscuity

Deliberately expose yourself to ideas from distant fields:

- Read books outside technology (history, psychology, philosophy, science)
- Attend talks on topics you know nothing about
- Have conversations with people in completely different professions
- Travel to places with different cultures and approaches
- Learn skills unrelated to engineering (music, cooking, woodworking)

This seems inefficient—why learn about neuroscience if you're a web developer? Because mental models transfer. The web developer who understands how attention works (neuroscience) builds better interfaces. The backend engineer who understands thermodynamics (physics) reasons better about entropy and system states.

The most valuable insights often come from unexpected sources. But you only get them if you're intellectually promiscuous—willing to explore far from your specialization.

Curiosity in the Age of AI

AI changes how curiosity manifests productively. Traditional curiosity might involve extensive reading and research. AI-augmented curiosity looks different:

- *Rapid hypothesis generation.* Use AI to quickly explore many possible answers to a question, then use human judgment to evaluate which are most promising.

- *Depth on demand.* Instead of shallowly learning many things, use AI to explain fundamentals deeply on-demand, focusing human curiosity on synthesis and application.
- *Comparative analysis.* Ask AI to compare multiple approaches, then use human curiosity to question the comparison, identify gaps, and evaluate based on context AI lacks.
- *Counterfactual exploration.* Ask AI "what if" questions that explore alternative scenarios, using human creativity to pose interesting counterfactuals.

The pattern: AI accelerates the exploration phase, allowing human curiosity to focus on the synthesis, evaluation, and application phases where humans add unique value.

- *Example of AI-augmented curiosity in action.*

Traditional curiosity path:

```
Question: "Why do some programming languages use
    garbage collection
while others use manual memory management?"

Process:
- Google search
- Read multiple articles
- Read language documentation
- Read research papers
- Synthesize understanding over days
```

AI-augmented curiosity path:

```
Question to AI: "Explain the trade-offs between
    garbage collection and
manual memory management. Include performance
    implications, safety
considerations, and when each is appropriate."

AI provides comprehensive comparison in 60
    seconds.

Human curiosity follow-ups:
- "Why haven't we solved the performance overhead
```

```
    of GC?"
- "Are there hybrid approaches?"
- "How does Rust's ownership model differ from
    both?"
- "Could these concepts apply outside memory
    management?"
- "What's the history—why was GC invented when?"

Each question gets instant exploration, allowing
    curiosity to go deeper
and broader faster than traditional research.
```

The time saved on basic exploration frees time for deeper questions that AI struggles with—the "why this matters" and "how does this connect to other ideas" questions that drive genuine insight.

Curiosity as Career Insurance

In a rapidly changing field, curiosity is the best insurance against obsolescence.

The engineer who's curious will: - Learn about emerging technologies before they're mainstream (early mover advantage) - Understand why changes are happening, not just what is changing (deeper insight) - Make connections between new and old approaches (transfer knowledge effectively) - Question whether new approaches are actually better (critical thinking) - Explore multiple domains (create optionality)

The engineer who isn't curious will: - Learn only what's required for current job (no buffer against change) - Follow trends without understanding them (shallow knowledge) - Miss connections between ideas (siloed expertise) - Accept new approaches uncritically (poor judgment) - Specialize narrowly (fragile career)

Curiosity is what keeps you learning when formal education ends. It's what drives you to understand problems deeply rather than apply solutions superficially. It's what makes you interesting to work with and valuable to organizations.

Most importantly: curiosity is intrinsically rewarding. The curious engineer enjoys their work more because learning itself is satisfying. This creates a virtuous cycle—curiosity leads to learning, learning leads to capability, capability leads to interesting work, interesting work sustains curiosity.

In contrast, the incurious engineer experiences work as obligation, learning as chore, and change as threat. This is a fragile psychological state that makes career longevity difficult.

Curiosity isn't just career strategy—it's the foundation of a sustainable, enjoyable career that adapts to whatever changes emerge.

Chapter Summary

- **Specialization has become fragile.** Deep expertise in specific tools or narrow domains creates single points of failure. Meta-specialization in problem-solving approaches transcends any specific technology (Taleb 2012).
- **Optionality is antifragile.** Building skills that transfer across contexts, creating multiple income streams, developing portable reputation, and avoiding locked-in expertise all create career resilience through optionality.
- **The barbell strategy balances safety and upside.** Invest heavily in enduring fundamentals (70%), experiment with emerging technologies (20-30%), and maintain just enough current skills for productivity (10-20%). Avoid overinvesting in mainstream technologies that will be commoditized.
- **Embrace volatility as information.** Change reveals what's valuable, creates opportunities for the positioned, and provides learning that stability cannot. Treating disruption as threat rather than intelligence is fragile thinking.
- **Build redundancy deliberately.** Skill redundancy, network redundancy, knowledge redundancy, income redundancy, and identity redundancy all protect against specific failures while positioning for multiple successes (Taleb 2012).
- **Learning debt compounds like technical debt.** Using without understanding creates future costs. Systematic paydown through weekly reflection, monthly deep-dives, and quarterly audits prevents accumulation that limits growth.
- **The 70-20-10 framework optimizes learning.** Most learning (70%) comes from reflected experience, significant learning (20%) from others through teaching and mentorship, and formal study (10%) provides structured

knowledge. Inverting this is inefficient (Lombardo and Eichinger 1996; Ericsson et al. 1993).

- **Just-in-time learning beats speculative learning.** Learning immediately before application improves retention, motivation, and contextualization while avoiding waste on unused knowledge (Bjork 1994; Cepeda et al. 2006).
- **Personal knowledge systems compound.** Simple capture habits (daily logging, weekly review, monthly consolidation) create invaluable personal resources. Favor search over hierarchy, connections over categories (Ahrens 2017).
- **Curiosity is the scarce resource.** AI makes knowledge abundant but makes knowing which knowledge matters scarce. Curiosity—asking better questions, exploring broadly, digging deeply, challenging assumptions, connecting ideas—creates competitive advantage.
- **Move up the curiosity spectrum.** From passive consumption to directed investigation to active exploration to generative creation. Generative curiosity that produces artifacts (writing, teaching, tools) compounds most effectively.
- **AI amplifies curiosity's value.** AI handles exploration breadth, human curiosity focuses on synthesis depth. This allows deeper questions, faster iteration, and more comprehensive understanding than either alone (Mediratta and Bick 2007).
- **Curiosity is career insurance.** In rapidly changing fields, curiosity about emerging technologies, understanding of why change happens, connections between domains, and critical evaluation of trends all protect against obsolescence while making work intrinsically rewarding.

In the next chapter, we'll explore vertical mastery—how developing deep expertise in increasingly valuable domains creates compounding career advantages, and why going deep in the right areas is more powerful than going broad across many.

Chapter 14

Vertical Mastery: The Engineer's New Advantage

"I fear not the man who has practiced 10,000 kicks once, but I fear the man who has practiced one kick 10,000 times." — Bruce Lee

---

In Chapter 13, we explored the antifragile career—building resilience through optionality, embracing change, and cultivating curiosity. We argued for the barbell strategy: invest heavily in enduring fundamentals while experimenting with emerging technologies, avoiding the middle ground of current mainstream skills.

But there's a tension in this advice. On one hand, we advocate for breadth—multiple skills, transferable knowledge, avoiding narrow specialization. On the other hand, genuine expertise requires depth—thousands of hours mastering specific domains, developing intuition that can't be quickly replicated.

How do we reconcile breadth and depth? When does specialization become fragile, and when does it become valuable? In an era where AI commoditizes generalist knowledge, what kind of depth creates lasting competitive advantage?

This chapter introduces the concept of *vertical mastery*—deep expertise in domains where human understanding compounds rather than depreciates. We'll explore why certain kinds of depth become more valuable as AI becomes more capable, how to identify domains worth mastering vertically, and how vertical expertise creates career advantages that horizontal breadth cannot.

The central insight: AI doesn't eliminate the value of expertise—it changes *which* expertise matters. The engineers who thrive will be those who go deep in domains where depth multiplies value, rather than those who go broad across commoditizing skills.

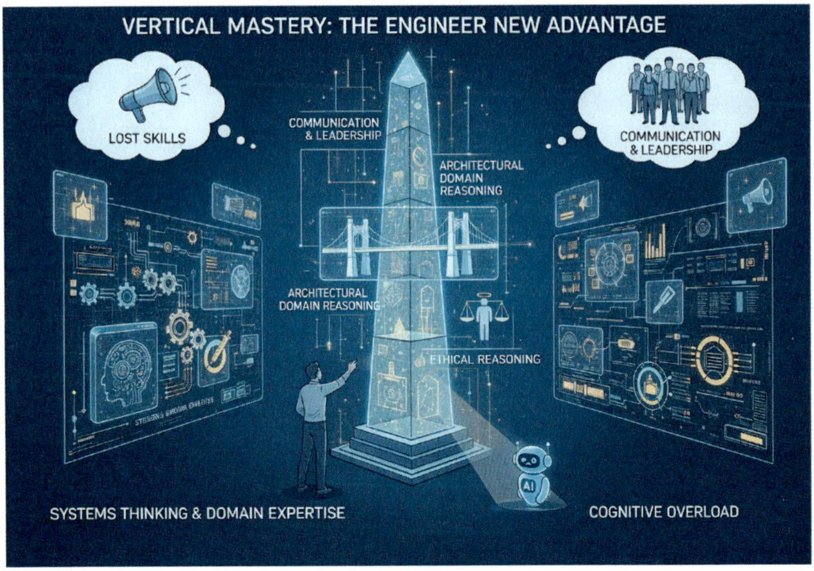

The Horizontal-Vertical Dichotomy

Scaling Systems: A Technical Foundation

Software engineers intuitively understand the difference between horizontal and vertical scaling—it's a fundamental concept in system architecture.

- *Vertical scaling* (scaling up) means making a single machine more powerful. Add more RAM, upgrade the CPU, increase disk space. You're making the one thing you have better at what it does.
- *Horizontal scaling* (scaling out) means adding more machines. Rather than making one server more powerful, you add ten servers and distribute the load across them.

Each approach has characteristic trade-offs:

Vertical scaling is *simple*. One machine means one configuration, one point of management, no distributed systems complexity. But it's *limited*—there's a ceiling to how powerful a single machine can become. It's also *risky*—that one powerful machine is a single point of failure.

Horizontal scaling is *unbounded*. You can keep adding machines indefinitely. It's *resilient*—if one machine fails, others continue. But it's *complex*—you need load balancers, data synchronization, distributed consensus, all the challenges of distributed systems.

The engineering judgment: use vertical scaling until you hit limits or need redundancy, then transition to horizontal scaling despite the complexity it introduces.

This technical metaphor extends powerfully to career strategy.

Scaling Businesses: From Technical to Strategic

The horizontal-vertical dichotomy also appears in business strategy, where it describes how companies grow and compete (Porter 1985).

- *Horizontal integration* means expanding at the same level of the value chain—acquiring competitors, entering new markets with similar products, scaling the same business model. Disney acquiring Pixar. Meta acquiring Instagram. The strategy: create one product and sell it to millions.
- *Vertical integration* means controlling more of the value chain—owning suppliers, distribution, or complementary products. Apple designing its own chips. Netflix producing original content. Tesla manufacturing batteries. The strategy: create an integrated system where each piece enhances the others.

Why do companies pursue vertical integration despite its complexity? Three compelling reasons:

- *Supplier power risk.* When you depend on external suppliers for critical components, they can dictate terms, erode margins, or favor competitors. Owning the supply chain eliminates this vulnerability.
- *Supply chain disruption risk.* Global supply chains are fragile. Geopolitical events, natural disasters, or component shortages can cripple businesses dependent on external vendors. Vertical integration provides resilience.
- *Differentiation risk.* If you're using the same components as competitors, differentiation becomes difficult. Vertical integration creates proprietary advantages that competitors can't easily replicate.

Consider Apple's vertical integration strategy. Apple designs its own chips (backward integration into component manufacturing), develops iOS alongside iPhone hardware (product integration), and controls retail through Apple Stores and the App Store (forward integration into distribution). This vertical control creates a user experience competitors using off-the-shelf components and third-party retail cannot match.

The result: premium pricing, customer loyalty, and profit margins that horizontally-integrated competitors envy. Apple's vertical strategy isn't just about controlling costs—it's about creating *differentiation* that's difficult to replicate.

The Career Parallel

The horizontal-vertical dichotomy maps powerfully onto engineering careers, especially in an AI era.

- *Horizontal career breadth* means accumulating many skills at similar levels of the stack. You can work across front-end, back-end, mobile, DevOps. You know many frameworks, languages, and tools. You're the generalist who can contribute to various parts of the codebase.

This horizontal breadth was valuable when engineering work was primarily about *building things*. Organizations needed engineers who could work on whatever task needed doing. Breadth meant flexibility, and flexibility meant employability.

- *Vertical career depth* means mastering specific domains deeply—going far beyond surface competence to develop genuine expertise in specialized areas. You understand not just the technical implementation but the domain context, business logic, regulatory constraints, and user needs that shape the problem space.

AI changes the value equation. As we've explored throughout this book, AI excels at horizontal tasks—generating code across many domains, implementing standard patterns, working with various technologies. The generalist who knows "a little about everything" competes directly with AI's strength: breadth at scale.

But AI struggles with vertical depth—the domain-specific knowledge, contextual understanding, and judgment that comes from years immersed in a particular problem space. The specialist who knows a domain deeply possesses something AI cannot easily replicate: expertise that transcends what's documented and that adapts to novel situations within the domain.

This is the career insight: horizontal skills commoditize under AI automation, while vertical expertise appreciates in value.

Why Vertical Mastery Matters in the AI Era

The Commoditization of Generalist Skills

Throughout this book, we've examined how AI automates work at the Execution layer—syntax, standard patterns, boilerplate code. But the commoditization extends beyond just low-level implementation.

AI is increasingly competent at *horizontal generalist work*—tasks that span many domains but don't require deep specialization:

- Building standard CRUD applications
- Implementing common architectural patterns
- Writing tests for straightforward functionality
- Creating basic documentation
- Deploying applications using standard tools
- Monitoring with conventional metrics

These tasks don't require deep domain expertise. They're well-documented, have established best practices, and appear frequently in training data. AI handles them with increasing competence.

The engineer whose value proposition is "I can build standard web applications" faces direct competition from AI. The engineer whose value proposition is "I can build compliant healthcare applications that handle protected health information correctly within HIPAA regulations" faces much less AI competition—because the latter requires vertical expertise that's harder to automate.

- *The key distinction.* Generalist skills are *portable but commoditizing.* Specialist skills are *less portable but appreciating.*

This creates a genuine strategic choice. Do you invest in breadth that keeps you flexible but exposes you to AI commoditization? Or do you invest in depth that reduces flexibility but creates defensible expertise?

The answer isn't binary—you need both. But the balance is shifting. In 2015, 70% breadth and 30% depth might have been optimal. In 2026, 40% breadth and 60% depth may be more defensible. By 2030, perhaps 30% breadth and 70% depth.

The reason for this shift is structural, not speculative.

The fracturing of the generalist full-stack role is not hypothetical — it is already producing a distinct set of AI-native specialist positions that did not exist three years ago. Agent Systems Architects design the boundaries, data flow, and trust layers between multiple autonomous agents. AI Platform Engineers build and operate the LLMOps (Large Language Model Operations) infrastructure that serves, monitors, and secures models at scale. Telemetry and Observability Engineers manage the data volumes required to keep non-deterministic systems predictable. AI Governance Leads ensure that AI-generated code is compliant, auditable, and free of the systemic debt described elsewhere in this book. Each of these roles rewards deep vertical knowledge in a specific layer of the new stack. None of them can be performed adequately by someone whose expertise is evenly distributed across the surface.

The Compounding Returns of Depth

There is a pattern worth examining in how engineers get real value from AI tools: domain expertise acts as a multiplier, and the multiplier compounds across the entire workflow.

At the input stage, depth improves what we described in Chapter 9 as context engineering — not because the engineer has studied "prompt engineering" as an isolated discipline, but because deep domain knowledge provides the vocabulary, the mental models, and the intuition to shape the entire informational environment around the model, not just the immediate question. You do not ask "How do I make my database faster?" You ask about index selectivity on a composite key with high cardinality in the leading column, or about the tradeoffs between a covering index and a filtered index given your specific query workload. The model responds with dramatically higher quality because you provided dramatically higher specificity.

At the output stage, depth improves verification. As we explored in Chapter 10, AI fluency makes verification essential but domain knowledge makes verification possible. The expert catches errors that the generalist cannot see.

At the integration stage, depth improves what you do with the output. Knowing where a correct AI response fits in the architecture, what downstream services it affects, what operational constraints it must satisfy — requires the contextual understanding that only vertical expertise provides. AI can generate a well-structured Kubernetes deployment manifest. It cannot tell you whether that configuration is the right choice for your cluster's resource profile, your team's on-call capacity, or your compliance requirements around data residency.

This three-stage compounding — better inputs, better filters, better application — is why depth of expertise does not become less valuable as AI improves. It becomes more valuable, because it is precisely that depth which determines the quality of the collaboration at every stage. The returns on vertical mastery are not linear. They compound.

The horizontalization of software accelerates this shift. Modern development stacks are overwhelmingly horizontal—authentication, payments, notifications, analytics, deployment, monitoring. Each layer has mature, well-documented solutions that AI can implement competently. The engineer who assembles horizontal components is doing work that is increasingly indistinguishable from what an AI agent can do: connecting APIs, configuring services, wiring standard patterns together.

This is why the engineer's role is migrating from *programmer* to *architect*. Not architect in the formal title sense, but in the cognitive sense: someone who understands how pieces fit together, why certain combinations create problems that won't surface for months, and which trade-offs are acceptable given the specific domain and organizational context. A programmer asks "how do I implement this?" An architect asks "should this exist, and if so, what shape should it take?" AI is increasingly competent at the first question. The second remains stubbornly human.

The Three Layers and Vertical Expertise

Let's map vertical expertise onto the three-layer framework from Chapter 1 to understand where it operates.

Execution Layer (implementation mechanics): - Horizontal at this layer: Knowing how to implement authentication in general - Vertical at this layer: Knowing how to implement authentication that meets specific regulatory requirements for your domain (HIPAA for healthcare, PCI DSS for payments, SOC 2 for SaaS)

Design Layer (architectural decisions): - Horizontal at this layer: Understanding general system design patterns - Vertical at this layer: Understanding which patterns work in your specific domain given its constraints (eventual consistency is acceptable in social media, unacceptable in financial transactions)

Intent Layer (purpose and value): - Horizontal at this layer: Understanding software should solve user problems - Vertical at this layer: Understanding which problems matter most in your domain, why users behave the way they do, what success actually means in domain-specific terms

Vertical expertise operates most powerfully at the Design and Intent layers. This is where domain knowledge compounds: understanding not just *how* to build systems but *what* systems should be built and *why* certain approaches work better in specific contexts.

AI can increasingly help at the Execution layer even for vertical domains—once you've specified the constraints precisely, AI can implement them. But specifying those constraints correctly requires vertical expertise. Understanding why those constraints exist and how they interact requires even deeper vertical expertise. Deciding which problems to solve in the first place requires the deepest vertical expertise.

- *This is why vertical mastery creates antifragile careers.* As AI handles more Execution-layer work, value concentrates at Design and Intent layers where vertical expertise operates.

Domain Knowledge as Moat

In business strategy, a "moat" is a competitive advantage that's difficult for competitors to replicate—like a moat around a castle (Buffett 1993). Vertical expertise creates personal moats in analogous ways.

- *Knowledge moat.* Deep domain expertise takes years to develop. An engineer who's spent a decade in fintech understands financial regulations, trading systems, risk management, and compliance in ways that can't be quickly replicated. This knowledge is a moat—new entrants (including AI) can't easily match it.
- *Relationship moat.* Vertical specialization means working repeatedly with the same stakeholder types—traders, doctors, lawyers, whoever your domain serves. These relationships create trust and shared vocabulary that make collaboration efficient. An engineer who speaks the language of the domain and understands stakeholder needs adds value beyond pure technical skill.
- *Pattern recognition moat.* After solving hundreds of problems within a domain, you develop intuition about what works and what doesn't. You recognize patterns that others miss. You know why certain approaches that seem good fail in practice. This tacit knowledge is extremely difficult to transfer—even to other humans, let alone to AI.
- *Context moat.* Every domain has unwritten rules, institutional knowledge, and historical context that shape decisions. Why was this system built this way? What assumptions does it encode? What constraints are no longer relevant but still embedded in the architecture? Vertical experts understand this context in ways that documentation can never capture.

These moats compound. The longer you work in a domain, the wider your moat becomes. This is exactly the opposite dynamic from horizontal generalist skills, which face constant erosion from new frameworks, changing best practices, and now AI automation.

The Horizontal AI / Vertical Expertise Symbiosis

Here's the pattern emerging: horizontal AI handles generalist work, while vertical human expertise handles specialist work. But they don't just coexist—they multiply each other's value.

- *The engineer with vertical expertise uses horizontal AI to:*
- Implement domain-specific logic faster (AI handles syntax, engineer provides domain specifications)
- Generate variations of domain patterns (AI explores options, engineer evaluates which fits domain constraints)
- Document domain-specific systems (AI drafts, engineer corrects domain inaccuracies)
- Prototype domain solutions rapidly (AI builds quickly, engineer validates domain correctness)
- *The key insight.* Vertical expertise makes you *better* at using AI, not redundant to it. You can leverage AI's execution speed because you can specify precisely what needs executing and evaluate whether the execution is domain-appropriate.

The generalist engineer without domain depth struggles to use AI effectively in specialized contexts. They don't know what to ask for, can't evaluate whether AI-generated solutions fit domain constraints, and can't adapt AI outputs to domain-specific requirements.

This creates a multiplier effect: Vertical expertise × Horizontal AI = Dramatically increased capability.

The math: An engineer with deep fintech expertise using AI can accomplish perhaps 3-5x what they could accomplish manually. A generalist engineer using AI might accomplish 2x what they could manually, but in fintech contexts their output requires extensive review and revision by someone with domain expertise.

The vertically expert engineer isn't just more productive—they're producing work that's actually useful in the domain without extensive remediation.

Choosing Your Vertical: Strategic Domain Selection

If vertical mastery is the strategy, the next question is: which vertical? Not all domains are equally valuable for developing career-defining expertise.

Criteria for Valuable Verticals

Criterion 1: Complexity That Resists Commoditization

Some domains are inherently more complex than others—they involve more regulations, more edge cases, more stakeholders, more constraints. This complexity creates barriers that protect specialist value.

- *High complexity domains.*
- Healthcare (regulations, privacy, interoperability, clinical workflows)
- Finance (compliance, risk management, real-time trading, fraud detection)
- Legal (case law, precedent, jurisdiction-specific rules, document analysis)
- Manufacturing (supply chains, physical constraints, safety, quality control)
- Enterprise security (threat models, compliance frameworks, incident response)
- *Lower complexity domains.*
- Consumer social media (fewer regulations, more room for experimentation)
- Basic e-commerce (well-established patterns, many similar implementations)
- Simple content management (commoditized functionality)

The higher the domain complexity, the more valuable vertical expertise becomes—and the longer it takes for AI to commoditize that expertise.

Criterion 2: Economic Value and Growth

Some domains are simply more economically important than others. Vertical expertise in high-value domains commands premium compensation and has more career opportunities.

Questions to evaluate economic value: - How much money flows through this domain? - What's the growth trajectory? (Shrinking domains are risky even with expertise) - How much does the domain pay for engineering talent? - How critical is software to the domain's operation?

Healthcare software and fintech command premium salaries because the domains are economically massive and software is increasingly central to their operations. Gaming or social media may be culturally visible but aren't necessarily as economically valuable.

Criterion 3: Durability of Knowledge

Some domains change constantly, making expertise ephemeral. Others have deep fundamentals that remain stable even as surface details evolve.

- *Durable knowledge domains.*
- Finance (financial instruments and risk management principles persist across technological changes)
- Healthcare (human physiology doesn't change; regulations evolve but foundational compliance concepts persist)
- Manufacturing (physical constraints and supply chain principles are fundamental)
- Security (threat models evolve but cryptographic principles and adversarial thinking remain relevant)
- *Less durable domains.*
- Consumer app trends (what's popular shifts rapidly)
- Specific platform ecosystems (dominant platforms change over decades)
- Particular technology stacks (frameworks come and go)

Invest in domains where fundamentals are durable even if implementations change.

Criterion 4: Alignment With Personal Interest

This is often overlooked but crucial: deep expertise takes years to develop. You won't sustain the effort required unless you're genuinely interested in the domain.

Ask yourself: - Do I find this domain intellectually engaging? - Do I enjoy conversations with domain experts? - Am I curious about domain-specific problems? - Would I read about this domain even if it weren't my job?

If the answers are no, you won't develop genuine vertical expertise no matter how economically valuable the domain is. Sustained interest is a prerequisite for depth.

Criterion 5: Access and Entry Points

Some domains are difficult to enter without specific credentials or prior experience. Others are more accessible.

Consider: - Can I work in this domain with my current background? - What's the path from where I am to domain expertise? - Are there companies hiring engineers to learn the domain? - Can I contribute to open source or side projects in this domain?

The best vertical is one you can actually access and where there's a plausible path from current state to expertise.

The Portfolio Approach: Primary and Secondary Verticals

Rather than specializing in exactly one domain, a more resilient approach is developing a *primary vertical* deeply while maintaining a *secondary vertical* with moderate depth.

Primary vertical (60-70% of domain learning time): - Where you develop genuine expertise - Where you're known in the community - Where you can teach others - Where you have deep pattern recognition and intuition

Secondary vertical (20-30% of domain learning time): - Adjacent domain that shares some concepts - Provides diversification if primary vertical changes - Creates interesting cross-pollination opportunities - Maintains some optionality

Foundational breadth (10-20% of learning time): - General software engineering principles - New paradigms and tools - Emerging technologies - Skills that transfer across domains

- *Example combinations.*
- Primary: Healthcare systems | Secondary: Privacy/security | Breadth: Systems architecture
- Primary: Fintech | Secondary: Data systems | Breadth: Distributed systems
- Primary: ML infrastructure | Secondary: Developer tools | Breadth: Performance optimization

This portfolio approach provides the antifragile benefits of vertical depth (primary creates defensible expertise) while maintaining some optionality (secondary provides fallback) and connection to broader engineering trends (breadth prevents isolation).

Recognizing When to Pivot

Vertical specialization doesn't mean permanent commitment. Career-long learning sometimes means recognizing when a vertical is losing value and pivoting to another.

- *Signals that suggest pivoting.*
- *Industry contraction.* If the domain is shrinking economically (fewer companies, less investment, declining compensation), even deep expertise loses value. Example: Vertical expertise in desktop application development became less valuable as software moved to web and mobile.
- *Commoditization acceleration.* If tools and platforms are rapidly commoditizing domain-specific work, vertical expertise may be losing its moat faster than you can deepen it. This is rare but possible.
- *Personal misalignment.* If you've tried for several years and still don't find the domain engaging, your lack of genuine interest will prevent you from developing the deep expertise that creates value. Better to pivot to a domain that sustains your curiosity.
- *Better opportunities emerge.* Sometimes new domains open up that offer higher value and better fit. Being willing to pivot when genuinely better opportunities appear is antifragile, not inconsistent.
- *How to pivot effectively.*
- Identify transferable concepts from current vertical to new one
- Leverage existing horizontal skills to gain entry
- Accept that you'll be less expert initially—the investment pays off over years
- Maintain some connection to previous vertical (it took years to build, don't abandon completely)

The key: Don't pivot frequently or opportunistically. Vertical expertise takes years to develop. But do pivot deliberately when evidence suggests your current vertical won't provide long-term value.

Developing Vertical Expertise: Practical Strategies

Understanding why vertical mastery matters and choosing a domain are necessary but insufficient. How do you actually develop deep domain expertise as a software engineer?

Immersion Over Tourism

The difference between vertical expertise and superficial familiarity is *immersion*—sustained, focused engagement with the domain over years, not months.

Tourist approach (doesn't build expertise): - Work on a healthcare project for six months - Move to a fintech project for six months - Then e-commerce, then gaming, then… - Never stay long enough to move beyond surface understanding

Immersion approach (builds expertise): - Commit to a domain for 3-5+ years minimum - Work on multiple projects within the domain - Solve increasingly complex problems as understanding deepens - Build relationships with domain experts - Stay long enough to see consequences of decisions play out

- *The 3-5 year horizon is crucial.* First year you're learning domain basics. Second year you're becoming competent. Third year you're developing intuition. Fourth and fifth years you're accumulating the pattern recognition and contextual understanding that creates genuine expertise.

Engineers who change domains every 1-2 years never develop vertical expertise—they're perpetual beginners. This was viable when horizontal breadth was valuable. It's increasingly risky as horizontal skills commoditize.

Learning From Domain Experts

Software engineers developing domain expertise cannot do so in isolation. The fastest path to vertical depth is learning from people who already have it—and those people usually aren't engineers.

Strategy 1: Shadow domain experts

Ask to observe domain experts doing their work: - Doctors seeing patients (with appropriate privacy protections) - Traders executing trades - Lawyers reviewing contracts - Manufacturing engineers managing production

This observation reveals workflows, decision-making processes, and pain points that no amount of requirements documentation captures.

Strategy 2: Conduct structured interviews

Regular conversations with domain experts where you ask: - "Walk me through how you do [task]" - "What's the hardest part of your job?" - "What workarounds do you use because the software doesn't support your workflow?" - "What information do you wish you had that you don't?" - "Tell me about a time when things went wrong—what happened?"

Strategy 3: Read domain literature

Don't just read technical documentation. Read what domain experts read: - Academic papers in the field - Industry publications and trade journals - Regulatory guidance and compliance frameworks - Case studies and post-mortems - Books written by and for domain practitioners

This builds vocabulary and mental models that make you a more effective collaborator.

Strategy 4: Attend domain conferences

Go to conferences in the domain, not just software engineering conferences. Healthcare engineers should attend medical informatics conferences. Fintech engineers should attend quantitative finance conferences. The conversations you overhear teach you what matters to domain experts.

Strategy 5: Earn domain credentials (when feasible)

Some domains have professional certifications that demonstrate knowledge: - Healthcare: Clinical informatics certification - Finance: CFA, FRM, or other financial credentials - Security: CISSP, CEH, or other security certifications - Legal technology: Familiarity with legal research and writing

You don't need to become a doctor or lawyer, but having some formal domain credentials signals commitment and provides structured learning.

Building Domain Intuition Through Repetition

Expertise emerges from encountering many variations of similar problems until patterns become automatic (Ericsson et al. 1993). This requires working on multiple projects within the domain, not just one.

- *The pattern recognition trajectory.*

Stage 1: Rule-following (Year 1) - "I need to implement HIPAA-compliant logging. Let me check the requirements and implement exactly what they say." - Mechanical application of documented rules

Stage 2: Understanding context (Year 2) - "I understand why HIPAA requires audit logs—it's about accountability and detecting breaches. That changes how

I think about what to log." - Beginning to understand the *why* behind requirements

Stage 3: Recognizing patterns (Year 3) - "This access pattern looks like previous projects where we had compliance issues. Let me think about how to structure this to avoid those problems." - Seeing similarities across projects, anticipating issues

Stage 4: Intuitive judgment (Year 4+) - "Something feels wrong about this architecture from a compliance perspective. Let me think through the implications..." - Gut-level sense of what works without always articulating why

This trajectory requires repetition. You can't reach stage 4 by working on one project for four years. You need to encounter many instances of domain-specific challenges so pattern recognition develops.

- *Practical tactics.*
- Volunteer for diverse projects within your domain vertical
- Seek code review opportunities across domain-related codebases
- Contribute to multiple domain-focused open source projects
- Consult or advise on domain problems outside your primary job

Each additional project in the domain adds to your pattern library.

Contributing to Domain Knowledge

True expertise manifests in the ability to contribute knowledge back to the domain community—not just consume it.

- *Ways to contribute.*

- *Write about domain-specific engineering challenges.* Blog posts, white papers, or conference talks about technical solutions to domain problems. Example: "Implementing real-time fraud detection at scale" (fintech) or "Building HIPAA-compliant microservices" (healthcare).

- *Create open source tools for the domain.* Libraries, frameworks, or utilities that solve common domain problems. These demonstrate expertise and build reputation.

- *Speak at domain conferences.* Present as a technologist at domain conferences (not just tech conferences). This forces you to communicate in domain language and builds credibility with domain experts.

- *Teach domain-focused courses or workshops.* Creating educational content for other engineers entering the domain requires organizing your knowledge clearly and reveals gaps in your understanding.

- *Contribute to domain standards or working groups.* Many domains have technical standards bodies or committees. Participation demonstrates deep engagement and influences how the domain evolves.

This contribution serves multiple purposes: it solidifies your own understanding (teaching deepens learning), builds your reputation in the domain (you become known), and creates artifacts that demonstrate expertise (useful for career advancement).

Maintaining Vertical Expertise Over Time

Vertical expertise is not static—domains evolve, regulations change, technologies advance. Maintaining expertise requires ongoing investment.

Strategy: Domain learning budget

Allocate specific time to domain learning, separate from technical skill development: - 3-5 hours per week reading domain literature - Quarterly conversations with domain experts to understand what's changing - Annual review of major regulatory or technology shifts in the domain - Regular participation in domain communities (online forums, local meetups)

Strategy: Project diversity within domain

Avoid working on identical projects within the domain. Seek variety: - Different company sizes (enterprise vs. startup) - Different regulatory contexts (if applicable) - Different technical challenges (real-time systems vs. batch processing vs. data pipelines) - Different user types (internal tools vs. customer-facing applications)

This diversity prevents your expertise from becoming narrow even within your vertical.

Strategy: Cross-pollination with adjacent domains

Deliberately learn from adjacent domains that share concepts: - Healthcare -> Life sciences research, medical devices - Fintech -> Insurance, accounting systems - Manufacturing -> Supply chain, logistics

Adjacent domains often have insights that transfer while maintaining your primary vertical focus.

Vertical Mastery and Career Leverage

Vertical expertise creates career advantages that compound over time. Let's examine the specific ways deep domain knowledge multiplies your effectiveness and value.

The Specification Advantage

In Chapter 4, we discussed how AI handles implementation increasingly well but struggles with specification—determining *what* should be built and *why*. Vertical expertise makes you exceptional at specification.

- *What this looks like in practice.*

A product manager requests: "We need to improve transaction processing speed."

- *Generalist engineer response.* "Okay, I'll optimize the database queries and add caching."
- *Vertically expert engineer response.* "Transaction processing has three distinct flows—retail point-of-sale, business-to-business settlements, and cross-border transfers. Each has different performance requirements and regulatory constraints. Which flow is causing problems? What's the actual user pain—is it latency they experience, or is it batch processing delays they don't see? What regulatory timing requirements apply? Let me talk to the compliance team and traders to understand the real requirements before we start optimizing."

The vertically expert engineer asks better questions, understands context the PM didn't specify, and avoids building the wrong solution optimally.

This specification advantage compounds: better specifications lead to more appropriate solutions, which lead to happier stakeholders, which lead to more trust and influence, which lead to better access to information, which lead to even better specifications.

The Review Advantage

Code review in specialized domains requires domain expertise to be effective. The vertically expert engineer provides review that generalists cannot.

Surface-level review (any engineer can do): - "This code has a syntax error" - "This variable name is unclear" - "This function should be split into smaller functions"

Domain-informed review (requires vertical expertise): - “This implementation violates PCI DSS requirement 3.4 about rendering full PAN unreadable—you’re storing card numbers in plaintext in logs” - “This caching strategy will cause issues with real-time trading because market data can become stale between cache updates” - “This data model doesn’t handle the regulatory requirement to maintain immutable audit trails for all account changes”

The domain expert catches issues that will become expensive production problems. This makes them invaluable to organizations working in the domain.

The Architecture Advantage

System architecture in specialized domains requires understanding both technical constraints and domain constraints. Vertical expertise enables architectures that generalists wouldn’t consider.

- *Example from healthcare.*

A generalist might design a patient data system with a standard microservices architecture—separate services for patient records, appointments, billing, etc.

A healthcare specialist recognizes additional requirements: - HIPAA requires tracking every access to protected health information - Clinical workflows require offline access for reliability - Interoperability standards (HL7, FHIR) impose specific data formats - Clinical decision support needs real-time access to complete patient history - Regulatory audits require immutable audit logs

These requirements shape architecture in ways that aren’t obvious without domain knowledge. The result: the specialist designs a system that meets both technical and domain constraints from the start, avoiding expensive refactoring later.

The Trust Multiplier

Perhaps the most important advantage: vertical expertise builds trust with stakeholders in ways that pure technical skill cannot.

When you speak the domain language, understand domain challenges, and demonstrate domain knowledge, stakeholders trust you to make good decisions. This trust creates a virtuous cycle:

1. Stakeholders share more context because they trust you’ll understand it
2. Better context leads to better decisions
3. Better decisions increase trust further
4. Higher trust leads to more responsibility
5. More responsibility provides more learning opportunities

6. More learning deepens expertise
7. Deeper expertise increases trust even more

This multiplier effect means the vertically expert engineer operates at a different level than equally technically skilled generalists. They're included in strategic conversations, consulted on product decisions, and given autonomy that others must earn more slowly.

The Compensation Premium

All of the above advantages translate to economic value. Vertical expertise commands premium compensation for several reasons:

- *Scarcity.* Fewer engineers have deep domain expertise than have broad technical skills. Supply and demand favor the scarce.
- *Impact.* Domain experts solve more valuable problems (right solutions vs. wrong solutions implemented well) and solve them faster (no learning curve on every project).
- *Retention value.* Organizations invest heavily in helping engineers develop domain expertise. Once developed, that expertise is valuable to competitors. Organizations pay to retain domain experts.
- *Multiplier effect.* A domain expert multiplies the effectiveness of entire teams by providing review, architectural guidance, and specification clarity that prevents expensive mistakes.

Data from specialized domains (anecdotal but consistent): - Healthcare software engineers with clinical domain knowledge: 20-30% premium over generalist engineers - Fintech engineers with trading or risk management expertise: 25-40% premium - Security engineers with deep expertise in specific domains (cloud, network, application): 30-50% premium at senior levels

These premiums grow with seniority—the gap between a generalist junior engineer and a domain specialist junior engineer is modest. The gap between a generalist principal engineer and a domain specialist principal engineer is substantial.

Vertical Mastery and the Three-Layer Framework

Let's synthesize vertical expertise with the three-layer framework that structures this book's argument.

Execution Layer: Vertical Syntax

Even at the Execution layer—where AI is most competent—vertical expertise matters. Domain-specific implementation has nuances that general implementation lacks.

Consider implementing data validation:

Generic validation (any engineer + AI can do):

```
function validateEmail(email) {
  return /^[^\s@]+@[^\s@]+\.[^\s@]+$/.test(email);
}
```

Domain-specific validation (requires vertical expertise):

```
function validateHealthcareEmail(email, context) {
  // Basic format validation
  if (!/^[^\s@]+@[^\s@]+\.[^\s@]+$/.test(email)) {
    return { valid: false, reason:
        'INVALID_FORMAT' };
  }

  // HIPAA compliance: email domains must be on
  // approved list
  // for PHI transmission
  const domain = email.split('@')[1];
  if (!context.isApprovedDomain(domain)) {
    return {
      valid: false,
      reason: 'UNAPPROVED_DOMAIN_FOR_PHI',
      requiresEncryption: true
    };
  }

  // Clinical context: verify email for patient
  // communication
  // matches consent preferences
  if (context.isPatientEmail && !context.
      hasEmailConsent()) {
    return {
      valid: false,
      reason: 'MISSING_COMMUNICATION_CONSENT'
```

```
    };
  }

  return { valid: true };
}
```

The vertically expert implementation handles domain-specific requirements that the generic version misses. AI can implement the generic version easily. The domain-specific version requires knowledge that's harder to prompt for because it's based on understanding regulatory and clinical contexts.

Design Layer: Vertical Architecture

At the Design layer, vertical expertise becomes crucial. Architectural decisions that seem equivalent technically have very different implications in different domains.

- *Generic architectural question.* "Should we use event sourcing?"
- *Domain-specific considerations.*

In **fintech**: Event sourcing is often ideal—financial regulations require audit trails of all transactions, event sourcing provides this naturally. Regulatory audits benefit from being able to replay events to reconstruct state at any point in time.

In **healthcare**: Event sourcing has complications—regulations such as the GDPR's "right to erasure" and evolving US state privacy laws can require patient data deletion, which conflicts with immutable event logs. Even HIPAA's amendment requirements add complexity to append-only architectures.

In **manufacturing**: Event sourcing makes sense for process tracking but may be overkill for simpler inventory management. The physical constraints (parts are physical objects that can't be "replayed") change how you think about state.

The vertically expert engineer knows these domain-specific considerations and makes architectural decisions accordingly. The generalist engineer implements event sourcing because it's an interesting pattern, then discovers domain incompatibilities late.

Intent Layer: Vertical Strategy

At the Intent layer—where we decide what to build and for whom—vertical expertise is irreplaceable. This is where domain knowledge determines whether you're solving real problems or imagined ones.

- *Generic product thinking.* "We should add machine learning to predict user behavior and personalize the experience."
- *Domain-specific thinking.*

In **healthcare**: "Predictive ML for clinical outcomes requires FDA approval as a medical device in many jurisdictions. We need to understand regulatory pathway, clinical validation requirements, and liability implications before building. Also, clinicians will require explainability for any ML system affecting patient care—black-box predictions are unacceptable in this context."

In **finance**: "ML for trading decisions must handle market regime changes that weren't in training data. We need to think about model drift detection, risk management integration, and regulatory reporting of algorithmic trading strategies. Also, wrong predictions can lose millions—we need robust confidence intervals and fallback strategies."

In **legal tech**: "ML for document analysis needs to maintain attorney-client privilege, handle jurisdiction-specific terminology, and provide audit trails for why documents were flagged. The model must be explainable because lawyers need to defend its decisions in court if challenged."

The Intent-layer decisions—what to build, why it matters, what success looks like—require vertical expertise that operates far beyond technical capabilities.

Chapter Summary

- **The horizontal-vertical dichotomy applies to careers.** Horizontal breadth (many skills at similar depth) is becoming commoditized by AI. Vertical depth (mastery in specific domains) creates defensible competitive advantage (Porter 1985; Taleb 2012).
- **AI commoditizes generalist skills while appreciating specialist skills.** Horizontal AI handles generalist work increasingly well. Vertical expertise in complex domains remains difficult to automate and increases in value.
- **Vertical expertise operates across all three layers.** Even at Execution, domain-specific implementation has nuances. At Design, domain constraints shape architecture. At Intent, domain knowledge determines what's worth building.
- **Domain knowledge creates multiple moats.** Knowledge moats (deep ex-

pertise), relationship moats (stakeholder trust), pattern recognition moats (intuitive judgment), and context moats (institutional knowledge) all compound to create defensible expertise (Buffett 1993).

- **Not all verticals are equally valuable.** Choose domains with high complexity (resists commoditization), strong economics (well-compensated), durable knowledge (fundamentals persist), personal alignment (sustains interest), and accessible entry points.
- **Portfolio approach balances depth and optionality.** Develop primary vertical deeply (60-70%), maintain secondary vertical moderately (20-30%), preserve foundational breadth (10-20%). This provides antifragile benefits of both depth and diversification.
- **Expertise requires immersion over tourism.** 3-5+ years minimum in a domain to develop genuine expertise. First year learning basics, second year becoming competent, third year developing intuition, fourth and fifth years accumulating pattern recognition (Ericsson et al. 1993).
- **Learn from domain experts, not just documentation.** Shadow domain practitioners, conduct structured interviews, read domain literature, attend domain conferences, and consider domain credentials to accelerate learning.
- **Build intuition through repetition.** Work on multiple projects within the domain to develop pattern recognition that eventually becomes intuitive judgment. Each additional project adds to your pattern library.
- **Contribute knowledge back to the domain.** Write about domain challenges, create domain-focused tools, speak at domain conferences, teach courses, and participate in standards bodies. Contribution solidifies expertise and builds reputation.
- **Vertical expertise creates multiplicative advantages.** Better specification (asking right questions), better review (catching domain-specific issues), better architecture (balancing technical and domain constraints), higher trust (stakeholder confidence), and compensation premiums (20-50% at senior levels).
- **Vertical × Horizontal AI = Force Multiplier.** Domain expertise makes you dramatically more effective at using AI because you can specify what needs building and evaluate whether AI output fits domain constraints. This symbiosis creates outsized capability.

In the next chapter, we'll explore how vertical expertise and technical leadership combine—examining how the engineer as leader shapes not just systems but teams, organizations, and the culture of engineering itself.

Chapter 15

The Engineer as Leader

> "Leadership is not about being in charge. It's about taking care of those in your charge." — Simon Sinek

---

In the previous chapters, we've explored how to build an antifragile career (Chapter 13) and develop vertical mastery (Chapter 14). These strategies position individual engineers for success in an AI-augmented world. But engineering excellence isn't purely individual—it happens in teams, shaped by leaders who create environments where excellent work becomes possible.

This chapter examines leadership in software engineering—not as formal authority or management hierarchy, but as the capacity to influence outcomes, shape culture, and multiply the capabilities of those around you. In an era where AI handles more technical execution, the human work of leadership becomes even more important.

Leadership in engineering has always been about more than technical prowess. But AI changes the equation in specific ways. When implementation speed is less of a bottleneck (AI assists), the bottlenecks become: clarifying what to build, aligning teams around purpose, making good decisions under uncertainty, developing people's capabilities, and maintaining the culture that makes all of this possible.

These are leadership responsibilities—and they resist automation because they're fundamentally about humans working with other humans.

The central insight: As AI commoditizes technical execution, the premium on *human-centered leadership*—the ability to understand people, build trust, communicate clearly, develop others, and create environments where teams thrive—increases dramatically. The engineers who develop leadership capabilities alongside technical depth will have opportunities unavailable to those who remain purely technical.

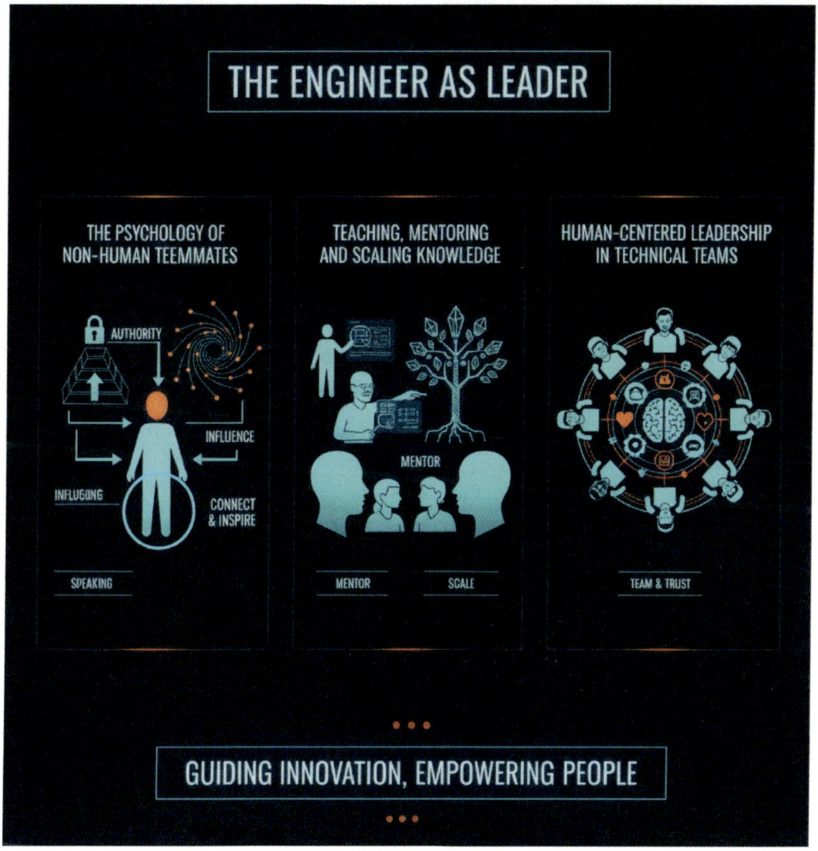

Influence vs. Authority

The Distinction That Matters

Software engineering cultures often conflate leadership with formal authority. "Who's the tech lead?" "Who's the manager?" These questions seek to identify the person with positional power—the one who can make final decisions, allocate resources, and direct work.

But the most effective engineering leadership often comes from engineers *without* formal authority. The senior engineer whose architectural opinions carry weight. The staff engineer who sets technical direction through influence rather than mandate. The individual contributor who mentors juniors and shapes team culture through example.

This distinction—**influence versus authority**—is fundamental to understanding leadership in technical contexts.

Authority is granted by organization: - Manager assigns you as tech lead - You get the title and the responsibility - You can make binding decisions - People must at least nominally follow your direction

Influence is earned through behavior: - People trust your technical judgment - Your ideas are adopted because they're good, not because you can mandate them - Teams seek your input voluntarily - Culture shifts because of your example

Authority is faster to acquire (get promoted) but more fragile (lose the title, lose the authority). Influence is slower to build (requires demonstrated capability over time) but more durable (persists even as formal roles change).

The best leaders have both: formal authority that enables certain decisions, and earned influence that makes those decisions accepted rather than just obeyed. But if you could only have one, influence is more valuable—it works across organizational boundaries, survives role changes, and creates lasting impact.

Why Influence Matters More in AI Era

As AI handles more technical execution, the nature of engineering work shifts toward judgment, context, and collaboration. These activities benefit from influence more than authority.

Example: Technical Direction

- *Authority-based approach.* "I'm the tech lead. We're using microservices architecture. Start implementing."

This works if you're right. If you're wrong, the team implements a poor decision because authority compelled them. The team learns not to question your decisions, even when they should.

- *Influence-based approach.* "I've been thinking about our architecture. Microservices could help us scale different components independently, but they add operational complexity. Let's discuss trade-offs as a team. Here's what I think, but I want your perspectives."

This invites collaboration. If you're right, the team understands *why* and can execute effectively. If you're wrong, someone catches it early. The team learns to think architecturally, not just implement instructions.

The influence-based approach is slower initially but creates better outcomes and develops team capability. In an AI era where implementation is faster but judgment is critical, this capability development is exactly what teams need.

Example: Code Review

- *Authority-based approach.* "I'm the principal engineer. This code doesn't meet standards. Rewrite it."

This gets compliance but not learning. The engineer rewrites without understanding why their approach was problematic.

- *Influence-based approach.* "I see what you're trying to accomplish here. The current approach works but will be hard to test and maintain because [specific reasons]. Have you considered [alternative approach]? It would [specific benefits]. What do you think?"

This teaches. The engineer learns not just what to change but *why*. Next time, they'll write better code without needing correction. This is leadership that scales—each interaction improves future work.

Building Influence: The Foundation

Influence isn't bestowed—it's earned through consistent behavior that builds trust. Several principles guide this:

Principle 1: Competence First

You cannot have technical influence without demonstrated technical competence. This doesn't mean being the best coder on the team—it means having sound judgment that proves correct over time.

People trust your technical opinions when: - Your architectural decisions lead to maintainable systems - Your warnings about risks turn out to be prescient - Your suggestions solve problems effectively - Your code reviews catch real issues, not just style nitpicks

This competence is table stakes. You can't skip it. But alone, competence isn't sufficient for influence.

Principle 2: Consistency

Influence requires that people can predict your behavior. If you're enthusiastic about an idea one day and dismissive the next, people don't know what you actually think. If you enforce standards for some team members but not others, your standards seem arbitrary.

Consistency builds trust. People learn: "When [person] raises a concern, it's usually worth investigating" or "When [person] suggests an approach, it's usually well-thought-out." This predictability makes your input valuable.

Principle 3: Transparency in Reasoning

Authority says: "Do it this way." Influence explains: "Here's why I think this approach is better..."

When you make reasoning visible, people can: - Evaluate whether your logic applies to their context - Learn the thinking process, not just the conclusion - Disagree productively when they have different information - Apply similar reasoning to future problems

This transparency is leadership as teaching. Every interaction becomes a learning opportunity.

Principle 4: Admitting Uncertainty

Perhaps counterintuitively, influence increases when you're honest about limitations. "I'm not sure" or "I might be wrong about this" builds more credibility than false certainty.

Why? Because people know everyone is uncertain sometimes. When you admit uncertainty, it signals: - You're honest about limitations - You won't lead them astray with overconfidence - It's safe for them to admit uncertainty too - You're focused on finding good answers, not being right

This psychological safety—the ability to admit uncertainty without loss of status—is essential for teams tackling hard problems. Leaders who model it create environments where others can too.

Principle 5: Giving Credit, Taking Blame

This old leadership principle applies powerfully in technical contexts. When projects succeed, attribute success to the team. When projects fail, accept responsibility as the leader.

This asymmetry seems unfair—why take more blame than credit? Because it creates trust and psychological safety. The team knows: - You'll protect them when things go wrong - They can take risks without fear of being thrown under the bus - Success is genuinely theirs to own - You're more focused on team performance than personal status

This trust compounds. Teams work harder for leaders who operate this way because they know the leader has their back.

The Technical Leadership Paradox

Here's a paradox: the best technical leaders often spend less time on purely technical work than less effective leaders.

Why? Because leadership is about multiplication. Writing code yourself creates 1x value. Helping five engineers write better code creates 5x value. Shaping architectural direction for a twenty-person team creates 20x value. Mentoring engineers who become leaders themselves creates exponential value.

But this multiplication requires time spent on non-code activities: - Reviewing and providing thoughtful feedback - Architecting systems and documenting decisions - Mentoring and pair programming - Clarifying requirements and technical direction - Building consensus across teams - Writing documentation that preserves knowledge

Early-career engineers sometimes resist this transition: "I became an engineer to write code, not sit in meetings." This is understandable but misses the point. Leadership isn't about meetings—it's about impact. If you can create more impact by shaping direction and developing others than by writing code directly, that's where you should spend time.

The paradox resolves: the best technical leaders aren't necessarily the best individual coders. They're the people who multiply the effectiveness of everyone around them.

Influence Without Authority: Practical Tactics

If you don't have formal authority, how do you exercise leadership?

Tactic 1: Volunteer for coordination work

Every team has work nobody wants: documenting decisions, organizing knowledge, facilitating discussions, managing technical debt tracking. Volunteer for these. They're opportunities to create structure that shapes how work happens.

The person who writes the design doc often shapes the design. The person who maintains the architecture decision records influences future decisions. The person who facilitates technical discussions guides conversations toward clarity.

Tactic 2: Become the organizational memory

Remember why decisions were made, what was tried before, what tradeoffs were considered. When discussions revisit old ground, you can provide context: "We tried that approach two years ago. Here's what we learned..." This makes you valuable and positions you to guide decisions.

Tactic 3: Ask good questions

Leadership isn't always about having answers—it's often about asking questions that clarify thinking: - "What problem are we really solving?" - "What are we optimizing for?" - "What happens if we're wrong?" - "Have we considered [alternative]?"

Good questions shape discussions more than strong opinions do. They guide groups toward better thinking without requiring authority.

Tactic 4: Make others successful

Help colleagues solve problems, review their code thoughtfully, introduce them to people who can help them, advocate for their ideas in other forums. When you consistently make others successful, they trust you and seek your input.

This creates influence through reciprocity and genuine relationship-building, not manipulation.

Tactic 5: Build artifacts that others use

Create tools, templates, documentation, or frameworks that make the team more effective. When people use what you've built, you've shaped how work gets done without requiring authority.

Examples: - Internal libraries that enforce good patterns - Documentation templates that clarify thinking - Decision frameworks that improve architectural discussions - Scripts that automate tedious work

These artifacts multiply your impact beyond what you could do directly.

Teaching, Mentoring, and Scaling Knowledge

In Chapter 11, we explored the apprenticeship problem—how junior engineers develop expertise when AI handles implementation work. Leadership in this context means creating learning environments where expertise can develop despite AI's presence.

Why Teaching Is Leadership

The traditional view: leaders set direction, make decisions, and delegate execution. Teaching is separate—something educators do, not leaders.

The AI-era view: teaching *is* leadership. When AI can generate code but can't develop judgment, the leader's role is helping engineers develop the judgment AI lacks. This is fundamentally about teaching.

Consider two team leads:

Team Lead A (traditional approach): - Makes all architectural decisions personally - Reviews code to catch errors but doesn't explain reasoning - Answers questions with solutions rather than teaching problem-solving - Measures success by team output

Result: Team is productive while Team Lead A is present. If they leave, the team struggles because they've been executing instructions, not developing judgment.

Team Lead B (teaching approach): - Involves team in architectural decisions, making reasoning explicit - Reviews code with explanations that teach principles - Answers questions with questions that develop thinking - Measures success by team capability growth

Result: Team becomes increasingly autonomous. They develop judgment that persists after Team Lead B leaves. The team's capability compounds over time.

Team Lead B creates more lasting value because they're teaching, not just directing.

The Socratic Method in Code Review

Code review is one of the most powerful teaching opportunities in software engineering, yet it's often reduced to finding bugs and enforcing style. The Socratic method—teaching through questions rather than answers—transforms code review into learning.

- *Traditional code review.*

```
Reviewer: "This function is too complex. Split it
    into smaller functions."
```

The author splits it, but they haven't learned how to recognize complexity themselves.

- *Socratic code review.*

```
Reviewer: "What does this function do? Can you
    explain it in one sentence?"
Author: "It validates the user input, processes
    it, updates the database,
sends notifications, and logs the result."
Reviewer: "That's five responsibilities. Which
    ones are core to this
function's purpose?"
Author: "Oh... really just validation and
```

```
    delegation. The others could be
separate."
Reviewer: "Right. How would you restructure it to
    separate those concerns?"
```

The author discovers the problem themselves through guided questions. They learn not just to fix this code but to recognize complexity in future code.

- *Keys to effective Socratic review.*
- *Ask, don't tell.* "What happens if this field is null?" rather than "This will crash if the field is null."
- *Guide toward principles.* "What principle of good design does this violate?" rather than "This is bad design."
- *Invite explanation.* "Walk me through how this works" rather than "This is confusing."
- *Acknowledge good thinking.* "Why did you choose this approach?" (even when you'd choose differently) teaches that choices should be reasoned, not arbitrary.

This takes more time initially. But it builds capability that pays dividends—engineers who've learned through Socratic review make better decisions independently.

Creating Mental Models Through Analogy

Expertise consists largely of mental models—frameworks for understanding problems that enable pattern recognition and intuitive judgment (Chi et al. 1989). Teaching these mental models is leadership work.

The most effective way to transfer mental models is through analogy—connecting unfamiliar concepts to familiar ones.

Example: Teaching Distributed Systems

Abstract explanation (correct but hard to internalize): "In distributed systems, you can't have both strong consistency and high availability during network partitions. This is the CAP theorem."

Analogical explanation (creates mental model): "Imagine two bank branches that need to stay synchronized. If they can talk to each other (no partition), they can stay consistent and available. If the network fails, they have two choices:

Option 1: Stay consistent by shutting down until they can sync (sacrifice availability). This is like saying 'Sorry, we can't process transactions until we can confirm with the other branch.'

Option 2: Stay available by operating independently (sacrifice consistency). This is like letting customers withdraw money at both branches, even though they might see different balances.

CAP theorem says during network failures, pick one—consistent or available—because you can't have both."

The analogy creates a mental model that helps engineers reason about distributed systems intuitively, not just memorize theorems.

- *Keys to effective analogies.*
- *Use familiar concepts.* Connect to things engineers already understand (bank branches, phone calls, physical mail).
- *Preserve structure.* The analogy should mirror the key relationships in the technical concept.
- *Acknowledge limits.* "This analogy breaks down when..." teaches nuance.
- *Iterate.* If an analogy doesn't land, try another. Different engineers need different mental models.

The Deliberate Practice Framework

In Chapter 11, we introduced deliberate practice as essential for skill development. Leaders create environments where deliberate practice happens.

- *What leaders do to enable practice.*
- *Create safe spaces for struggle.* Juniors need to work on problems at the edge of their capability without fear that mistakes will be career-limiting. Leaders protect this space:
- "This is a learning project. Mistakes are expected and valuable."
- "Let's try this approach. If it doesn't work, we'll learn from it."
- "I made similar mistakes when I was learning. Here's what I discovered..."
- *Provide appropriate scaffolding.* Too much help and juniors don't learn. Too little and they thrash unproductively. The skill is calibrating support:
- Early on: Work together, think aloud, show the process
- Middle stage: Offer hints when stuck, but let them work
- Later stage: Observe from distance, intervene only if significantly off track

- *Structure reflection.* Practice without reflection doesn't build expertise (Schön 1983). Leaders structure reflection:
- Post-project retrospectives: "What did you learn? What would you do differently?"
- Weekly 1-on-1s: "What was the hardest problem you solved this week? How did you approach it?"
- Design review: "Explain your reasoning. What alternatives did you consider?"
- *Increase difficulty progressively.* As engineers master one level, provide challenges at the next:
- Junior: Implement specified features
- Mid: Propose implementation approaches for features
- Senior: Design features that solve underlying problems
- Staff: Identify which problems are worth solving

This progressive challenge is how expertise develops. Leaders orchestrate it deliberately.

Scaling Knowledge Through Documentation

Leadership includes preserving and scaling knowledge beyond direct teaching. Documentation is how knowledge scales to many people and across time.

But most documentation fails because it's written for the wrong audience or purpose. Effective leaders understand documentation types:

Type 1: Decision Records

Document *why* decisions were made, not just what was decided. Future engineers (including future you) need context:

```
# Architecture Decision Record: Use Event
# Sourcing for Orders

## Context
Order processing requires audit trails for
    compliance. We've had issues with
data consistency during concurrent updates.
    Previous architecture made
debugging difficult because we couldn't
```

```
    reconstruct historical state.

## Decision
Implement event sourcing for order domain:
    persist events rather than state,
reconstruct state from events.

## Consequences
Pros: Audit trail built-in, easier debugging,
    natural fit for compliance
Cons: More complex than CRUD, requires team to
    learn event sourcing,
      eventual consistency model

## Alternatives Considered
1. Transaction logs + snapshots (complex to
    implement correctly)
2. Audit tables alongside state tables
    (consistency issues)
3. Time-travel database features (vendor lock-in)

## Date
2026-01-15

## Participants
@alice (architect), @bob (domain expert),
    @charlie (ops lead)
```

This preserves reasoning so future engineers understand context.

Type 2: Onboarding Guides

Reduce the ramp-up time for new team members by documenting what you wish you'd known when you joined: - How to set up development environment - How to run and test locally - Where things are (repos, docs, monitoring) - Who to ask about different domains - Common pitfalls and how to avoid them

Good onboarding documentation is leadership multiplied—it helps every new hire become productive faster.

Type 3: Domain Context

Document domain knowledge that engineers need but that isn't in code: - Why this domain is complex - Key concepts and terminology - Regulatory or business constraints - Common workflows and user journeys - Integration points with other systems

This is vertical expertise made scalable (Chapter 14). When you document domain knowledge, you multiply your expertise across the team.

Type 4: Post-Mortems

When things go wrong, document what happened and what you learned. This turns failures into learning for the whole organization: - What happened (timeline) - Why it happened (root cause) - How we fixed it (resolution) - How we prevent recurrence (action items) - What we learned (insights)

Post-mortems without blame are powerful teaching tools and demonstrate the psychological safety discussed earlier.

Mentorship Beyond "Have a 1-on-1"

Formal mentorship programs often fail because they're too structured or too vague. Effective mentorship is relationship-based and context-specific.

- *What makes mentorship effective.*
- *Specificity.* Don't mentor "in general." Focus on specific areas: "Let's work on your system design thinking" or "I'll help you navigate stakeholder communication."
- *Observation.* Watch the person work—pair programming, sitting in on their meetings, reviewing their designs. You can't mentor effectively if you only talk about work, not observe it.
- *Modeling.* Let them observe you work. Explain your thinking aloud. Show them how an expert approaches problems, makes decisions, handles ambiguity.
- *Challenge.* Good mentors push mentees beyond comfort zones. "You're ready for this. I'll be here if you need backup, but I think you should lead this design."
- *Connection.* Introduce mentees to people who can help them. Expand their network. Advocate for them when they're not in the room.
- *Patience.* People learn at different rates. The mentee who struggles now may become exceptional later. Patient investment in people pays off over years.

Human-Centered Leadership in Technical Teams

The most important leadership skill, especially in an AI era, is understanding humans. Technical problems are increasingly solvable (often with AI assistance). Human problems—motivation, conflict, communication, trust—remain as difficult as ever and determine whether technical solutions succeed.

The People Side of Technical Decisions

Every technical decision is also a people decision. Leaders understand this dual nature.

Example: Choosing a Technology

- *Purely technical view.* "Framework X has better performance than Framework Y."
- *Leadership view.* "Framework X has better performance, but our team knows Framework Y well and Framework X would require significant retraining. We're also about to launch two major features that need the team at full productivity. Do we gain enough from X to justify the switching cost now, or should we wait until after launch?"

The technical view sees only technical trade-offs. The leadership view sees technical trade-offs *and* impact on people, timing, organizational context.

Example: Refactoring Decision

- *Purely technical view.* "This code is messy and should be refactored."
- *Leadership view.* "This code is messy, but it was written under intense deadline pressure by someone who just left the company. The team who maintains it now is already stretched thin and demoralized by technical debt they inherited. Another refactoring project might break morale. Can we improve it incrementally as we add features, or do we need dedicated time? If dedicated time, how do we frame it so it's motivating rather than punitive?"

The leadership view considers morale, workload, perception, and motivation alongside technical quality.

- *The pattern.* Technical decisions affect people. Leaders think about both dimensions.

Motivation: Autonomy, Mastery, Purpose

Research on motivation consistently identifies three intrinsic drivers: autonomy, mastery, and purpose (Pink 2009). Technical leaders create environments where these drivers flourish.

- *Autonomy.* People want agency over their work.
- *Bad leadership.* "Here's exactly what to build and exactly how to build it. Let me know when it's done."
- *Good leadership.* "Here's the problem we need to solve and the constraints. I trust you to figure out the best approach. Come back if you want to discuss alternatives or if you get stuck."

Autonomy doesn't mean abandonment—it means trust combined with support. Let people make decisions, provide guidance when needed, but don't micromanage.

- *Mastery.* People want to develop skills and become better at their craft.
- *Bad leadership.* Assign the same types of tasks repeatedly. People stagnate.
- *Good leadership.* "You've mastered feature implementation. Ready for the next challenge? I'd like you to lead the design for the next module. I'll be involved, but you'll drive."

Mastery requires stretch assignments—work slightly beyond current capability that develops new skills. Leaders provide these opportunities intentionally.

- *Purpose.* People want work that matters.
- *Bad leadership.* "Just implement the ticket. Don't worry about why."
- *Good leadership.* "Let me explain why this feature matters. Users are frustrated because [specific problem]. This feature will [specific benefit]. Your work will make their experience significantly better."

Purpose connects daily work to larger impact. Leaders provide this context regularly.

- *The AI connection.* As AI handles more routine work, human work becomes more focused on problems requiring judgment—inherently more purposeful. But leaders must make this purpose explicit. "You're not just coding anymore—you're solving problems that AI can't handle" is motivating if framed correctly.

Psychological Safety: The Foundation of High Performance

Google's research on team effectiveness found psychological safety—the belief that you can take risks without being punished or humiliated—was the most important factor distinguishing high-performing teams (Edmondson 1999; Rozovsky 2015).

In technical contexts, psychological safety means: - You can admit you don't know something without seeming incompetent - You can propose ideas without fear they'll be dismissed - You can make mistakes without fear of blame - You can disagree with senior engineers without career risk - You can ask for help without seeming weak

- *How leaders build psychological safety.*
- *Model vulnerability.* Admit when you don't know something. "I'm not familiar with this technology. Can someone explain it?" If the leader can admit ignorance, others can too.
- *Respond to failures constructively.* When mistakes happen, focus on learning rather than blame. "What happened? What can we learn? How do we prevent this?" not "Who screwed up?"
- *Invite dissent.* "I think we should do X, but I might be wrong. What am I missing?" Actively seeking disagreement signals it's safe to disagree.
- *Protect people who take risks.* When someone tries something ambitious and fails, defend them. "They took a calculated risk. That's exactly what we need people doing. The issue was [technical problem], not judgment."
- *Celebrate learning.* Make learning visible and valued. "Here's what I learned this week" in team meetings. Public learning normalizes not knowing.

Psychological safety is especially important in AI-augmented work. If engineers are afraid to admit AI-generated code might be wrong, or afraid to ask whether an AI suggestion makes sense, bad code reaches production. Safety enables honest evaluation.

Managing Conflict Productively

Technical teams experience conflict constantly—disagreements about architecture, technology choices, priorities, approaches. Bad leaders suppress conflict or let it fester. Good leaders channel it productively.

- *Healthy vs. unhealthy conflict.*

Healthy conflict (about ideas): - "I think we should use approach A because [reasons]. You prefer approach B. Let's evaluate trade-offs." - Focus: Technical merits - Tone: Respectful, curious, focused on finding best solution - Outcome: Better decision through diverse perspectives

Unhealthy conflict (about people): - "You always want to over-engineer things." - Focus: Personal characteristics, past grievances - Tone: Defensive, attacking, focused on winning - Outcome: Damaged relationships, poor decisions, reduced psychological safety

- *How leaders manage conflict.*
- *Reframe personal as technical.* When conflict becomes personal, redirect to technical merits. "Let's focus on the approaches rather than who's proposing them. What are the trade-offs?"
- *Make criteria explicit.* "We're evaluating based on: maintainability, performance, team familiarity. Let's assess each option against these criteria."
- *Acknowledge emotions.* "I see this matters deeply to both of you. That's good—we want people who care. Let's find the best solution together."
- *Create structured discussion.* Ad-hoc arguments are often unproductive. "Let's schedule an architecture discussion where each of you presents your approach, and we evaluate them systematically."
- *Model humility.* "I had a strong opinion about this, but after hearing the arguments, I've changed my mind. Here's why..." This shows changing positions based on evidence is strength, not weakness.

The Delegation Challenge

As we discussed in Chapter 9, effective delegation to AI requires skill. Effective delegation to humans is even more complex—and it's central to leadership.

- *Why engineers struggle with delegation.*
- *Perfectionism.* "If I do it myself, it'll be done right." But this doesn't scale and prevents others from developing skills.
- *Speed.* "It's faster to do it myself than explain it." True in the short term, false in the long term. Teaching takes time but creates capability.
- *Identity.* "I'm an engineer—I'm supposed to write code." Leadership requires shifting identity from doing to enabling.

- *Trust.* "I'm not sure they can handle it." Sometimes true—but people develop capability by being trusted with challenges.
- *Keys to effective delegation.*
- *Delegate outcomes, not tasks.* "We need to improve query performance" not "Optimize these three queries." The first develops thinking; the second is just execution.
- *Provide context.* Explain why something matters, what constraints apply, what success looks like. Context enables good decisions.
- *Match challenge to capability.* Delegate slightly beyond current capability—enough to be challenging, not so much that it's overwhelming.
- *Stay available.* "I've delegated this to you, but I'm available if you get stuck or want to discuss approaches."
- *Accept different approaches.* If the outcome is good, the approach doesn't have to match what you would have done. Different doesn't mean wrong.
- *Review and reflect.* After delegated work completes, discuss: "What went well? What was challenging? What did you learn?"

Communication: The Meta-Skill

If there's one skill that separates good technical leaders from great ones, it's communication. Not just speaking clearly—though that matters—but the ability to:

- *Translate between technical and non-technical.* Explain technical concepts to non-engineers, business constraints to engineers, and uncertainty to stakeholders who want certainty.
- *Tailor message to audience.* The same architectural decision requires different explanations for developers (technical trade-offs), managers (business implications), and executives (strategic fit).
- *Write effectively.* Documentation, design proposals, post-mortems, technical strategy—all require clear writing. Writing is thinking made visible.
- *Listen actively.* Understanding not just what people say but what they mean, what concerns they have, and what they're not saying.
- *Facilitate discussion.* Guide conversations toward clarity and decisions without dominating them. Ask questions that help groups think together.

- *Give feedback constructively.* Deliver criticism in ways that improve performance without damaging relationships or motivation.

These communication skills multiply impact. A technically brilliant engineer who can't communicate is limited to their own output. An engineer with strong communication skills multiplies the output of everyone they interact with.

The Leadership Journey

Leadership isn't binary—you're not "not a leader" one day and "a leader" the next. It's a gradual progression:

Stage 1: Individual Contributor (Years 0-3) - Focus: Your own technical growth - Leadership opportunity: Model good practices, help teammates with specific technical problems - Primary learning: Technical competence, professional behavior

Stage 2: Peer Influencer (Years 3-5) - Focus: Team's technical quality - Leadership opportunity: Code review, pair programming, proposing improvements, building consensus - Primary learning: Influence without authority, communication, feedback

Stage 3: Team Multiplier (Years 5-8) - Focus: Team capability and effectiveness - Leadership opportunity: Mentoring, architectural guidance, facilitating decisions, cultural influence - Primary learning: Teaching, delegation, people understanding

Stage 4: Organizational Leader (Years 8+) - Focus: Organization's technical direction and capability - Leadership opportunity: Strategy, culture, cross-team coordination, developing leaders - Primary learning: Systems thinking, organizational dynamics, long-term thinking

These stages aren't age or experience dependent—they're capability dependent. Some engineers reach Stage 3 in four years; others never leave Stage 1. The progression requires deliberate development of leadership skills alongside technical skills.

Leadership as Service

Perhaps the most important mindset shift: leadership is not about status, power, or recognition. It's about service—using your capabilities to make others more effective.

The leader who asks "How can I make my team successful?" rather than "How can I look good?" creates trust and enables high performance.

The leader who asks "What does this person need to grow?" rather than "What can I get from this person?" develops people who become leaders themselves.

The leader who asks "What does the organization need?" rather than "What benefits my career?" makes decisions that compound positively over time.

This service orientation is especially important in technical contexts where engineers often become leaders reluctantly and resist "soft skills" as less valuable than technical skills. The truth: in AI-augmented environments where technical execution is faster, the "soft" skills of understanding people, building trust, communicating clearly, and developing others are the hardest and most valuable skills of all.

Chapter Summary

- **Influence matters more than authority.** Authority is granted by organization, influence is earned through behavior. Influence is more durable, works across boundaries, and creates lasting impact through trust rather than compliance.
- **AI amplifies the value of human leadership.** As technical execution becomes faster through AI assistance, the bottlenecks are: clarifying what to build, aligning teams, developing capabilities, making good decisions under uncertainty. These are leadership responsibilities that resist automation.
- **Building influence requires consistent demonstration.** Technical competence, consistency in behavior, transparency in reasoning, honest admission of uncertainty, and asymmetric credit/blame (give credit, take blame) all build the trust that creates influence.
- **Technical leaders multiply through others.** Writing code yourself creates 1x value; helping five engineers creates 5x value; shaping direction for twenty creates 20x value. Leadership is about multiplication, not individual productivity (Pink 2009).
- **Teaching is leadership.** When AI generates code but can't develop judgment, the leader's role is helping engineers develop judgment. Socratic code review, mental models through analogy, deliberate practice frameworks, and scaling knowledge through documentation all multiply impact.
- **Every technical decision is a people decision.** Technology choices affect

morale, motivation, and workload. Leaders consider both technical and human dimensions when making decisions.

- **Motivation requires autonomy, mastery, purpose.** People want agency over work (autonomy), opportunities to develop skills (mastery), and understanding of why work matters (purpose). Leaders create environments where these flourish (Pink 2009).
- **Psychological safety enables performance.** The belief that you can take risks, admit ignorance, propose ideas, make mistakes, and disagree without punishment is the foundation of high-performing teams. Leaders build this through vulnerability, constructive failure response, and protecting risk-takers (Edmondson 1999; Rozovsky 2015).
- **Conflict is healthy when about ideas, not people.** Leaders reframe personal conflict as technical disagreement, make evaluation criteria explicit, acknowledge emotions, structure discussions, and model humility about changing positions based on evidence (Chi et al. 1989).
- **Effective delegation develops capability.** Delegate outcomes not tasks, provide context, match challenge to capability, stay available, accept different approaches, and review to enable learning. This takes more time initially but builds sustainable team capability (Schön 1983).
- **Communication is the meta-skill.** Translating between audiences, tailoring messages, writing clearly, listening actively, facilitating discussions, and giving constructive feedback all multiply impact more than pure technical skill.
- **Leadership is a progression, not a binary.** From individual contributor to peer influencer to team multiplier to organizational leader—each stage requires deliberate development of leadership capabilities alongside technical depth.
- **Leadership as service, not status.** The most effective leaders ask "How can I make my team successful?" rather than "How can I look good?" This service orientation builds trust and enables high performance.

Having explored the skills, collaboration patterns, career strategies, and leadership capabilities that define engineering excellence, we now turn to the broader landscape: how work itself is transforming, what ethical responsibilities accompany these changes, and what kind of engineer will thrive in the decades ahead.

Chapter 16

Work in the Age of Intelligent Machines

"The future is already here—it's just not evenly distributed." — William Gibson

---

In 1960, psychologist J.C.R. Licklider published "Man-Computer Symbiosis," envisioning a future where humans and computers would work together in ways that transcended the capabilities of either alone (Licklider 1960). Licklider imagined computers handling "routinizable" tasks while humans focused on "goal-setting, problem definition, hypothesis generation, and decision-making." He predicted this symbiosis would emerge "in a few years"—optimistically underestimating by about six decades.

We are now, finally, entering the era Licklider anticipated. But the reality is stranger and more complex than his mid-century optimism suggested. AI systems don't simply handle the "routinizable" while leaving humans the interesting work. They reshape the entire topology of knowledge work, creating new categories of labor while eliminating others, amplifying some skills while rendering others obsolete, and fundamentally altering what it means to "program" or "engineer" or "create."

The Obsolescence Paradox operates at multiple scales. At the task level, automation makes judgment more valuable. But what happens at the structural level—when AI doesn't just automate tasks but reshapes the very nature of engineering work itself?

This chapter confronts three questions that probe the paradox's limits:

First: If AI can now operate at the Design layer—not just executing specified tasks but making architectural decisions—where does irreducible human contribution begin? Has the boundary moved?

Second: As AI systems become capable of sustained, agentic work—operating autonomously over hours or days—what new forms of human-AI collaboration emerge? Do our existing interaction patterns suffice?

Third: If AI can unbundle knowledge work into discrete, automatable tasks, does this represent the ultimate revaluation of human skills—or does it threaten the coherence of engineering as a profession?

These questions aren't comfortable. But they're essential if we want to understand—and shape—the transformation we're living through.

AI, Software, and the Return of Infrastructure

For years, we told ourselves that software was the easy part.

Building applications wasn't the challenge anymore. Distribution was solved. Cloud made deployment trivial. SaaS abstracted away complexity. The real value shifted to process—encoding how a business operates, complies, reports, and scales. That's what companies were really buying.

AI doesn't fundamentally change that truth. What it changes is how we access it.

Instead of navigating dashboards, learning tooling, or relying on specialists to extract insight, we now interact directly. We ask questions. We describe outcomes. We request formats. The interface collapses into language.

This feels revolutionary—and it is—but it doesn't erase the underlying systems. It simply lowers the friction between intent and execution.

And that distinction matters.

Coding Is Easier. Engineering Is Harder.

There's a temptation to say that AI is killing coding. That's only partially true.

What AI is really doing is lowering the barrier to entry. More people can now express logic, generate code, and assemble systems. The floor drops. Participation explodes.

But the ceiling doesn't come down.

In fact, it rises.

As systems become easier to create, they also become more numerous, more interconnected, and more operationally demanding. The hard problems shift upward—into architecture, state management, security, reliability, compliance, and long-term evolution.

AI can help you write code. It cannot yet own a complex, stateful system over time. It doesn't close the feedback loop between behavior in production and architectural refinement. It doesn't run operations.

That's why the most aggressive adopters of AI are not shrinking their engineering teams—they're hiring more experienced ones.

The paradox is simple: when creation gets cheaper, responsibility gets heavier (Autor 2015).

One concrete marker of this shift is the unit of cost accounting. The infrastructure engineer of the previous decade calculated cost in CPU-hours, memory allocation, and network egress. The infrastructure engineer of 2026 calculates Total Cost of Ownership per token — the fully-loaded expense of processing a unit of language model inference across compute, latency, and model tier. This is not a trivial reframing. It changes how capacity is planned, how architectural trade-offs are evaluated, and which engineers sit closest to the financial decisions. The engineers who internalise token economics think like owners of the new infrastructure layer. Those who do not remain consumers of it.

SaaS Was Never About Screens

Much of the anxiety around AI and SaaS misses the point.

SaaS didn't win because of better interfaces. It won because it captured business reality. It embedded workflows, approvals, constraints, audits, and compliance into software. That complexity doesn't disappear just because the interface becomes conversational.

What changes is interaction, not obligation.

Humans—and increasingly autonomous agents—now sit closer to decision-making. Software becomes something that is queried, instructed, and orchestrated, rather than navigated. Pricing, purchasing, and control models will shift accordingly.

But the core burden remains: software must still reflect how the real world works.

This Doesn't Look Like a Bubble—It Looks Like a Bottleneck

If AI demand is so real, why does everything feel tight?

Because this is what every major technological transition looks like.

In the early phase of a new epoch, we assume the hard problems are behind us. We treat infrastructure as complete. Then usage explodes—and the cracks appear.

Systems built for a smaller world begin to strain. Networks saturate. Power becomes scarce. Physical footprint, coordination, and regulation reassert themselves as first-order constraints.

We've seen this before: with the internet, with cloud, with mobile, with 5G. Each time, the story repeats. Each time, we have to rebuild the stack (Perez 2002; Brynjolfsson et al. 2023).

AI is not different. It is simply the next forcing function.

The demand isn't speculative. Budgets are moving. Models are deployed. Productivity gains are measurable. And yet compute is scarce, data centers take years to build, power is constrained, and governance lags far behind capability (Sevilla et al. 2022; Strubell et al. 2019).

This isn't a bubble dynamic. It's an infrastructure lag.

Why Scale Isn't Saving Us (Yet)

Two simplistic narratives dominate the conversation.

One claims AI is overhyped and will collapse under its own expectations.

The other assumes scale will magically smooth everything out.

Neither explains reality.

What's actually happening is that demand is outpacing every layer beneath the models. The biggest constraints are no longer inside the algorithms—they sit in energy, hardware supply chains, physical buildout, organizational readiness, and institutional inertia.

Enterprise software exposes this most clearly. The harder parts were never the UI. They were the rules, the guarantees, and the operational truth embedded underneath.

AI doesn't remove that weight. It redistributes it.

The Quiet Shift in Decision-Making

There is a deeper, more subtle change underway.

If agents can generate code, provision infrastructure, select tools, and orchestrate workflows—where does decision-making actually live?

Who is accountable when choices are automated, layered, and partially invisible?

This isn't a tooling question. It's a governance one.

As AI systems move closer to intent and further from explicit human control, the locus of responsibility becomes harder to see—but more important than ever to define.

That's why infrastructure is not fading away.

It's moving back to the center of the story.

The Pattern Repeats

Every technical epoch convinces us that we've reached the end of complexity.

And every time, the next wave proves us wrong.

AI is not the end of software, engineering, or infrastructure. It is the reason we will have to take them more seriously than we have in years.

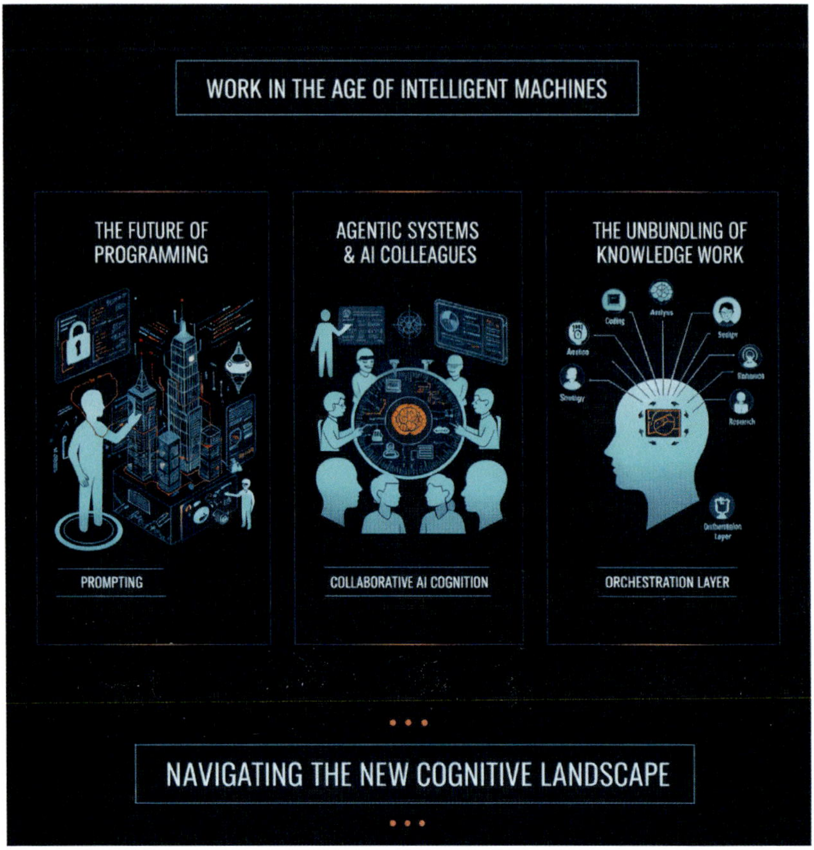

The Future of Programming

Let's begin with a question that cuts to the heart of engineering identity: if AI systems can now operate at the Design layer—making architectural decisions, evaluating trade-offs, proposing solutions—what exactly is left for human engineers to do?

The Historical Arc of Abstraction

To understand where programming is going, we need to understand where it's been. The history of programming is a history of *rising abstraction*—each generation of technology allowing developers to work at higher conceptual levels while automating away lower-level concerns.

- *Machine code (1940s-1950s).* Programming meant directly manipulating processor instructions—load this value into register A, add register B, store the result. Every operation was explicit. Every memory address was manual. The "program" was indistinguishable from the machine's operation.

- *Assembly language (1950s-1960s).* Symbolic names replaced numeric opcodes. `ADD` instead of `0x83`. The assembler automated the translation to machine code. This was controversial—some programmers insisted real programming required working directly with machine code, that assembly was a crutch for the less skilled (Knuth 1997).
- *High-level languages (1960s-1980s).* FORTRAN, COBOL, C. Abstract data types, functions, control flow structures. The compiler automated register allocation, instruction scheduling, and optimization. Again, controversy—"real" programmers worked in assembly; high-level languages were for those who didn't understand the machine (Dijkstra 1972).
- *Memory-managed languages (1990s-2000s).* Java, Python, JavaScript. The runtime automated memory management, removing an entire class of bugs and cognitive load. Once more, skepticism—"real" programmers understood memory; garbage collection was training wheels (Pike 2012).
- *Frameworks and libraries (2000s-2010s).* React, Rails, Django. Vast amounts of functionality pre-packaged and composed. Configuration over code. Convention over configuration. The framework automated entire architectural layers. And yes, debate—"real" programmers built from first principles (Fowler 2003).

Each abstraction layer was met with resistance from those who had mastered the previous layer. Each was accused of lowering the bar, producing programmers who didn't "really" understand what was happening. And each, eventually, became the new baseline—the taken-for-granted foundation that the next generation built upon.

- *AI-assisted programming (2020s-present).* Natural language descriptions generate code. The AI automates not just execution but increasingly participates in design decisions. And predictably, we hear that "real" programming requires writing code by hand, that AI assistance produces engineers who never develop true expertise.

The pattern is unmistakable. As Dijkstra observed about structured programming, each new abstraction layer "alters the way in which we have to think about the program" (Dijkstra 1972). The question isn't whether AI will change programming—it already has. The question is whether this change is continuous with previous transitions, or whether it represents something qualitatively different.

Programming as Protocol Design

The historical arc of abstraction reveals something deeper: programming in the AI era is less about speaking to silicon and more about negotiating a shared language between humans and increasingly capable machine collaborators. The same compilation machinery that once targeted CPUs now mediates intent between teams of engineers, large models, and heterogeneous hardware.

Intent preservation in an AI world. Traditional languages were designed to preserve a human's intent as it moves from source code to machine code. AI tooling adds a new, powerful reader and co-author into that loop. Code now has three audiences at once: future maintainers, optimizing compilers, and generative models learning from and acting on that codebase.

For engineers, this shifts the design challenge. The question is no longer "How do I make this clear to the compiler?" but "How do I make this intent robust under transformation by compilers, refactorings, and AI agents that will rewrite, specialize, and recompose it over time?" The best engineers treat code as a long-lived **protocol** for intent, not just a one-off artifact to be compiled.

From ASTs to AI-readable structure. The compilation pipeline still begins with parsing source code into an abstract syntax tree (AST), but the AST is increasingly the substrate on which AI tools operate rather than merely a staging area for code generation. Refactoring assistants, automated reviewers, and code-understanding models all lean on structural representations that strip away noise and expose the semantic skeleton of a system.

This changes how structure should be viewed:

- The AST is now a contract for both classical compilers and learned tools, defining where intent is explicit versus implicit.
- Semantic passes such as type inference and data-flow analysis become features that AI systems can consume to reason about invariants and propose safe transformations.
- Engineers who design APIs and domain-specific languages with clean structural and semantic boundaries are effectively designing better training data and control surfaces for the AI tools that will work on their systems.

Intermediate representations as optimization playgrounds. Intermediate representations (IRs) used to be the quiet middle layer of compilers—a bridge between high-level source and low-level machine code. In the AI era, they have become the battleground where search and learning decide how intent is realized in hardware. Systems like TVM treat IR not just as a bridge but as the definition of a search space over all programs equivalent to a given high-level specification (Chen et al. 2018).

Three shifts are apparent:

- IRs are becoming more *declarative*, making it easier to apply learned cost models and reinforcement learning to explore schedules, layouts, and parallelization strategies.
- Optimization is increasingly framed as a continuous experiment: the compiler tries variants, measures behavior, updates a model, and converges on hardware-specific strategies.
- Engineers who can reason about IR-level tradeoffs—tensor layouts, fusion boundaries, scheduling primitives—gain leverage because they can shape the search space AI optimizers explore, rather than hand-tuning each outcome.

JVM-style architectures as adaptive ecosystems. The Java Virtual Machine pioneered an architecture where a stable intermediate representation (bytecode) sits between human intent and machine execution, and where runtime profiling drives speculation, inlining, and deoptimization. In an AI-saturated toolchain, that architecture looks less like a historical curiosity and more like a template for adaptive software ecosystems.

Modern runtimes continuously profile behavior and recompile hot paths, treating execution as feedback that can reshape code layout and specialization. They use speculative optimizations that assume patterns observed so far will persist, then roll back safely when those assumptions fail. They provide hooks where external optimizers—potentially AI schedulers or layout planners—can influence decisions traditionally reserved for built-in compilers.

Engineers who understand these feedback loops are positioned to integrate AI-driven optimizers safely: they know which invariants must hold, which assumptions may change, and where guardrails belong.

The deeper lesson. The compilation pipeline reveals that engineering in the AI era is no longer a one-way translation; it is a continuous negotiation between human-specified intent, AI-driven search, and hardware constraints. The same technology that makes code generation "automatic" also amplifies the consequences of unclear intent, leaky abstractions, and poorly chosen boundaries.

Engineers who thrive will:

- Design systems with clear semantic contracts, so that automated transformations—by compilers or AI agents—have less room to misinterpret the underlying intent.
- Think in terms of optimization *spaces* and constraints instead of single "optimal" solutions, providing AI tools with well-shaped search landscapes rather than brittle hand-tuned code.
- Treat intermediate representations, runtime feedback, and AI tooling as part of the architectural design space, not as opaque magic layers below the application.

In that light, the obsolescence paradox resolves: as more of the mechanics of code generation and tuning are automated, the premium shifts toward engineers who can specify intent precisely, shape the representations that carry it, and architect systems that remain intelligible to both humans and machines over decades.

The Three Layers Under Pressure

AI's rapid evolution challenges our understanding of where human contribution remains essential. Consider how capabilities have shifted across the three layers of engineering work:

- *At the Execution Layer.* AI systems now generate syntactically correct code, write comprehensive tests, produce documentation, and perform complex refactoring with remarkable reliability. For well-specified tasks, execution is largely automated. This was predictable—execution has always been most amenable to automation.
- *At the Design Layer.* This is where things get interesting. Modern AI systems can:
- Propose architectural patterns based on requirements
- Evaluate trade-offs between competing design approaches
- Suggest optimizations for performance or maintainability
- Identify integration points in existing codebases
- Generate multiple design alternatives for comparison

These are Design-layer activities. The AI isn't just executing specified plans—it's participating in planning itself. This represents a genuine capability expansion beyond what was possible even two years ago.

- *At the Intent Layer.* AI has made less progress here, and the reasons are fundamental rather than incidental. Intent involves:

- Understanding whose problems matter and why
- Navigating organizational politics and stakeholder conflicts
- Making ethical judgments about acceptable trade-offs
- Aligning technical solutions with business strategy
- Deciding what to build, not just how to build it

These remain stubbornly human domains. AI can assist—clarifying requirements, surfacing implications, identifying stakeholders—but it cannot originate purpose.

So has the boundary moved? Yes and no. The crucial distinction is between *design within constraints* and *design of constraints*. AI can explore the design space defined by human-specified requirements and constraints. It can optimize, suggest, and even innovate within that space. But it struggles with the meta-design question: *what constraints should we impose?*

Consider a concrete example. Ask an AI to "design a caching layer for our API" and it will generate reasonable options—Redis with TTL-based expiration, CDN caching with cache-control headers, application-level memoization. It understands caching patterns and can apply them competently.

But ask the deeper question: "Should we optimize for read latency at the expense of consistency guarantees, given our user base and business model?" and the AI's limitations become apparent. It can explain the trade-offs technically, but it cannot make the value judgment about which trade-off aligns with organizational priorities, user expectations, and long-term strategic direction.

This is the Design/Intent boundary, and it remains meaningful. AI operates at Design within Intent-specified constraints. The human role at Design is evolving from *implementation of design decisions* to *specification of design constraints and evaluation of design proposals.*

The Revaluation Intensifies

Here's the key insight: AI's incursion into the Design layer doesn't contradict the pattern we've observed—it *intensifies* it.

When AI handles routine tasks, the remaining tasks requiring creativity and judgment become a larger proportion of the work. The same dynamic is now playing out at the Design layer.

As AI handles routine design decisions—selecting standard patterns, optimizing for well-understood metrics, implementing best practices—the human role at Design concentrates in the non-routine:

- **Novel architectural challenges** where established patterns don't apply
- **Contextual design decisions** requiring deep organizational knowledge
- **Trade-off evaluation** where competing values must be balanced
- **Design review and critique** where judgment about quality matters
- **Cross-system coherence** where multiple components must align

These activities were always valuable. They're now becoming the primary work of the Design layer, as routine design work migrates toward automation. Engineers who excel at these activities become more valuable precisely because AI handles everything else.

The same pattern holds at the Intent layer. As AI assists with intent clarification and requirement specification, human work at Intent concentrates in the hardest parts:

- **Stakeholder mediation** when requirements conflict
- **Strategic alignment** between technical and business objectives

- **Value judgments** about acceptable risks and trade-offs
- **Ethical considerations** about impact and responsibility

This is the paradox operating at higher levels of abstraction. Each time AI automates a layer of work, human value concentrates in the next layer up—and in the most challenging parts of the automated layer.

From Operational to Intentional Programming

What's genuinely different about AI-assisted programming is the shift from *operational* to *intentional* thinking.

When you write in C instead of assembly, you're still specifying exactly what operations to perform—you're just doing it at a higher level of abstraction. The compiler figures out *how* to map those operations to machine instructions, but you're still thinking operationally: allocate memory, iterate over arrays, call functions.

When you use AI to generate code from natural language, something different happens. You describe a goal—"implement user authentication with JWT tokens"—and the AI determines what operations are needed. You're operating at the level of *intent*, not operations.

This shift has profound implications for what "programming" means. The programmer becomes less an implementer and more a *specifier and evaluator of intent*. But intent is ambiguous, contextual, and value-laden in ways that operations are not.

Consider Fred Brooks's observation that "the hardest single part of building a software system is deciding precisely what to build" (Brooks 1987). For decades, this seemed to support the centrality of human judgment in software development. Since specifications are hard to create and inherently incomplete, human programmers would always be essential.

AI changes the equation in an unexpected way: by being *tolerant of ambiguous specifications*. Large language models trained on vast corpora of code develop something like "common sense" about what programmers typically mean by vague descriptions (Chen et al. 2021). Ask for "a function to validate email addresses" and the AI generates something reasonable—not perfect, but reasonable—without requiring precise specification of all edge cases.

This is both powerful and dangerous. Powerful because it reduces the specification burden. Dangerous because it hides the gap between what you said and what you meant. The AI fills that gap with statistical defaults—the most common interpretation in its training data—which may or may not match your actual intent.

Here's a simple example. You ask an AI to "generate a function to calculate user age from birthdate." The AI produces:

```
def calculate_age(birthdate):
    today = datetime.date.today()
    age = today.year - birthdate.year
    if today.month < birthdate.month or (today.
        month == birthdate.month
        and today.day < birthdate.day):
        age -= 1
    return age
```

This looks reasonable. It handles the case where the birthday hasn't occurred yet this year. But it doesn't handle: - Invalid dates (February 30th) - Future dates (birthdate after today) - Dates before certain epochs - Time zone considerations - Edge cases in leap year calculations

An experienced programmer would recognize these edge cases and either handle them explicitly or consciously decide they don't matter for the use case. The AI filled the specification gap with a statistically common implementation—which might be exactly what you want or might be subtly wrong in ways that don't emerge until production.

This creates a new kind of challenge: *intent is harder to verify than code*. When you write code yourself, you're continuously testing your implementation against your mental model of the problem. When AI writes code, you must verify that the generated code matches your intent—but intent exists only in your head, not in any artifact you can diff or test.

This is where human value concentrates. As AI gets better at inferring intent from ambiguous specifications, the skill that becomes valuable is *precise intent specification*—the ability to articulate exactly what you mean, including constraints, edge cases, and contextual requirements that might not be obvious.

Interaction Modes Evolve

As AI becomes more capable at Design-layer work, the ways humans and AI collaborate must evolve. Consider how the four interaction modes play out at higher levels of abstraction:

- *Delegation at Design.* When design patterns are well-established and context is clear, engineers can delegate design decisions to AI. "Design a REST API for this data model following OpenAPI 3.0 standards" is delegable—the constraints are specified, the patterns are known, verification is straightforward.

But delegation at Design is riskier than delegation at Execution. A delegated execution error (syntax mistake, logic bug) is usually caught quickly by tests or compilers. A delegated design error (wrong architectural pattern, inappropriate trade-off) may only manifest under load, during maintenance, or when requirements evolve.

The skill required for effective delegation at Design is *constraint specification*—knowing what to specify upfront versus what can be left to AI judgment.

- *Collaboration at Design.* This is where the most interesting work happens. Engineer and AI engage in iterative dialogue:
- Engineer: "Design a caching layer for high-read, low-write data"
- AI: Proposes Redis with read replicas
- Engineer: "What about cache invalidation when writes occur?"
- AI: Suggests cache-aside pattern with TTL-based expiration
- Engineer: "How does this handle cache stampedes during cold starts?"
- AI: Proposes probabilistic early expiration and request coalescing

This back-and-forth explores the design space collaboratively. The AI provides pattern knowledge and implementation details. The human provides context, asks probing questions, and evaluates proposals against unstated requirements.

Research on human-AI collaboration in creative domains suggests this co-creative mode is both productive and cognitively engaging (Fan et al. 2023). The human remains the primary agent—setting direction, asking questions, making decisions—while the AI acts as a knowledgeable collaborator who can quickly explore possibilities.

- *Supervision at Design.* When AI systems operate autonomously at Design—making architectural decisions without human approval at each step—we enter Supervision mode. This is powerful but risky.

An AI agent that designs an entire microservice architecture, selects data stores, defines API contracts, and implements service boundaries might produce something functional. But does it align with organizational standards? Does it create maintainability challenges? Does it introduce security vulnerabilities through design choices?

Effective supervision at Design requires the ability to *evaluate designs holistically*—to see not just whether the design works technically but whether it's the *right* design given organizational context. This is where deep expertise becomes essential. The supervising engineer must maintain sufficient understanding of system architecture to recognize when AI-generated designs diverge from organizational norms or create future problems.

- *Augmentation at Design.* AI can augment human design thinking without taking over the design process. Examples include:
- Suggesting design patterns based on requirements
- Identifying potential bottlenecks in proposed architectures
- Generating diagrams from textual descriptions
- Comparing proposed design against known anti-patterns
- Simulating design alternatives to evaluate trade-offs

Augmentation preserves human agency—the engineer remains the designer—while extending their capabilities. This is often the safest mode for critical design decisions where judgment matters most.

The Solutions Engineer at Higher Abstraction

As AI encroaches on the Design layer, what differentiates the valuable engineer?

The traditional "software engineer" was defined by their ability to write code and make design decisions. If AI can do both, the engineer's value proposition must lie elsewhere—in meta-level capabilities that resist automation:

- *Clear thinking.* The ability to cut through ambiguity and identify the core problem. When AI proposes three design alternatives, the solutions engineer can evaluate which actually addresses the real problem versus which solves a surface issue.
- *Context engineering.* Providing AI with the right constraints, requirements, and background to generate useful designs. This requires deep domain knowledge—understanding not just the technical problem but the organizational, operational, and strategic context.
- *Judgment about quality.* Distinguishing elegant designs from merely functional ones. AI can generate designs that work, but the solutions engineer recognizes whether a design is maintainable, evolvable, and aligned with team capabilities.
- *Systems thinking.* Seeing how components fit together at levels beyond individual design decisions. The solutions engineer ensures coherence across multiple AI-generated designs, preventing local optimizations that create global problems.

These skills become *more* valuable as AI handles routine design work. When the floor rises, the ceiling rises faster. The engineer who excels at these meta-level skills can now apply their judgment across ten AI-proposed designs instead of laboriously crafting one design themselves.

This is amplification, not replacement. The role evolves from *making design decisions* to *making decisions about design decisions*—operating at a higher level of abstraction while AI handles lower levels.

What This Means for Programming

So what does "programming" mean in this landscape? Not obsolescence, but evolution—the continuation of the abstraction trajectory we've traced through seven decades.

Programming is becoming less about writing code and more about:

- **Specifying intent precisely** enough that AI can infer correct implementations
- **Evaluating designs** proposed by AI against contextual requirements
- **Maintaining coherence** across AI-generated components

- **Making trade-off decisions** that require organizational and domain context
- **Ensuring quality** through effective testing and review strategies
- **Providing oversight** for increasingly autonomous AI systems

These activities are still programming—they're just programming at a higher level of abstraction. Just as C programmers don't write assembly but are still programmers, engineers who orchestrate AI systems rather than writing every line by hand are still programmers.

The pattern holds: as AI automates routine programming, the value concentrates in the programming that resists automation. The engineers who thrive will be those who operate effectively at these higher levels—not because they've stopped programming, but because they understand that programming has always been about problem-solving, and the tools for problem-solving have evolved.

The uncomfortable truth is this: programming isn't ending, but it is transforming in ways that will feel disorienting to many practitioners. Engineers who defined their identity around "writing code" will need to redefine it around "solving problems"—a shift that requires not just new skills but a new professional self-concept.

Yet this transformation creates opportunity as much as disruption. Engineers who can operate at higher levels of abstraction, who can think clearly about complex systems, who can translate between stakeholder needs and technical implementation—these engineers become force multipliers. They don't write ten times more code; they accomplish ten times more impact by directing AI systems effectively.

The question for individual engineers is not "will I be replaced?" but "can I evolve?" And the answer, for those willing to develop meta-level skills and embrace new modes of work, remains yes.

A necessary caution: the "become an architect" narrative can itself become a trap. Not every engineer wants to operate at the architectural level, and not every organization needs all its engineers there. Systems still need people who understand implementation deeply—who can diagnose performance problems at the instruction level, who can reason about memory layouts and cache behavior, who can write the code that AI cannot yet generate reliably. The risk is that "architect" becomes a euphemism for "person who doesn't actually build things," and that we lose the hands-on understanding that makes architectural judgment trustworthy in the first place. The best architects never fully leave implementation behind. They maintain enough contact with the concrete to keep their abstractions honest.

Agentic Systems and AI Colleagues

The discussion above assumes a particular interaction model: humans prompt AI systems, which generate responses, which humans evaluate. This prompt-response cycle—regardless of whether we call it delegation, collaboration, or augmentation—assumes humans remain the primary agents, initiating each interaction.

But this assumption is rapidly becoming obsolete. The emerging paradigm isn't AI as *tool* but AI as *agent*—autonomous systems that pursue goals over extended periods, make decisions independently, and interact with other systems (human and artificial) without constant human direction (Wooldridge 2009).

This shift from tool to agent represents a fundamental change in the nature of human-AI interaction. It doesn't just add a new interaction mode to our existing framework—it creates an entirely new category of collaboration that challenges our assumptions about control, responsibility, and what it means to "engineer" software.

Before we explore what agentic AI means for engineering work, it's worth grounding the term. Strip away the marketing language, and an *agent* is remarkably simple: it is an LLM with access to tools. A language model that can not only generate text but also execute code, query databases, call APIs, read files, and take actions in the world. The intelligence comes from the model; the agency comes from the tools.

This definition is clarifying because it reveals both the power and the limits. An agent is not a new form of intelligence—it is a familiar form of intelligence (pattern-matching, token prediction) connected to unfamiliar affordances (real-world actions). The model's judgment hasn't improved because it gained tool access; it simply has more ways to be right—and more ways to be wrong. An agent that can execute code can also execute *bad* code. An agent that can modify databases can also corrupt them. Agency amplifies capability and risk in equal measure.

From Function Calls to Goal Delegation

Traditional software is *reactive*: it waits for input, processes it according to predetermined logic, and returns output. Even sophisticated systems like databases or web servers follow this pattern—they respond to requests but don't initiate action.

AI agents are *proactive*: given a goal, they plan actions, execute them, observe results, and adapt their approach based on feedback (Russell and Norvig 2010). The "program" isn't a fixed sequence of instructions but an emergent behavior arising from goal pursuit in a complex environment.

Consider the difference:

- *Tool paradigm.* "Generate a function to parse CSV files with error handling." -> AI produces code -> Human reviews, tests, integrates
- *Agent paradigm.* "Implement a robust data import pipeline for our customer database." -> AI analyzes existing codebase -> AI identifies integration points -> AI generates multiple components (parser, validator, error handler, database interface) -> AI writes tests -> AI runs tests, debugs failures -> AI iterates on failures, refactors based on test results -> AI submits pull request with documentation -> Human reviews final result

The agent paradigm is already reality. Systems like Devin, AutoGPT, and various "coding agent" frameworks demonstrate sustained autonomous work over hours (Yang et al. 2024). They don't just generate code—they debug, test, refactor, and iterate until tests pass or error budgets are exceeded.

This changes the human role fundamentally. Rather than directing every step, humans set goals, provide constraints, and evaluate outcomes. The relationship shifts from *craftsperson using a tool* to something more like *architect directing a contractor*.

But "contractor" isn't quite right either. Contractors have experience, intuition, and the ability to push back on unrealistic requirements. AI agents have none of these qualities. They have speed, tirelessness, and the ability to explore solution spaces exhaustively—but they lack judgment about whether the solution space being explored is the right one.

This asymmetry creates a new category of cognitive work: *strategic direction of autonomous systems*. It's not management in the traditional sense—AI agents don't have careers or feelings. It's not tool use in the traditional sense—you don't directly control their actions. It's something in between, and we're still developing the vocabulary and mental models to understand it.

The Manager-Engineer Convergence

Here's a genuinely weird implication: as AI systems become more agentic, engineering work starts to resemble *management* more than traditional programming.

Managers in organizations don't typically do the work themselves—they delegate tasks, set priorities, resolve conflicts, communicate with stakeholders, and ensure overall coherence. They operate at a meta-level, orchestrating the work of others.

This is increasingly what "engineering" looks like with agentic AI:

- **Task decomposition**: Breaking high-level goals into subtasks appropriate for AI agents
- **Priority setting**: Deciding which tasks are urgent and which can wait
- **Resource allocation**: Distributing computational resources and API budgets
- **Quality assurance**: Reviewing outcomes rather than implementation details
- **Integration**: Ensuring different AI-generated components work together coherently
- **Communication**: Translating between stakeholder requirements and AI-actionable specifications

The irony is striking: the "individual contributor" role—traditionally distinct from management—takes on managerial characteristics when the "individuals" being coordinated are artificial.

This convergence has profound implications. Many engineers enter the field precisely because they prefer *making things* to *managing people*. The appeal of engineering has always been direct creation—the satisfaction of building something with your own hands (or keyboard). If engineering becomes primarily about directing AI agents, does it retain that appeal?

Research on job satisfaction consistently shows that autonomy and creative expression are major motivators for knowledge workers (Pink 2009). The direct experience of creation—seeing your ideas take concrete form through your own effort—provides intrinsic satisfaction that transcends compensation.

If agentic AI removes this direct experience, replacing it with meta-level direction, does the work remain satisfying? We don't yet know. Early reports from engineers working with AI agents are mixed. Some describe liberation from tedious implementation work, allowing them to focus on creative problem-solving. Others describe a sense of disconnection—feeling like project managers rather than builders.

The resolution may be that different personality types thrive in different eras. Engineers who loved the craft of implementation may struggle in an agent-directed world. Engineers who always found implementation tedious and preferred system-level thinking may flourish. The profession isn't disappearing—it's selecting for different characteristics.

The Colleague Metaphor and Its Limits

As AI agents become more sophisticated, a natural metaphor emerges: the AI as *colleague*. Companies building AI systems use this framing extensively. Anthropic describes Claude as "a collaborative partner" (Anthropic 2024). OpenAI discusses "AI teammates" (OpenAI 2024). The language suggests peer relationships, collaborative work, shared goals.

But the colleague metaphor is misleading in important ways:

- *Asymmetric knowledge.* Human colleagues learn about organizational context, past decisions, and interpersonal dynamics through continuous presence. They build institutional memory. They remember that time three years ago when a similar approach failed for subtle reasons.

AI agents have discontinuous context—they know what's in their current context window and nothing more. Each session starts with partial amnesia (Huang et al. 2023). You must constantly re-establish context, re-explain constraints, re-specify preferences. This isn't collaboration in the human sense—it's more like working with an extremely capable but perpetually amnesiac assistant.

- *Misaligned incentives.* Human colleagues have careers, reputations, and personal stakes in outcomes. They care about code quality not just because it's specified but because their professional identity is tied to their work. They push back on technical debt because they'll have to maintain it.

AI agents optimize for reward functions that may or may not align with actual project success. They have no intrinsic motivation toward quality, maintainability, or long-term thinking. The principal-agent problem—ensuring that agents act in the principal's interest—takes new forms when the agent lacks any self-interest at all (Hadfield-Menell et al. 2016).

- *Unequal responsibility.* When human colleagues make mistakes, they experience consequences—damaged reputation, career setbacks, potentially termination. This accountability shapes behavior. Humans are careful because they bear the costs of errors.

When AI agents make mistakes, the humans who deployed them bear the consequences. This asymmetry distorts accountability (Elish 2019). The AI agent experiences no consequences for generating buggy code or making poor architectural decisions. The engineer who trusted the agent's output does.

This creates a moral hazard: AI agents can take risks that humans wouldn't, because they don't bear the downside. The engineer must compensate by being *more* cautious when reviewing AI-generated work than when reviewing human-generated work—counterintuitively, since the AI often generates correct code faster than humans.

- *Scalability.* You can't clone human colleagues. You can't pause them when budget is tight and resume them when funding returns. You can't run thousands of copies in parallel. You can't reset them to a known-good state when they develop bad habits.

AI agents have fundamentally different resource economics than human labor (Agrawal et al. 2019). This creates temptations that don't exist with human teams. Why carefully scope work when you can spin up fifty AI agents to brute-force the problem? Why invest in code quality when you can regenerate components on demand?

These temptations often lead to poor outcomes. Throwing AI agents at a problem without clear direction produces quantity without coherence. The result is repositories full of AI-generated code that technically works but lacks what Fred Brooks called "conceptual integrity" in *The Mythical Man-Month* (Brooks 1975)—the sense that a system was designed by a single coherent mind.

Perhaps more accurate than "colleague" would be "specialized contractor"—capable of skilled work but with bounded context, temporary engagement, and external accountability. Or "power tool"—extremely capable but requiring expert operation, regular maintenance, and careful attention to safety.

The metaphor matters because it shapes expectations. Treating AI agents as colleagues suggests a level of trust and autonomy they don't deserve. Treating them as mere tools suggests a level of direct control we don't actually have. We need metaphors that capture the reality of human-agent collaboration without misleading ourselves about its nature.

The Span of Control Problem

If engineers become directors of AI agents, a classical management problem re-emerges: *span of control*—how many agents can one human effectively supervise? (Urwick 1937)

Management research suggests optimal span of control ranges from 5-10 direct reports for complex knowledge work, depending on task similarity and autonomy level (Ouchi and Dowling 1977). Beyond this range, managers struggle to maintain adequate oversight, leading to coordination failures and quality problems.

But AI agents aren't human reports. They work faster, require different forms of supervision, and fail in different ways. The optimal span of control for AI agents is an empirical question we're only beginning to explore.

Some factors suggest high span of control is feasible:

- **Parallelism**: AI agents can work simultaneously on independent tasks without coordination overhead
- **Speed**: Agents complete tasks faster than humans, allowing rapid iteration through supervision cycles
- **Consistency**: Agents don't have bad days, get sick, or become demotivated. Their performance is more predictable than human performance.
- **Restart capability**: When an agent produces poor results, you can reset and retry without the interpersonal costs of redirecting a human colleague

Other factors suggest low span of control is necessary:

- **Error rates**: If agents make mistakes 15% of the time, supervising 10 agents means catching 1.5 errors per task. The cognitive load of constant error detection is substantial.
- **Context gaps**: Each agent may need extensive context provided, and context doesn't transfer between agents automatically. Supervising many agents means constantly re-establishing context.
- **Integration complexity**: More agents mean more interfaces to keep coherent. AI-generated components may solve local problems while creating global inconsistencies.
- **Verification burden**: As we explored in Chapter 10, verifying AI-generated work requires different cognitive effort than producing it yourself. Verification doesn't scale linearly with the number of agents supervised.

The answer likely depends on task characteristics. For well-specified, independent tasks (writing unit tests, generating documentation), high span of control may be viable. For interdependent tasks requiring shared context (implementing a feature across multiple components), low span of control may be necessary.

This has direct implications for productivity gains from AI. If one engineer can effectively supervise 20 AI agents, productivity multiplies 20x. If effective supervision is limited to 3 agents, productivity gains are more modest—perhaps 3-4x accounting for agent speed advantages.

The research on optimal human-AI ratios will profoundly shape the economics of software development (Brynjolfsson et al. 2023). Early evidence from companies deploying AI agents suggests the answer varies dramatically by task type and engineer skill level. Senior engineers with strong system-level understanding can supervise more agents effectively than junior engineers still developing that understanding.

This creates a potential widening gap: experts who can effectively leverage AI agents become dramatically more productive, while those still developing expertise struggle to supervise even a few agents effectively. The amplification effect we've discussed throughout this book may create winner-take-most dynamics in engineering labor markets.

When Agents Disagree

Here's a scenario that sounds like science fiction but is already happening: multiple AI agents working on the same codebase generate conflicting implementations. Agent A optimizes for performance and generates code with complex caching. Agent B optimizes for maintainability and generates code with simple, readable logic. Both satisfy the stated requirements. How does the human supervising these agents resolve the conflict?

This isn't hypothetical. Multi-agent systems for code generation already exist, and coordination problems emerge regularly (Li et al. 2024). The human finds themselves not writing code but *mediating between AI agents*—evaluating competing approaches, making trade-off decisions, providing tie-breaking judgment.

This is genuinely novel territory. Traditional software engineering doesn't have "competing implementations" from different parts of your own brain. There's one mind, one set of preferences, one implementation. With multiple agents, you have multiple "opinions" that must be reconciled.

The skills required are more managerial than technical: conflict resolution, trade-off analysis, stakeholder communication (where the "stakeholders" are AI agents with different optimization functions). The engineer must understand *why* each agent made its choices and decide which reasoning is more appropriate for the context—even when both are technically valid.

Consider a concrete example. You ask two agents to implement a data processing pipeline:

Agent A (optimizing for throughput): - Uses batch processing with large buffers - Implements parallel workers with shared-nothing architecture - Minimal error handling to avoid latency - Result: 10x throughput but 90th percentile latency spikes

Agent B (optimizing for latency): - Uses stream processing with small buffers - Implements single-threaded processing for predictability - Comprehensive error handling and retries - Result: Consistent low latency but 3x lower throughput

Both implementations are "correct" given their optimization targets. Neither agent is wrong. But they can't both be deployed. The human must decide—and that decision requires understanding not just the technical trade-offs but the business context: Are users more sensitive to average experience or worst-case experience? What's the cost of additional infrastructure versus the cost of user frustration? What are competitors doing?

These aren't questions AI agents can answer, because they require value judgments grounded in organizational strategy and user psychology. The human engineer must maintain enough system-level understanding to make these calls—even when they didn't write any of the code being evaluated.

Research on multi-agent AI systems emphasizes coordination mechanisms—protocols for agents to negotiate, share information, and reach consensus (Durfee 2001). But when humans are in the loop, these mechanisms must be human-interpretable. We need not just agent-agent coordination but agent-human-agent triadic coordination. The interaction patterns are more complex than anything in traditional software development.

This points toward a future where engineering includes a new skill: *agent orchestration*—the ability to coordinate multiple AI agents with different capabilities and optimization functions, resolve conflicts between their outputs, and synthesize their contributions into coherent systems. This skill doesn't exist in traditional software engineering education. We're inventing it in real-time.

The Autonomy-Control Trade-off

As agentic AI becomes more capable, organizations face a fundamental trade-off: *autonomy* versus *control.*

- *More autonomy.* Agents operate with minimal human oversight, making decisions independently, potentially achieving higher productivity but with greater risk of errors or misalignment.
- *More control.* Humans maintain tight supervision, reviewing each agent action, reducing risks but also reducing productivity gains and potentially bottlenecking on human review capacity.

This trade-off isn't binary—it's a continuous spectrum that can be adjusted per-task and per-agent. But the meta-question is challenging: *who decides where on the spectrum each task belongs?*

This is a governance problem. Organizations need frameworks for deciding: - Which tasks can be fully delegated to AI agents - Which require human-in-the-loop approval at each step - Which require human-on-the-loop monitoring with intervention capability - Which remain fully human-performed

These aren't purely technical decisions. They involve risk assessment, liability considerations, regulatory compliance, and organizational values. An AI agent that autonomously refactors code in an internal tool poses different risks than an AI agent that autonomously modifies code in a medical device or financial system.

Research on algorithmic governance and "algorithmic management" in gig economy contexts provides cautionary lessons (Lee et al. 2015; Möhlmann et al. 2021). When algorithms manage human workers with minimal oversight, exploitation and poor outcomes often result. Workers find themselves subject to opaque decision-making processes they can't contest or understand.

The inverse scenario—humans managing AI workers—may face similar challenges. If AI agents operate with excessive autonomy, they may produce technically correct but contextually inappropriate solutions. If they operate with insufficient autonomy, human review becomes the bottleneck, negating productivity gains.

The autonomy-control trade-off also evolves with AI capabilities. As agents become more reliable, appropriate autonomy levels increase. But reliability isn't uniform across task types—an agent might be highly reliable at implementing standard patterns while unreliable at novel architectural decisions. Organizations must continuously recalibrate—making this an ongoing organizational challenge, not a one-time decision.

Some companies are developing "AI agent policies" analogous to cloud service usage policies—formal guidelines about which agents can be used for which tasks, what level of human oversight is required, and who bears responsibility for agent outputs. This formalization of human-AI collaboration represents a new category of organizational governance that didn't exist five years ago.

The engineers who thrive in this environment will be those who can navigate these governance questions thoughtfully—understanding not just what AI agents *can* do but what they *should* be allowed to do in different organizational contexts. This is judgment that transcends technical skill, drawing on ethics, risk assessment, and organizational understanding.

Beyond the Colleague Metaphor: A New Mental Model

If the colleague metaphor misleads, what mental model should we use for agentic AI?

Perhaps the most useful framing is *cognitive prosthetics*—tools that extend human cognitive capabilities in specific domains while requiring human direction and judgment for effective use.

Cognitive prosthetics aren't autonomous agents in the full sense—they don't have goals of their own. But they're more than simple tools—they exhibit sophisticated behavior and can operate with limited guidance. The relationship is neither peer collaboration nor tool use but something in between.

This framing has several advantages:

- *It acknowledges capability without overstating autonomy.* Prosthetics are sophisticated and powerful, but they don't replace the human—they extend human capability in specific ways.
- *It emphasizes the need for human direction.* Prosthetics require someone who knows how to use them effectively. A prosthetic limb doesn't move on its own—it responds to neural signals from the user. Similarly, AI agents require human direction to be effective.
- *It highlights the learning curve.* Using prosthetics effectively requires practice. Early use is often clumsy. Over time, the prosthetic becomes an extension of the user's intention. The same learning curve applies to AI agents—effective use requires developing intuition about their capabilities and failure modes.
- *It suggests customization and fit.* Prosthetics must be tailored to indi-

vidual users. Generic prosthetics work poorly. Similarly, effective use of AI agents requires customization—training them (through prompting and example) on organizational context, coding standards, and domain-specific knowledge.

This mental model helps calibrate expectations. You wouldn't expect a prosthetic limb to work perfectly the first time you use it, or to operate effectively without your direction, or to replace your own judgment about where to move. The same realistic expectations should apply to AI agents.

The engineers who succeed with agentic AI will be those who develop this nuanced understanding—seeing AI agents neither as infallible colleagues nor as simple tools, but as powerful cognitive prosthetics that extend their capabilities when used skillfully and with appropriate caution.

The Unbundling of Knowledge Work

Let's now confront the most economically consequential question raised by AI: what happens to engineering as a *profession* when AI can unbundle knowledge work into discrete, automatable tasks?

The traditional engineering "job" is a *bundle* of tasks—some routine, some complex, some creative, some tedious. Employers hire humans to perform the entire bundle because the coordination costs of splitting work across multiple workers historically exceeded the efficiency gains (Coase 1937).

AI changes this calculus dramatically. When routine tasks can be automated cheaply and complex tasks can be delegated to AI agents, it becomes economically rational to unbundle: let AI handle automatable components, humans handle the remainder. This isn't just automation—it's *decomposition* of the coherent role we call "software engineer" into constituent parts that can be optimized, automated, or outsourced independently.

But here's the crucial question: does this unbundling represent the ultimate *revaluation* of human skills—concentrating engineering work in the tasks that truly require human judgment—or does it threaten the coherence of engineering as a stable profession? The answer, uncomfortably, may be both.

The Anatomy of Unbundling

Consider a traditional software engineering role and decompose it into its constituent tasks:

- *Tasks now substantially automated.*
- Writing boilerplate code (getters/setters, CRUD operations)
- Generating unit tests for existing code
- Writing documentation from code
- Basic debugging (syntax errors, simple logic bugs)
- Code formatting and style enforcement
- Translating between similar codebases
- Generating API clients from specifications
- *Tasks partially automated.*
- Feature implementation from specifications
- Refactoring for maintainability
- Performance optimization
- Integration with existing systems
- Writing integration and end-to-end tests
- Database schema design and migration
- *Tasks resistant to automation.*
- System architecture design
- Requirement elicitation from stakeholders
- Technical decision-making under uncertainty
- Code review requiring domain judgment
- Incident response and complex debugging
- Mentoring and knowledge transfer
- Technical leadership and strategy
- Cross-functional communication and alignment

This decomposition reveals something important: the tasks that resist automation aren't just "harder" versions of automatable tasks. They're qualitatively different—they require contextual judgment, organizational knowledge, stakeholder empathy, and strategic thinking that AI systems currently lack.

Now ask: if the first category is fully automated and the second substantially automated, what remains?

One answer—the optimistic one we've been building toward—is that the role shifts upward. Engineers focus on architecture, leadership, and judgment while AI handles implementation. The "software engineer" becomes a "solutions engineer" in the fullest sense: someone defined not by artifacts produced but by problems solved and systems designed.

This is revaluation in action. The remaining tasks aren't trivial—they're the tasks that were always most valuable but were obscured by the time engineers spent on mechanical work. As AI handles the mechanical, the valuable becomes visible and properly compensated.

But there's another possibility—one that's less comfortable but equally plausible: the role *fragments*. The remaining tasks don't constitute a full-time job for most engineers. Organizations need fewer full-time engineers and more specialized roles: architects (for system design), integrators (for coordination), reviewers (for quality assurance), strategists (for technical direction).

The coherent "software engineer" job—the bundle of tasks we've recognized for decades—dissolves into specialized functions that can be staffed independently. Some of these functions command high compensation (architecture, strategy). Others become commoditized (verification, basic integration). The middle—routine implementation work—disappears into automation.

The Barbell Labor Market

Labor economists studying automation have identified what they call the "barbell effect" or "job polarization": technology simultaneously increases demand for workers at both ends of the skill distribution while hollowing out the middle (Autor et al. 2006; Acemoglu and Restrepo 2019).

High-skill end (increasing demand and compensation): - System architects who design overall technical strategy - Domain experts who understand business context deeply - Technical leaders who make organizational decisions - Specialists in emerging or critical technologies - Engineers who can effectively direct and supervise AI agents

Low-skill end (stable or increasing demand, modest compensation): - Verification and testing (checking AI-generated work) - Monitoring and maintenance (watching automated systems) - Context provision (feeding information to AI systems) - Exception handling (dealing with cases AI can't handle) - First-line support and triage

Middle-skill hollowing (decreasing demand): - Routine implementation work - Standard feature development - Basic debugging and maintenance - Documentation and test writing - Straightforward integration tasks

This barbell pattern has been observed across industries undergoing automation—manufacturing, clerical work, service industries. Software engineering, long considered immune due to its creative and cognitive nature, now faces the same dynamics.

The challenge: most software engineers currently occupy the middle of this distribution. They're competent implementers who handle routine-to-moderate complexity work effectively. They're not architects or technical leaders, but they're solid contributors who form the backbone of engineering organizations.

If AI automates this middle tier, where do these engineers go?

The optimistic answer: they move up. Professional development at scale. Companies invest in upskilling. Engineers develop the architectural thinking, domain expertise, and leadership skills needed for high-end roles. The middle tier doesn't disappear—it ascends.

This is plausible. We've seen skill shifts before. The spreadsheet didn't eliminate accountants—it eliminated bookkeepers and made remaining accountants more analytical. Word processors didn't eliminate writers—they eliminated typists and made writers more productive. Perhaps AI eliminates implementers and makes remaining engineers more architectural.

But there's a pessimistic counter-narrative: upskilling is hard, especially for mid-career professionals with established skills and identities. Many engineers became engineers because they enjoyed *implementing*—solving concrete problems, seeing immediate results, building things. Forcing everyone toward architecture or leadership roles assumes preferences and aptitudes that may not match reality (Card et al. 2020).

Not everyone wants to be an architect. Not everyone wants to manage AI agents. Not everyone finds satisfaction in meta-level work. Some engineers are drawn to the craft of implementation itself—the aesthetic pleasure of writing elegant code, the satisfaction of debugging complex issues, the tangible sense of building something with your own hands (metaphorically).

If AI removes this craft dimension—if "engineering" becomes primarily direction and oversight—the profession may lose appeal for personality types it historically attracted. We may see an exodus not because engineers can't upskill but because they don't *want* to do the work that remains.

This is a more subtle form of displacement: not "you can't do this job anymore" but "the job you loved has transformed into something you don't love."

The Credentialization Trap Revisited

Here's where the unbundling creates a genuine crisis: as AI handles more implementation work, how do engineers develop the expertise needed for high-level roles?

Expertise develops through practice. Specifically, through what Ericsson calls "deliberate practice"—effortful engagement with tasks at the edge of current capability (Ericsson et al. 1993). Junior engineers write simple code and make mistakes. They debug those mistakes and build intuition. They encounter edge cases and develop pattern recognition. They implement increasingly complex features and ascend the skill ladder.

But if AI eliminates the early rungs of that ladder—if simple code is now generated rather than written—where does practice happen?

Consider the traditional skill development path: 1. Junior engineer writes simple functions, learns syntax and patterns 2. Intermediate engineer handles complex features, encounters edge cases 3. Senior engineer makes architectural decisions informed by implementation experience 4. Staff/principal engineer provides technical leadership based on deep pattern recognition

AI threatens to remove steps 1 and 2. Junior engineers can't spend their first year writing simple CRUD endpoints because AI generates them instantly. They can't learn from implementing straightforward features because AI handles that work.

The result: juniors arrive at senior-level problems without junior-level experience. They must review and debug AI-generated code without having internalized the patterns that code implements. They must make architectural decisions without the tacit knowledge that comes from hands-on implementation.

This is what educational researchers call the "credentialization trap"—when the credentials required for a role increase while the opportunities to gain those credentials decrease (Brown et al. 2001). Employers want senior engineers with implementation experience. But implementation opportunities are being automated. How do you gain experience that's no longer available?

Some proposed solutions:

- *Deliberate practice environments.* Organizations create "AI-free zones"—

protected contexts where engineers write code manually to develop skills, even when AI could do it faster. This is analogous to flight simulators for pilots—practice that happens outside production to maintain skills that production systems have automated (Casner et al. 2014).

But this feels artificial. Engineers know they're doing "practice work" rather than "real work." The motivational structure is different. And it's expensive—organizations pay engineers to do things slower than necessary, purely for skill development.

- *Apprenticeship through verification.* Instead of learning by implementing, juniors learn by verifying AI implementations. They develop pattern recognition by seeing thousands of AI-generated solutions and identifying problems in them.

This is promising but incomplete. Verification develops *critical* skills but not *generative* skills. You learn to spot bad code but not necessarily to create good code. It's like learning to write by only reading and critiquing others' work—valuable, but missing something essential.

- *Staged autonomy.* Junior engineers start by working with heavily restricted AI agents—systems that generate only simple code that juniors can fully understand. As engineers develop expertise, they graduate to more capable agents. The AI capability scales with human capability.

This preserves the skill development ladder but creates new coordination challenges. Organizations must maintain multiple "tiers" of AI capability, manage engineer progression through tiers, and ensure juniors don't access too-capable agents prematurely.

- *Hybrid roles.* Career tracks that blend verification, context engineering, and limited implementation. Rather than progressing from implementation to architecture, progress from assisted implementation to sophisticated orchestration. The role changes shape but remains continuous.

This may be the most realistic path. Engineering becomes less about writing code from scratch and more about working *with* AI at increasing levels of sophistication. The junior engineer directs simple AI agents on well-specified tasks. The senior engineer orchestrates complex multi-agent systems on ambiguous problems. Different work, but still a developmental arc.

None of these solutions is proven at scale. We're experimenting in real-time with how to develop expertise when traditional development paths are disrupted. The risk is that we discover the solutions too late—after a generation of engineers has missed the foundational experiences that earlier generations took for granted.

The Gig Economy Comes to Engineering?

The most radical unbundling scenario: software development becomes *task-based* rather than role-based. Organizations don't hire "software engineers" for full-time employment. Instead, they post discrete tasks—"implement this API endpoint," "debug this performance issue," "review this architecture proposal"—which are claimed by available engineers (human or AI) and compensated per task.

This is the "gig economy" model applied to knowledge work (Lehdonvirta 2018). It has precedents: platforms like Upwork and Toptal already enable task-based engineering work for certain contexts. AI could accelerate this trend by making task specification and verification cheaper, reducing the coordination costs that currently favor full-time employment.

- *The economic logic.* When tasks are highly decomposable and verification is reliable, hiring full-time employees for the entire bundle becomes inefficient. Why pay a full salary when you can pay per task? Why maintain fixed headcount when demand fluctuates? Why offer benefits when work can be atomized?

Potential benefits (from the platform/organization perspective): - **Flexibility**: Scale engineering capacity up or down with demand - **Specialization**: Match tasks to engineers with specific expertise - **Efficiency**: Pay for outcomes, not time or presence - **Global talent**: Access engineers worldwide without geographic constraints - **Cost reduction**: Eliminate overhead of full-time employment

Potential harms (from the engineer perspective): - **Income instability**: No guaranteed salary, income fluctuates with task availability and pricing - **Loss of benefits**: No health insurance, retirement contributions, paid leave, or job security - **Reduced learning**: Narrow task focus prevents broad skill development and career progression - **Skills atrophy**: Without exposure to full project lifecycles, engineers lose systemic understanding - **Power asymmetry**: Platforms and organizations have structural advantages over individual workers in price negotiations - **Diminished collaboration**: Without stable teams, building shared context and trust becomes difficult - **Race to the bottom**: Competition between human and AI task-takers drives down compensation

Research on gig work in other domains shows deeply mixed outcomes (Goods et al. 2019). Drivers for Uber and delivery workers often experience precarity, low pay, and lack of autonomy despite platform rhetoric about flexibility. Whether knowledge work gig economy would differ is uncertain.

Some argue high-skilled workers have more bargaining power—engineering tasks are complex enough that platforms need human expertise and can't purely commoditize. Others suggest platform dynamics are fundamentally exploitative regardless of skill level, concentrating value in platform owners while workers bear risk (Rosenblat 2018).

The question isn't just economic—it's about what kind of working life we want. The traditional engineering "job" provided: - **Stable income** for planning life decisions (housing, family, education) - **Benefits** tied to employment (healthcare, retirement) - **Team membership** providing collaboration, learning, and social connection - **Career progression** with clear advancement paths - **Professional identity** grounded in organizational affiliation

Task-based work sacrifices these for flexibility and autonomy. Is the trade-off worth it? The answer depends heavily on individual circumstances—highly skilled engineers with strong reputations might thrive in a gig model, while those earlier in their careers or with less portable skills might struggle.

But the choice may not be individual. If unbundling becomes economically dominant—if organizations find that task-based AI-mediated work is sufficiently more efficient than full-time employment—the traditional job may become rare regardless of worker preferences. Market forces may push toward unbundling even if most engineers would prefer stable employment.

Historical Precedent: The Putting-Out System

There's a historical analogy worth considering: the "putting-out system" of preindustrial textile production (Kriedte et al. 1981).

Before factories, textile merchants would "put out" raw materials to rural workers who would spin or weave at home, returning finished goods for payment. Workers had flexibility—they could work when they wanted, at their own pace. But they also bore risks: income fluctuated with demand, they supplied their own tools, they had no bargaining power against merchants who controlled access to raw materials and markets.

The factory system replaced putting-out with centralized production—fixed hours, guaranteed wages, and eventually collective bargaining. This was initially seen as oppressive (and often was), but eventually led to labor protections, benefits, and the middle-class stability of the mid-20th century

(Thompson 1963).

Task-based AI-mediated work resembles putting-out in structural ways: Distributed workers perform discrete tasks for platforms that control access to work. Workers have flexibility but bear precarity. The coordination benefits that firms traditionally provided—stable income, benefits, career development, shared context—are lost.

Are we seeing a full historical cycle? Artisanal production -> putting-out -> factory employment -> knowledge work firms -> gig economy -> ???

The pattern may not repeat exactly. Knowledge work differs from textile production in important ways—tasks are more heterogeneous, verification is harder, expertise matters more. But the structural dynamics—tension between flexibility and security, individual autonomy versus collective power—feel eerily similar.

Labor history suggests that workers eventually organize to reclaim power lost in market transitions. The factory system was initially exploitative until workers formed unions and governments imposed regulations. Perhaps task-based knowledge work will follow a similar arc—initial exploitation followed by collective organization and regulatory protection.

But the timescale matters. If the transition to task-based work happens over decades, workers have time to organize. If it happens over years—accelerated by AI capabilities—the disruption may outpace institutional adaptation.

What Stable Employment Survives?

Let's ask directly: if AI can handle most implementation work and economic forces push toward task unbundling, what stable full-time employment remains in software engineering?

The economic answer emphasizes *complementarity*: work that complements AI rather than competes with it survives (Acemoglu and Restrepo 2019). This includes:

- *Work requiring continuous organizational context.*
- System architecture that evolves with business strategy
- Technical leadership informed by organizational politics and culture
- Stakeholder relationships built over time
- Knowledge of legacy system constraints and historical decisions

These roles require continuous presence and deep organizational embedding. They're hard to decompose into tasks or outsource to gig workers who lack context.

- *Work requiring trust and accountability.*
- Security-critical decisions where liability matters
- Ethical judgment about product impact and user welfare
- Financial decisions with regulatory implications
- Strategic technical choices with long-term consequences

Organizations need identifiable humans responsible for these decisions. Task-based work diffuses accountability in ways that create legal and ethical risks.

- *Work requiring cross-functional coordination.*
- Product engineering bridging user needs and technical implementation
- DevOps managing the interface between development and operations
- Technical program management orchestrating multiple teams
- Engineering management handling people and process

These roles are fundamentally about coordination across boundaries. They don't decompose into discrete tasks because the value lies in maintaining continuous relationships and shared understanding.

- *Work requiring mentorship and culture-building.*
- Training and developing other engineers
- Building and maintaining engineering culture
- Defining technical standards and practices
- Creating knowledge-sharing systems

These are investments in organizational capability rather than direct value creation. They're hard to justify in a task-based model focused on immediate outcomes.

This list is narrower than current engineering employment. Perhaps 30-40% of current engineering roles fit these categories clearly. The remaining 60-70%—routine implementation, standard feature development, maintenance work—are vulnerable to automation or task unbundling.

This doesn't necessarily mean 60-70% displacement. As we've argued throughout this book, AI that automates routine work creates demand for complex work. New tasks emerge. The question is whether new tasks emerge *fast enough* and whether *enough engineers* can transition to them.

Historical precedent is mixed. The Industrial Revolution eventually created more jobs than it destroyed, but the transition took generations and involved significant suffering. The computer revolution eliminated many jobs but created new industries and occupations. The AI revolution may follow similar patterns—but the pace is faster, and we're still early in the transition.

The Revaluation Thesis Holds—With Caveats

So does unbundling contradict the Obsolescence Paradox? Not fundamentally—but it reveals important caveats.

The paradox holds: as AI automates routine work, human value concentrates in tasks requiring judgment, context, and strategic thinking. Engineers who excel at these tasks become more valuable, not less. The ceiling rises even as the floor rises.

But unbundling reveals two important qualifications:

- *First caveat—distribution of value changes.* Even if aggregate value of engineering work remains constant or increases, its distribution across the workforce becomes more unequal. The high-skill engineers who can effectively leverage AI and provide strategic direction capture more value. The middle-tier engineers who primarily performed routine implementation capture less.

This is revaluation, but revaluation that creates winners and losers. It's not a tide that lifts all boats—it's a redistribution that lifts some boats dramatically while leaving others stranded.

- *Second caveat—transition costs are real.* Even if the long-term equilibrium is positive—more valuable work for skilled engineers—the transition may involve significant disruption. Engineers must develop new skills, organizations must restructure, institutions must adapt. This adaptation takes time and involves costs that aren't evenly distributed.

The engineers who thrive will be those who: - **Develop meta-level skills**: Architecture, strategy, AI orchestration rather than pure implementation - **Build contextual expertise**: Deep domain knowledge and organizational understanding that AI can't replicate - **Maintain adaptability**: Willingness to evolve their role as AI capabilities expand - **Cultivate judgment**: The ability to make good decisions under uncertainty with incomplete information

These are the engineers for whom unbundling represents opportunity rather than threat—for whom AI eliminates tedious work and frees capacity for high-leverage activities.

But we must be honest about the transition costs. Not every engineer will make this shift successfully. Not every organization will support the necessary professional development. Not every displaced engineer will find equivalent work in the new landscape.

The Obsolescence Paradox describes the opportunity space—the ways in which AI can make skilled humans more valuable. But seizing that opportunity requires navigating genuine disruption. The engineers who understand both the opportunity and the challenge—who prepare deliberately rather than hoping the transition happens smoothly—will be best positioned for the future we're building.

Chapter Summary

- **The semantic shift**: AI programming moves from operational (specifying *how*) to intentional (specifying *what*), fundamentally changing what "programming" means while continuing the historical trajectory toward higher abstraction (Dijkstra 1972; Chen et al. 2021).
- **The three layers under pressure**: AI now operates substantially at the Design layer, not just Execution. Human value concentrates in Design-layer activities requiring contextual judgment and in the Intent layer where purpose originates (Brooks 1987).
- **Revaluation intensifies**: As AI handles routine design decisions, human design work concentrates in novel problems, contextual decisions, quality judgment, and system-level coherence—making these skills more valuable (Autor 2015).
- **Interaction modes evolve**: Delegation, Collaboration, Supervision, and Augmentation take on new meaning when AI operates at higher abstraction levels. Effective use requires understanding when each mode is appropriate (Fan et al. 2023).
- **From tool to agent**: AI systems are becoming autonomous agents that pursue goals over extended periods, fundamentally changing human-AI interaction from prompt-response to goal-delegation (Wooldridge 2009; Yang et al. 2024).
- **The manager-engineer convergence**: Engineering with agentic AI increasingly resembles management—delegating tasks, setting priorities, ensuring coherence. This may appeal to different personality types than traditional engineering (Pink 2009).
- **The colleague metaphor misleads**: AI agents have discontinuous context, misaligned incentives, unequal responsibility, and different resource

economics than human colleagues. Better mental model: cognitive prosthetics requiring skillful use (Hadfield-Menell et al. 2016; Elish 2019).

- **Span of control matters**: How many AI agents one engineer can effectively supervise profoundly shapes productivity gains and labor market outcomes. Early evidence suggests wide variation by task type and engineer skill (Urwick 1937; Brynjolfsson et al. 2023).
- **Agent coordination challenges**: Multi-agent systems create novel coordination problems requiring mediation, trade-off analysis, and judgment synthesis across AI-generated alternatives (Li et al. 2024; Durfee 2001).
- **Unbundling decomposes roles**: AI enables breaking engineering jobs into discrete tasks (automated, partially automated, resistant). This is economic revaluation but creates questions about role coherence (Coase 1937; Malone and Laubacher 2004).
- **The barbell effect**: Automation increases demand at high-skill (architecture, leadership) and low-skill (verification, monitoring) ends while hollowing out middle-skill routine implementation (Autor et al. 2006; Acemoglu and Restrepo 2019).
- **The credentialization trap**: Expertise develops through practice, but AI eliminates practice opportunities. How engineers develop senior-level skills without junior-level experience remains unsolved (Brown et al. 2001; Ericsson et al. 1993).
- **Gig engineering risks**: Task-based work offers flexibility but threatens income stability, benefits, collaboration, skill development, and worker bargaining power. Historical parallels (putting-out system) suggest eventual organization and regulation (Lehdonvirta 2018; Rosenblat 2018; Kriedte et al. 1981).
- **Stable employment categories**: Work requiring continuous organizational context, trust and accountability, cross-functional coordination, or mentorship resists unbundling. But this may represent only 30-40% of current roles (Acemoglu and Restrepo 2019).
- **The paradox holds—with caveats**: Human value concentrates in judgment, context, and strategy (revaluation). But distribution becomes more unequal (winners and losers), and transition costs are real. Engineers who develop meta-level skills, contextual expertise, and judgment will capture increasing value.

In the next chapter, we'll examine the ethical dimensions of AI-augmented engineering—exploring questions of responsibility when AI systems make autonomous decisions, the moral hazards of delegation, and how engineers can maintain ethical agency in systems where consequences are increasingly mediated by artificial intelligence.

Chapter 17

Ethics, Responsibility, and Human Agency

"With great power comes great responsibility." — Voltaire (paraphrased in popular culture)

On March 23, 2018, a self-driving Uber test vehicle struck and killed Elaine Herzberg as she crossed a street in Tempe, Arizona. The vehicle's sensors detected her six seconds before impact. The autonomous system classified her first as an unknown object, then as a vehicle, then as a bicycle, never settling on "pedestrian." It failed to predict her path correctly. The emergency braking system had been disabled to prevent erratic behavior. The human safety driver, monitoring the system but not the road, noticed the pedestrian less than a second before impact—too late to intervene (National Transportation Safety Board 2019).

Who was responsible? The AI system that misclassified the pedestrian? The engineers who tuned the perception algorithms? The company that disabled automatic emergency braking? The safety driver who was supposed to monitor but had no way to maintain situational awareness during hours of uneventful autonomous driving? The city that approved testing on public roads?

The answer, uncomfortably, is all of them—and none of them felt sufficient responsibility to prevent the tragedy. This is the ethics problem of AI-augmented systems: responsibility becomes diffused across humans and machines in ways that undermine accountability. No single actor caused the failure, yet a human died.

This chapter examines the moral dimensions of engineering in an age of increasingly autonomous AI systems. We'll explore how automation changes the nature of responsibility, why engineers bear a distinctive form of ethical obligation when building AI-driven systems, and how to design systems that preserve rather than erode human agency.

The central insight, consistent with this book's thesis: as AI handles more technical execution, human judgment about *what should be built and for whom* becomes more consequential, not less. The Obsolescence Paradox has an ethical dimension—automation amplifies the importance of human values, judgment, and responsibility.

The Responsibility Stack: Where Ethics Lives in AI Systems

Before we can discuss ethical AI engineering, we need to understand where responsibility resides in AI-augmented systems. The three-layer framework from Chapter 1 provides a useful starting point.

Ethics at the Execution Layer

At the Execution layer—where code runs, tests execute, and artifacts are produced—ethical concerns are relatively straightforward. Does the code do what it claims to do? Are there security vulnerabilities? Does it handle edge cases correctly?

These are technical questions with technical answers. A buffer overflow is a bug regardless of intent. A race condition is a flaw regardless of who wrote the code. When AI generates execution-layer code, responsibility is clear: the engineer who accepts and deploys that code is responsible for verifying its correctness.

This is why verification skills, discussed in Chapter 10, have an ethical dimension. An engineer who deploys AI-generated code without adequate testing isn't just being negligent—they're abdicating a moral responsibility. The fact that an AI wrote the code doesn't transfer responsibility to the AI; it concentrates responsibility on the human who decided to trust it.

Ethics at the Design Layer

At the Design layer—where architectural decisions shape system behavior—ethical concerns become more subtle. Design choices embed assumptions about users, contexts, and acceptable trade-offs. A caching strategy that optimizes for throughput at the expense of consistency makes an implicit judgment about which matters more. A database schema that makes some queries fast and others slow prioritizes certain use cases over others.

These design decisions are value-laden even when they appear purely technical. As we explored in Chapter 16, AI systems are increasingly capable of making design-layer decisions autonomously. An AI agent that architects a microservice system makes dozens of implicit trade-offs—between performance and maintainability, between simplicity and flexibility, between immediate functionality and long-term evolvability.

Who is responsible for these design-level value judgments when an AI makes them?

The answer cannot be "the AI." AI systems optimize for specified objectives, but they cannot decide which objectives should be specified. They can balance explicitly stated trade-offs, but they cannot identify which trade-offs matter for a particular organizational context.

Responsibility remains with the human engineer who: 1. Specifies the constraints and objectives that guide AI design decisions 2. Reviews and approves AI-generated designs 3. Maintains sufficient understanding to recognize when designs are technically correct but contextually inappropriate

This is why context engineering and design judgment—skills we've emphasized throughout this book—have ethical weight. An engineer who blindly accepts AI-generated architectures without understanding their implications has failed an ethical obligation, not just a technical one.

Ethics at the Intent Layer

The Intent layer—where we decide *why* to build systems, whose problems to solve, and what success looks like—is where ethics becomes most explicit and most consequential.

AI has minimal capability at the Intent layer. It can help clarify goals by asking questions, surface implications of stated objectives, and identify stakeholders who might be affected. But it cannot originate purpose. It cannot decide that one person's needs matter more than another's. It cannot make the value judgments that determine what should be built.

This is where human responsibility is irreducible. The Intent layer is where engineers make decisions like:

- **Whose problems do we solve?** Building a system that optimizes for paying customers may neglect the needs of vulnerable users who can't pay. This is an ethical choice, not just a business decision.
- **What counts as success?** Optimizing for engagement metrics might increase time-on-site while decreasing user wellbeing. Defining success determines what gets built.
- **Who bears the risks?** Systems that provide benefits to organizations while imposing risks on users or third parties create ethical asymmetries that someone must consciously accept or reject.
- **What happens when we're wrong?** All systems have failure modes. Who experiences the consequences when failures occur? How severe are those consequences? Are safeguards proportional to risks?

These questions don't have algorithmic answers. They require moral judgment—the kind of judgment that cannot be automated and that makes human engineers essential.

As AI systems become more autonomous, operating with less moment-to-moment human direction, Intent-layer decisions become more important, not less. Someone must decide what these systems should optimize for, whose interests they should serve, and what trade-offs are acceptable. That "someone" must be human, and in software development, it's often the engineer.

The Diffusion of Responsibility Problem

The Uber incident that opened this chapter illustrates a pervasive challenge in AI-augmented systems: responsibility becomes diffused across humans and machines in ways that undermine accountability.

The "Many Hands" Problem

When multiple actors contribute to an outcome—some human, some algorithmic—responsibility fragments. The AI researchers who developed the perception algorithms didn't deploy them. The engineers who integrated the system didn't set company policy. The safety driver who was supposed to intervene was placed in a role that research shows humans cannot perform reliably (monitoring automation for rare failures over extended periods). The executives who approved testing on public roads didn't write the code.

This is what philosophers call the "many hands" problem (Thompson 1980). When everyone is partially responsible, no one is fully accountable. Each actor can point to others who also contributed to the outcome. The result is a responsibility gap—harm occurs, but no identifiable party bears clear accountability.

AI systems exacerbate this problem because they introduce a non-agent into the causal chain. The perception algorithm that misclassified the pedestrian cannot be held responsible—it lacks the moral agency required for responsibility. But its presence in the causal chain creates ambiguity about who should be held responsible.

Did the algorithm fail? Yes. Does that absolve the humans who built and deployed it? No. But determining *which* humans bear *how much* responsibility becomes genuinely difficult.

Automation Bias and Moral Crumple Zones

Research on human-automation interaction has documented a phenomenon called *automation bias*—the tendency to favor suggestions from automated systems and to ignore contradictory information from other sources (Parasuraman and Riley 1997a). We discussed this in Chapter 10 in the context of trust calibration. But automation bias has an ethical dimension as well.

When engineers over-trust AI systems, they create what anthropologist M.C. Elish calls "moral crumple zones"—locations in a system where responsibility accumulates, even though the human in that position has limited ability to prevent failures (Elish 2019). Like the crumple zone in a car that absorbs impact during a crash, these humans absorb blame when AI systems fail.

The Uber safety driver was in a moral crumple zone. She was nominally responsible for preventing accidents, but the system design made that responsibility practically impossible to discharge. Monitoring a well-functioning autonomous system for hours creates vigilance decrements—attention naturally wanders. When a failure finally occurs, the human is blamed for not intervening, even though the system design predictably degraded their ability to do so.

Engineers who design AI-augmented systems create moral crumple zones—often unintentionally—whenever they:

- Place humans in supervisory roles without preserving the skills needed to intervene effectively
- Require sustained monitoring of rare failure modes (which humans are neurologically bad at)
- Remove humans from decision loops during normal operations but expect them to intervene during anomalies
- Design systems that operate faster than human reaction time allows meaningful oversight

These design choices concentrate moral responsibility on humans who lack the practical capability to exercise it. This is not just poor design—it's ethically problematic.

The Engineer's Distinctive Responsibility

Given these challenges, where does responsibility properly reside?

A useful framework comes from philosopher Hans Jonas, who argued that responsibility scales with power (Jonas 1984). Those who have the greatest ability to foresee and prevent harm bear the greatest responsibility to do so. In AI-augmented systems, engineers occupy a unique position: they understand system capabilities and failure modes in ways that users, managers, and even executives typically do not.

This specialized knowledge creates what we might call *epistemic responsibility*—responsibility that flows from knowing things others don't. The engineer who understands that an AI system hallucinates 15% of the time bears responsibility for communicating that limitation, designing appropriate safeguards, and pushing back when the system is deployed in contexts where 15% error rates are unacceptable.

This responsibility cannot be discharged by simply building what's specified. "I just implemented the requirements" is not an adequate ethical defense when the engineer knew—or should have known—that those requirements would lead to harmful outcomes.

Some will object: engineers aren't ethically trained, they're not empowered to make business decisions, they'll be replaced if they push back too hard. These objections have force. But they don't eliminate the responsibility—they create a tension between moral obligation and practical constraint that each engineer must navigate.

The engineers who thrive in the AI era will be those who can navigate this tension effectively—who understand that technical skill includes the ability to foresee consequences, communicate risks, and refuse to build systems that predictably cause harm.

Designing Systems That Preserve Human Agency

The previous section identified problems—responsibility diffusion, moral crumple zones, epistemic obligations. But critique without constructive alternatives is incomplete. How should engineers design AI systems to avoid these ethical pitfalls?

The Human Override Principle

A fundamental design principle: AI systems should be designed so humans can always intervene, correct, or override system decisions (Shneiderman 2020).

This sounds obvious, but it's routinely violated. AI systems often operate at speeds that preclude human intervention. They make decisions based on features humans can't observe or understand. They're deployed in contexts where override mechanisms exist in theory but not in practice.

Meaningful human override requires:

- *Transparency.* Humans must be able to understand what the system is doing and why. This doesn't mean full explainability of neural network weights—that's often impossible. It means providing enough information for a human to form a judgment about whether the system's output is reasonable for the context.

Transparency is not an all-or-nothing property. Different contexts require different levels: - For high-stakes decisions (medical diagnosis, credit approval, criminal sentencing), humans need detailed explanations of reasoning - For lower-stakes decisions (movie recommendations, spam filtering), humans need only rough intuitions about system behavior - For safety-critical systems, humans need immediate visibility into system state and confidence levels

Engineers should design transparency appropriate to stakes, not transparency sufficient to publish papers about interpretable AI.

- *Appropriate timescales.* Override must be possible before irreversible consequences occur. A trading algorithm that executes transactions in milliseconds cannot be meaningfully overseen by humans who think in seconds. If the system must operate faster than human reaction time allows, it requires additional safeguards—circuit breakers, confidence thresholds, or architectural constraints that prevent catastrophic failures even without human intervention.

This is an architectural principle: systems that remove humans from decision loops must be designed to fail safely when operating beyond human oversight capabilities.

A precise example of where human accountability cannot be delegated sits at the boundary between autonomous agents and production systems. Giving an AI agent access to a terminal, a browser, or a database connection is operationally necessary in an Agentic SDLC — and operationally dangerous without deliberate containment. The discipline that has emerged around this problem is called agent sandboxing: the design of secure execution environments that grant an agent the access it needs to perform a task without exposing systems it should never reach. No framework automates this decision. A human architect must draw the boundary, test the containment, and accept responsibility for where the line was placed. When that line is drawn incorrectly and a production system is affected, the accountability chain leads to a person — not to the agent, and not to the model vendor. That asymmetry is the definitive argument for treating human oversight not as a compliance requirement, but as a load-bearing element of any AI-integrated system.

- *Competence preservation.* Humans who might need to override the system must maintain the skills and understanding necessary to do so effectively. This connects directly to the skill atrophy problem we explored in Chapter 11.

Consider autopilots in aviation. As autopilots became more capable, airlines discovered that pilots were losing manual flying skills. When autopilots failed—as they inevitably do—pilots sometimes couldn't recover (Casner et al. 2014). The solution wasn't to eliminate autopilots but to mandate regular manual flying practice, ensuring pilots maintained the competence required for override.

The same principle applies to AI-augmented engineering. If engineers might need to debug AI-generated code, they must maintain debugging skills. If they might need to evaluate AI-proposed architectures, they must maintain architectural judgment. Systems that eliminate practice opportunities for critical skills undermine the competence required for oversight.

- *Organizational support.* Override decisions must be supported rather than punished by organizational culture. If engineers are penalized for questioning AI recommendations—if "the algorithm said so" becomes sufficient justification—override becomes theoretical rather than practical.

This is partly an organizational problem beyond individual engineers' control. But engineers can influence culture by: - Documenting when and why they override AI systems - Creating shared knowledge about AI failure modes - Establishing norms that override is a sign of good judgment, not insufficient technical sophistication - Building override mechanisms into systems rather than leaving them as afterthoughts

Design for Amplification, Not Replacement

Throughout this book, we've emphasized the distinction between replacement and amplification. This distinction has direct ethical implications.

Systems designed for replacement—to fully automate human decision-making—create the problems we've discussed: skill atrophy, responsibility diffusion, moral crumple zones. They remove humans from loops they might need to re-enter and erode the capabilities required for meaningful oversight.

Systems designed for amplification—to extend human capabilities while keeping humans in control—avoid many of these problems. They preserve human agency because humans remain the primary actors. They maintain competence because humans continue exercising judgment. They clarify responsibility because humans make the consequential decisions.

Consider two approaches to AI-assisted code review:

- *Replacement approach.* AI automatically approves code that passes certain checks, merging without human review. Humans only see code that AI flags as problematic. This is efficient but creates several problems: engineers stop reading code carefully (skill atrophy), responsibility for merged code is ambiguous (who approved it—the AI or the human who didn't override?), and the system fails precisely when it encounters code patterns not in its training data.
- *Amplification approach.* AI highlights potential issues—likely bugs, style inconsistencies, performance concerns—but humans make all approval decisions. Engineers review AI's observations, investigate when they seem relevant, dismiss when they don't, and maintain responsibility for everything that merges. This is less "efficient" in the narrow sense

but preserves competence, clarifies responsibility, and keeps humans engaged with the code.

The amplification approach is ethically superior not because it's slower but because it maintains human agency. The human remains the decision-maker, using AI as a powerful assistant rather than delegating decisions to AI.

Engineers who internalize this principle will build different systems than those who default to replacement logic. They'll design systems where: - AI suggests rather than decides - Humans can always see what AI is doing and why - Override is easy, expected, and encouraged - System failure doesn't require heroic human intervention

These design choices have ethical weight. They determine whether the systems we build empower humans or replace them.

The Power User Principle

One concrete implication of designing for amplification: systems should be designed to support expert users, not just average ones.

This might seem like a tangent, but it connects to agency in important ways. Systems designed around "average user" assumptions often remove controls, hide complexity, and automate decisions that expert users would prefer to make themselves. This serves simplicity but sacrifices agency.

Research on human-computer interaction identifies "power users" as individuals who push systems beyond intended defaults, combining deep domain knowledge with advanced usage to achieve outcomes that novice users cannot (Hippel 1986; Carroll 2003). Power users are important not because they're a large segment but because they're a signal—they reveal where a system's capabilities can be extended, where automation should be overrideable, where expert judgment adds value that automation eliminates.

In AI systems, this principle suggests:

- *Expose controls.* Rather than hiding AI's configuration behind simplicity, allow expert users to adjust confidence thresholds, override classifications, provide correction signals, and tune behavior to their specific contexts.
- *Allow customization.* Let users train or fine-tune AI systems on their particular workflows, domains, or preferences. Generic AI serves average cases; customizable AI serves experts.
- *Respect expertise.* When expert users override AI suggestions, treat that

as valuable signal rather than user error. Systems that learn from expert corrections become more valuable over time.

- *Preserve traditional workflows.* Don't force users to adopt AI-mediated workflows if they prefer direct control. Provide AI assistance as an option, not a requirement.

The ethical argument is this: systems that prevent expert users from exercising their expertise erode agency. They reduce humans to consumers of AI outputs rather than skilled practitioners who use AI as a tool.

Engineers who care about human agency will design systems that support expertise rather than replacing it—systems that get out of the way when users know what they're doing, while still offering assistance when it's wanted.

The Intent Layer Is Where Ethics Lives

Let's return to the three-layer framework and make the ethical argument explicit. While ethical considerations appear at all three layers, the most consequential moral decisions happen at the Intent layer.

At Execution, ethics is mostly about correctness and safety—does the system do what it claims, without causing harm? These are important but relatively constrained.

At Design, ethics involves trade-offs—performance versus maintainability, simplicity versus flexibility, immediate benefit versus long-term cost. These trade-offs have stakeholders who are affected differently, creating genuine ethical complexity.

But at Intent, ethics becomes central. This is where we decide: - **Whose problems are worth solving**—which stakeholders' needs matter, whose pain points justify investment - **What we optimize for**—which metrics define success, what counts as "better" - **Who bears the costs and who receives the benefits**—how value and risk are distributed - **What happens when we're wrong**—who experiences consequences of our mistakes

These are not technical questions. They're moral questions that require moral judgment. And they're questions that AI cannot answer, because answering them requires the very thing AI lacks: the ability to care about human welfare for its own sake, not as an optimization target.

This is where the Obsolescence Paradox manifests ethically. As AI becomes more capable at Execution and Design, the Intent layer doesn't diminish in importance—it becomes more critical. Someone must still decide what to build and for whom. That someone must be human. And in software development contexts, that someone is often the engineer.

Values Cannot Be Automated

There's a temptation to frame ethics as another optimization problem. Define "fairness" mathematically, encode it as a constraint, train AI systems to satisfy it. This approach has produced important research on algorithmic fairness, bias mitigation, and value alignment (Mehrabi et al. 2021).

But ethics fundamentally resists full formalization. Here's why:

- *Values are contested.* What counts as "fair" depends on whose perspective you adopt. Fairness as "equal treatment" conflicts with fairness as "equal outcomes." Fairness as "proportional to merit" conflicts with fairness as "according to need." These aren't technical disagreements—they're philosophical ones, reflecting different theories of justice (Binns 2018).
- *Context matters.* Whether an outcome is ethical depends on context that's hard to specify completely. An AI that denies someone a loan might be making a statistically sound prediction that nonetheless perpetuates historical injustice. The ethics depend on facts about history, social structure, and individual circumstances that no model can fully capture.
- *Priorities shift.* What matters most changes over time and across situations. During a pandemic, public health might override privacy in ways that would be unacceptable in normal times. An ethical framework that doesn't allow for this kind of contextual recalibration is too rigid to be useful.
- *Moral responsibility requires agency.* Ethics isn't just about achieving good outcomes—it's about taking responsibility for our choices. An AI system that automatically optimizes for "fairness" hasn't made a moral choice; it's executed code. The moral choice was made by whoever decided what fairness meant and how to encode it.

This doesn't mean engineers should ignore algorithmic fairness research. It means they should understand its limits. Fairness metrics are tools for thinking about ethics, not replacements for ethical thinking.

The engineer who understands this occupies a position of genuine moral responsibility. They cannot outsource value judgments to AI systems. They cannot hide behind "the algorithm decided." They must exercise moral agency—

make value judgments, take responsibility for consequences, advocate for the vulnerable when systems threaten harm.

This is not a burden that AI will lift. It's a responsibility that AI makes more salient.

When to Refuse to Build

The previous sections assumed that AI systems are being built and focused on how to build them responsibly. But sometimes the right answer is not to build at all.

Engineers are not neutral implementers of other people's decisions. They have moral agency and, with it, the right—sometimes the obligation—to refuse to build systems they believe will cause harm.

Recognizing Red Flags

Certain system characteristics should trigger serious ethical scrutiny:

- *Systems targeting vulnerable populations.* When the primary users are people with limited power—children, prisoners, immigrants, the poor—engineers should ask whether the system serves their interests or exploits their vulnerability. Systems that make existing power imbalances worse rather than better deserve skepticism.
- *Systems with irreversible consequences.* When errors cannot be easily corrected—decisions about employment, credit, immigration status, criminal justice—the bar for deployment should be extremely high. AI systems that get these decisions wrong don't just cause inconvenience; they cause lasting harm.
- *Systems optimizing for addiction.* When the explicit goal is to maximize engagement through mechanisms that exploit human psychology—variable reward schedules, social comparison, fear of missing out—engineers should question whether this serves human welfare or undermines it.
- *Systems that deceive users.* When systems are designed to appear more capable than they are, hide their limitations, or manipulate users through dark patterns, engineers are participating in deception. This includes AI systems that simulate empathy or understanding they don't possess.
- *Systems with massive power asymmetries.* When one party has complete information and control while another party has neither—algorithmic

management systems, surveillance tools, predictive policing—engineers should ask whether this arrangement is just, regardless of its efficiency.

None of these characteristics automatically makes a system unethical. Context matters. But they're warning signs that deserve serious thought.

The Engineer's Right to Refuse

Professional codes of ethics in engineering typically include obligations to public welfare that supersede obligations to employers (IEEE 2020). In principle, engineers have not just the right but the duty to refuse work they believe will cause harm.

In practice, this is difficult. Engineers who refuse work risk their jobs, their reputations, and their careers. Organizations have strong incentives to portray engineers who raise ethical concerns as difficult, uncommitted, or naive. The power asymmetry between individual engineers and large organizations makes principled refusal costly.

But the cost of refusing is often less than it appears:

- *Reputational benefits.* Engineers known for ethical backbone are often more, not less, employable. Organizations serious about responsible AI want engineers who will push back on bad ideas.
- *Legal protections.* In many jurisdictions, whistleblower protections exist for employees who report illegal or dangerous practices. These protections are imperfect but real.
- *Collective action.* Individual engineers are vulnerable, but collective refusal by teams or professional groups is more powerful. Cultures where ethical pushback is normalized make principled refusal less costly for individuals.
- *Exit options.* Engineers with valuable skills often have alternatives. The ability to walk away from unethical work—to choose a different employer, start something new, or even leave the field temporarily—is a form of power that shouldn't be underestimated.

The calculation is personal. Not every engineer is in a position to refuse work without serious consequences. But many engineers who imagine themselves powerless actually have more power than they think.

Drawing Lines

Each engineer must decide where their ethical lines are. There's no universal answer, but here are questions worth considering:

- **Would I be comfortable explaining this system to the people it affects?** If you'd be embarrassed or defensive describing what you're building to those who will experience its consequences, that's a signal.
- **Am I being asked to work on something whose societal impact I genuinely don't understand?** Sometimes the ethical problem is that engineers don't know enough about the social context to evaluate impact. "I don't know enough to judge if this is ethical" is a reason to pause, learn more, or involve people with relevant expertise.
- **Is this a system I'd want used on people I care about?** If you wouldn't want your family subjected to this system, why is it acceptable for strangers?
- **Does this work align with the kind of engineer I want to be?** Professional identity matters. Engineers who pride themselves on building things that matter, that help people, that make the world better have reason to refuse work that contradicts those values.

These aren't algorithms for ethical decision-making. They're heuristics that might help engineers notice when they're building something they shouldn't.

From Answer Production to Judgment Stewardship

Let's synthesize the ethical argument we've been building. In an AI-augmented world, the engineer's role transforms from *producing technical artifacts* to *exercising judgment about which artifacts should exist and how they should behave.*

This transformation has an ethical dimension that amplifies, rather than diminishes, human responsibility.

- *AI excels at generating options.* Given a problem specification and training data, AI can produce solutions faster and in greater volume than any human. It can optimize, iterate, and explore solution spaces exhaustively.
- *But AI cannot own consequences.* When an AI-generated solution causes harm, the AI experiences nothing. It cannot feel regret, learn from moral mistakes, or take responsibility. Only humans can do these things.

This asymmetry defines the ethical relationship between humans and AI. AI systems are extraordinarily powerful tools, but they remain tools—instruments of human purposes, not moral agents in their own right.

The engineers who build and deploy these systems bear responsibility for:

- *Interpreting outputs in context.* AI-generated solutions are abstractions from training data. Whether they're appropriate for a particular context requires contextual judgment that AI lacks. The engineer who deploys a solution without verifying its contextual appropriateness has failed an ethical obligation.
- *Making value trade-offs.* AI optimizes for specified objectives, but choosing which objectives to optimize for is a value judgment. When objectives conflict—speed versus safety, innovation versus stability, individual versus collective benefit—humans must decide which matters more. These are moral choices that cannot be automated.
- *Designing for human welfare.* The ultimate measure of system success is not technical sophistication but human benefit. Engineers bear responsibility for ensuring that systems serve human flourishing, not just organizational efficiency or their own technical interests.
- *Maintaining ability to intervene.* As systems become more autonomous, maintaining human ability to intervene becomes both harder and more important. Engineers must design systems that preserve human agency even when automation is extensive.
- *Taking responsibility for outcomes.* When AI systems cause harm, someone must be accountable. That someone cannot be the AI. It must be humans—and often, the humans with the deepest understanding of what could go wrong are the engineers who built the systems.

This is not a diminished role. It's an elevated one. The engineer who merely implemented specifications was replaceable—another skilled practitioner of a learnable craft. The engineer who exercises moral judgment over AI systems, who decides what should be built and for whom, who takes responsibility for consequences that algorithms cannot foresee—this engineer occupies a position that no AI can fill.

The Solutions Engineer as Moral Agent

In Chapter 1, we introduced the concept of the "solutions engineer"—someone defined not by artifacts produced but by problems solved and value delivered. This concept has an ethical dimension we can now make explicit.

The solutions engineer is not just a technical problem-solver. They are a *moral agent* who:

- **Asks "should we?" not just "can we?"**: Technical capability doesn't imply ethical obligation. The solutions engineer evaluates whether a technically feasible solution serves human interests.
- **Considers whose problems are being solved**: Not all problems are equally worth solving. Some problem definitions privilege powerful stakeholders while ignoring vulnerable ones. The solutions engineer attends to whose interests are being served.
- **Evaluates long-term consequences**: Solutions that work in the short term may create problems in the long term. The solutions engineer thinks beyond immediate deliverables to systemic effects.
- **Takes responsibility for outcomes**: When solutions cause harm, the solutions engineer doesn't blame the AI or the requirements or the organization. They take ownership of their contribution to the outcome and work to prevent similar harms in the future.

This expanded conception of engineering excellence requires skills beyond technical competence. It requires: - **Ethical reasoning**: The ability to identify moral dimensions of technical choices and reason about them carefully - **Empathy**: Understanding how different stakeholders will experience a system, especially those with less power - **Courage**: The willingness to raise concerns, push back on problematic requirements, and refuse unethical work when necessary - **Humility**: Recognition that technical expertise doesn't imply ethical expertise, and willingness to learn from ethicists, social scientists, and affected communities

These capabilities cannot be automated. They are distinctively human. And as AI handles more technical execution, they become not less important but more important—because they're what separates responsible engineering from mere implementation.

Chapter Summary

- **The three-layer framework applies to ethics**: Execution-layer ethics concerns correctness and safety; Design-layer ethics concerns trade-offs and stakeholder impacts; Intent-layer ethics concerns fundamental questions of purpose and value that only humans can answer.

- **Responsibility diffuses dangerously**: The "many hands" problem means that when multiple actors (human and AI) contribute to outcomes, accountability weakens. Engineers must resist this diffusion by maintaining clear ownership of their decisions (Thompson 1980; Elish 2019).
- **Automation bias creates moral crumple zones**: Over-trusting AI systems places humans in positions of nominal responsibility without practical ability to intervene. Engineers who design these systems bear responsibility for the moral crumple zones they create (Parasuraman and Riley 1997a; Elish 2019).
- **Engineers have epistemic responsibility**: Technical knowledge creates ethical obligation. Engineers who understand system capabilities and failure modes bear responsibility to communicate limitations, design safeguards, and push back when systems are misused (Jonas 1984).
- **Design for human override**: AI systems should preserve human ability to intervene through transparency, appropriate timescales, competence preservation, and organizational support for override decisions (Shneiderman 2020).
- **Amplification over replacement**: Systems designed to augment human capabilities preserve agency better than systems designed to replace human decision-making. This distinction has ethical weight beyond efficiency considerations (Casner et al. 2014).
- **Support power users**: Systems that enable expert users to exercise expertise preserve agency better than systems that optimize for average users. Exposing controls and allowing customization respects human competence (Hippel 1986).
- **Values cannot be fully automated**: Ethical judgments require contextual understanding, value trade-offs, and moral agency that AI lacks. Fairness metrics are tools for ethical thinking, not replacements for it (Mehrabi et al. 2021; Binns 2018).
- **Engineers have the right to refuse**: When systems will predictably cause harm, engineers have not just the right but the obligation to refuse to build them. Professional codes support this, even when organizational pressures work against it (IEEE 2020).
- **The solutions engineer as moral agent**: Engineering excellence in the AI era requires not just technical skill but ethical reasoning, empathy, courage, and humility. These distinctively human capabilities become

more valuable as AI handles more execution.

- **Judgment becomes stewardship**: As AI takes over answer production, the human role shifts to judgment stewardship—interpreting outputs, making value trade-offs, designing for human welfare, maintaining intervention capability, and taking responsibility for outcomes.

In the final chapter, we'll synthesize these themes—technical excellence, ethical responsibility, and human judgment—into a portrait of the Renaissance Engineer: the kind of practitioner who thrives not despite this era of transformation, but because of it.

Chapter 18

The Renaissance Engineer

"The future belongs to those who learn more skills and combine them in creative ways." — Robert Greene, *Mastery*

In 1452, Leonardo da Vinci was born into a world undergoing profound technological transformation. The printing press was reshaping how knowledge spread. New instruments were revolutionizing navigation and astronomy. Mathematical innovations were enabling architectural achievements previously thought impossible.

Leonardo didn't resist these changes. He embraced them—while remaining distinctively, irreplaceably human. He was a painter who understood optics. An engineer who studied anatomy. An inventor who combined mechanical principles with artistic vision. He didn't specialize narrowly in one domain; he synthesized knowledge across domains in ways that created entirely new possibilities.

The Renaissance produced polymaths like Leonardo not despite technological change but *because* of it. When printing made specialized knowledge more accessible, the value shifted to those who could combine knowledge in novel ways. When new tools expanded what was possible, the value shifted to those who could imagine what should be possible.

We stand at a similar inflection point. AI is not replacing human engineers—it's creating conditions for a new Renaissance in engineering, where the most valuable practitioners are those who combine technical skill with judgment, creativity, ethics, and deep contextual understanding.

This final chapter synthesizes the themes we've explored throughout this book into a vision of the Renaissance Engineer—the qualities that endure across technological change, the skills that compound rather than depreciate, and why this moment represents opportunity rather than threat for those who understand what makes humans irreplaceable.

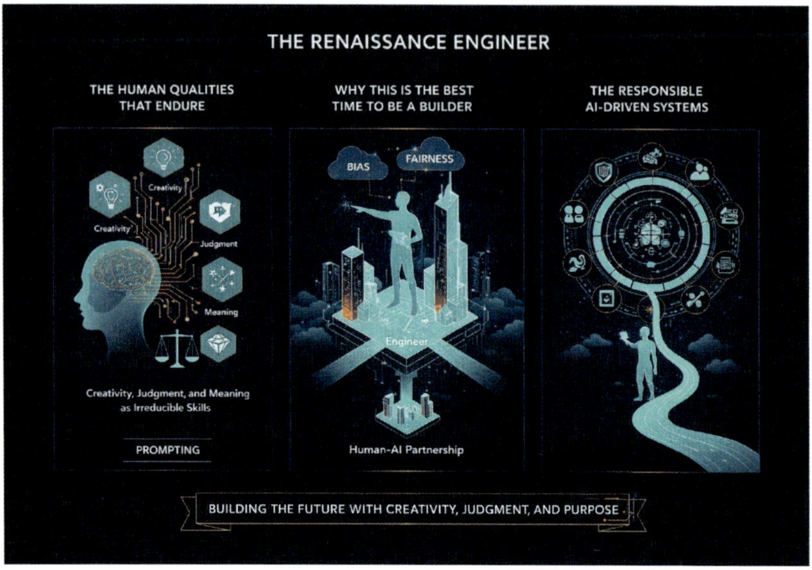

The Human Qualities That Endure

Throughout this book, we've argued that AI automation doesn't diminish human value—it concentrates it in distinctively human capabilities. But what exactly are these capabilities? What qualities of mind and character will define engineering excellence in an age of increasingly capable machines?

The answer isn't a list of technical skills—those will evolve too rapidly to catalog. Instead, it's a set of *meta-capabilities*: qualities that enable engineers to adapt to change, exercise judgment in novel situations, and create value in ways that resist automation.

Clear Thinking in Ambiguous Contexts

The ability to cut through complexity and identify the core of a problem is perhaps the most fundamental engineering skill. It's what separates those who solve real problems from those who implement solutions to imagined ones.

AI excels at pattern matching within well-defined problem spaces. It struggles when problem definition itself is the challenge—when requirements are vague, stakeholders disagree, constraints conflict, and the "right" problem to solve isn't obvious.

Consider a common scenario: a product manager requests "a feature to improve user retention." An engineer who thinks clearly recognizes this isn't actually a problem specification—it's a desired outcome. The real problems might be: - Users don't understand core value proposition (onboarding problem) - Users understand value but forget to return (notification problem) - Users return but encounter friction (performance problem) - Users complete their goals and have no reason to return (product-market fit problem)

Each requires a different solution. AI can implement any of them competently. But identifying *which problem is real* requires talking to users, analyzing behavior patterns, understanding business context, and making judgment calls about which evidence matters most.

This is clear thinking: the ability to question assumptions, distinguish symptoms from causes, recognize when you're solving the wrong problem, and reframe questions to make them answerable.

Clear thinking isn't innate—it's a skill that develops through practice. Engineers develop it by: - **Asking "why" repeatedly** until surface requirements reveal underlying problems - **Challenging their own assumptions** before building solutions - **Seeking disconfirming evidence** rather than just confirming evidence - **Explaining problems to non-experts** to test whether they actually understand - **Reflecting on failures** to understand where their problem diagnosis was wrong

As AI handles more implementation, clear thinking becomes more valuable, not less. The engineer who can correctly identify problems will be more productive by an order of magnitude than the engineer who efficiently implements solutions to the wrong problems.

Simplifying Complexity Without Losing Truth

Perhaps the most underrated engineering skill is the ability to take something complex and make it simple—not simplistic, but genuinely simple in a way that preserves essential truth while discarding incidental detail.

AI tends toward verbosity and completeness. Given a question, it will provide comprehensive answers that cover edge cases, acknowledge uncertainties, and include caveats. This is useful for certain purposes, but it often obscures rather than clarifies.

Human engineers who can distill complexity provide value that AI cannot replicate:

- *Creating abstractions.* The best engineers build abstractions that hide complexity without losing power. A well-designed API makes simple things easy and complex things possible—hiding complexity without removing power. This is a human art—knowing what to expose, what to hide, where to draw boundaries.

- *Explaining technical concepts.* The ability to explain a complex system to different audiences—executives who need strategic implications, users who need to understand behavior, junior engineers who need to learn principles—requires understanding at a level beyond surface implementation.
- *Making architectural decisions.* Good architecture isn't about using the most sophisticated patterns. It's about using the simplest patterns that solve the actual problems. Choosing simple over complex requires judgment about what complexity is essential versus what's accidental.

Research on expertise consistently shows that experts see simplicity where novices see chaos (Chi et al. 1981). They've internalized patterns that allow them to compress complex situations into coherent models. They recognize that five edge cases are really instances of one underlying principle.

This simplification skill compounds over time. Early-career engineers who practice explaining their code, questioning complexity, and seeking simpler alternatives build a capacity that makes them exponentially more valuable as they gain experience.

As AI generates increasingly complex implementations, the engineer who can see through complexity to identify simple solutions becomes invaluable. They don't just implement requirements—they question whether requirements can be met more simply, whether complexity is essential or accidental, whether there's an insight that makes the problem easier.

Contextual Judgment

We've emphasized throughout this book that AI lacks access to context—the organizational history, political dynamics, team capabilities, and unwritten constraints that shape real-world software decisions.

This contextual judgment is what separates adequate solutions from excellent ones. Two architectures might be technically equivalent but have radically different outcomes based on: - *Team skills.* A sophisticated microservices architecture might be optimal in theory but disastrous if the team lacks distributed systems expertise - *Organizational politics.* The "best" technical solution might be one that's acceptable to stakeholders who control budget and priorities - *Operational realities.* A system that's elegant in development might be unmaintainable in production given actual operational capabilities - *Historical constraints.* Past architectural decisions create path dependencies that make some changes easier and others harder

AI can learn these contexts if they're explicitly documented. But much organizational knowledge is tacit—known by people but never written down. The engineer who's been with an organization for years knows that "we tried that approach three years ago and it failed for subtle reasons." They know which stakeholders care about which concerns. They know which shortcuts are acceptable and which will create future problems.

This contextual judgment is what makes experienced engineers valuable even when AI can implement solutions faster. They don't just build what's specified—they build what's appropriate given everything that isn't specified.

Developing contextual judgment requires: - *Active listening* to understand stakeholder concerns beyond stated requirements - *Institutional memory* about what's been tried and why it succeeded or failed - *Empathy* for users, operators, and maintainers who will live with decisions - *Systems thinking* about how technical choices interact with organizational dynamics

These capabilities take time to develop, but they're precisely what AI cannot replicate without continuous organizational presence that current AI systems lack.

Intellectual Curiosity and Learning Appetite

Technology evolves faster than any curriculum can track. The tools, frameworks, and best practices that define "modern" engineering shift every few years. What remains constant is the need for engineers who can learn continuously.

But curiosity is more than just keeping up with new tools. It's a disposition toward understanding—asking not just "how does this work?" but "why was it designed this way?" and "what problems was it meant to solve?"

Engineers with genuine curiosity: - **Read code to understand patterns**, not just to fix bugs - **Explore domains they're not working in** to build broader context - **Question why things are the way they are** rather than accepting conventions uncritically - **Experiment with new approaches** even when current approaches work adequately - **Learn from failures** systematically rather than just moving on

This curiosity compounds because each thing you learn makes the next thing easier to learn. The engineer who understands three programming paradigms picks up a fourth more quickly than someone learning their first. The engineer who's worked in three industries recognizes patterns across domains that specialists miss.

In an AI-augmented world, curiosity becomes even more important. AI systems work by pattern matching on training data. They can't be curious about domains they haven't encountered. They can't wonder "what if we approached this differently?" in ways that lead to genuine innovation.

The engineers who remain valuable indefinitely are those who never stop learning—not because they're keeping up with technology, but because they're genuinely interested in understanding how things work and why.

Emotional Resilience and Grit

Engineering is fundamentally about confronting problems that don't have obvious solutions. This requires psychological qualities that AI lacks entirely: the willingness to struggle with hard problems, the ability to tolerate ambiguity and uncertainty, and the persistence to keep trying when initial approaches fail.

Research on expertise emphasizes that deliberate practice—effortful engagement with tasks at the edge of current capability—is essential for skill development (Ericsson et al. 1993). But deliberate practice is uncomfortable. It means repeatedly facing problems you can't yet solve, making mistakes, getting feedback, and trying again.

AI doesn't experience this discomfort. It optimizes according to loss functions, but it doesn't "struggle" in any meaningful sense. It doesn't feel frustration when stuck or satisfaction when breakthroughs occur.

Human engineers who can tolerate discomfort, persist through setbacks, and maintain motivation despite uncertainty have a fundamental advantage. They can work on problems that don't yield to first attempts. They can learn from failure rather than being discouraged by it. They can maintain performance during the ambiguous early phases of projects when success isn't assured.

This resilience isn't about raw talent. Research consistently shows that grit—sustained effort toward long-term goals—predicts success better than innate ability (Duckworth et al. 2007). The engineer who's willing to spend hours debugging a subtle concurrency issue, who keeps trying different approaches when the first five don't work, who treats failure as information rather than defeat—this engineer will solve problems that defeat more talented but less persistent colleagues.

As we discussed in Chapter 5, AI that makes easy things easier risks creating engineers who've never developed this resilience. If every obstacle is immediately overcome by AI assistance, engineers never build the psychological muscle required for genuinely hard problems.

The engineers who thrive will be those who deliberately practice resilience—who take on problems that require sustained effort, who push past frustration to understanding, who build the capacity to work productively with uncertainty.

Ethical Judgment and Moral Courage

As we explored in Chapter 17, engineering in the AI era carries distinctive ethical responsibilities. The engineer who exercises moral judgment—who asks "should we build this?" not just "can we build this?"—provides value that cannot be automated.

This requires: - *Ethical sensitivity.* The ability to recognize when technical decisions have moral implications - *Stakeholder empathy.* Understanding how different people will experience a system's consequences - *Moral reasoning.* The capacity to think carefully about competing values and make defensible judgments - *Courage.* The willingness to raise concerns, push back on problematic requirements, and refuse unethical work

These qualities don't naturally emerge from technical training. They require deliberate cultivation through exposure to ethics literature, engagement with diverse stakeholders, and practice making values-based decisions.

But they're increasingly essential. As AI systems make more consequential decisions affecting more people, the engineers who build these systems bear greater responsibility for outcomes. The ability to exercise ethical judgment will separate engineers who are merely technically competent from those who are professionally excellent.

Creativity, Judgment, and Meaning as Irreducible Skills

The qualities described above—clear thinking, simplification, contextual judgment, curiosity, resilience, ethical reasoning—can be grouped into three meta-capabilities that define the Renaissance Engineer: creativity, judgment, and the capacity for meaning-making.

Creativity: Genuine Novelty vs. Sophisticated Recombination

AI systems are often described as "creative"—they can generate novel images, compose music, write poetry. But there's a crucial distinction between *recombinative creativity* (combining existing elements in new ways) and *transformative creativity* (introducing genuinely new concepts or paradigms) (Boden 2004).

Current AI excels at recombinative creativity. Given exposure to millions of images, it can generate new images that are novel combinations of patterns it has seen. Given exposure to codebases, it can generate new code that combines familiar patterns in contextually appropriate ways.

But transformative creativity—the kind that introduces genuinely new paradigms, reconceptualizes problems in ways that make them solvable, or imagines possibilities that don't exist in training data—remains distinctively human.

Consider the invention of relational databases. This wasn't just a new implementation of existing ideas—it was a fundamentally different way of thinking about data storage and retrieval. Edgar Codd's insight that data could be represented as relations and manipulated through algebraic operations wasn't a recombination of existing database approaches; it was a conceptual leap that created a new paradigm (Codd 1970).

Or consider the development of version control systems. Early approaches treated versions as snapshots—complete copies of files at different points in time. The insight that versions could be represented as *diffs*—changes from one state to another—enabled distributed version control systems like Git that fundamentally changed how software development teams collaborate (Chacon and Straub 2009).

These innovations weren't predictable from patterns in existing solutions. They required seeing problems from entirely new angles, questioning assumptions that everyone else took for granted, and imagining approaches that didn't yet exist.

AI trained on historical data cannot reliably produce this kind of creativity because, by definition, transformative creativity goes beyond what exists in training data. It requires: - **Questioning foundational assumptions** that define the problem space - **Drawing insights from unrelated domains** and applying them in novel contexts
- **Imagining possibilities** that don't currently exist - **Taking intellectual risks** on approaches that might fail entirely

These are distinctively human capabilities that emerge from our ability to reason abstractly, form analogies across distant domains, and pursue ideas even when success isn't assured.

The engineers who create transformative innovations in the AI era will be those who use AI for recombinative creativity—rapidly exploring variations within known solution spaces—while reserving their own cognitive effort for the transformative leaps that AI cannot make.

Judgment: Deciding Under Irreducible Uncertainty

Throughout this book, we've emphasized that judgment—the ability to make good decisions despite incomplete information, competing values, and irreducible uncertainty—is what makes human engineers valuable.

Judgment differs from optimization. Optimization finds the best solution given fully specified objectives and constraints. Judgment makes reasonable choices when objectives are ambiguous, constraints are unknown, and "best" depends on values that resist quantification.

Consider a common engineering decision: should we refactor this messy code now or ship it and refactor later? This question has no algorithmic answer because it requires weighing incommensurable values: - **Code quality** (favors refactoring now) - **Time to market** (favors shipping now) - **Team morale** (engineers frustrated by messy code vs. pressure to deliver) - **Future costs** (technical debt that compounds vs. opportunity cost of delay) - **Uncertainty** (maybe this code will be replaced soon anyway)

AI can provide information relevant to each consideration. It can estimate refactoring time, predict bug likelihood, analyze code complexity. But it cannot make the trade-off decision itself because the trade-off depends on organizational priorities, risk tolerance, and strategic context that vary by situation.

Good judgment in software engineering requires:

- *Pattern recognition from experience.* Having seen similar situations and their outcomes, recognizing which past cases are analogous to current ones and which are meaningfully different.
- *Balancing multiple perspectives.* Understanding how different stakeholders view the decision and what each values most, then finding solutions that respect competing concerns.
- *Calibrated confidence.* Knowing when you have enough information to decide versus when you should gather more, and adjusting confidence

based on how similar current situations are to past experiences.

- *Comfort with ambiguity.* Making reasonable choices despite irreducible uncertainty rather than waiting for impossible levels of certainty.

Research on expert judgment consistently shows that experts develop fast, intuitive judgment through years of experience with varied cases (Klein 1998). They build mental libraries of situations and outcomes that allow rapid assessment of new situations. They've learned which factors matter most in which contexts.

This expertise cannot be fully transferred to AI because much of it is tacit—the expert often can't fully articulate why they lean one way or another. They "just know" that a particular approach feels risky, that a stakeholder's concern is more important than it seems, that this refactoring is worth doing while another can wait.

The Renaissance Engineer develops this judgment deliberately by: - **Seeking diverse experiences** across different projects, domains, and organizations - **Reflecting on decisions** to understand what worked, what didn't, and why - **Learning from others' experiences** through mentorship, case studies, and post-mortems - **Practicing explanation** to make tacit knowledge explicit - **Accepting fallibility** and updating judgment based on outcomes

As AI systems handle more routine decisions, the judgment required for non-routine decisions becomes more valuable. The engineer who can navigate ambiguity, weigh competing values, and make defensible choices despite uncertainty will be indispensable precisely because these capabilities resist automation.

Meaning-Making: Why We Build What We Build

The final irreducible skill is perhaps the most fundamental: the capacity to create and recognize meaning.

Software engineering isn't just about solving technical puzzles. It's about building things that matter—that solve real problems for real people, that create value in the world, that contribute to human flourishing in some form.

AI systems optimize for specified objectives, but they cannot determine which objectives are meaningful. They can maximize engagement metrics, but they can't judge whether engagement serves human wellbeing. They can optimize for efficiency, but they can't decide what's worth being efficient at.

Meaning-making requires asking and answering questions like: - **Why does**

this problem matter? Not just to the organization but to actual humans whose lives might be affected. - **What does success look like?** Not just in metrics but in terms of human experiences and outcomes. - **What are we really trying to achieve?** Not just the stated objectives but the deeper purposes they serve. - **Is this worth doing?** Given limited time and resources, is this the most valuable contribution we can make?

These questions don't have algorithmic answers because meaning is a human construct. What counts as meaningful depends on values, purposes, and judgments about what makes life worth living.

The Renaissance Engineer doesn't just build what's specified—they think carefully about why they're building it. They question whether technical solutions address real problems or just symptoms. They consider whether systems serve genuine human needs or optimize for metrics that correlate poorly with actual wellbeing.

This capacity for meaning-making is what allows engineers to be more than implementers. It's what makes them *builders* in the fullest sense—people who don't just construct artifacts but create value that matters.

Research on meaningful work consistently shows that people derive satisfaction not just from technical achievement but from contribution to purposes they find meaningful (Wrzesniewski and Dutton 2003). Engineers who connect their daily work to larger purposes—improving healthcare, enabling education, solving climate challenges, making people's lives easier—report higher satisfaction and maintain motivation through difficulties that would defeat those working purely for compensation.

As AI handles more implementation, the meaning layer becomes more important. Organizations need engineers who can identify what's worth building, articulate why it matters, and maintain purpose through the inevitable frustrations of complex projects.

Why This Is the Best Time to Be a Builder

Throughout this book, we've documented genuine challenges: automation of routine work, unbundling of traditional roles, the need to develop new skills, uncertainty about career trajectories. It would be easy to conclude that we're witnessing the decline of engineering as a viable profession.

But that conclusion would be precisely wrong. This moment of transformation isn't the worst time to be an engineer—it's the best.

The Democratization of Implementation

For most of computing history, the bottleneck has been implementation. Ideas were abundant; the ability to translate ideas into working software was scarce. Organizations needed armies of engineers to maintain legacy systems, handle routine feature development, and keep infrastructure running.

This scarcity created a particular kind of engineering career: stable, well-compensated work implementing specifications, maintaining systems, and incrementally improving products. It was good work, but it wasn't particularly creative or high-leverage. Most engineers spent most of their time on routine implementation rather than solving genuinely novel problems.

AI is changing this dynamic. As implementation becomes easier, the bottleneck shifts from execution to judgment—from "can we build this?" to "should we build this?" and "what should we build?"

This is liberating for engineers who want to work on interesting problems. Instead of spending months implementing routine features, you can generate first drafts in hours and spend your time on higher-level concerns: - **Architectural decisions** that shape how systems evolve - **Problem discovery** to identify which problems are worth solving - **Stakeholder alignment** to ensure technical solutions serve real needs - **Quality and correctness** verification that AI-generated code does what it should - **Innovation** on genuinely novel problems that AI can't solve from patterns

For engineers who found routine implementation tedious, this is a massive upgrade. The work becomes more interesting, more strategic, and more creative.

The Amplification of Expertise

We've argued throughout this book that AI amplifies expertise rather than replacing it. This creates an unprecedented opportunity for engineers who develop high-level skills.

Consider the productivity multiplier. A senior engineer who can effectively leverage AI might accomplish in a day what previously took a week. This isn't just incremental improvement—it's a qualitative change in what's possible.

The engineer who can: - Rapidly prototype multiple approaches to compare them - Generate comprehensive test suites in minutes rather than days - Explore architectural alternatives without full implementation costs - Iterate through design options at speeds that were previously impossible

...operates at a fundamentally different level than engineers without effective AI collaboration skills.

This amplification compounds. The engineer who accomplishes 5x more this year learns 5x more, builds 5x more intuition, encounters 5x more edge cases. Next year, they're not just more productive—they're more capable in ways that lead to even greater productivity.

For engineers committed to excellence, this compounding is extraordinary. You can achieve in a career what might have taken multiple careers in previous eras. You can work on bigger problems, explore more ideas, have greater impact.

The gap between excellent engineers and mediocre ones will widen dramatically. But that's opportunity for those willing to develop excellence.

The Expansion of the Possible

Perhaps most exciting: AI expands what's possible to build.

Projects that were previously too expensive, too complex, or too labor-intensive become feasible. Solo developers can build applications that once required teams. Small teams can build systems that once required organizations. Organizations can tackle problems that were previously intractable.

This expansion creates opportunities:

- *For entrepreneurs.* The cost of building software products drops dramatically. Ideas that weren't economically viable become viable. Experiments that were too expensive become cheap enough to try.
- *For researchers.* Prototyping research ideas becomes faster. Testing hypotheses becomes easier. The gap between idea and working system shrinks.
- *For problem-solvers.* Problems that weren't worth engineering time become worth solving. Automation of routine work frees resources for addressing harder, more important challenges.
- *For learners.* Building complex systems becomes accessible to people earlier in their learning journey. Students can create sophisticated projects that demonstrate mastery.

The democratization of building capability means that good ideas can flourish regardless of resource constraints that previously limited who could build what. This is profoundly empowering for engineers who care about impact more than credentials or organizational resources.

The Return to First Principles

When implementation is difficult, engineers focus on how to build things efficiently within existing paradigms. When implementation becomes easy, attention shifts to whether we're building the right things—whether our paradigms themselves are optimal.

This creates opportunity for innovation at the paradigm level. Questions that were settled because changing approaches was too costly become unsettled. Assumptions that were locked in by legacy systems become questionable again.

Consider how AI might reshape debates about: - **Programming paradigms**: If AI can translate fluently between paradigms, maybe we should optimize for expressiveness rather than popularity - **System architectures**: If AI can handle boilerplate, maybe we should optimize for conceptual clarity rather than implementation convenience - **Development practices**: If AI generates tests automatically, how should test-driven development evolve?

The engineers who can think from first principles—who can question assumptions baked into current practices—have opportunity to reshape how software engineering works. This is rare in any field—most of the time, you're optimizing within existing paradigms. When paradigms themselves are in flux, creative thinkers can have outsized impact.

The Revaluation of the Human

The most profound opportunity is psychological: as AI handles mechanical work, human qualities become more visible and more valuable.

For decades, software engineering has been defined primarily by technical skill—the ability to write code, debug systems, understand algorithms. These skills mattered, but they sometimes obscured equally important human qualities: judgment, creativity, empathy, ethical reasoning, communication.

As technical execution becomes more automated, these human qualities come to the foreground. The engineer who thinks clearly, communicates effectively, understands human needs, makes sound judgments, and takes ethical responsibility becomes recognizably more valuable than the engineer who just writes code quickly.

This is revaluation in the fullest sense. Engineers who cultivated these human qualities—who developed judgment, who learned to communicate, who thought about ethics—were always valuable. But their value was sometimes obscured by the sheer volume of implementation work that needed doing.

Now, that value is more visible. Organizations are discovering that their most valuable engineers aren't necessarily those who write the most code. They're those who make good decisions, align teams, communicate with stakeholders, mentor others, and exercise judgment about what should be built.

This is profoundly good news for engineers who want to be more than coding machines. It means that developing fully as a human—cultivating wisdom, judgment, empathy, creativity—is not tangential to engineering excellence but central to it.

Building the Future You Want

Finally, this moment creates opportunity for agency. When paradigms are stable, individuals have limited ability to shape the future—they can optimize within existing systems but can't easily change the systems themselves.

When paradigms are in flux, individual agency increases. The engineers who build the first widely-adopted AI coding assistants are shaping how millions of engineers will work. The engineers who establish best practices for human-AI collaboration are defining professional standards for decades. The engineers who build systems that preserve human agency versus those that erode it are determining what kind of technological future we get.

This is not just opportunity for career success—it's opportunity for impact. The choices engineers make now, about what to build and how to build it, will influence how AI transforms work for billions of people.

You can be passive in this transformation—accepting whatever systems emerge, adapting to whatever practices become standard, following wherever the field goes.

Or you can be active—building systems that embody your values, establishing practices you believe are wise, shaping the field toward futures you think are better.

The Renaissance Engineer chooses agency. They don't just adapt to change; they participate in creating it.

The Renaissance Engineer: A Synthesis

Let's bring together the threads we've been weaving throughout this book.

The Obsolescence Paradox reveals a counterintuitive truth: as AI automates routine work, high-level human skills become more valuable, not less. This paradox operates at multiple scales—from individual tasks to entire career arcs to the profession as a whole.

The three-layer framework (Execution, Design, Intent) clarifies where human value concentrates: increasingly at Design and Intent, where contextual judgment and value alignment matter most.

The four interaction modes (Delegation, Collaboration, Supervision, Augmentation) provide patterns for effective human-AI collaboration, each appropriate for different tasks and contexts.

The solutions engineer concept reframes engineering excellence: from artifact production to problem-solving, from technical skill to judgment, from implementation to impact.

The ethical dimension recognizes that as AI handles more execution, moral responsibility intensifies rather than diminishes. Engineers become stewards of judgment, accountable for consequences that algorithms cannot foresee.

Synthesized, these themes paint a picture of the Renaissance Engineer:

- *Technically capable but not defined by technique.* They understand technology deeply enough to direct AI systems effectively, evaluate proposals critically, and recognize when technical solutions are contextually appropriate. But they don't define themselves primarily as "coders"—they define themselves as problem-solvers who use whatever tools are most effective.
- *Broadly knowledgeable rather than narrowly specialized.* Like Renaissance polymaths, they draw connections across domains. They understand business, psychology, ethics, and design alongside technical architecture. This breadth allows them to see solutions that specialists miss.
- *Judgment-centric rather than execution-centric.* They recognize that the scarce resource isn't the ability to implement but the ability to decide what should be implemented. They invest in developing judgment, contextual understanding, and wisdom alongside technical skill.
- *Ethically engaged rather than morally neutral.* They take responsibility for what they build and for whom. They question whether technical solutions serve genuine human needs. They refuse to build systems they believe will cause harm, even when that refusal is professionally costly.
- *Continuously learning rather than static.* They embrace change rather

than resist it. They're curious about new approaches, willing to discard practices that no longer serve, and committed to growth throughout their careers.

- *Creative in the full sense.* They generate not just novel code but novel concepts, paradigms, and ways of thinking about problems. They're not satisfied with recombining existing ideas—they pursue transformative insights that create new possibilities.
- *Collaboratively excellent rather than heroically individual.* They work effectively with both human teammates and AI systems. They communicate clearly, mentor generously, and elevate those around them. They recognize that the best solutions emerge from collaboration, not isolation.

This Renaissance Engineer isn't a mythical figure—it's a description of real engineers who are thriving now, in this moment of transformation. They're the engineers who: - Welcomed AI tools early and learned to use them effectively - Invested in judgment and communication alongside technical skill - Questioned what they were building, not just how to build it - Took responsibility for outcomes rather than hiding behind specifications - Adapted their skills continuously rather than clinging to legacy approaches - Found meaning in building things that matter

These engineers aren't being displaced by AI. They're being amplified by it. They're accomplishing more, having greater impact, and creating more value than ever before.

A Call to Action

This book has argued that the Obsolescence Paradox creates opportunity for engineers who understand where human value concentrates in an AI-augmented world. But understanding is insufficient without action.

If you've read this far, you've invested time in understanding. The question now is: what will you do with that understanding?

Here are concrete actions worth taking:

- *Develop meta-level skills.* Don't just learn the next framework or language. Develop clear thinking, simplification ability, contextual judgment, and ethical reasoning. These capabilities compound over years in ways that technical knowledge alone doesn't.

- *Practice direction, not just implementation.* When using AI tools, force yourself to specify goals clearly, evaluate outputs critically, and maintain responsibility for decisions. Resist the temptation to passively accept AI suggestions.
- *Cultivate breadth alongside depth.* Don't just specialize in one technical domain. Learn about adjacent fields—design, business, ethics, psychology. The connections you make between domains will generate insights that specialists miss.
- *Build things that matter.* Choose projects that solve real problems for real people. Build systems that improve lives, that address genuine needs, that create value beyond metrics. Meaning isn't optional—it's what sustains motivation through difficulty.
- *Take responsibility seriously.* Don't hide behind "I just implemented the requirements" or "the AI generated it." Own the consequences of what you build. Push back on systems that will predictably cause harm. Exercise moral agency.
- *Teach and mentor.* Share what you learn. Help others develop the skills you've developed. Build communities of practice around effective human-AI collaboration. The profession advances when knowledge spreads.
- *Stay curious.* Never stop learning. Not because you need to keep up with technology (though you do), but because curiosity is what makes engineering interesting. Follow your interests. Explore domains that fascinate you. Build things to understand them.
- *Embrace change rather than resist it.* AI will continue evolving. New capabilities will emerge that create new opportunities and new challenges. Engineers who adapt thrive; those who resist stagnate. Be in the first group.
- *Exercise agency.* Remember that you're not just responding to change—you can shape it. The systems you build, the practices you establish, the values you embody influence how AI transforms engineering. Choose wisely.

The Renaissance is happening now. The question isn't whether you'll be affected by it—you will be. The question is whether you'll be passive or active, whether you'll be shaped by change or participate in shaping it.

Conclusion: The Paradox Resolved

We opened this book with a paradox: as AI systems become more capable of performing engineering tasks, the value of human engineers paradoxically increases.

Having explored this paradox from multiple angles—historical, technical, cognitive, ethical—we can now see why it's not truly paradoxical. It's the natural consequence of how automation interacts with human capability.

Automation doesn't make humans less valuable. It changes where human value resides. As AI handles execution, value concentrates in design and intent. As routine work is automated, expertise in non-routine work becomes more valuable. As technical skills become more accessible, judgment about how to apply those skills becomes scarcer.

The engineers who understand this dynamic position themselves correctly. They don't compete with AI at execution—they leverage AI for execution while focusing their own efforts on judgment, creativity, and meaning-making.

They don't fear automation—they embrace it as a tool that makes them more capable. They don't resist change—they adapt continuously, developing skills that compound rather than depreciate.

They don't view AI as a threat to their relevance—they view it as an amplifier of their capabilities, allowing them to tackle problems that were previously beyond reach.

Throughout this book, we have argued that the engineers who thrive will not be those who resist AI or those who surrender to it, but those who understand the paradox and position themselves on the right side of it. The evidence points to a conclusion that is simple to state and difficult to shortcut: AI is not coming for the experts. It is coming for the people who thought they could skip becoming one.

The best engineers do not use AI to avoid thinking. They use it to think faster, explore more broadly, and verify more rigorously. The tool amplifies what is already there. If what is already there is deep — built through years of deliberate practice, hard-won domain knowledge, and the kind of judgment that only comes from making real decisions with real consequences — then the amplification is extraordinary.

Build the depth. The tools will follow.

Most fundamentally, they recognize that engineering excellence has always been about more than technical execution. It's been about clear thinking, sound judgment, ethical responsibility, and the capacity to create value that matters.

AI doesn't eliminate the need for these human qualities. It makes them more visible, more valuable, and more central to what it means to be an excellent engineer.

This is why this is the best time to be a builder. Not despite AI, but because of it. The tools are more powerful, the possibilities are more expansive, and the opportunity for impact is greater than ever before—for those who develop the skills that matter.

The Renaissance Engineer understands the paradox and resolves it through action: by developing excellence in distinctively human capabilities, by using AI to amplify rather than replace human judgment, and by taking responsibility for building a future worth building.

The transformation is happening. The opportunity is real. The choice is yours.

Chapter Summary

- **The Renaissance analogy**: Like 15th-century polymaths who synthesized knowledge across domains during technological transformation, modern engineers thrive by combining technical skill with judgment, creativity, and contextual understanding (Greene 2012).
- **Enduring human qualities**: Clear thinking in ambiguous contexts, simplifying complexity without losing truth, contextual judgment, intellectual curiosity, emotional resilience, and ethical reasoning define engineering excellence in the AI era (Chi et al. 1981; Ericsson et al. 1993; Duckworth et al. 2007).
- **Three irreducible skills**: Creativity (transformative vs. recombinative), judgment (deciding under irreducible uncertainty), and meaning-making (determining what's worth building) resist automation because they require capabilities AI fundamentally lacks (Boden 2004; Klein 1998; Wrzesniewski and Dutton 2003).
- **Why this is the best time to build**: AI democratizes implementation, amplifies expertise, expands what's possible, enables paradigm-level innovation, and makes human qualities more visible and valuable than ever.

- **The solutions engineer synthesized**: Technically capable but not technique-defined; broadly knowledgeable; judgment-centric; ethically engaged; continuously learning; fully creative; collaboratively excellent.
- **The paradox resolved**: Automation doesn't make humans less valuable—it concentrates value in distinctively human capabilities. Engineers who understand this dynamic position themselves correctly for amplification rather than replacement.
- **Call to action**: Develop meta-level skills, practice direction over passive acceptance, cultivate breadth, build meaningful systems, take responsibility, teach others, stay curious, embrace change, and exercise agency in shaping the future.

The transformation is happening. The opportunity is real. The choice is yours.

References

Abelson, Harold, Gerald Jay Sussman, and Julie Sussman. 1996. *Structure and Interpretation of Computer Programs*. 2nd ed. MIT Press.

Acemoglu, Daron, and Pascual Restrepo. 2019. "Automation and New Tasks: How Technology Displaces and Reinstates Labor." *Journal of Economic Perspectives* 33 (2): 3–30. https://doi.org/10.1257/jep.33.2.3.

Agrawal, Ajay, Joshua Gans, and Avi Goldfarb. 2019. "Artificial Intelligence: The Ambiguous Labor Market Impact of Automating Prediction." *Journal of Economic Perspectives* 33 (2): 31–50.

Ahrens, Sönke. 2017. *How to Take Smart Notes: One Simple Technique to Boost Writing, Learning and Thinking*. CreateSpace Independent Publishing Platform.

Allspaw, John. 2012. *Blameless PostMortems and a Just Culture*. Blog post. https://codeascraft.com/2012/05/22/blameless-postmortems/.

Amodei, Dario, Chris Olah, Jacob Steinhardt, Paul Christiano, John Schulman, and Dan Mané. 2016. "Concrete Problems in AI Safety." *arXiv Preprint arXiv:1606.06565*.

Andreessen, Marc. 2026. *On Voyager and the Future of AI Planning Systems*. Interview and public commentary.

Anthropic. 2024. *Claude as a Collaborative Partner: Design Principles and Use Cases*. Anthropic.

Arrow, Kenneth J., and Anthony C. Fisher. 1974. "Environmental Preservation, Uncertainty, and Irreversibility." *The Quarterly Journal of Economics* 88 (2): 312–19.

Autodesk. 2024. *How AI in Architecture Is Shaping the Future of Design and Construction*. Autodesk Design & Make. https://www.autodesk.com/design-make/articles/ai-in-architecture.

Autor, David H. 2015. "Why Are There Still so Many Jobs? The History and Future of Workplace Automation." *Journal of Economic Perspectives* 29 (3): 3–30. https://doi.org/10.1257/jep.29.3.3.

Autor, David H., Lawrence F. Katz, and Melissa S. Kearney. 2006. "The Polarization of the u.s. Labor Market." *American Economic Review* 96 (2): 189–94. https://doi.org/10.1257/aer.96.2.189.

Autor, David H., Frank Levy, and Richard J. Murnane. 2003. "The Skill Content of Recent Technological Change: An Empirical Exploration." *The Quarterly Journal of Economics* 118 (4): 1279–333. https://doi.org/10.1162/003355303322552801.

Bainbridge, Lisanne. 1983. "Ironies of Automation." *Automatica* 19 (6): 775–79. https://doi.org/10.1016/0005-1098(83)90046-8.

Barke, Steve, Benjamin Bichsel, and Veselin Raychev. 2023. "Grounded Copilot: How Programmers Interact with Code-Generating Models." *Proceedings of the 45th International Conference on Software Engineering.*

Bartlett, Frederic C. 1932. *Remembering: A Study in Experimental and Social Psychology.* Cambridge University Press.

Bender, Emily M., Timnit Gebru, Angelina McMillan-Major, and Shmargaret Shmitchell. 2021. "On the Dangers of Stochastic Parrots: Can Language Models Be Too Big?" *Proceedings of the 2021 ACM Conference on Fairness, Accountability, and Transparency*, 610–23. https://doi.org/10.1145/3442188.3445922.

Binns, Reuben. 2018. "Fairness in Machine Learning: Lessons from Political Philosophy." *Proceedings of Machine Learning Research* 81: 149–59.

Bjork, Robert A. 1994. "Memory and Metamemory Considerations in the Training of Human Beings." *Metacognition: Knowing about Knowing* (Cambridge, MA), 185–205.

Boden, Margaret A. 2004. *The Creative Mind: Myths and Mechanisms.* 2nd ed.

Routledge.

Bowman, Samuel R. 2022. "The Dangers of Underclaiming: Reasons for Caution When Reporting How NLP Systems Fail." *Proceedings of ACL*, 7484–99.

Brooks, Frederick P. 1975. *The Mythical Man-Month: Essays on Software Engineering*. Addison-Wesley.

Brooks, Frederick P. 1987. "No Silver Bullet: Essence and Accidents of Software Engineering." *Computer* 20 (4): 10–19. https://doi.org/10.1109/MC.1987.1663532.

Brown, Phillip, Anthony Hesketh, and Sara Williams. 2001. *The Mismanagement of Talent: Employability and Jobs in the Knowledge Economy*. Oxford University Press.

Brown, Tom B., Benjamin Mann, Nick Ryder, et al. 2020. "Language Models Are Few-Shot Learners." *Advances in Neural Information Processing Systems* 33: 1877–901.

Brynjolfsson, Erik, and Andrew McAfee. 2014. *The Second Machine Age: Work, Progress, and Prosperity in a Time of Brilliant Technologies*. W. W. Norton & Company.

Brynjolfsson, Erik, Daniel Rock, and Chad Syverson. 2023. "The Productivity j-Curve: How Intangibles Complement General Purpose Technologies." *American Economic Journal: Macroeconomics* 15 (1): 333–76.

Buffett, Warren E. 1993. *Berkshire Hathaway Annual Letter to Shareholders*. Berkshire Hathaway Inc.

Card, David et al. 2020. "Wage Inequality and Technological Change." *Annual Review of Economics*.

Carlini, Nicholas, Florian Tramer, Eric Wallace, et al. 2021. "Extracting Training Data from Large Language Models." *USENIX Security Symposium*, 2633–50.

Carroll, John M. 2003. *HCI Models, Theories, and Frameworks: Toward a Multidisciplinary Science*. Morgan Kaufmann.

Casner, Stephen M., Lael J. Schooler, and John D. McDonnell. 2014. "Aviation Automation: The Mechanisms Behind Human Performance Problems." *Human Factors* 56 (3): 477–88.

Cepeda, Nicholas J., Harold Pashler, Edward Vul, John T. Wixted, and Doug Rohrer. 2006. "Distributed Practice in Verbal Recall Tasks: A Review and Quantitative Synthesis." *Psychological Bulletin* 132 (3): 354–80. https://doi.org/10.1037/0033-2909.132.3.354.

Chacon, Scott, and Ben Straub. 2009. *Pro Git*. Apress. https://git-scm.com/book.

Chen, Mark, Jerry Tworek, Heewoo Jun, et al. 2021. "Evaluating Large Language Models Trained on Code." *arXiv Preprint arXiv:2107.03374*.

Chen, Tianqi, Thierry Moreau, Ziheng Jiang, et al. 2018. "TVM: An Automated End-to-End Optimizing Compiler for Deep Learning." *13th USENIX Symposium on Operating Systems Design and Implementation*, 578–94.

Chi, Michelene T. H., Miriam Bassok, Matthew W. Lewis, Peter Reimann, and Robert Glaser. 1989. "Self-Explanations: How Students Study and Use Examples in Learning to Solve Problems." *Cognitive Science* 13 (2): 145–82. https://doi.org/10.1207/s15516709cog1302_1.

Chi, Michelene T. H., Nicholas De Leeuw, Mei-Hung Chiu, and Christian LaVancher. 1994. "Eliciting Self-Explanations Improves Understanding." *Cognitive Science* 18 (3): 439–77. https://doi.org/10.1207/s15516709cog1803_3.

Chi, Michelene T. H., Paul J. Feltovich, and Robert Glaser. 1981. "Categorization and Representation of Physics Problems by Experts and Novices." *Cognitive Science* 5 (2): 121–52. https://doi.org/10.1207/s15516709cog0502_2.

Coase, Ronald H. 1937. "The Nature of the Firm." *Economica* 4 (16): 386–405. https://doi.org/10.1111/j.1468-0335.1937.tb00002.x.

Codd, Edgar F. 1970. "A Relational Model of Data for Large Shared Data Banks." *Communications of the ACM* 13 (6): 377–87. https://doi.org/10.1145/362384.362685.

Csikszentmihalyi, Mihaly. 1990. *Flow: The Psychology of Optimal Experience.*

Harper & Row.

Dakhel, Arghavan Moradi, Vahid Majdinasab, Amin Nikanjam, Foutse Khomh, Michel C. Desmarais, and Zhen Ming Jack Jiang. 2023. "GitHub Copilot AI Pair Programmer: Asset or Liability?" *Journal of Systems and Software* 203: 111734. https://doi.org/10.1016/j.jss.2023.111734.

Davis, Ernest, and Gary Marcus. 2015. "Commonsense Reasoning and Commonsense Knowledge in Artificial Intelligence." *Communications of the ACM* 58 (9): 92–103. https://doi.org/10.1145/2701413.

Dawes, Robyn M., David Faust, and Paul E. Meehl. 1989. "Clinical Versus Actuarial Judgment." *Science* 243 (4899): 1668–74.

Dietvorst, Berkeley J., Shyam Bharti, and Dylan Rivers. 2018. "Algorithm Appreciation: People Prefer Algorithmic to Human Judgment." *Organizational Behavior and Human Decision Processes* 151: 90–103.

Dietvorst, Berkeley J., Joseph P. Simmons, and Cade Massey. 2015. "Algorithm Aversion: People Erroneously Avoid Algorithms After Seeing Them Err." *Journal of Experimental Psychology: General* 144 (1): 114–26.

Dijkstra, Edsger W. 1972. "The Humble Programmer." In *Communications of the ACM*, vol. 15.

Duckworth, Angela L., Christopher Peterson, Michael D. Matthews, and Dennis R. Kelly. 2007. "Grit: Perseverance and Passion for Long-Term Goals." *Journal of Personality and Social Psychology* 92 (6): 1087–101. https://doi.org/10.1037/0022-3514.92.6.1087.

Durfee, Edmund H. 2001. "Distributed Problem Solving and Multi-Agent Systems: Comparisons and Examples." *AI Magazine* 20 (4): 81–90.

Dweck, Carol S. 2006. *Mindset: The New Psychology of Success*. Random House.

Edmondson, Amy C. 1999. "Psychological Safety and Learning Behavior in Work Teams." *Administrative Science Quarterly* 44 (2): 350–83. https://doi.org/10.2307/2666999.

Elhage, Nelson, Neel Nanda, Catherine Olsson, et al. 2022. "Toy Models of Superposition in Neural Networks." *arXiv Preprint arXiv:2209.10652.*

Elicit. 2024. *AI for Scientific Research.* Company documentation. https://elicit.com.

Elish, Madeleine Clare. 2019. "Moral Crumple Zones: Cautionary Tales in Human-Robot Interaction." *Engaging Science, Technology, and Society* 5: 40–60.

Endsley, Mica R. 1995. "Toward a Theory of Situation Awareness in Dynamic Systems." *Human Factors* 37 (1): 32–64. https://doi.org/10.1518/001872095779049543.

Ericsson, K. Anders, Ralf Th. Krampe, and Clemens Tesch-Römer. 1993. "The Role of Deliberate Practice in the Acquisition of Expert Performance." *Psychological Review* 100 (3): 363–406. https://doi.org/10.1037/0033-295X.100.3.363.

Fan, Angela et al. 2023. "Human-AI Co-Creation in Creative Writing and Art." *arXiv Preprint arXiv:2303.00000.*

Fielding, Roy Thomas. 2000. "Architectural Styles and the Design of Network-Based Software Architectures." Doctoral dissertation, University of California, Irvine. https://www.ics.uci.edu/~fielding/pubs/dissertation/top.htm.

Fitts, Paul M. 1951. *Human Engineering for an Effective Air-Navigation and Traffic-Control System.* (Washington, DC).

Fitzgerald, Sue, Gary Lewandowski, Renée McCauley, et al. 2008. "Debugging: Finding, Fixing and Flailing, a Multi-Institutional Study of Novice Debuggers." *Computer Science Education* 18 (2): 93–116. https://doi.org/10.1080/08993400802114508.

Fogarty, Kevin. 1988. *The Shootdown of Iran Air Flight 655: Anatomy of a Tragedy.* U.S. Naval Institute Proceedings.

Foote, Brian, and Joseph Yoder. 1997. "Big Ball of Mud." *Pattern Languages of Program Design 4* (Reading, MA).

Fowler, Martin. 2003. *Patterns of Enterprise Application Architecture*. Addison-Wesley.

Gelman, Andrew, John B. Carlin, Hal S. Stern, David B. Dunson, Aki Vehtari, and Donald B. Rubin. 2013. *Bayesian Data Analysis*. 3rd ed. Chapman; Hall/CRC.

Glass, Robert L. 2002. *Facts and Fallacies of Software Engineering*. Addison-Wesley.

Goodfellow, Ian, Jean Pouget-Abadie, Mehdi Mirza, et al. 2014. "Generative Adversarial Nets." *Advances in Neural Information Processing Systems* 27: 2672–80.

Goods, Caleb, Alex Veen, and Tom Barratt. 2019. "Is Your Gig Any Good? Analysing Job Quality in the Australian Platform-Based Food-Delivery Sector." *Journal of Industrial Relations* 61 (4): 502–27. https://doi.org/10.1177/0022185618802168.

Greene, Roland. 2012. *Five Words: Critical Semantics in the Age of Shakespeare and Cervantes*. University of Chicago Press.

Hadfield-Menell, Dylan, Stuart J. Russell, Pieter Abbeel, and Anca Dragan. 2016. "Cooperative Inverse Reinforcement Learning." *Advances in Neural Information Processing Systems* 29: 3909–17.

Hickey, Rich. 2011. *Simple Made Easy*. Strange Loop Conference.

Hiebert, James, and Douglas A. Grouws. 2003. "The Effects of Classroom Mathematics Teaching on Students' Learning." *Second Handbook of Research on Mathematics Teaching and Learning* (Charlotte, NC), 371–404.

Hinds, Pamela J. 1999. "The Curse of Expertise: The Effects of Expertise and Debiasing Methods on Prediction of Novice Performance." *Journal of Experimental Psychology: Applied* 5 (2): 205–21. https://doi.org/10.1037/1076-898X.5.2.205.

Hippel, Eric von. 1986. "Lead Users: A Source of Novel Product Concepts." *Management Science* 32 (7): 791–805. https://doi.org/10.1287/mnsc.32.7.791.

Huang, Minxuan et al. 2023. "Memory and Context in Large Language Models." *arXiv Preprint arXiv:2305.00000*.

IEEE. 2020. *IEEE Code of Ethics*. Institute of Electrical; Electronics Engineers. https://www.ieee.org/about/corporate/governance/p7-8.html.

Ji, Ziwei, Nayeon Lee, Rita Frieske, et al. 2023. "Survey of Hallucination in Natural Language Generation." *ACM Computing Surveys* 55 (12): 1–38. https://doi.org/10.1145/3571730.

Jonas, Hans. 1984. *The Imperative of Responsibility: In Search of an Ethics for the Technological Age*. University of Chicago Press.

Kadavath, Saurav, Sam Marks, Sandipan Kundu, et al. 2022. "Language Models (Mostly) Know What They Know." *arXiv Preprint arXiv:2207.05221*.

Kahneman, Daniel. 2011. *Thinking, Fast and Slow*. Farrar, Straus; Giroux.

Kalliamvakou, Eirini, Albert Ziegler, X. Alice Li, et al. 2024. *Research: Quantifying GitHub Copilot's Impact on Developer Productivity and Happiness*. GitHub Blog. https://github.blog/news-insights/research/research-quantifying-github-copilots-impact-on-developer-productivity-and-happiness/.

Kaplan, Jared, Sam McCandlish, Tom Henighan, et al. 2020. "Scaling Laws for Neural Language Models." *arXiv Preprint arXiv:2001.08361*.

Kasneci, Enkelejda, Kathrin Sessler, Stefan Küchemann, et al. 2023. "ChatGPT for Good? On Opportunities and Challenges of Large Language Models for Education." *Learning and Individual Differences* 103: 102274. https://doi.org/10.1016/j.lindif.2023.102274.

Klein, Gary. 1998. *Sources of Power: How People Make Decisions*. MIT Press.

Knuth, Donald E. 1974. "Structured Programming with Go to Statements." *Computing Surveys* 6 (4): 261–301. https://doi.org/10.1145/356635.356640.

Knuth, Donald E. 1997. *The Art of Computer Programming, Volume 1: Fundamental Algorithms*. 3rd ed. Addison-Wesley.

Kolb, David A. 1984. *Experiential Learning: Experience as the Source of Learning and Development*. Prentice Hall.

Kosmyna, Nataliya, Eugene Hauptmann, Ye Tong Yuan, et al. 2025. "Your Brain on ChatGPT: Accumulation of Cognitive Debt When Using an AI Assistant for Essay Writing Task." *arXiv Preprint arXiv:2506.08872*.

Kriedte, Peter, Hans Medick, and Jürgen Schlumbohm. 1981. *Industrialization Before Industrialization: Rural Industry in the Genesis of Capitalism*. Cambridge University Press.

Krizhevsky, Alex, Ilya Sutskever, and Geoffrey E. Hinton. 2012. "ImageNet Classification with Deep Convolutional Neural Networks." *Advances in Neural Information Processing Systems* 25: 1097–105.

Kruger, Justin, and David Dunning. 1999. "Unskilled and Unaware of It: How Difficulties in Recognizing One's Own Incompetence Lead to Inflated Self-Assessments." *Journal of Personality and Social Psychology* 77 (6): 1121–34. https://doi.org/10.1037/0022-3514.77.6.1121.

Lakoff, George, and Mark Johnson. 1999. *Philosophy in the Flesh: The Embodied Mind and Its Challenge to Western Thought*. Basic Books.

Lee, John D., and Katrina A. See. 2004. "Trust in Automation: Designing for Appropriate Reliance." *Human Factors* 46 (1): 50–80.

Lee, Min Kyung, Daniel Kusbit, Evan Metsky, and Laura Dabbish. 2015. *Working with Machines: The Impact of Algorithmic and Data-Driven Management on Human Workers*. 1603–12. https://doi.org/10.1145/2702123.2702548.

Lehdonvirta, Vili. 2018. *Cloud Empires: How Digital Platforms Are Overtaking the State and How We Can Regain Control*. MIT Press.

Li, Guohao, Hasan Abed Al Kader Hammoud, Hani Itani, Dmitrii Khizbullin, and Bernard Ghanem. 2024. "Camel: Communicative Agents for "Mind" Exploration of Large Language Model Society." *Advances in Neural Information Processing Systems* 36.

Licklider, J. C. R. 1960. *Man-Computer Symbiosis*. In *IRE Transactions on Human*

Factors in Electronics, HFE-1.

Lin, Stephanie, Jacob Hilton, and Owain Evans. 2022. “Teaching Models to Express Their Uncertainty in Words.” *Transactions on Machine Learning Research.*

Logg, Jennifer M., Julia A. Minson, and Don A. Moore. 2019. “Algorithm Appreciation: People Prefer Algorithmic to Human Judgment.” *Organizational Behavior and Human Decision Processes* 151: 90–103.

Lombardo, Michael M., and Robert W. Eichinger. 1996. “The Career Architect Development Planner.” *Human Resource Planning* 19 (2): 50–55.

Malone, Thomas W., and Robert J. Laubacher. 2004. “The Dawn of the e-Lance Economy.” *Harvard Business Review* 82 (9): 145–52.

Martin, Robert C. 2008. *Clean Code: A Handbook of Agile Software Craftsmanship*. Prentice Hall.

Maslach, Christina, and Susan E. Jackson. 1981. “The Measurement of Experienced Burnout.” *Journal of Occupational Behavior* 2 (2): 99–113. https://doi.org/10.1002/job.4030020205.

McCarthy, John, Marvin L. Minsky, Nathaniel Rochester, and Claude E. Shannon. 2006. “A Proposal for the Dartmouth Summer Research Project on Artificial Intelligence.” *AI Magazine* 27: 12–14.

McCloskey, Michael, and Neal J. Cohen. 1989. “Catastrophic Interference in Connectionist Networks: The Sequential Learning Problem.” *Psychology of Learning and Motivation* 24: 109–65. https://doi.org/10.1016/S0079-7421(08)60536-8.

McCulloch, Warren S., and Walter Pitts. 1943. “A Logical Calculus of the Ideas Immanent in Nervous Activity.” *Bulletin of Mathematical Biophysics* 5 (4): 115–33.

Meadows, Donella H. 2008. *Thinking in Systems: A Primer*. Edited by Diana Wright. Chelsea Green Publishing.

Mediratta, Bharat, and Julie Bick. 2007. “The Google Way: Give Engineers Room.” *Harvard Business Review* 85 (10): 56–62.

Mehrabi, Ninareh, Fred Morstatter, Nripsuta Saxena, Kristina Lerman, and Aram Galstyan. 2021. “A Survey on Bias and Fairness in Machine Learning.” *ACM Computing Surveys* 54 (6): 1–35. https://doi.org/10.1145/3457607.

Miller, George A. 1956. “The Magical Number Seven, Plus or Minus Two: Some Limits on Our Capacity for Processing Information.” *Psychological Review* 63 (2): 81–97. https://doi.org/10.1037/h0043158.

Mitchell, Melanie. 2019. *Artificial Intelligence: A Guide for Thinking Humans*. Farrar, Straus; Giroux.

Möhlmann, Mareike, Lior Zalmanson, Ola Henfridsson, and Robert Wayne Gregory. 2021. “Algorithmic Management of Work on Online Labor Platforms: When Matching Meets Control.” *MIS Quarterly* 45 (4): 1999–2022.

Mosier, Kathleen L., Linda J. Skitka, Matthew Dunbar, and Lisa McDonnell. 1998. “Automation Bias: Decision Making and Performance in High-Tech Cockpits.” *International Journal of Aviation Psychology* 8 (1): 47–63.

Mosier, Kathleen L., Linda J. Skitka, Susan Heers, and Mary Burdick. 2001. “Automation Bias, Accountability, and Verification Behaviors.” *International Journal of Human-Computer Studies* 55 (6): 815–28.

Muller, Michael, Ian Lange, Dakuo Wang, et al. 2019. “How Data Science Workers Work with Data: Discovery, Capture, Curation, Design, Creation.” *Proceedings of the 2019 CHI Conference on Human Factors in Computing Systems*, 1–15. https://doi.org/10.1145/3290605.3300356.

Musk, Elon. 2013. *First Principles Thinking*. Interview and public commentary.

National Transportation Safety Board. 2019. *Collision Between Vehicle Controlled by Developmental Automated Driving System and Pedestrian*. NTSB/HAR-19/03. National Transportation Safety Board.

Nye, Maxwell, K. Balasubramanian, I. Mei, G. Gur-Ari, Joshua B. Tenenbaum, et al. 2021. “Show Your Work: Scratchpads for Intermediate Computation with Language Models." *arXiv Preprint arXiv:2112.00114*.

Nygard, Michael. 2011. *Documenting Architecture Decisions*. Blog post. https://cognitect.com/blog/2011/11/15/documenting-architecture-decisions.

OpenAI. 2024. *AI Teammates: Designing Collaborative AI Systems*. OpenAI.

Ouchi, William G., and John B. Dowling. 1977. "Defining the Span of Control." *Administrative Science Quarterly* 22 (3): 357–65.

Parasuraman, Raja, R. Molloy, and I. L. Singh. 1993. "Performance Consequences of Automation-Induced Complacency." *The International Journal of Aviation Psychology* 3 (1): 1–23.

Parasuraman, Raja, and Victor Riley. 1997a. "Humans and Automation: Use, Misuse, Disuse, Abuse." *Human Factors* 39 (2): 230–53.

Parasuraman, Raja, and Victor Riley. 1997b. *Humans and Automation: Use, Misuse, Disuse, Abuse*. In *Human Factors*, vol. 39. https://doi.org/10.1518/001872097778543886.

Parnas, David L. 1972. "On the Criteria to Be Used in Decomposing Systems into Modules." *Communications of the ACM* 15 (12): 1053–58. https://doi.org/10.1145/361598.361623.

Peng, Sida, Eirini Kalliamvakou, Peter Cihon, and Mert Demirer. 2023. "The Impact of AI on Developer Productivity: Evidence from GitHub Copilot." *arXiv Preprint arXiv:2302.06590*.

Perez, Carlota. 2002. *Technological Revolutions and Financial Capital: The Dynamics of Bubbles and Golden Ages*. Edward Elgar Publishing.

Perez, Ethan, Sam Ringer, Kamilė Lukošiūtė, et al. 2022. "Discovering Language Model Behaviors with Model-Written Evaluations." *arXiv Preprint arXiv:2212.09251*.

Pike, Rob. 2012. "Go at Google: Language Design in the Service of Software Engineering." *Communications of the ACM* 55 (11): 44–49.

Pink, Daniel H. 2009. “Drive: The Surprising Truth about What Motivates Us.” *Riverhead Books.*

Popper, Karl. 1959. *The Logic of Scientific Discovery*. Hutchinson.

Porter, Michael E. 1985. *Competitive Advantage: Creating and Sustaining Superior Performance*. Free Press.

Poursabzi-Sangdeh, Forough, Daniel G. Goldstein, Jake M. Hofman, Jennifer Wortman Vaughan, and Hanna Wallach. 2021. “Manipulating and Measuring Model Interpretability.” *ACM Conference on Human Factors in Computing Systems (CHI).*

Prather, Joseph et al. 2023. “When Developers Don’t Understand Their Tools: Code Comprehension with AI Assistance.” *arXiv Preprint arXiv:2310.00000.*

Reuters. 2023. *ChatGPT Sets Record for Fastest-Growing User Base.* Reuters. https://www.reuters.com/technology/chatgpt-sets-record-fastest-growing-user-base-analyst-note-2023-02-01/.

Robins, Anthony, Janet Rountree, and Nathan Rountree. 2003. “Learning and Teaching Programming: A Review and Discussion.” *Computer Science Education* 13 (2): 137–72. https://doi.org/10.1076/csed.13.2.137.14200.

Rosenblat, Alex. 2018. *Uberland: How Algorithms Are Rewriting the Rules of Work*. University of California Press.

Royal Institute of British Architects. 2024. *RIBA AI Report 2024*. Royal Institute of British Architects.

Rozovsky, Julia. 2015. *Re:work: The Five Keys to a Successful Google Team*. Google. https://rework.withgoogle.com/blog/five-keys-to-a-successful-google-team/.

Russell, Stuart J., and Peter Norvig. 2010. *Artificial Intelligence: A Modern Approach*. 3rd ed. Prentice Hall.

Sah, Sunita, David Tannenbaum, P. Daniel Cleary, et al. 2021. “Blaming the Algorithm: On the Effect of Responsibility Bias When Using Algorithmic Decision Aids." *Journal of Behavioral Decision Making* 34 (4): 533–46.

Scholarcy. 2024. *AI-Powered Research Summarization*. Product documentation. https://www.scholarcy.com.

Schön, Donald A. 1983. *The Reflective Practitioner: How Professionals Think in Action*. Basic Books.

Sculley, D., Gary Holt, Daniel Golovin, et al. 2015. "Hidden Technical Debt in Machine Learning Systems." *Advances in Neural Information Processing Systems* 28: 2503–11.

Sevilla, Jaime, Lennart Heim, Anson Ho, Tamay Besiroglu, Marius Hobbhahn, and Pablo Villalobos. 2022. "Compute Trends Across Three Eras of Machine Learning." *arXiv Preprint arXiv:2202.05924*.

Sharma, Mrinank, Meg Tong, Tomasz Korbak, et al. 2023. "Towards Understanding Sycophancy in Language Models." *arXiv Preprint arXiv:2310.13548*.

Shneiderman, Ben. 2020. "Human-Centered Artificial Intelligence: Reliable, Safe & Trustworthy." *International Journal of Human-Computer Interaction* 36 (6): 495–504. https://doi.org/10.1080/10447318.2020.1741118.

Strubell, Emma, Ananya Ganesh, and Andrew McCallum. 2019. "Energy and Policy Considerations for Deep Learning in NLP." *Proceedings of the 57th Annual Meeting of the Association for Computational Linguistics*, 3645–50. https://doi.org/10.18653/v1/P19-1355.

Sutherland, Jeff. 2014. *Scrum: The Art of Doing Twice the Work in Half the Time*. Crown Business.

Sweller, John. 1988. "Cognitive Load During Problem Solving: Effects on Learning." *Cognitive Science* 12 (2): 257–85. https://doi.org/10.1207/s15516709cog1202_4.

Taleb, Nassim Nicholas. 2012. *Antifragile: Things That Gain from Disorder*. Random House.

Thompson, Dennis F. 1980. "Moral Responsibility of Public Officials: The Problem of Many Hands." *American Political Science Review* 74 (4): 905–16. https://doi.org/10.2307/1954312.

Thompson, E. P. 1963. *The Making of the English Working Class*. Victor Gollancz.

Turing, Alan M. 1950. "Computing Machinery and Intelligence." *Mind* 59 (236): 433–60. https://doi.org/10.1093/mind/LIX.236.433.

Urwick, Lyndall. 1937. "The Span of Control." *Harvard Business Review* 15 (3): 39–47.

Vaccaro, Kristen, Karrie Karahalios, Amy Bruckman, Christian Sandvig, and Kevin Hamilton. 2018. *The Illusion of Choice: An Ethnography of Algorithmic Systems in Practice*. 1–12. https://doi.org/10.1145/3173574.3174100.

Vaithilingam, Priyan, Tianyi Zhang, and Elena L. Glassman. 2023. "Expectations and Experience of Software Engineers Using AI-Powered Code Completion." *Proceedings of the 2023 CHI Conference on Human Factors in Computing Systems*, 1–12.

Vaswani, Ashish, Noam Shazeer, Niki Parmar, et al. 2017. "Attention Is All You Need." *Advances in Neural Information Processing Systems* 30: 5998–6008.

Wang, Guanzhi, Xiaohui Ren, Yihan Tang, et al. 2023. "Voyager: An Open-Ended Embodied Agent with Large Language Models." *arXiv Preprint arXiv:2305.16291*.

Wei, Jason, Yi Tay, Rishi Bommasani, et al. 2022. "Emergent Abilities of Large Language Models." *Transactions on Machine Learning Research*.

Wiener, Norbert. 1948. *Cybernetics: Or Control and Communication in the Animal and the Machine*. MIT Press.

Wooldridge, Michael. 2009. *An Introduction to MultiAgent Systems*. 2nd ed. Wiley.

Wrzesniewski, Amy, and Jane E. Dutton. 2003. "Crafting a Job: Revisioning Employees as Active Crafters of Their Work." *Academy of Management Review* 26 (2): 179–201. https://doi.org/10.5465/amr.2001.4378011.

Yang, Liu et al. 2024. "Devin and Beyond: Software Engineering with Autonomous Coding Agents." *arXiv Preprint arXiv:2403.00000.*

Zeller, Andreas. 2009. *Why Programs Fail: A Guide to Systematic Debugging.* 2nd ed. Morgan Kaufmann.

Made in United States
Orlando, FL
04 November 2026

90208247R00274